THE IMPOSSIBILITY
OF MOTHERHOOD

feminism, individualism, and the problem of mothering

PATRICE DIQUINZIO

ROUTLEDGE • New York • London

Published in 1999 by
Routledge
29 West 35th Street
New York, NY 10001

Published in Great Britain by
Routledge
11 New Fetter Lane
London EC4P 4EE

Designed by Cynthia Dunne

Printed in the United States of America on acid-free paper.

10 9 8 7 6 5 4 3 2 1

LIBRARY OF CONGRESS CATALOGING-IN-PUBLICATION DATA

DiQuinzio, Patrice, 1955–
        The impossibility of motherhood: feminism, individualism, and the problem of mothering / Patrice DiQuinzio.
        p.   cm.
Includes bibliographical references and index.
ISBN 0-415-91022-6 (hc). — ISBN 0-415-91023-4 (pb)
1. Motherhood—Political aspects—United States.   2. Mothers—United States—Social conditions.   3. Feminist theory—United States.   I. Title.
HQ759.D56   1999
306.874'3—dc21   98-49163
        CIP

CONTENTS

ACKNOWLEDGMENTS

THE PRESENCE IN my life of many teachers, colleagues, friends, and family members made the completion of this work possible. Three teachers—John Immerwahr and John D. Caputo, Philosophy, Villanova University; and Stephen G. Salkever, Political Science, Bryn Mawr College—particularly inspired me and supported my work in feminist theory. George Weaver, Philosophy, Bryn Mawr, was also my friend and advocate, which I appreciate all the more because I was completely inept in his subject area.

Communities of women have supported me everywhere I have worked. The intellectual and personal support of the women of the Society for Women in Philosophy, especially Kate Wininger and Donna Serniak, who organized a Philadelphia chapter of SWIP in the early 1980s, has been very important to me. Friendship and philosophical engagement with SWIP women, especially Jana Sawicki, Peg Walsh, and Iris Young, continue to sustain me. Sara Ruddick's work first challenged me to think philosophically about mothering, and her personal support and encouragement are invaluable to me. As assistant dean and coordinator of women's studies at Bryn Mawr College, I enjoyed working with many extraordinary and accomplished women, including Erika Behrend, Joyce Miller (now at The American Friends Service Committee), and Karen Tidmarsh of the undergraduate dean's office, women's studies faculty Jane Caplan, Jane Hedley, and Carole Joffe (now at UC Davis), Provost Judith Shapiro (now president of Barnard College), and President Pat MacPherson

(now at the Mellon Foundation). At the University of Scranton, I greatly bene-
fited from the intelligence, commitment, and friendship of the women's studies faculty, especially Sharon Meagher, Philosophy. As I began work on this
book, the enthusiastic support of Maureen MacGrogan, formerly of Routledge,
was invaluable. I am deeply grateful to Linda Nicholson, SUNY Albany, not
only for her critical engagement with and painstaking editing of my work, but
also for all the work she has done in bringing us the Thinking Gender series.

At Muhlenberg College I am multiply blessed in my colleagues and friends.
Larry Hass, Margie Hass, Da'an Pan, Ted Schick, Lud Schlecht, and Christine
Sistare have generously made a collegial home for me in the philosophy depart-
ment. The faculty with whom I work as director of women's studies—Anna
Adams, Jim Bloom, Michael Carbone, Penny Dunham, Jane Flood, Margie
Hass, Paula Irwin, Sue Curry Jansen, Mary Lawlor, Patt McCrae, Fred Norling,
Marilyn Roberts, Christine Sistare, Laura Snodgrass, Jill Stephen, Carol Shiner
Wilson, and Dan Wilson—are true colleagues in interdisciplinary work.
Sharing my work and reading theirs with Barri Gold, Margie Hass, Susan
Leggett, Lisa Perfetti, and Sheryl Welte (now at the University of Iowa) in our
1997–98 feminist theory work-in-progress group has been enormously helpful
and enjoyable. I am also very grateful for the support of my work by
Muhlenberg deans Dick Hatch, Curtis Dretsch, and Carol Shiner Wilson, and
by President Arthur Taylor and Kathryn Taylor. Muhlenberg College's financial
support, in the form of a summer research grant, was crucial to the completion
of this book.

Most importantly, I am deeply grateful for my family—my parents Bernice
and P .J. DiQuinzio, my brothers Mark and David, my dear sister Mary, and
their families; Doug and Irene Waitzman, my children's father and step-
mother; and the sons I love beyond any expressing, Tom and Brian Waitzman.
I cannot thank them enough for all their love, support, and assistance.

MOTHERING AND FEMINISM

essential motherhood and the dilemma of difference

— mothering and feminism —

MOTHERING IS FREQUENTLY a subject of contention in American society and culture, and controversies about mothering usually have an urgent tone that suggests that fundamental issues and crucially important values are at stake. The resurgence of the women's movement in the second half of the twentieth century has intensified the contention surrounding mothering. The women's movement has made a wide variety of choices with respect to motherhood more available to and more socially acceptable for more women. But this outcome has also increased both the difficulty of women's decision making about motherhood and the public debate about the relative value of women's varied options concerning motherhood. Such conflicts and debates are evident in the significant number of real and fictional mothers and groups of mothers who have recently been the object of public scrutiny in the United States and beyond. Mary Beth Whitehead, Susan Smith, Deborah Eappen and Louise Woodward, Murphy Brown and Madonna; single mothers, teenage mothers, lesbian mothers, welfare mothers, and soccer moms have all been the focus of such scrutiny and debate. Teenage pregnancy, surrogate mothering, multiple births resulting from fertility treatments, mothering through IVF for women fifty, sixty, and older; extra-uterine gestation and cloning; abortion and day care; adoption and child custody law—all continue to generate controversy.

Much of this controversy surrounding mothering is a function of its social context. In Western, industrial capitalist societies like the United States, the nuclear family in which women have primary responsibility for child rearing—what Nancy Chodorow calls the male-dominated, father-absent family (1978: 181)—is a crucial component of social organization and individual development. The nuclear family and female child rearing sustain other structures of these societies, and persons' experiences of being mothered in this sort of family are pervasive and powerful. Thus, being a mother and being mothered are both imbued with tremendous social, cultural, political, economic, psychological, and personal significance. Everyone has a stake in the social organization of mothering, but these stakes can vary greatly. Although few persons share exactly the same position with respect to mothering, none has an unconflicted relationship to it.

Conflicts among women also play out in relationship to mothering. Some women do not want to be mothers and never do so; some women do not want to become mothers but nonetheless do; some women want to be mothers but are unable to do so for a variety of reasons; some women find great satisfaction and a sense of accomplishment in mothering; some women become mothers in circumstances that prevent their experiencing such satisfaction in mothering; and some women regret having become mothers. Many mothers report that mothering is a deeply ambivalent experience in which, at one time or another, they feel exaltation, despair, and many other emotions in between. In addition, the needs and interests of women who are mothers and women who are not, as well as the needs and interests of some mothers compared to others, can be at odds. The needs and interests of mothers who work for wages and those who do not, and of mothers who hire other women to care for their children, and of the women, often mothers themselves, whom they hire can come into conflict. Mothers who work for wages, mothers who are provided for by husbands or children's fathers, and mothers who receive public funds for their support can have opposing needs and interests.

Mothers can occupy many different positions with respect to the family; they can be married mothers, single mothers who are either divorced or never married, step-mothers, adoptive mothers, lesbian mothers with or without partners, foster mothers, surrogate mothers, other-mothers (Collins 1991: 119–22), or mothers who do not live with their children or do not have physical and/or legal custody of their children. Some of these positions are much more socially accepted and validated than others, and the needs and interests of mothers in more socially accepted relationships to the family can conflict with the needs and interests of mothers in delegitimated relationships to the family. At the same time, other kinds of social conflict, especially conflicts involving race, ethnicity, socioeconomic class, and sexual orientation, can be particularly intense in relationship to mothering. For example, "welfare" mothers are often coded as African-American, family dysfunctions such as spousal or child abuse are often understood to involve mothers who are poor and/or members of minority groups, the enforcement of laws and social policies that criminalize pregnant women who drink alcohol or use drugs as child abusers often target mothers who are poor and/or members of minority groups, and lesbian mothers are often stigmatized as unfit, for instance, in legal proceedings regarding custody of their children.

Mothering is also a very contentious issue in American feminism, and many critics of feminism focus on what they believe feminism says or implies about mothering. Feminism in the United States, however, has never been characterized by a monolithic position on mothering. Some feminists have argued that mothering is the source of women's limitations or the cause of women's oppression, because it is the experience in which women most suffer under the tyranny of nature, biology, and/or male control. Others have argued that mothering is an important source of women's identity, a scene of women's most joyful accomplishments, a basis of women's value as members of society, and an impetus for women's political participation. Some feminist assessments of mothering agree that it can unite women in many shared experiences. But of such assessments, some emphasize women's deep and abiding love for their children and/or their pleasures and sense of accomplishment in child rearing, while others focus on the stifling confinement to home and family, the annoyances and frustrations of caring for children, the agonizing losses that mothering can entail, and the lack of control over the circumstances of their mothering that many women experience. Some feminist analyses of mothering emphasize that mothers of different racial and ethnic groups, religions, ages, socioeconomic classes, and sexual orientations can have much in common in their day-to-day existence, their ongoing interests and concerns, and the shape and trajectory of their lives. But others focus on the specificity of different women's experiences of mothering, arguing that socially significant differences such as race, ethnicity, religion, age, socioeconomic class, and sexual orientation so thoroughly shape women's situations and experiences of mothering as to preclude much commonality among mothers. Feminists have argued that mothering can unite women in political action, from local struggles for better schools and safer neighborhoods to global peace activism and antimilitarism. But they have also recognized that mothering can divide women, creating misunderstanding, suspicion, and hostility among women whose opportunities, choices, or experiences with respect to mothering are different. And feminists have seen that political activism conducted under the sign of mothering can alienate women who are not mothers, women who don't like being mothers, or women who don't want to be identified primarily in terms of their mothering.

Some of feminism's most pressing, but also most contradictory, demands are issued in the name of mothering. For example, feminism demands that women have freedom, autonomy, and choice with respect to reproduction and child rearing. But feminism also demands that men participate at least equally in child rearing, which may limit mothers' autonomy. Feminism demands that social institutions, policies, and practices treat women as human individuals, with no reference to their actual or potential mothering, but also demands that social institutions, policies, and practices accommodate the needs and interests of mothers. Feminists have seen that when social institutions, policies, and practices treat women and men equally, without consideration of women's actual or potential mothering, this can benefit women who are not mothers (and all or most men) and disadvantage mothers (and men who do take significant responsibility for caring for children). But when social institutions, policies, and practices do take the needs and interests of mothers (and child rearing men) into account, this may benefit mothers and disadvantage women who are not mothers and men who have few or no child rearing responsibilities. In addition, feminists struggle among themselves over the meaning, significance, and control of medical interventions in reproduction, and of laws, social policies, and cultural practices that affect reproduction and mothering. Controversies among feminists about whether fertility treatments and surrogacy arrangements enhance women's freedom, autonomy, and choice with respect to mothering; reinforce the view that all women should be mothers; or enable some women to become mothers by exploiting other women are only a few instances of contention among feminists about mothering. Feminists also continue to struggle among themselves over the question of how best to reorganize social institutions, such as workplaces and schools, so that they will accommodate both mothering and women's freedom and equal opportunity.

— mothering and feminist theory —

It is not surprising, then, that mothering is a very contentious issue in feminist theory. The central concepts of feminist theory, including sex, gender, embodiment, desire, consciousness, experience, representation, oppression, equality, freedom, and liberation are all relevant to understanding mothering and are regularly invoked in feminist analyses of mothering. But analyzing mothering also raises questions or problems about the meaning and implications of these concepts, problems that may only become apparent when these concepts are deployed in connection with mothering. Thus, mothering is both an important site at which the central concepts of feminist theory are elaborated, and a site at which these concepts are challenged and reworked. In addition, the issue of mothering often functions as a sort of lightning rod in feminist theory: other issues and disagreements in feminist theory are expressed in terms of mothering or get attached to the issue of mothering, and this brings all the intensity and contention associated with mothering to these disagreements. Furthermore, the various proposals for reorganizing mothering that feminism has articulated and attempted to put into practice have met with strenuous resistance in the United States, particularly compared to the reception and implementation of feminist proposals for change in other areas of social life. For example, feminism's demand for women's equal access to and participation in paid labor and public life has been much more widely accepted and put into practice than the corresponding demand that men take greater responsibility for child rearing and other domestic activities. This has left many mothers to face the "second shift," taking all or most responsibility for child rearing and domestic work while also meeting the demands of paid work (Hochschild 1989). Feminism's demand for women's greater sexual freedom and for destigmatizing mothering outside of marriage, combined with men's failure to take greater responsibility for child rearing, has left many women struggling to raise children alone, with little or no support of any kind from the fathers of their children (Folbre 1994). This uneven progress of feminism has especially complicated the lives of mothers, and has generated further feminist analyses of mothering, that are not necessarily consistent with each other.

But precisely for these reasons neither feminism nor feminist theory can afford to ignore the issue of mothering. To the extent that mothering, in all its diverse forms, remains an important aspect of many women's lives and that decisions about whether, when, and how to mother continue to face almost all women, feminism cannot claim to give an adequate account of women's lives and to represent women's needs and interests if it ignores the issue of mothering. And to the extent that mothering has been a primary site of women's oppression, it is likely that sexists and supporters of an antifeminist backlash will continue to insist that mothering be theorized and organized in their own terms. This will certainly have significant consequences, few of them consistent with feminist goals and values. The problematic outcomes of the uneven progress of feminism and the strong resistance to feminist ideas about reorganizing mothering also suggest that feminism and feminist theory need to explore further the issue of mothering, at least in order to determine the basis of this resistance to reorganizing mothering. Certainly it is possible to theorize women's situations and experiences, or to theorize gender, in ways that minimize the issue of mothering, or do not address it at all. But assumptions about women's mothering are so deeply embedded in U.S. society and culture and are so complexly intertwined with other fundamental beliefs and values that these assumptions are likely to be implicit in accounts of women's situations and experiences and in theories of gender that do not explicitly address mothering.

In this study of feminist thinking about mothering, I consider the difficulties of theorizing mothering and doing feminist theory in light of the relationship of feminism and individualism, the theory of subjectivity presupposed by the ideological formation that predominates in the United States. Feminism has to rely on individualism in order to articulate its claims that women are equal human subjects of social and political agency and entitlement. But, I argue, feminism has found it impossible to theorize mothering adequately in terms of an individualist theory of subjectivity. Thus, I ask, in what ways has feminism relied on individualism and in what ways has feminism challenged it? How has individualism facilitated feminism, and in what ways has it been an obstacle to feminism? In what ways have feminist theories of mothering participated in the complex relationship of feminism and individualism and in what ways have they reconfigured this relationship? What alternative theories of subjectivity has feminist theory looked to or devised in order to analyze mothering, and what have been the implications and effects of these alternatives for theorizing mothering, for analyzing other aspects of women's situations and experiences, for theorizing gender, and for representing women's needs and interests?

Briefly, my response to these questions takes the following form: I offer a theory of ideology in order to analyze the conflicted relationship of feminism and individualism. I understand individualism as the theory of subjectivity presupposed by the individualist ideological formation that is dominant in the modern United States. Thus, it is the theory of subjectivity that supports the material conditions and social relations sustained and justified by this ideological formation, and that mediates more or less successfully the contradictions that emerge in the attempt to maintain both liberal democratic political practices and capitalist economic arrangements. I show that, as a theory of subjectivity, individualism represents subjectivity in terms of identity, denies the effectivity of difference in subjectivity, and construes subjectivity in terms consistent with traditional Western conceptions of masculinity. Individualism relies on the metaphysics of substance, the modern, Western philosophical tradition that understands subjectivity in terms of mind/body dualism and includes an analysis of embodiment, social relations, and social contexts as instrumental to rather than constitutive of subjectivity.

Individualism is complexly related to what I call 'essential motherhood'. Essential motherhood is an ideological formation that specifies the essential attributes of motherhood and articulates femininity in terms of motherhood so understood. According to essential motherhood, mothering is a function of women's essentially female nature, women's biological reproductive capacities, and/or human evolutionary development. Essential motherhood construes women's motherhood as natural and inevitable. It requires women's exclusive and selfless attention to and care of children based on women's psychological and emotional capacities for empathy, awareness of the needs of others, and self-sacrifice. According to essential motherhood, because these psychological and emotional capacities are natural in women, women's desires are oriented to mothering and women's psychological development and emotional satisfaction require mothering. Essential motherhood also represents women's sexuality in terms of mothering; it holds that the primary goal of women's sexuality is motherhood and that women value sexual activity and pleasure primarily as a means to motherhood rather than as ends in themselves. Essential motherhood's account of women's sexuality thus requires women's heterosexuality, which it also construes as natural. Essential motherhood dictates that all women want to be and should be mothers and clearly implies that women who do not manifest the qualities required by mothering and/or refuse mothering are deviant or deficient as women. Essential motherhood is not only an account of mothering, but also an account of femininity.

So, while individualism is ostensibly gender neutral, insisting on the equal human subjectivity of men and women, essential motherhood posits a specifically feminine/maternal subjectivity and requires this subjectivity of all women. Essential motherhood represents mothering and femininity in terms that are at odds with subjectivity as individualism defines it, and so it has the effect of excluding mothers and women from individualist subjectivity. Individualism and essential motherhood together position women in a very basic double bind: essential motherhood requires mothering of women, but it represents motherhood in a way that denies mothers' and women's individualist subjectivity. Essential motherhood also masks the contradiction implicit in social formations that are based on an individualist theory of subjectivity but also deny women's individualist subjectivity. It does so by specifying mothering as women's proper function, and implying that women's mothering, rather than sexism or male dominance, explains women's exclusion from individualist subjectivity. Without questioning the individualist conception of subjectivity, essential motherhood's specification of femininity in terms of mothering implies that women fail to meet individualism's criteria for subjectivity. Thus, it also obscures the extent to which individualism defines subjectivity in terms that are derived from or based on situations and experiences more typical of men than of women.

Feminism in the United States has to rely on individualism to claim women's equal human subjectivity, because the intelligibility and political effectiveness of this claim are a function of its being expressed in terms consistent with the dominant ideology. If feminism cannot show that women are subjects as individualism defines subjectivity, then it cannot argue for women's equal political agency and entitlement. By relying on individualism to make this argument, feminism includes what I call an identity-based challenge to sexism and male dominance. But feminism also resists and challenges individualism—because of its relationship to essential motherhood, because it inadequately conceptualizes important aspects of women's situations and experiences, and ultimately because it inadequately conceptualizes subjectivity itself. Feminist theory argues that these effects of individualism are the result of its denial of the significance of difference for understanding subjectivity. Thus, feminism also includes what I call a difference-based challenge to individualism, or difference feminism, which reconceptualizes subjectivity in terms of difference. This reconceptualization of subjectivity recognizes the effects for subjectivity of socially significant differences among persons and of elements of difference operating within individual subjects. Ideological determination, however, is never total—there are always elements of contradiction within ideological formations, and among ideological formations, material conditions, and social relations. Thus, that which an ideological formation seeks to exclude or contain may nonetheless be effective within it, and thereby may be available for critique and rearticulation. The concepts of identity and difference are complexly interwoven and mutually dependent for their articulation in the individualist ideological formation. This means that the concept of difference persists—even in its disavowal—in feminism's identity-based challenge to sexism and male dominance, and the concept of identity persists—even as it is challenged—in feminism's difference-based challenge to individualism.

As a result of this interplay of identity and difference, feminism and feminist theory are characterized by 'the dilemma of difference'. This dilemma refers to the way in which feminism and feminist theory must deny or disavow women's difference, and differences among women, in order to argue for women's equality and to mobilize women as a group, but must also rely on the concept of difference to analyze the specificity of women's situations and experiences and to theorize differences among women. An important aspect of the dilemma of difference is that neither identity nor difference is without risks for feminist theory, so that whether it relies on or challenges individualism, feminist theory faces complex problems and often makes contradictory claims. I illustrate this aspect of the dilemma of difference by showing how this dilemma manifests itself in a number of paradoxes concerning embodiment, gender, and representation in feminist theory. I argue that in feminist theory the dilemma of difference and its resulting paradoxes are most salient and most difficult to resolve at the site of mothering. To show this, I focus on the ideological moments that occur in the accounts of mothering I consider. By 'ideological moments' I mean those points in an account of mothering at which certain key concepts attempt to mediate, reconcile, and/or disguise the dilemma of difference and the paradoxes it produces for feminist theory. My analysis of feminist accounts of mothering shows that mothering is an important site at which the individualist ideological formation is elaborated and imposed, but it is also a site at which this ideological formation can be contested and reworked.

I proceed by way of close reading of a number of feminist analyses of mothering, and I juxtapose these analyses in ways that I believe generate productive discussion among them. My analysis of the theories of subjectivity at work in these accounts of mothering is the basis of my conclusion of the impossibility of motherhood. I argue that motherhood as essential motherhood specifies it cannot be adequately conceptualized in individualist terms; it is impossible to be a mother in the sense implied by the notion of mother*hood*, which suggests an essential identity or state of being. (For this reason I use the term 'mothering' to refer to birthing and rearing children, and reserve the term 'motherhood' to refer to the ideological construct of essential motherhood.) This impossibility of motherhood means that all attempts to theorize mothering inevitably encounter and must negotiate the dilemma of difference. But the risks of difference in theorizing mothering are formidable. These risks include the reconsolidation of all or most aspects of essential motherhood, including the social organization of mothering based on it, the social organization of mothering that oppresses women and that feminism intends to challenge and change. Theorizing mothering in terms of difference also risks capitulating to the double bind in which individualism and essential motherhood position women. By insisting on women's difference, for instance in analyzing women's situations and experience of mothering and their effects on women's consciousness and social relations, difference feminism jeopardizes feminism's claim to women's equal human subjectivity. On the other hand, the possible benefits for feminism and feminist theory of taking these risks of difference are also considerable. These benefits include the rearticulation of understandings of mothering that more adequately conceptualize mothering, more strenuously challenge individualism, and thus more strongly support the changes in the social organization of mothering that feminism advocates. The difficulty for feminist theory is that, in an individualist ideological context, the subversive and liberatory possibilities of accounts of mothering that challenge individualism in terms of difference are never far removed from the risks of reconsolidating elements of essential motherhood that occur in the project of theorizing mothering. My readings of a number of feminist accounts of mothering show that the possible benefits of theorizing mothering in terms of difference nonetheless outweigh the risks it poses, and suggest how the project of theorizing mothering might best negotiate the dilemma of difference in feminism's current ideological context. I also argue that feminist theory must accept the inevitability of the dilemma of difference and its resulting paradoxes in theorizing mothering, and thus must embrace, or at least reconcile itself to, what I call a 'paradoxical politics of mothering.'

I begin with an analysis of the debate about the social reorganization of mothering between Charlotte Perkins Gilman and Ellen Key that took place in the United States at the beginning of the twentieth century to argue that the dilemma of difference and the prominence of this dilemma in connection with mothering have characterized feminism in the United States since its inception. I next consider the work of political philosopher Jean Bethke Elshtain, analyzing the account of mothering presupposed by the form of feminism for which she argues. I conclude that, not withstanding her explicit critique of individualism, Elshtain's account of mothering is so closely aligned with essential motherhood that it generates a very conservative form of feminist politics. Because the conservatism of Elshtain's version of feminism is partly a result of Elshtain's dematerializing account of mothering, I turn to Simone de Beauvoir's analysis of mothering in *The Second Sex* to see how a theorist explicitly concerned to theorize embodiment, especially female embodiment, deals with mothering. Here I argue that Beauvoir's existentialist theory of subjectivity relies on a version of mind/body dualism and an oppositional account of the self/other relation that are in many ways consistent with individualism. For this reason, her account of mothering is characterized by contradictions and reconsolidates crucial elements of the sexism and male dominance that she means to challenge. But I also argue that the figure of the pregnant woman as represented by Beauvoir suggests an alternative approach to theorizing subjectivity, and thus to theorizing mothering, than that on which Beauvoir relies. I read the figure of the pregnant woman in *The Second Sex* as suggesting an account of subjectivity according to which embodiment and subjectivity are reciprocally permeable and mutually over-determining, so that subjectivity is divided, partial, and fragmentary. My reading of the figure of the pregnant woman in *The Second Sex* raises the question of whether such an account of subjectivity can more adequately conceptualize mothering than individualism while also more adequately resisting the risks of difference.

With this possibility in mind I look to Sara Ruddick's work on mothering and to Julia Kristeva's representation of mothering in her essay "Stabat Mater." I argue that each of these accounts of mothering points in different ways to the need for a theory of subjectivity as partial, divided, and fragmented, and thus each extends the implications of my reading of Beauvoir's account of mothering. Ruddick's work on mothering and Kristeva's "Stabat Mater" also suggest how a theory of subjectivity such as the one I elicit from Beauvoir's account of mothering enables the reconceptualization of mothering in ways consistent with feminist practical and theoretical goals while also avoiding some of the most serious risks of difference. But neither Ruddick's nor Kristeva's account of mothering is entirely successful in negotiating the dilemma of difference. I explore the difficulties that Ruddick encounters in trying to theorize embodiment in terms that both support her practicalist account of mothering and adequately represent women's experiences of mothering, especially pregnancy and birth. Exploring these difficulties requires an analysis of Ruddick's use of feminist standpoint theory, including an analysis of what standpoint theory presupposes about experience. I also consider the difficulties presented by Kristeva's reliance on a Lacanian psychoanalytic framework for her account of mothering. The Lacanian framework of Kristeva's account of mothering generates her analysis of what I call the desire of/for the mother, which undermines Kristeva's goal of developing what she calls a 'herethics', problematizes maternal subjectivity, and thus risks the recuperation of significant elements of essential motherhood.

To further consider the difficulties of theorizing mothering in psychoanalytic terms, I turn to Nancy Chodorow's *The Reproduction of Mothering*:

Psychoanalysis and the Sociology of Gender. I argue that the object relations version of psychoanalysis that Chodorow deploys in order to explain the social reproduction of women's mothering allows a broader focus on, and thus a more complete analysis of, the determinants of the social contexts in which women's mothering is done than does Lacanian psychoanalysis. But I also show how the elements of Lacanian and Freudian versions of psychoanalysis to which Chodorow also appeals problematize her account of mothering. Chodorow's combination of object relations theory, Lacanian, and Freudian versions of psychoanalysis recuperates many elements of individualism that are more strenuously resisted by Kristeva's Lacanian psychoanalytic frame. But, while Lacanian psychoanalysis is a more promising basis on which to theorize mothering in resistance to individualism, its representations of the desire of/for the mother and maternal subjectivity are problematic. In addition, Chodorow's account of mothering, like Kristeva's, recuperates certain elements of essential motherhood, especially the requirement of maternal heterosexuality. For this reason, I bring Ruddick's critique of psychoanalysis to bear on these two psychoanalytically based accounts of mothering, and show that this critique has considerable validity in relationship to Kristeva's and Chodorow's accounts of mothering.

In light of Ruddick's critique of psychoanalytic approaches to mothering, I return to a consideration of the theoretical framework of Ruddick's analysis of maternal practice and birthgiving, including the difficulties she encounters in her attempt to theorize maternal embodiment and represent women's experience of mothering. I do so by considering two additional analyses of mothering in which the concept of experience plays a significant role: Adrienne Rich's account in *Of Woman Born: Motherhood as Experience and Institution*, and the account of black women's mothering presented by Patricia Hill Collins in *Black Feminist Thought: Knowledge, Consciousness and the Politics of Empowerment*. Here I argue that the concept of experience in these two accounts of mothering represents, not so much the reality of women's experience that is available for interpretation by feminist theory, as the expression of a desire for the kind of subjectivity promised but never provided by individualism. I particularly question the significance of the way that this concept of experience represents the desire for subjectivity as a desire for the mother, which resembles the desire of/for the mother that is also operative in psychoanalysis, especially Lacanian psychoanalysis. Just as I caution against the possible individualist elements of psychoanalysis and its tendency to recuperate aspects of essential motherhood, here I caution against the demand implicit in the appeal to women's experience and in psychoanalysis, that the mother represent a guarantee of the coherence and stability of subjectivity or that the mother console for the lack of any such guarantee. Feminist analyses of women's experiences must resist more strenuously the desire for the experience of subjectivity that individualism promises but does not deliver than do Rich's and Collins's accounts of mothering.

On the basis of my readings of these feminist accounts of mothering, I conclude that feminist theory must reconcile itself to an ongoing engagement with the dilemma of difference, especially in connection with mothering. Feminist theory must recognize that, especially in connection with mothering, it will have "only paradoxes to offer" (Scott 1996) as a result of its conflicted relationship to—its simultaneous reliance on and challenge to—individualism. But, while feminist analyses of mothering will inevitably encounter the dilemma of difference and thereby come to include paradoxical or contradictory conclusions, this does not mean that any particular account of mothering is just as useful and valuable as any other for feminist politics. Rather, feminism must determine which of its accounts of mothering or which aspects of its analyses of mothering to foreground in each of its multiple and contradictory struggles on behalf of women and/or mothers. Thus, I end with my views as to how feminism might decide the deployment of the paradoxical analyses of mothering that feminist theory generates.

Some of the feminist accounts of mothering on which I focus I chose because they have been much discussed by feminist thinkers, and their ideas and claims have been put to use in other feminist theoretical contexts; for example, Beauvoir's *The Second Sex* and Chodorow's *The Reproduction of Mothering*. Others I chose because I believe that they make important contributions to or illustrate important conflicts in feminist thinking about mothering, even though they have received somewhat less attention from and use by feminist theorists or are generally not thought of primarily in connection with mothering; for example, the work of Collins and Elshtain. For all of the thinkers whose work I examine, I focus on what they have written about mothering, even when the issue of mothering is one of many they address, as is the case with Beauvoir, Collins, Elshtain, Kristeva, and Rich. Thus, my readings of their analyses of mothering are by no means exhaustive or even representative of the entirety of their work in feminist theory. Most importantly, I have chosen to work with these thinkers and texts because when I consider them separately I find in them suggestive and illuminating tensions or conflicts, and when I consider them in relationship to each other I am able to bring them into productive discussion. This of course also means that I have left out of consideration many important works, such as Jessie Bernard's *The Future of Motherhood*

(1972), Elizabeth Badinter's *Mother Love: Myth and Reality* (1980), Mary O'Brien's *The Politics of Reproduction* (1981), Jane Lazarre's *The Mother Knot* (1985), and Ann Ferguson's *Blood at the Root: Motherhood, Sexuality, and Male Dominance* (1989), as well as thinkers such as Jane Gallop (1988), Virginia Held (1993), Luce Irigaray (1991, 1985a, 1985b), and Audre Lorde (1984), whose work includes important analyses of mothering. This does not mean that this work is any less worthy of close reading and critical attention, but rather that I was not able to bring it into the discussion I hoped to stage here.

My goal in staging this discussion of feminist accounts of mothering is not to determine which of them is the best or most adequate account of mothering, although my conclusions as to which of them I find more or less problematic are fairly clear. Neither is it my goal to criticize these accounts of mothering in order to present my own account of mothering. Instead, I hope to contribute to feminist theory at one of its most conflicted sites by articulating some of the complexities and difficulties at stake in the issue of mothering. Feminist theory can only continue to theorize mothering, even though this necessitates feminist theory's continued engagement with the dilemma of difference and its resulting paradoxes. This is another way in which motherhood is impossible: it is impossible for feminist theory to avoid the issue of mothering and it is impossible for feminist theory to resolve it.

FEMINISM
AND INDIVIDUALISM

identity and difference, ideology and rearticulation

— ideology: theory and contexts —

CENTRAL TO MY analysis of feminist accounts of mothering is my view that no theoretical practice can be adequately understood apart from its ideological context. Theory construction may appear to be an activity in which individuals freely choose to engage, alone or with others. Such a view of theory construction may include the view that the practice of theorizing is always located in historical and cultural contexts or traditions, and that individuals must engage such contexts or traditions when they decide to participate in theorizing. According to this view of theoretical practice, contexts or traditions may constrain theory construction in certain ways, but do not determine it. My view of theoretical practice rejects this concept of the autonomous individual freely choosing to engage in this activity and determining for himself or herself its conditions, materials, methods, and outcomes. Instead I hold that theoretical practice is over-determined by its ideological context, but that this over-determination can be less than total. I understand the term 'ideology' to refer to a discursive formation or a set of ideas deeply connected to and dependent on each other for their coherent articulation. Ideological formations attempt to systematize, rationalize, and justify particular material conditions and the social relations, structures, institutions, and practices to which these material conditions give rise. At the same time, ideological formations contribute to the production and maintenance of the material conditions and the social relations, structures, institutions, and practices that these formations claim simply to describe.

A characteristic feature of ideological formations is that they can be hegemonic. This means that at the level of individual consciousness they are understood as "common sense" or as a description of "the way things are"; ideological formations are not perceived as determinants of consciousness with specific relationships to and specific effects on material conditions, social relations, and social contexts. In order to be hegemonic, ideological formations must mask or obscure both the contradictions that can be implicit in these formations themselves and the contradictions that can exist between ideological formations and their corresponding material conditions and social relations, structures, institutions, and practices. To the extent that ideological formations prevent such contradictions from becoming evident and becoming a concern to a significant number of people, the vision of "the way things are" that these formations embody tends to be widely accepted and infrequently questioned.[1] In my analysis of accounts of mothering that have been developed in or influenced by modern U.S. feminism, I argue that individualism and essential motherhood have tended to be hegemonic. At the same time, however, because ideological formations are discursive phenomena, they are also characterized by the fundamental undecidability that is an element of language itself. All signification is an exclusion that points indirectly to what it excludes, and there are inevitably gaps or slippages between signifiers and what they signify. For these reasons, a complex interplay of identity and difference is characteristic of discursivity. The operation and effects of undecidability in language can themselves be recognized and theorized, and deconstructive reading practices can focus on the exclusions, slippages, and contradictions implicit in a discursive formation so as to produce alternative readings of such formations (Derrida 1974, 1978, 1981, 1982). Within ideological formations there is a similar interplay of identity and difference, and the operations and effects of this interplay can also be recognized and theorized. Thus, ideological formations can also be subject to deconstructive reading practices that enable their analysis, critique, and rearticulation. I believe that bringing such reading practices to bear on essential motherhood, as well as on feminist accounts of mothering, can be an important contribution to dislodging essential motherhood.

While it may be difficult in theory and in practice to distinguish an ideological formation and its material conditions, I believe that their relationship is best characterized as mutually over-determinative. The concept of over-determination refers to a phenomenon's having multiple and varied causes that do not necessarily bring about the same effects, or do not necessarily bring about their effects in the same way. These varied and multiple causes bring about varied and multiple effects, and some of these varied and multiple causes produce effects that are at odds with or in opposition to the effects of other causes also operating to determine the phenomenon in question. Thus, over-determined phenomena tend to be complex, characterized by tensions, oppositions, and contradictions that destabilize them.[2] Ideological formations are over-determined; they are produced and maintained by specific material conditions, but as causes these conditions can be multiple, varied, and contradictory, so that the ideological formations they produce and maintain are also destabilized by tensions, oppositions, and contradictions. With a sufficient degree of coherence and stability, ideological formations can operate more or less successfully to keep their over-determining conditions in place and unchanged. Furthermore, ideological formations are effective—they bring about and sustain the material conditions, social relations, structures, institutions, and practices that they claim simply to describe. Ideological formations thus also over-determine the material and social conditions they produce. Ideological formations produce a variety of subjects of power (Foucault 1980, 1987), and those more powerful individuals, groups, and institutions, especially those with access to or control over "ideological apparatuses" (Althusser 1971), articulate, more or less consciously, the elements of ideological formations in ways that more or less successfully advance their interests and preserve their power. But they also produce inconsistencies and contradictions, and individuals and groups may be able to use these inconsistencies and contradictions as a basis to critique and rearticulate the ideological formation that produced them.[3]

In other words, as a result of the interplay of identity and difference within ideological formations and the over-determination of ideological formations, their conditions, and their effects, ideological formations can be unstable. Within an ideological formation there are contradictions or inconsistencies that are only more or less managed and/or concealed by its terms, and there are contradictions or inconsistencies among ideological formations, material conditions, social relations, and social contexts. The various elements of an ideological formation—the material conditions that generate it and that it sustains and manages, the subjectivity and agency that it produces and deploys, the social relations and contexts that it sustains and rationalizes, and its own operations that it seeks to obscure—may be at odds to such an extent that their contradictions and inconsistencies are relatively evident. This instability of ideological formations means that processes of ideological determination can become accessible to analysis and critique, as the contradictions and inconsistencies implicit in them become available as a basis for this analysis and critique. Such analysis and critique can lead to the disarticulation and rearticulation of the elements of an ideological formation, so that the formation can be subverted and reworked by subjects who are nonetheless still over-determined by it. In other words, while there is no possibility of taking up a position outside of an ideological formation and undoing it externally, there sometimes occurs room for maneuver within it that allows for disarticulation and rearticulation of some of its elements. But this also means that ideology critique and the reorganization and redetermination of material conditions, social relations, and social contexts are also always partial and incomplete (Laclau and Mouffe 1985; Hennessy 1993).

In any ideological formation, certain terms, concepts, or images do "ideological work" (Poovey 1988). Ideological work is the work of containing or managing contradictions within an ideological formation that might otherwise be sites of disarticulation and rearticulation. Thus, the terms, concepts, or images that do ideological work are crucial in enabling an ideological formation to impinge on consciousness in such a way as to make it seem commonsensical. This containment or management of contradiction is not always entirely successful, however, so that these terms, concepts, or images may also provoke the sort of questions that are the starting point of ideology critique. In other words, the terms, concepts, or images that do ideological work are both an important component of ideological over-determination and a locus of the instability of an ideological formation that enables rearticulation. In feminist accounts of mothering, concepts and images of mothering and terms and concepts deployed in theories of mothering do just such ideological work. The concept of mothering and the image of the mother represented in essential motherhood are perhaps the two most significant elements of dominant definitions of femininity, the determination of women's inequality and oppression, and the rationalization and justification of sexism and male dominance. But concepts of mothering and images of the mother can also be powerful elements of feminist critique of the ideology of essential motherhood; they can represent this ideological formation's internal contradictions or the contradictions among this ideological formation, its material conditions, and its social relations and contexts. So concepts of mothering and images of the mother can be a basis for feminist rearticulation of essential motherhood. In addition, concepts such as embodiment, desire, dependence, and care in feminist accounts of mothering can both contribute to and challenge individualism and essential motherhood. Given the complexities of ideological over-determination, however, a term, concept, or image can and often does function in both of these ways at the same time. And, I argue, this is often the case with mothering and the concepts feminist theory relies on to theorize mothering. Their potential for subversive disarticulation and rearticulation is never far removed from their role in perpetuating sexism and male dominance, and they remain available to fulfill this latter role even in the course of their subversive deployment. Feminist theory's subversive rearticulation and deployment of mothering always risks the recuperation of elements of the ideological formations feminist theory means to challenge by deploying it, and feminist challenges to dominant ideological formations in terms of mothering never entirely avoid this risk.

The version of ideology critique that I propose and carry out in these readings begins by locating the ideological moments—the moments in which significant ideological work occurs—in feminist theories of mothering. I specify several kinds of ideological moments including exclusion, equation, displacement, naturalization, and recuperation. Feminist accounts may theorize mothering in ways that exclude certain activities from the practice of mothering, exclude certain versions or instances of mothering, or exclude certain possibilities for mothering. Feminist theories of mothering may equate certain activities with mothering, see certain activities as definitive of mothering, or equate mothering with other activities, social relations, or institutions. They may raise problems or issues with respect to mothering but displace these problems by attributing them to other activities, social relations, or institutions. They may naturalize dominant forms of the social organization of mothering, insisting that the assignment of the work of mothering to women and the material conditions, social relations, and social contexts that support it are determined by natural and therefore unchangeable causes, such as the nature of female embodiment or human evolutionary development. The ideological naturalization of women's mothering recuperates elements of sexism and male dominance, by positing that the oppressive aspects of dominant social organizations of mothering are inevitable and/or not really oppressive, thereby making these aspects of mothering more difficult to dislodge in practice. The explanatory frameworks and basic concepts on which feminist theory relies to explicate mothering may all have similar ideological effects. Feminist theory's use of theories such as psychoanalysis and feminist standpoint epistemologies, distinctions such as natural/social and private/public, and concepts such as situation and experience may include ideological moments, even as feminist theory struggles to rearticulate these theories, distinctions, and concepts. To analyze these ideological moments, I focus on the "slippage of signifiers" (Spivak 1988b: 275), considering in these accounts of mothering what subtle—or not so subtle—reinscriptions of essential mothering and/or of terms and concepts consistent with individualism occur in them. A number of concepts central to contemporary feminist theory, such as sex, gender, desire, standpoint, situation, experience, and consciousness, and a number of social structures, particularly family and state, are the subjects of such slippage in feminist theories of mothering. This form of ideology critique is appropriate for analyzing feminist accounts of mothering, given the dilemma of difference in feminist theory that is a result of feminism's difficult and conflicted relationship to the dominant ideology in the United States.

— feminism and individualism —

The dilemma of difference in feminist theory is a function of feminism's conflicted relationship to individualism. As a social, political, and theoretical practice, feminism in the United States finds itself operating in an individualist ideological context. As a result feminism must appeal to individualism to assert women's individualist subjectivity so that it can argue for women's equal political entitlement and agency. But individualism problematizes certain aspects of women's situations and experiences, especially women's situations and experiences having to do with mothering, that feminism also wants to represent and analyze. Thus, when feminism appeals to individualism, it risks the misrepresentation or denial of those aspects of women's situations and experiences that are exclusive to or more typical of women. For this reason, contemporary feminism in the United States has come to include a theoretical discourse that emphasizes the significance of difference for theorizing women's subjectivity and representing women's situations and experiences, or difference feminism. The various forms of difference feminism that have emerged in the past thirty years in the United States are generally more successful than identity-based, individualist forms of feminism at theorizing the specificity of women's subjectivity, situations, and experiences. But, when feminist theory appeals to accounts of subjectivity that, unlike individualism, recognize the significance of difference for subjectivity, it may weaken feminism's claim of women's equal subjectivity and thus jeopardize its claim of women's equal political entitlement and agency. Given the hegemony of individualism, I argue, this dilemma of difference is inevitable in feminist theory.[4]

Individualism attempts to provide a rationale for liberal democratic capitalism and to mediate the contradictions that emerge in the attempt to maintain both liberal democratic political practices and capitalist economic structures. Individualism theorizes subjectivity in terms of identity, relying on the dominant tradition of Western philosophy, the metaphysics of substance, for its foundations. The metaphysics of substance privileges identity by conceptualizing everything that exists—substances—in terms of essence. 'Essence' refers to the fixed and unchanging properties of a substance that make it what it is. These properties can be clearly distinguished from the accidental properties of a substance, which can be changed without altering its essence. Thus, the metaphysics of substance disavows difference; it emphasizes the significance of the sameness or identity of a substance and it overlooks the significance of difference, both for a thing's being a substance, and for understanding substances. The metaphysics of substance holds that differences among substances are ontologically and epistemologically less significant than their essences; differences are appearances or accidents that are insignificant in relation to the essential attributes that make a substance what it is. The metaphysics of substance also denies that difference operates within substances, arguing that for a thing to be a substance is for it to be or to manifest—entirely, unambiguously, consistently, and coherently—its essence.[5]

According to individualism, the essence of human subjectivity is a set of capacities, primarily reason, consciousness, or rational autonomy, which enable rational, independent self-determination and action. These capacities are distinct from embodiment, which is the ground of the accidental or particular attributes that distinguish human subjects from each other but do not define subjectivity itself. While the expression of subjectivity is embodied, subjectivity is independent of the particulars of the body. The body is instrumental to subjectivity; the body may constrain or facilitate subjectivity but does not determine it. In other words, the individualist theory of subjectivity also relies on the mind/body dualism that is a basic element of modern versions of the metaphysics of substance. Mind/body dualism—the view that subjectivity is a function of immaterial, mental, or spiritual self-consciousness that is ontologically distinct from embodiment—privileges identity in the two ways characteristic of the metaphysics of substance. First, it holds that all human beings are identical in essence, that is, identical in possessing the capacities that define subjectivity. Second, it holds that subjectivity itself is internally identical, or self-present, and that this quality of subjectivity guarantees its stability and coherence.

Individualism's mind/body dualism leads to a theory of knowledge according to which the individualist subject can in principle know anything and everything. Because consciousness is fundamentally disembodied, it includes the capacity to abstract itself from or transcend the material, social, and ideological contexts of its existence, take up a universal, objective perspective, and thus to know its objects entirely and as they truly are. Individualist consciousness includes the capacity to know itself, so one aspect of subjectivity is the capacity to know that one is a human subject and to understand all that this means. Subjectivity is present to consciousness in a way that none of its other objects are, because, according to individualism, subjectivity is constituted entirely by consciousness. In practice the body is an obstacle to this abstraction or transcendence, so that in practice no one subject can know anything and everything. But individualism nonetheless holds out the achievement of an entirely disembodied consciousness as an ideal and as a criterion for the adequacy of knowledge claims. According to individualism, the more successfully subjects abstract themselves from or transcend their material, social, and ideological contexts, the greater the truth of the knowledge they then acquire.[6] On the basis of my account of ideology, however, the ideological significance of this theory of knowledge is evident. Since it construes material, social, and ideological contexts as obstacles to rather than constituents of knowledge, this theory of knowledge deflects analysis of the relationship of the materially, socially, and ideologically over-determined contexts in which subjects exist and the knowledge claims they articulate.

Within the ideological context defined by individualism and the metaphysics of substance, the possession of the capacities that according to individualism define subjectivity is the only basis on which persons can claim social and political agency and entitlement. Individualism insists that all claims to agency and entitlement be articulated in its terms, and individualism operates so as to bring this about; it interpellates the individual, both producing the effect of subjectivity and obscuring this production. Individualism constitutes a self-concealing grid or matrix of intelligibility that organizes social fields. Subjects must be intelligible as individuals in order to be recognized as such by others (who themselves require such recognition if they are to count as subjects) and to exercise agency within the social structures, institutions, and practices characteristic of social contexts in which this ideological formation is hegemonic.[7] Agency is thus a function of subjectivity; like the body, the social contexts of subjectivity may constrain or facilitate agency but they do not determine it. Entitlement is also a function of subjectivity, and one of the fundamental human entitlements is the right to exercise agency, especially the right to participate in creating and maintaining social structures, institutions, and practices that preserve opportunities for agency and provide all else to which subjects are entitled.

According to this individualist account of subjectivity, social relations are not essential to subjectivity, agency, and entitlement. Rather, interactions and ongoing relationships with other subjects are a function of individual preferences and choices, even if these choices are limited or constrained. This means that social contexts are also instrumental to, rather than constitutive of, subjectivity. According to individualism, subjects exercise agency as a function of their essential capacity for rational autonomy. They assess their needs, desires, and interests, consider their social relations and the social contexts in which they find themselves, determine what action is most likely to produce what they need or desire or bring about what is in their interests, and take that action. Subjectivity and agency are thus the internal ground and motivating source of action. Needs, desires, and interests originate within subjects, and, more or less self-consciously considered, they propel subjects to action. Subjects act on or within their social contexts, but express their essence and maintain the stability and coherence of their subjectivity in so doing. Social relations and social contexts determine neither subjectivity nor agency.

Individualism includes not only a metaphysical account of subjectivity but also an epistemological mode predicated on a logic of binaries. If all that exists is identified by its essence and distinguished from everything else by what it is not, then all that exists can be conceived of in binary terms based on the binary of identity and difference. This epistemological mode is consistent with the metaphysics of substance in privileging identity and opposing it to difference. Individualism presents itself in terms of binary logic and requires binary thinking; subjects are compelled to present themselves, as well as to conceive of themselves, others, their social relations, and social contexts, in binary terms. The binary of identity and difference is the foundation for a number of other binaries in which one term is understood in relationship to identity and thus opposed to and privileged over the other, understood in terms of difference. Two of the most important of such binaries are the distinction of the natural and the social, and the distinction of the private and the public. Together they do significant ideological work, primarily by inscribing mind/body dualism on social existence. This ideological work renders the over-determination of social existence by individualism itself opaque, by suggesting that social existence is naturally organized in terms reflective of individualist subjectivity.

The distinction of the natural and the social builds on the distinction of body and mind to mark off a realm of social existence and experience—the private sphere—in which natural, bodily needs are expressed and satisfied, and a realm that is the appropriate context for the exercise of rational autonomy—the public sphere—in which social matters are decided and these decisions are

implemented through the exercise of agency. These distinctions thus determine both the body and its corresponding social realm as natural, meaning
inaccessible to human action, unchangeable, or changeable primarily with
harmful consequences. In this view, 'the social'—those structures, institutions,
and practices that human agents create—does not determine the natural and
must adjust to or accommodate it in order to avoid the harmful consequences
of interfering in or disturbing that which is natural. Naturalization is thus an
important ideological moment, for when some aspect of human existence is
theorized as natural, it is also understood as that which cannot and/or should
not be changed. Essential motherhood represents women's mothering as natural in this sense, determining it as inevitable, instinctive, and properly contained in its appropriate social realm, the private sphere. So, whatever the
consequences of mothering for women, women's mothering is natural and thus
cannot and should not be changed. This naturalization of women's mothering
obscures the extent to which sexism and male dominance have usually
included intervention of one kind or another into human reproduction, and
the demands and constraints of modern industrialized capitalism require the
continual intervention of human agency into the natural. The natural/social
and private/public binaries do the ideological work of obscuring the extent to
which the natural and the private are not and have never been immune from
human interference. Thus, it is the imposition of these binaries as a framework
for conceptualizing mothering, rather than any natural and objectively
observed characteristics of mothering, that render women's mothering and its
psychological, social, economic, political, and cultural consequences inevitable
and unchangeable.

   A binary conception of social relations, based on the distinction of self and
other, also does significant ideological work in individualist social contexts.
Individualism's insistence on the radical alterity of the other reflects and sustains its view of subjectivity as the possession of essential attributes bounded
or contained by the body and uninfluenced by that which is external to the
self. The self/other distinction minimizes the importance of social relations for
subjectivity. It posits an atomistic social world in which rational, autonomous
agents strive to preserve and extend their control over that which is external to
them, including other persons, so as to preserve and extend their freedom and
autonomy. In this way the self/other distinction both rationalizes and obscures
the extent to which one person's choices and actions can have significant consequences for others. For these reasons the self/other distinction does not allow
for the mutual constitution of subjects in social relations, and theorizes dependence as a failure of subjectivity. Individualism's conception of the self/other

relationship thoroughly problematizes feminist theory's analysis of mothering and the mother-child relationship. An account of mothering that presupposes the radical alterity and opposition of interests of mother and child implied by individualism's binary conception of the self/other relationship cannot adequately analyze pregnancy and childbirth. In pregnancy mother and child are distinct but not separate, and in pregnancy and childbirth mother and child can have both common and conflicting needs and interests. Neither can such an account of mothering adequately analyze the mutual and reciprocal transformations of the mother's and the child's subjectivity that pregnancy, childbirth, and child rearing bring about.

Furthermore, in the context of sexism and male dominance, the binary of man and woman operates ideologically and other binaries are gendered. The 'male' comes to stand for the mind, the social, and the public, and the 'female' for the body, the natural, and the private. Embodiment, the natural, and the private are feminized, and the mind, the social, and the public are masculinized. That the mind, the social, and the public are not only privileged but also masculinized means that subjectivity itself, as premised by individualism, is implicitly masculine. In an individualist ideological context, all human experience comes to be more or less gendered—understood in terms of the masculine or the feminine—and this understanding of experience in gendered terms obscures the ideological imposition of binary logic that genders experience, including the experience of subjectivity itself. An analysis of the ideological work done by the binaries that individualism generates shows that individualism and essential motherhood together position women and mothers in a fundamental double bind. Essential motherhood holds that all women want to be and should be mothers, so that women who are not or do not want to be mothers are deviant. But individualism holds that the capacities and actions characteristic of mothering are not the capacities and actions characteristic of subjectivity. Taken together, individualism and essential motherhood render the subjectivity of mothers questionable and preclude the possibility of a subjectivity that is both human and specifically maternal, but also insist that women who are not and/or do not want to be mothers are inadequate, abnormal, or deviant as women.

In an individualist ideological context, feminism's identity-based challenge to sexism and male dominance explicitly relies on individualism to claim women's human subjectivity and equal entitlement. But feminism finds it almost impossible to theorize the specificity of women's situations and experiences, especially mothering, in individualist terms. Individualism's privileging of identity and masculinization of subjectivity require that feminist theory conceptualize women's subjectivity, agency, and entitlement in ways that bring them in line with an account of subjectivity that can only deny or disavow the specificity of women's situations and experiences. For any gesture toward the specificity of women's situations and experiences constitutes a recognition of women's difference and thus of women's failure to meet the individualist criteria for subjectivity. This does not mean that feminist theory can make no claims about mothering in individualist terms. Rather it means that such claims tend to disavow important aspects of mothering and to deny its significance in women's lives, including the significance of the ideological construct of essential motherhood in all women's lives. The claim of women's individualist subjectivity means that women's actual or potential mothering is irrelevant to women's agency and entitlement. This claim is clearly crucial to feminism's demand for women's equal treatment and self-determination. By claiming women's individualist subjectivity, feminism can demand that women's rights and opportunities are and should be a function of their subjectivity, not of their actual or potential mothering. It can also demand women's freedom, autonomy, and choice with respect to mothering, including women's rights to use contraception and abortion, choose mothering on their own terms, refuse mothering altogether, and engage in mothering in whatever ways they think best. The claim of women's individualist subjectivity also facilitates feminism's demands for men's equal responsibilities for child rearing, for sufficient and high-quality day care, and for public policies that support mothering without requiring or limiting women to mothering, such as legally required family leave from paid work. From the perspective of individualism, all of these can be understood as demands for a social reorganization of mothering that enhances women's freedom and autonomy with respect to mothering while also ensuring that mothering is not an obstacle to women's social and political agency.

But the view that mothering is irrelevant to women's subjectivity, agency, and entitlement slips very easily into the view that mothering is not an exercise of subjectivity. From the perspective of individualism, pregnancy, childbirth, and the care of infants and children seem to require little if any exercise of the capacities that constitute subjectivity. Individualism implies that mothering is a natural or instinctive bodily function rather than an exercise of rational autonomy, and that it is concerned primarily with meeting the bodily and emotional needs of children. Caring for children may enable children to actualize their essential capacities, primarily by maintaining the conditions of this actualization such as healthy embodiment and proper social contexts. But this does not itself require or enhance the exercise of these capacities by mothers. Thus, feminism's reliance on individualism participates in individualism's construction of a gap between subjectivity and mothering that is consistent with essential motherhood and its effects. By relying on individualism, feminism risks the specification of the essence of mothering in terms that oppose it to individualist subjectivity. Individualism and essential motherhood operate together to determine that women can be subjects of agency and entitlement only to the extent that they are not mothers, and that mothers as such cannot be subjects of individualist agency and entitlement. Furthermore, essential motherhood naturalizes this social determination of women's situations and experiences, construing women's bodily, especially reproductive, differences or the course of evolutionary development, rather than human agency, as the factors that determine women's social positions. Thus, essential motherhood obscures the ways in which women's inequality and oppression are related to the social assignment of mothering to women.

In order to theorize mothering in more adequate terms, then, feminist theory must consider the specificity of female embodiment, of women's situations, experiences, and consciousness, and of women's social relations and contexts. In other words, the issue of mothering requires an account of embodiment, consciousness, experience, social relations, and social contexts that resists individualism and acknowledges difference. So feminist theory offers difference feminism, a difference-based challenge to individualism, even as it also relies on individualism to claim women's subjectivity, agency, and entitlement. This difference-based challenge to individualism rejects the privileging of identity and the binary logic of the metaphysics of substance. But it also runs the risks implicit in the dilemma of difference—among them the recuperation of essential motherhood—and draws feminist theory into a number of difficult paradoxes. The basic elements of individualism called into question by difference feminist theory are its mind/body dualism, including the view of subjectivity defined by a disembodied consciousness in principle capable of any and all knowledge; its binary account of social relations that privileges the independence and autonomy of subjectivity; and its instrumental view of the relationship of subjectivity and its material, social, and ideological contexts.

Feminist theory's appeal to difference can challenge individualism in several distinct ways. First, it challenges the gender neutrality that individualism claims for its account of subjectivity. Analyses of women's experiences and of sexual difference reveal the implicit masculinity of the individualist subject (Pateman 1988; Spelman 1988). If differences between men and women and women's oppression persist within social structures based on and justified by individualism, and if women's difference and/or oppression precludes their rational, autonomous self-determination and action, then for all practical purposes rational, autonomous self-determination and action are possible only for men. An analysis of the sex-based division of labor further shows that (masculine) subjects are capable of rational, autonomous self-determination and action only if their material, emotional, psychological, and social needs are met, and in many social contexts the work of meeting these needs is done primarily by women. To the extent that women's responsibility for child rearing is at the center of the sex-based division of labor, the issue of mothering is at the center of an analysis of this division of labor. This version of difference feminism's challenge to individualism thus argues that the continued hegemony of the individualist ideological formation and the persistence of the sex-based division of labor exclude women from individualist subjectivity, agency, and entitlement and obscure the ways in which women's activities sustain men's individualist subjectivity, agency, and entitlement. Given the material and social conditions that give rise to and support it, individualism produces the rational autonomous agency it claims to describe, produces it only for men, and obscures this production by naturalizing it.

Second, feminist theory's appeal to difference challenges the adequacy of individualism as an account of (masculine and feminine) subjectivity. Analyses of women's experiences of oppression, the specificities of female embodiment, and the activities assigned to women by the sex-based division of labor all point to the importance of the material, historical, social, cultural, and ideological contexts of human existence for subjectivity. So feminist theory challenges the individualist claim that subjectivity can and should be understood apart from these contexts and argues that an adequate account instead understands subjectivity in terms of these contexts. It argues that an adequate theory of subjectivity must take into account the over-determination of subjectivity and its various contexts. To do so, a theory of subjectivity must analyze and explain the complexities of human embodiment, material needs, sexual difference, and material and temporal finitude; the significance of interdependence and social relations for subjectivity; the multifaceted interaction of individual and collective action and social structures; and the multiple operations of power, language, and culture in constituting subjectivity. By calling for a theory of subjectivity that addresses these issues, difference feminist theory challenges the metaphysics of substance and the privileging of identity at work in individualism. It insists on the significance of difference for subjectivity by focusing on the importance of material conditions including embodiment, and of social relations, practices, and institutions for human existence.

Feminist accounts of mothering are closely related to difference feminism's challenge to the metaphysical foundations of individualism in several ways.

First, feminist accounts of mothering indicate that important aspects of mothering, as well as of infancy and childhood, cannot be adequately theorized in individualist terms. These include pregnant embodiment and childbirth, especially the indeterminate boundaries of self and other represented in pregnancy and childbirth; the significance of need and dependence, both the infant's and child's dependence on its mother and mothers' dependence on others; and the mutual and reciprocal transformations of self that occur in the relationship of mother and child, even into the child's adulthood. From a difference feminist perspective the failure of individualism to theorize these aspects of mothering indicates the inadequacy of individualism and its metaphysical foundations, rather than the failure of mothers and children to meet individualist standards of subjectivity. Since these aspects of mothering, infancy, and childhood all point to the significance of material conditions, embodiment, social relations, and social contexts in human existence, these feminist accounts of mothering suggest the need to theorize subjectivity in such terms. Second, feminist accounts of mothering indicate the centrality of mothering to women's experiences, including women's oppression, to the social construction of individualist (masculine) subjectivity, and to the naturalization of this construction. Thus, these accounts of mothering also indicate the need to theorize subjectivity in terms of the effects of social structures and the operations of power in the constitution of subjectivity. By recognizing the significance of difference in the constitution of subjectivity, including the different ways in which material, social, and ideological contexts can over-determine subjectivity, difference feminism intends to theorize the complexity of embodied, gendered subjectivity.

A close analysis of how difference feminism deploys the concept of women's difference to challenge these elements of individualism, and of the paradoxical results of this deployment, however, indicates that feminist theory risks recuperating elements of sexism and male dominance by challenging individualism in terms of difference. The appeal to difference implicitly retains the basic individualist terms of identity and difference, most obviously in the form of the binary of male and female. This means that the appeal to difference always retains some traces of individualism's identity-based account of subjectivity and of its binary logic. The appeal to difference in feminist theory thus always risks reinforcing rather than or in addition to challenging and subverting the distinction of male and female and the social structures, institutions, and practices based on it. The critical and subversive potential of the appeal to difference is always complexly interwoven with its potential for recuperating that which it is intended to challenge. The ideological effects of feminism's difference-based challenge to individualism can include the recuperation of analyses of women and the feminine that are consistent with sexism and male dominance, including the recuperation of essential motherhood, and the persistence within this challenge to individualism of elements of individualism sufficient to undermine the goals of feminism's appeal to difference.

— feminist paradoxes —

Given this conflicted relationship to the ideological formations in which they operate, feminism and feminist theory are inevitably characterized by a number of paradoxes (Scott 1996). With respect to mothering, the most difficult and pressing of these paradoxes concern embodiment, gender, and representation. The paradoxes of embodiment and gender emerge in feminist theory's attempts to theorize the significance of sexed embodiment and gender for subjectivity without recuperating the determination of femininity and women's social position by female embodiment. Such attempts to theorize the significance of sexed embodiment and gender require resistance to mind/body dualism, but the difficulty of theorizing sexed embodiment and gender without recuperating significant elements of mind/body dualism is considerable. The paradox of representation emerges in feminist theory's attempt to represent women's social and political interests while also representing women's specific situations and experiences. Representing women in these two ways means that feminism must create the conditions in which women can articulate their own situations and experiences and must recognize the epistemological significance of women's reports of their situations and experiences. But it also means that feminism must critically analyze the determination of women's reports of their situations and experiences by sexist and oppressive conditions, conditions that render at least some of women's articulations of their situations and experiences problematic and/or inaccurate. These paradoxes of embodiment, gender, and representation are more specific manifestations of the dilemma of difference that characterizes feminist theory as a result of its conflicted relationship to individualism and the metaphysics of substance.

If feminist theory must theorize the significance of sexed embodiment and gender for subjectivity without recuperating the determination of femininity and women's social position by female embodiment, then it must resist mind/ body dualism. Dualist theories of subjectivity, taken together with the binaries characteristic of the metaphysics of substance and with essential motherhood, lead to accounts of an ungendered subjectivity that is implicitly a masculine subjectivity and to accounts of the female body as an obstacle to individualist subjectivity that suits women primarily to the activity of mothering. Feminist theory's most sustained attempt to provide an alternative to dualist theories of embodied subjectivity is its distinction of sex and gender and its social constructivist account of their relationship. In this theory of embodied subjectivity, 'sex' refers to the genetic, hormonal, and anatomical differences that characterize the bodies of human males and females, and 'gender' refers to the psychological, social, political, and cultural meanings that these bodily differences come to have in specific social contexts. The sex/gender distinction assumes that sex is generally invariant, and calls for an explanation of gender, an explanation that feminist theory provides with the concept of social construction. Social constructivism argues that gender is a result of complex social processes, including the care and rearing of infants and children, the development of personal identity, the division of labor on the basis of sex, and organization of other elements of culture in terms of the distinction of male and female. These social processes solicit feminine self-understanding and behavior from women, and masculine self-understanding and behavior from men, and sanction those who do not respond appropriately. These social processes are so pervasive and so complexly interwoven that gender becomes a deeply rooted element of subjectivity and alternative meanings and enactments of gender become practically inconceivable.[8]

Social constructivist theories of embodied subjectivity based on the sex/gender distinction are intended to avoid the biological determinist analysis of gender according to which masculinity and femininity are determined by the sex of the body. They are also intended to allow the possibility of the reconstruction of gender, so that, while the sex of the body remains unchanged, masculinity and femininity might come to be something other than what they are in sexist and male-dominated social contexts. But social constructivist theories of embodied subjectivity also raise difficult questions about sexed embodiment, primarily by problematizing the relationship of sex and the body and the significance of the sexed features of the body for the social construction of gender. The concept of social construction implies that processes of social construction operate on something that exists apart from and prior to these processes. But what exactly is it that exists apart from and prior to the social construction of gender—is it the body, or is it sex, a feature of the body? In addition, how is knowledge of the body and/or its sex apart from gender possible? If gender is socially constructed and this social construction is distinct from the body's being sexed, does it matter that the body is sexed, and if so, how and why does it matter?

Social constructivism can offer two different responses to these questions about the significance of the body's being sexed. One response emphasizes the body's being sexed and argues that processes of social construction produce gender by establishing the social significance of the sexed features of bodies. A second response deemphasizes the body's being sexed and argues that processes of social construction operate on the body to produce gender. Both of these possible answers to the question of the significance of sexed embodiment, however, have problematic implications. Both can slip into a version of mind/body dualism, and neither is entirely successful in explaining the significance of gender as it is currently constructed in modern, industrialized social contexts while also explaining the possibility of the reconstruction of gender. The view that the social construction of gender operates on the sexed features of the body tends to slip into a version of mind/body dualism by detaching sex and gender, and aligning sex with the body and gender with the social. If processes of social construction operate primarily on sex, which happens to be a feature of the body, then female bodies are the basis of femininity and male bodies are the basis of masculinity. In this case social constructivism seems to do little more than elaborate the biological determinist account of gender by arguing that social processes are the mechanism by which the sex of the body determines the gender of the person. This explanation of the significance of sexed embodiment explains the persistence of two genders in most social and cultural contexts and the persistence of the social significance of gender, but it does not avoid the implication that gender is a function of sex, which is a natural, invariant feature of the body. Neither does it allow for significant reconstruction of gender, since it implies that the possible meanings of gender are limited by the dimorphism of sex. This explanation of the significance of sexed embodiment thus retains traces of mind/body dualism in its implication that gender, understood as the social significance of sex, is a function of the sexed features of the body and that both sex and gender are accidental features of an essentially ungendered subjectivity (Butler 1990: 4–9).

The account of gender that deemphasizes the body's being sexed and argues that processes of social construction operate on the body to produce gender, however, raises almost as many questions as it answers. For instance, if the sex of the body is less directly relevant to gender, then why does the social construction of masculinity and femininity tend to mimic sex so that male bodies are almost invariably gendered masculine and female bodies are almost invariably gendered feminine? On the other hand, if the social construction of gender does not operate primarily on the sex of the body, what is the explanatory value of the concept of sex distinguished from gender? If processes of social construction operate on the body, which happens to be sexed, then it would seem that the sex of the body is irrelevant to the gender of the person. In this case social constructivism implies that embodied persons might come to have all kinds of different personality traits, cognitive and emotional dispositions, social roles and functions, and styles of self-presentation that have nothing to do with their being genetically, hormonally, and anatomically male or female. This explanation of the significance of sexed embodiment avoids the implication that gender is determined by and is an effect of sexed embodiment. Instead it suggests that the social significance of sexed embodiment is an effect, rather than a cause, of the social construction of gender. It implies that sexual dimorphism becomes socially significant because the social construction of gender tends to be dimorphic. It also implies that theories of embodied subjectivity that posit the sex of the body as the material foundation of gender read back into the social construction of gender a material foundation that gender does not really have. This explanation of the significance of sexed embodiment allows for considerable reconstruction of gender by suggesting that the various components that constitute gender can be disentangled and recombined in so many different ways and to such an extent that the binary distinction of masculinity and femininity would be almost meaningless. But this explanation of the significance of sexed embodiment does not account for the persistence of two genders in most social and cultural contexts. It distinguishes sex and gender but then disembodies gender to such an extent that it slips into mind/body dualism by implying that gender is an attribute of a disembodied consciousness and that (sexed) embodiment is not significant to (disembodied) gender.

The difficulty of explaining the significance of sexed embodiment within the terms of social constructivist theories of gender based on the sex/gender distinction is evident in the way that these theories of gender simultaneously detach and reattach some combination of sex and gender to the body. The sex/gender distinction is implicitly an explanatory triad—body/sex/gender—with sex as a pivotally unstable term, always poised on the verge of collapsing into either the body or gender and thus of returning feminist theory to a version of mind/body dualism. To this extent, social constructivist theories of gender based on the sex/gender distinction do not provide an adequate alternative to individualism's dualist account of subjectivity. If social constructivism theorizes gender as a function of the sexed features of the body and thus as accidental to subjectivity, then it does not account for either the significance of gender in social relations or the significance of women's difference. But if it theorizes gender as an attribute of a disembodied consciousness, then it accounts for the significance of gender in social relations and the significance of women's difference, but it dematerializes both gender and women's difference.

Social constructivist accounts of embodied subjectivity based on the sex/
gender distinction also have paradoxical implications when they are deployed
in the analysis of mothering. On one hand, to the extent that such accounts of
embodied subjectivity deemphasize the significance of sexed embodiment for
gender, they resist essential motherhood's claim that the female body determines women's mothering. This resistance to essential motherhood enables
feminism's arguments for women's equal subjectivity, agency, and entitlement, including the argument that women's (potential or actual) mothering
is irrelevant to women's subjectivity, agency, and entitlement. In addition,
deemphasizing the significance of sexed embodiment for gender allows for
the reconstruction of gender that feminism advocates, especially the reconstruction of essential motherhood's linkage of the female body, femininity,
and mothering. But precisely as a result of this deemphasis of the significance
of female embodiment, analyses of mothering based on social constructivist
accounts of embodied subjectivity risk the misrepresentation of the significance of mothering in some women's lives and obscure the ideological effects
of essential motherhood in all women's lives. On the other hand, if analyses of
mothering emphasize the significance of gender for consciousness they can
theorize the significance of mothering in women's lives while also recognizing
the ideological effects of essential motherhood. But in this case they also risk
the recuperation of essential motherhood's insistence that femininity requires
or determines women's mothering and thus jeopardize feminism's arguments
for women's equal subjectivity, agency, and entitlement.

Apart from the difficulties of the sex/gender distinction, the concept of
social construction does not necessarily escape the terms of individualism and
the metaphysics of substance. The concept of social construction can presuppose some essence of subjectivity on which processes of social construction
operate. For instance, a dualist theory of subjectivity can posit as the essential
feature of subjectivity a disembodied potential for rational autonomy and
argue that the social construction of gender is one element of the social
processes that actualize this potential, namely, the element that engenders this
potential so that it is actualized as masculine or feminine. Social psychological
theories that explain gender in terms of learning, imitation, positive and negative reinforcement, and/or role socialization can be consistent with an individualist account of subjectivity as a disembodied, ungendered potential that is
actualized and gendered by processes of social construction. Psychoanalytic
theories of the establishment of a core self through processes of separation and
individuation occurring prior to or in the course of the acquisition of gender
can also be consistent with an individualist account of subjectivity as ungen-

dered potential. These explanations of social construction figure gender as a set of traits or personality dispositions acquired by essentially ungendered subjects, primarily as a result of others interacting with them in gender-specific ways. Further, social constructivism often argues that gender-specific social relations are themselves an object of knowledge that can be acted on by subjects, and that changing these social relations so that men and women are treated in the same ways would reveal the ungendered subjectivity that men and women share. This argument also implies that gender is an accidental attribute of subjectivity, which is defined by its essential attributes.

Thus to the extent that social constructivist theories of gender recuperate elements of individualism, they do not provide adequate conceptual foundations for theorizing women's difference because they can imply an ungendered subjectivity on which the social construction of gender operates. But when they try to provide such conceptual foundations, they may do so in terms of the sexed body; thus, they risk reconceptualizing women and the feminine in terms of embodiment, understood in individualist terms, and excluding women from subjectivity. These risks are especially salient in connection with mothering. In the context of the hegemony of individualism and the persistence of sexism and male dominance, the construct of essential motherhood is the most deep-seated version of the conceptualization of women and the feminine in terms of the female body. So an appeal to sexed embodiment to challenge individualism and theorize women's difference clearly risks recuperating the conceptualization of women and the feminine in terms of the female body on which essential motherhood relies. But a theory of gender that cannot account for the specificity of women's situations and experiences risks overlooking important aspects of women's situations and experiences of mothering, leaving them unanalyzed. It also risks overlooking important aspects of essential motherhood, leaving them unchallenged and in place.

These paradoxes of embodiment and gender are the most difficult elements of the dilemma of difference that emerge in relationship to theorizing mothering. But similar paradoxes concerning consciousness, social relations, and social contexts are also effects of feminist theory's appeal to difference to challenge individualism and theorize women's difference. On the grounds that an account of the specificity of women's situations and experiences requires a theory of consciousness other than the individualist view of consciousness as ontologically distinct from others and as undetermined by its processes of knowledge acquisition and/or its objects of knowledge, feminist theory has looked to phenomenological, psychoanalytic, and practicalist accounts of consciousness for this alternative. These accounts of consciousness attempt to allow, in one way or another, for the effects of sexed/gendered embodiment and gender-specific social relations and practices on consciousness, thus suggesting the gender specificity of consciousness. Theories of women's distinctive epistemological modes or standpoints and some feminist reinterpretations of psychoanalysis, for example, attempt to provide a basis for resisting the concept of disembodied consciousness.[9] But in the context of the continued hegemony of individualism, theorizing consciousness in terms of difference risks reinstantiating the male/female binary at the level of consciousness. Given the implicit masculinity of the individualist subject, theories of the gender specificity of consciousness risk conceptualizing women's epistemological positions as limited, partial, and inadequate, and thus reconsolidating women's exclusion from individualist subjectivity. Some feminist accounts of gender try to avoid these risks of devaluing women's consciousness by valorizing women's epistemological positions. But this valorization of women's epistemological positions, in terms of either the factors that determine these positions or in terms of their effects, does not remove this risk. Such a valorization of women's epistemological positions still relies on the male/female binary, even when it is based on a theory of the social construction of gender, and thus retains traces of the privileging of identity at work in individualism. This paradox concerning gender-specific consciousness is also very pressing in connection with mothering. The notion of women's consciousness or standpoint slips very easily into the notion of maternal consciousness or standpoint. This is also true of the notion of a feminist consciousness or standpoint, to the extent that 'feminist' here bears some mimetic relationship to 'woman'. The construct of essential motherhood insists on—while also naturalizing—a maternal consciousness or standpoint, explicitly for mothers and implicitly for all women, and in this way rationalizes mother's and women's oppression and exclusion from individualist subjectivity, agency, and entitlement. So the attempt to theorize a gender-specific consciousness risks recuperating essential motherhood's requirement of a maternal consciousness of all mothers, and all women.

If difference feminist theory rejects the individualist account of social relations that privileges the independence and autonomy of subjects in interaction with others, then it requires a theory of social relations that can account for interdependence and reciprocal constitution of subjectivity. Analyses of the social construction of gender can be understood as attempts to theorize social relations in these terms. These analyses reject both the view that gender is an accidental and insignificant attribute of individuals and the view that some combination of embodiment and sex determines gender apart from social relations. They argue instead that subjectivity is not only gendered, but is itself constructed in and through social relations, and that the gendered self comes into being only in and through interactions with others. But vestiges of individualism can persist in such theories of subject construction in several ways, as I have argued in connection with feminist theories of the social construction of gender. For example, these theories can accept the individualist view of the essential capacities that define subjectivity and nonetheless argue that the development or actualization of these capacities is a function of social relations. Social constructivist accounts of subjectivity thus retain a privileging of identity by locating the origins of the essential capacities defining subjectivity within the individual, as complete in potentiality and waiting to be drawn out or actualized in the individual's interactions with others. And, in an ideological context defined by individualism and essential motherhood, social constructivist theories of subjectivity risk reconsolidating the view that feminine subjectivity in particular is a function of women's relationships to others. Essential motherhood represents mothers as the persons most responsible for interacting with others, especially children, in ways that enable the actualization of their potentials for subjectivity and extends this responsibility to femininity as well. So theorizing subject constitution in terms of social relations can risk the recuperation of this element of essential motherhood.

Feminism's difference-based challenge to individualism also challenges the individualist view of subjects as acting in and on, but being undetermined by, the social structures, institutions, and practices of their social contexts. So it also requires an alternative account of the relationship of subjectivity and its social contexts. With respect to women, such an alternative must explain the effects of social contexts on women's situations, experiences, and consciousness but also allow for the change of social contexts to improve women's situations. If social contexts, however, shape women's experiences and consciousness, then change of social context would also change women's experiences and consciousness. Modern feminist theory has looked to both Marxist theories of subjectivity and existentialism for such accounts of the relationship of subjectivity and its social contexts (Jaggar 1983; Beauvoir 1989 [1952]). But if the effects of social contexts are gender specific, then what are the implications of change of social contexts for women's difference? Feminist theory needs to claim the reality of women's unequal social status and the oppression of women, explain their effects, and deflect the view that women's inequality is a result of women's being inadequate, less developed, or less capable than men. So it has argued that women's oppressive social contexts, rather than any innate female characteristics, limit women's development and accomplishment. But, given an account of subjectivity and social context that sees social context as influencing or determining subjectivity, what would liberation from this oppression mean for women and the feminine? Would liberation from oppression entail liberation from femininity? Would women so liberated no longer be women? In other words, can valorizing accounts of women's difference argue for the changes in social contexts required for the liberation of women without also contradicting, or at least problematizing, their arguments for the preservation of those aspects of women's difference that they valorize?

In other words, a theory of gender-specific effects of social contexts on subjectivity raises the possibility that change of social contexts does away with gender specificity itself, in which case this theory may obscure as much as it explains about the specificity of women's situations and experiences. In any case, the possibility that change of social contexts does away with gender specificity itself at least problematizes the concept of difference on which such a theory of gender and its social contexts would depend. This paradoxical result is also an effect of traces within feminist theory's difference-based challenge to individualism of the privileging of identity and the binary of male and female typical of individualism. And just as the paradox of a simultaneous detaching and reattaching of gender to (sexed) embodiment marks the persistence of individualism in feminist social constructivism, so too the paradox of an insistence on the specificity of women's situations and experiences that simultaneously raises the possibility of eradicating this specificity marks the persistence of individualism in feminist theory's attempt to theorize the gender-specific effects of social contexts on subjectivity while also allowing for their change. Theories of the gender-specific effects of social contexts risk recuperating rather than disrupting the link between gender and social contexts. This in turn risks perpetuating rather than changing the determination of the specificity of women and the feminine in terms of restrictive and/or oppressive social contexts. These risks are also especially serious in connection with essential motherhood. Essential motherhood determines the maternal and the feminine in part by locating them in specific social contexts, such as the family or the private sphere, and delegitimating and/or pathologizing forms of mothering and/or femininity that do not confine themselves to such social contexts. Theories of the gender-specific effects of social contexts risk a similar containment of mothering and/or femininity within social contexts taken to be appropriate to them.

Finally, the dilemma of difference in feminism and feminist theory also generates paradoxes with respect to representation. As a social and political movement, feminism claims to represent the interests of women. But the appeal to difference problematizes the representation of women and women's interests. In order to qualify as political subjects and agents women must be represented in terms of individualist subjectivity, especially when sexism and male dominance operate by constructing women as different. But, if feminism represents women in terms of their individualist subjectivity, it risks denying the specificity of women's experiences and situations. And if feminism represents women in terms of difference, it risks their disqualification for the very agency and entitlement that feminism insists on for women. This paradox is compounded when representation is understood to include presenting women's experiences and situations from women's point of view. Contemporary feminism and feminist theory have been particularly committed to representing women in the sense of creating the conditions under which women can speak for themselves—articulate their experiences and voice their interests. This concept of representation presupposes that women are in the best position to articulate their own experiences and interests. If sexism and male dominance operate by determining women as different, however, then women's reports of their experiences and their situations are likely to be determined at least in part by sexism and male dominance. In this case it is not obvious or inevitable that women occupy the best position from which to articulate their experiences, at least not without some analysis of what social forces have determined those experiences. Thus, creating the conditions in which women can speak for themselves may not produce the most adequate account of women's experiences, from the perspective of a feminist social and political agenda. At the same time, this appeal to difference paradoxically insists on the similarity of all women, thus denying differences among women and misrepresenting the needs, interests, situations, and experiences of at least some women. So, to the extent that feminist theory appeals to difference to represent the specificity of women's experiences and situations, it does not merely report or document difference, it participates in the determination of difference itself.

This paradox of representation is evident in feminist accounts of mothering in several ways. First, it is evident in feminism's difficulties in representing the interests of women and representing the interests of mothers, where feminism finds itself making contradictory claims about and on behalf of women and mothers. These contradictory claims signal the difficulties of feminism's reliance on individualism to represent women, in combination with an appeal to difference to represent mothers. To represent the interests of women, feminism appeals to individualism to insist on women's equal subjectivity, entitlement, and agency, thereby emphasizing those interests that women tend to have in common whether or not they are mothers. But to represent mothers, feminism appeals to difference to represent the specificity of mothers' situations, experiences, and interests. Representing women in terms of individualism, however, may misrepresent mothering and disavow the complex significance of mothering in women's lives, including the significance of essential motherhood as an ideological formation in all women's lives. But representing mothers in terms of difference jeopardizes feminism's claim to women's equal subjectivity, entitlement, and agency, thereby risking the recuperation of major elements of sexism and male dominance. At the same time, representing women in terms of individualism implicitly recognizes sexual difference by distinguishing men and women, and representing mothers in terms of difference implicitly emphasizes identity by implying the identity of all mothers' situations, experiences, and interests. Furthermore, both individualist, identity-based challenges to sexism and male dominance and difference-based challenges to individualism risk the recuperation of essential motherhood, although in different ways. Feminism's reliance on individualism risks recuperating essential motherhood's implication that mothering is not an exercise of subjectivity and its appeal to difference risks recuperating essential motherhood's implication that all women want to be and should be mothers. In other words, the complex interplay of identity and difference that gives rise to the dilemma of difference is evident in the difficulties of feminism's attempts to represent both women and mothers.

The paradox that emerges when the representation of women refers to enabling women to articulate their situations, experiences, and consciousness can also be illustrated in relationship to mothering. According to this view of representation, women's reports of their experience of mothering must at least be taken seriously, if not afforded a privileged epistemological position, by feminism and feminist theory. But, given the effects of individualism and essential motherhood, it is likely that women's experience of mothering, and their reports of it, are determined by the very ideological formations that feminism means to challenge. So feminist theory faces the difficulty of enabling the presentation of women's report of their experiences of mothering while also analyzing and critiquing women's situations and experiences of mothering, which includes analyzing and critiquing the conditions that determine women's reports of their experiences of mothering. This difficulty means that feminism may simultaneously represent women—to the extent that it enables women to report their experiences—and fail to represent women—to the extent that it undermines the conditions of women's reports of their experiences of mothering. Furthermore, a thorough consideration of women's reports of their experience of mothering reveals considerable differences among women. The very recognition of differences among women with respect to mothering problematizes the representation of women's experience; difference in this context fragments rather than unifies the experiences of women. This recognition of difference among women reveals the extent to which feminist theory may participate in the determination of women's difference in order to ground its claims to represent women. Such a recognition may be a good development in that it allows feminist theory to analyze critically the conditions of its own practices of representation. But it may be a problematic development from the point of view of the constraints imposed on feminist political practice by its ideological contexts. How is feminism to proceed if it requires both the constitution of women in terms of difference and the recognition of differences among women? These paradoxical aspects of representation in feminist theory point to difficult questions about the ideological over-determination of experience, and of perception, understanding, and articulation of experience.

— theorizing mothering and reconceptualizing feminist theory —

The analyses of feminist accounts of mothering that follow elaborate the ways in which the project of theorizing mothering is both crucially important and highly risky for feminist theory. None of these accounts of mothering succeeds entirely in addressing the dilemma of difference, if that is taken to mean avoiding or resolving the paradoxes generated by the dilemma of difference. My analyses of these feminist accounts of mothering instead show that the dilemma of difference is intractable in feminist theory and remains most pressing and most difficult in relation to mothering, as long as feminism and feminist theory must operate in an ideological context characterized by the hegemony of individualism and essential motherhood. In such a context, feminist analyses of mothering will always be characterized by inconsistencies and contradictory implications; indeed, the more directly an account of mothering addresses the paradoxes generated by the dilemma of difference, the more explicitly it leads to inconsistencies and contradictory implications. These conclusions indicate that feminist theory ought to abandon the project of developing a completely exhaustive and consistent account of mothering that entirely avoids the dilemma of difference and essential motherhood. Instead feminist theory must recognize that, given the hegemony of individualism and essential motherhood, mothers' situations and experiences themselves will be over-determined and contradictory and thus that feminist accounts of mothering will have to negotiate the dilemma of difference (Spivak 1993: 128–29). Feminist accounts of mothering will have to focus on specific instances of mothering in specific contexts, so as to analyze in detail the complex processes of over-determination that differently constitute mothering in different material, social, and ideological contexts. Feminist theory will have to resist the tendency to totalize such accounts of mothering; it will have to accept that its analyses of mothering will be partial and fragmentary, and that some feminist accounts of mothering will be inconsistent with other feminist accounts of mothering (Fraser and Nicholson 1990).

Giving up the goal of a completely exhaustive and consistent account of mothering further implies reconceptualizing the project of analyzing mothering in terms of resistance to individualism and essential motherhood. In the context of the hegemony of individualism and essential motherhood, it is impossible to refuse the terms of these ideological formations entirely, but it is possible to resist them to one extent or another (Spivak 1993: 42). No account of mothering will completely resolve the dilemma of difference and the paradoxes it generates for feminist theory. But reconceptualizing the goals of feminist theory in terms of resistance to individualism and essential motherhood leaves open the possibility that an account of mothering that is not completely exhaustive and entirely consistent can nonetheless provide a viable alternative to essential motherhood in specifically defined contexts or at specifically defined moments. So feminist theory must consider which resisting accounts of mothering are best for advancing which specific feminist social and political goals in which particular local contexts and at what specific moments. This means that feminist theory will have to accept what I will call a paradoxical politics of mothering.

Reconceptualizing the goals of feminist theory in terms of resistance to individualism and essential motherhood also implies the need for a persistent and critical interrogation of feminist theory itself. If elements of the individualist ideological formation will continue to exert some influence on and have some appeal to feminist theory as long as it is hegemonic, then feminist theory must be able to analyze the interests and desires that motivate its accounts of women, especially its accounts of mothering, and consider critically their presuppositions and effects. This implication of my views on reconceptualizing the goals of feminist theory in terms of resistance to individualism and essential motherhood does not mean that feminist theory should avoid or refuse the issue of mothering for fear of recuperating essential motherhood. On the contrary, the complexity of the ideological intersection of individualism and essential motherhood suggests that traces of essential motherhood will persist even in accounts of women's subjectivity, situations, and experiences that do not explicitly consider mothering. Feminist theory cannot avoid and should not refuse the issue of mothering, despite the formidable risks of theorizing mothering. For, if feminist thinkers do not theorize mothering, essential motherhood will continue to hold sway. Others will not only theorize mothering in these terms, but will also act to put into practice as much of their essentialist views of mothering as they can. In my view, the risks for feminism, and for women, of theorizing mothering are minimal in comparison to the risks of not doing so.

MOTHERING AND THE
EMERGENCE OF FEMINISM

challenging and recuperating individualism

— the emergence of feminism —

THE CONFLICTED RELATIONSHIP of feminism and individualism, the dilemma
of difference, and the paradoxes it generates have all characterized feminism
in the United States since its emergence at the beginning of the twentieth
century. The prominence and urgency of issues related to mothering are also
evident early in the development of feminism. As Nancy Cott argues, the
term 'feminism' marks a fundamental reconfiguration of the ideas of the
nineteenth-century woman movement. And, as Cott also points out, the emergence of feminism included a wide-ranging debate about mothering between
Charlotte Perkins Gilman and Ellen Key that was largely responsible for
"[bringing] the term 'feminism' and the question of its definition to public
attention" (1987: 48; see also Buhle 1981: 292–95). My analysis of this debate
shows that the interplay of identity and difference characteristic of feminist
theory in an individualist ideological context is evident in the theoretical
frameworks of Gilman's and Key's accounts of mothering. As my account of

the relationship of feminism and individualism suggests, neither Gilman nor Key is entirely successful in avoiding the risks of difference while theorizing mothering. Their arguments for reorganizing mothering indicate that feminist theory needs both an individualist appeal to identity to challenge sexism, male dominance, and essential motherhood, and an appeal to women's difference to challenge individualism. But their arguments also show that appealing to both identity and difference in order to theorize mothering leads to contradictions that are impossible to resolve without compromising the goal of challenging at once sexism and male dominance, essential motherhood, and individualism.

By the turn of the century the nineteenth-century woman movement had brought about major changes in American life, primarily by increasing women's access to endeavors from which they had been excluded, such as higher education, paid labor, business, the professions, and social reform. In addition, the suffrage cause was clearly on the verge of being won, and so women's greater political participation was imminent. But, as Cott argues, the culmination of the woman movement also revealed tensions or paradoxes that had been present but mediated, and to a certain extent reconciled, in the ideas and rhetoric of the movement itself. These paradoxes included a demand for political equality that appealed both to women's human subjectivity and to women's difference. Suffrage advocates, for instance, offered an identity-based challenge to sexism and male dominance in their argument that women are entitled to vote because of their equal human subjectivity and agency, that is, their equal possession of the capacity for rational autonomy. But they also made a difference-based challenge to individualism by arguing that women deserved the vote because, given their 'women's nature' or their specifically womanly experiences, their voting would make a uniquely feminine contribution to social improvement. Even when the woman movement demanded individual rights on the basis of women's equal subjectivity, it articulated this demand in terms of a group identity, thus implicitly highlighting women's difference. The demand for women's freedom of choice also recognized that specific women would make different choices of education, occupation, or other activities. Thus, the woman movement implicitly recognized differences among women, even as it insisted on the unity of women as a group.

These paradoxical demands are instances of the dilemma of difference that I have argued results from feminism's conflicted relationship to individualism. These demands both rely on individualism to claim women's subjectivity, agency, and entitlement, and challenge individualism by appealing to women's difference. According to Cott, the feminism that emerged early in the twentieth century resolved these paradoxes primarily by insisting on the importance of women's individual self-development and fulfillment. Rethinking the ideas of the woman movement in these individualist terms allowed feminism to continue to appeal to the specificity of women as a group, by referring to an interest in and entitlement to self-development and fulfillment shared by all women. At the same time it allowed feminism to avoid prescribing for women any specific form or path to such development and fulfillment, and so implicitly recognized differences among women. This individualist reconceptualization of the ideas of the nineteenth-century woman movement might have allowed feminism to demand women's equality and freedom in terms better suited to the material, social, and ideological conditions of American life at the turn of the century, when the effects of the development of industrial capitalism were being consolidated. But it also ensured that the paradoxes produced by the dilemma of difference would persist in modern feminism.

It is in this context that Charlotte Perkins Gilman and Ellen Key debated the reorganization of marriage, mothering, the family, and the home. Gilman was already well known as a feminist writer and speaker in the United States when she published *Women and Economics* in 1898. Here she argued for a reorganization of mothering based on socialist as well as feminist principles. Ellen Key was a Swedish writer whose *The Century of the Child* appeared in the United States in 1910. This was followed by *Love and Marriage* (1911), *The Woman Movement* (1912), and *The Renaissance of Motherhood* (1914). While identifying Key as a feminist involves some difficulties—for instance, she opposed woman's suffrage until 1905—she was read by U.S. feminists of this era as offering radical views on mothering and sexuality (Cott 1987: 46–48; see also Nystrom-Hamilton 1913: 106–13). The reorganization of mothering proposed by Key differed significantly from that which Gilman suggested, and Key argued against Gilman's ideas in some detail.[1] Gilman defended the position she presented in *Women and Economics* and explicitly criticized Key's proposals in reviews and articles, many of them published in *Forerunner*, which Gilman edited, between 1910 and 1916.[2] According to Cott, "The simultaneous influence of Gilman and Key represented Feminism's characteristic doubleness, its simultaneous affirmation of women's human rights and women's unique needs and differences" (1987: 49).

My reading of Gilman's and Key's analyses of mothering focuses on how each relies on and challenges individualism, encounters the dilemma of difference, and becomes entangled in the paradoxes generated by feminism's conflicted relationship to individualism. Gilman emphasizes women's equal subjectivity in order to challenge sexism and male dominance, as well as essential motherhood. Key argues for a specifically feminine form of self-development and fulfillment in which mothering is central, thus appealing to women's difference to challenge individualism, especially its masculinization of subjectivity, which she also saw in identity-based versions of feminism such as Gilman's. Both Gilman's and Key's views on mothering challenge but ultimately succumb to the dominant ideological formation in which they are articulated. Both Gilman and Key suggest a radical reorganization of mothering without calling for a radical reorganization of other material conditions and social structures fundamental to liberal democratic capitalism. This explains why nothing like their reorganizations of mothering has ever been implemented in the United States, and why such changes continue to be unlikely in the absence of radical change of other material conditions and social structures. Though their proposals for reorganizing mothering are quite different, each is in some way impossible, given the hegemony of individualism and essential motherhood.

My analysis of Gilman's and Key's positions argues that any feminist proposals for reorganizing mothering must take into account the complex relationship of mothering and the material, social, and ideological conditions in which mothering is done. In the U.S. context, these conditions include a free market economy that separates waged work from work done without direct economic remuneration, a separation that supports the nuclear family, the privatization of child rearing, and women's economic dependence on men. In addition, the ideological construct of essential motherhood is one of the conditions that arises from and contributes to the material conditions and social structures of liberal democratic capitalism. Any challenge to essential motherhood is implicitly a challenge to these conditions and structures, and for this reason is likely to provoke considerable resistance. Neither Gilman nor Key anticipates and responds to this likely resistance, and the fact that neither of their suggestions for reorganizing mothering has been seriously attempted indicates the strength and persistence of such resistance. On the basis of my analysis of their positions on mothering, I conclude that the simultaneous influence of Gilman and Key in the emergence of feminism also lays part of the ideological groundwork for the recuperation of essential motherhood in the form of the feminine mystique (Friedan 1963) in the United States after World War II. Since the components of Gilman's and Key's positions on mothering can be separated and combined differently, various parts of their analyses can appear in or be used to construct different accounts of mothering. Gilman's view that the purpose of women's sexuality is mothering can be detached from her argument for the social reorganization of housekeeping and mothering, and Key's view that women's psychological development and happiness requires mothering can be detached from her argument for the state support of mothers regardless of marriage. These components of their positions on mothering can then be combined to create a new version of the argument that all women and only women should be mothers.

— charlotte perkins gilman: social motherhood —

Gilman and Key shared an evolutionary functionalist perspective, based on Herbert Spenser's application of evolutionary principles to social behavior and institutions. Spenser's social Darwinism tends to argue for the functionality of capitalist economic and social structures. Gilman and Key, however, saw in evolutionary functionalism the basis for an argument for changing women's current economic and social position, and thus each adapted this perspective to her own uses. Both argued that the traditional organization of marriage and mothering had outlived its social evolutionary usefulness and was now hindering not only the emancipation of women but also the further development of the human race. Despite this common starting point, however, Key's emphasis on women's self-development and fulfillment yields an analysis of mothering, gender, and social evolution very different from that which follows from Gilman's emphasis on women's individualist subjectivity, agency, and entitlement.

According to Gilman, the principal tendency of social evolution is the increasing specialization and more complex organization of work; these are "the basis of human progress" and "the organic methods of social life" (1898: 67). From this perspective, the evolution of women so far, especially women's economic dependence on men, is inconsistent with human progress. Women's economic dependence on men might have been necessary in earlier times, when primitive modes of production and exchange required great strength, wide-ranging mobility, and single-mindedness, and the care of infants and children required complete attention to their needs and their constant protection from danger. But this arrangement does not serve the interests of men and women living in modern conditions. In these circumstances, women's economic dependence on men fosters excessive "sex distinction" in women (1898: 43–50). When women's survival depends on marriage, they develop those qualities of appearance, personality, and accomplishment most likely to attract husbands. They become pretty and dainty, acquiescent and submissive, rather than healthy and strong, assertive and autonomous. They develop few of the qualities required for self-sufficient existence. But, Gilman argues, while this may help women acquire husbands, it detracts from their capacity to be true companions or partners to their husbands, and it makes them weak and vacillating mothers. In other words, excessive sex distinction makes women incapable of

fulfilling even those duties and functions attributed to them by the most traditional nineteenth-century view of woman's nature or appropriate sphere.

Women's economic dependence on men in marriage restricts women to the
private home and to the work of cleaning, cooking, and child care for their individual families. But this division of labor never leads to the degree of specialization and organization needed to do this work efficiently. It also fosters
attitudes in mothers and children that are not adaptive for modern life.
Gilman argues that modern conditions of production and the further progress
of the human race depend on greater appreciation of interdependence in social
relations. But in private circumstances, mothers focus on the needs and interests of their family members and develop no appreciation of the needs and
interests of those outside their families and immediate social settings. And
children raised with a mother available and expected to meet their every need
become self-centered and selfish. They become adults who lack a sense of
social concern, and who are unable to see beyond themselves and their immediate needs and to recognize the common interests of all humanity. Finally,
women's economic dependence on men and their restriction to the private
home deprives society as a whole of the contributions to further progress that
women would make if they acquired the socially useful characteristics fostered
by education, paid work, and participation in political life.

This analysis of women's situation led Gilman to the conclusion that it is
not marriage and mothering per se, but rather women's economic dependence
on men and the traditional gender division of labor that limit women, hinder
progress, and ought to be changed. Gilman insisted that women should be able
to enjoy the benefits of marriage and mothering without having to forgo meaningful paid work and political participation. Thus, she argued for the socialization of the work traditionally done by women in the private home. She
envisioned homes and apartments in which several families share some living
quarters, while also having private quarters. She imagined neighborhoods in
which several family dwellings share a "baby garden," workshops, laundries,
and cleaning services all staffed by well-trained, efficient experts. Gilman
describes these circumstances: "The home, quiet, sweet, and kitchenless, will
be visited by swift, skilled cleaners to keep it up to the highest sanitary standards; the dishes will come in filled with fresh, hot food and go out in the same
receptacle, for proper cleansing; the whole labor of 'housekeeping' will be
removed from the home, and the woman will begin to enjoy it as a man does.
The man will also enjoy it more. It will be cleaner, quieter, more sanitary, more
beautiful and comfortable and far less expensive" (1910b: 6). At the same
time, women's paid work would be organized to require no more than four

hours away from home, and both women's work and expert child care would be available close to home. Gilman writes: "Think of the kindergarten. Think of the day-nursery. Multiply and magnify these a thousand fold; make them beautiful, comfortable, hygienic, safe and sweet and near—one for every twenty or thirty families perhaps; and put in each, not a casual young kindergarten apprentice or hired nurse; but Genius, Training and Experience" (1910b: 5).

This would be a great improvement for children and mothers over "[t]he mother, nervous, irritable, unfit for her work and not happy in it, a discontented person, her energies both exhausted and unused" and "the sullen misery, the horrible impotent rage, the fretful unhappiness of mishandled children" (1910b: 6). Such arrangements would also benefit society as a whole. Women freed from household labor and child care would be able to participate in the paid labor for which their talents and training best suited them, thus increasing production, providing better professional services, and improving civic life. Those women (and men) interested in and suited to the work of child care and education could be properly trained for it, give it their complete attention, acquire expertise, and earn their living by it. Women who experienced self-development through paid work and political participation would be better companions to their husbands, and children who received better care and education would be happier and healthier, developing the skills and personality traits required of good citizens and productive members of modern society.

Ellen Key, however, characterized Gilman's position as "amaternal feminism" and described it as a program for the abolition of the home. According to Key, in Gilman's work,

> Successive institutions are suggested for the bottle-period, kindergarten, and school-age, and so on. Thus . . . will the parents . . . be supplanted by trained and "born" educators; the children would stand in visiting relations to the individual home with its too warm and emasculating tenderness, while in the institutions they would get the bracing air and the training for the social life demanded in this age, instead of the egotistical attitude of family life. The social activities of the well-to-do classes and the outside work of the wage-earning mothers make mother-care only a figure of speech and the children are neglected. (1914: 127)

In defending her views against such criticism, Gilman insisted that what she called her 'human feminism' was not recommending the institutional care of children in place of mothering, nor communal living in place of private homes. She meant her proposals for child care by experts to supplement and enhance, not replace, care of children by their mothers. And she saw her proposals for socializing the work of the home as a way for both men and women to enjoy the true benefits of home life, such as companionship, emotional support, and respite from work. Gilman argued for a reorganization of mothering consistent with a challenge to sexism and male dominance based on an appeal to women's individualist subjectivity by arguing that this reorganization of mothering would allow women the same experiences of agency and entitlement enjoyed by men.

— ellen key: the renaissance of motherhood —

While Key also adopted an evolutionary functionalist perspective, she focused more on personal and psychological development than on the evolution of social structures. She emphasized the importance of personality and argued that "happiness signifies the development of the powers inherent in the personality" (1912a: 214). She held that the pursuit of such happiness is sanctioned by a "new ethics" that values personal freedom and the right to self-assertion as well as altruism, arguing that "[s]elf-preservation and self-development are the basic conditions for the practice of altruism" (1914: 13–14). Key supported the woman movement and, later, feminism, to the extent that they enhanced "social equilibrium," which requires "that every one . . . have the right and the opportunity to develop and exercise his own capacities" (1912a: 18). But Key's concepts of 'personality' and 'individuality' are gender specific; she ultimately argues that women's complete self-development requires mothering. Thus, she advocated a reorganization of mothering and a form of feminism, which she called 'maternal feminism,' directly opposed to Gilman's position. Key's position on mothering includes a more strenuous challenge to individualism, and a less strenuous challenge to essential motherhood, than Gilman's position.

Key agreed with Gilman that women ought to be economically independent, because this would foster both individual women's self-development and social progress. But she adamantly opposed mothers of young children working outside of the home, insisting that this is unhealthy and harmful for both children and mothers. According to Key, children's development requires their interaction with someone who observes them carefully and closely, and whose emotional attachment to them sustains a particularized attention to their specific needs. This loving care and attention, she argued, requires an individualized setting. Key believed that this care could not be provided in group child care settings, especially if these are modeled on schools, which emphasize conformity among children and provide children with a succession of teachers. She concluded that the only appropriate setting for child rearing is the private home: " . . . the more our laws, our habits of work, and our feelings become socialised, the more ought education itself in home and school to become *individualised*, to counteract the danger of getting fewer personalities while institutions increase. And individual upbringing can be carried on only in homes where mothers have preserved the nature-power of motherliness and given this power a conscious culture" (1914: 118, 136, Key's emphasis). Key was also convinced that it was impossible to do well both the work of mothering and paid work, especially in the traditionally male occupations and professions, and that any woman who tried would inevitably be torn between the demands of both and experience the satisfaction of neither (Nystrom-Hamilton 1913: 105–6, 111). Furthermore, the work done by most employed women, such as domestic, factory, or routinized office work, harms them physically and/or psychologically while providing little opportunity for self-development. While Key recognized that some women might be happier forgoing mothering for paid work, she believed that most women would find their development stunted and their lives incomplete without the experience of mothering.

For these reasons Key recommended legal and social reforms to allow mothers to be as economically independent as possible while still mothering in private circumstances. First, she argued for a variety of ways for women to be economically independent without doing paid labor. She favored married women's property rights, so that those who had some source of income other than their husbands could be economically independent. In those families where the husband's work is the sole source of income, husbands should give their wives a regular allowance to manage without interference. She also insisted that men should be legally required to support any children they father, whether in marriage or out of wedlock, and that divorce should be easier for women to obtain, so that they need not be burdened with the support of husbands who do not or cannot support themselves and their families. Finally, she proposed the state-supervised education of all young women for mothering, and the state support and supervision of mothers of children for whom no other source of support is available. This mother's pension, or social wages for mothering, should be paid out of the proceeds of a progressive tax, on the grounds that in rearing children women are doing society's most important work (1911: 229; 1912: 43). Like Gilman, Key recognized that mothering is a social, rather than private, activity, but she drew very different conclusions about this. Gilman envisioned a reorganization of mothering that would allow women to be mothers as well as paid workers and active citizens, which she believed would enhance women's experiences of all of these activities. Key, on the other hand, argued for a reorganization of mothering that would allow all women to experience mothering in what she took to be the best possible material and economic circumstances, which she believed would enhance women's specific fulfillment in mothering (Register 1982).

Despite their different positions on the reorganization of mothering, then, Key's and Gilman's arguments have in common the effects of the conflicted relationship to individualism that characterizes modern feminism. Gilman's argument for women's equality and freedom in mothering as well as in economic and public life relies on an individualist understanding of subjectivity, agency, and entitlement. But it also resists individualism in its recognition that the social contexts of women's experiences determine the extent of their equality and freedom, and in its insistence on theorizing social relations in terms of interdependence rather than autonomy. The individualist elements of Gilman's position on reorganizing mothering allow her to argue for women's equal opportunity to participate in other human endeavors. But they also make it almost impossible for her to challenge the masculinization of subjectivity implicit in individualism. Instead Gilman adopts the individualist concept of subjectivity as rational autonomy and argues that women are subjects in this sense. She accepts the implicit consequences of this position, namely, that experiences traditionally specific to women, such as mothering, have little to do with women's self-development and must be drastically altered to allow women equal opportunity for other (traditionally male) experiences.

Key's argument for reorganizing mothering relies on individualism in its demand for women's self-development and fulfillment. But it also challenges individualism in terms of difference by theorizing a specifically feminine form of self-development and fulfillment, and by insisting that mothering is a social rather than private accomplishment or contribution. Key's appeal to women's difference also allows her to challenge the individualist concept of subjectivity that Gilman accepts and to develop a concept of self-development and fulfillment specific to women. So Key can argue for the improvement of the conditions of mothering, but must also accept the consequence that women will not have the same opportunities as men to engage in other worthwhile endeavors. Gilman argues for freeing women from many if not most of the duties of mothering in private circumstances, thus significantly attenuating mothering itself, so that women can experience paid work and active citizenship. Key, however, subordinates women's paid work and active citizenship to mothering and subjects at least some mothers, and mothering, to state control, by allowing the state not only to support mothers, but also to define and enforce proper mothering. The individualist elements of Gilman's position undermine feminism's demand for recognition and respect of women's unique social contributions, while Key's implicit appeal to women's difference undermines feminism's demand for women's economic and political equality.

— the ideological work of teleology —

One of the most explicit challenges to individualism in Gilman's and Key's arguments is their attempts to articulate a form of feminism that reconciles individualism and socialism, which both understand as a reconciliation of the needs of society and the rights and desires of individuals.[3] Both Gilman and Key try to bring this about by means of their functionalist concept of evolution. This concept of evolution, however, ultimately turns back the challenge to individualism that is implicit in Gilman's and explicit in Key's arguments. Thus, an important ideological moment occurs in these arguments for reorganizing mothering when the concept of evolution, invoked to reconcile individualism and socialism, instead subordinates socialism—and feminism—to individualism. In Gilman's work the most important elements of socialism are an emphasis on the effects of material and economic conditions on social relations and a recognition that the improvement of the human race depends on collective action by persons who recognize their interdependence and work together to improve the quality of life for all. This materialist framework allows Gilman to concede the functionality of the traditional sex-based division of labor in earlier times, but also to argue that it has outlived its usefulness in changed material and economic conditions. Emphasizing the improvement of the human race through conscious, collective action allows Gilman to argue that women's contributions to all aspects of human work and life are necessary, and that the reorganization of home and family life required to free women to make this contribution is possible. This argument shows that socialism is compatible with feminism. For Gilman the claim that all persons should contribute to the improvement of their society and of the human race is consistent with the expansion of women's rights and opportunities. Her evolutionary functionalist presuppositions imply that, if women's rights and opportunities are expanded, women will use them in ways that inevitably contribute to social improvement. For, primarily as a result of their increased access to education, women's development now makes them just as desirous and capable as men of using their talents, abilities, and training to contribute to the social good (Egan 1989).

For Key the most important element of socialism is the claim that, given the proper conditions, all forms of human work can provide self-development and fulfillment, as well as self-sufficiency. Because all persons are entitled to work under such conditions, a society is obliged to provide them for all workers.

Emphasizing the self-development available through work done in appropriate conditions allows Key to argue that mothering and homemaking could be such experiences if they were reorganized as she recommends. Rather than encouraging women to enter the paid labor force and the professions and compete with men on men's traditional terms, feminism should work for the improvement of the working conditions of all workers, including mothers in private homes. Like Gilman, Key also argues that women's duty to contribute to the social good is consistent with the expansion of women's rights and opportunities. Given greater rights and opportunities, and the appropriate conditions for their work, women will choose activities that contribute to the social good because these activities are also those most likely to lead to their self-development and fulfillment. But, unlike Gilman, Key believed that under such conditions women would choose to devote themselves for some part of their lives to full-time mothering and private homemaking. Thus, Key argues that her maternal feminism is compatible with socialism.

These attempts to reconcile socialism and feminism, however, exclude other elements of socialism that neither Gilman nor Key addresses. Neither imagines worker control of the means of production, the abolition of private property, or collective ownership of the means of production. While both recognize that socioeconomic class division leads to social and political inequalities, neither explicitly argues for economic changes that would lessen or end class division. While both deplore war, neither argues for ending nationalism by means of an international worker's movement. And neither seems to have seriously considered that the class of owners and others who benefit from the capitalist mode of production and capitalist social relations would go to great lengths to prevent even the reformist changes they recommend in wages, working hours, working conditions, and social welfare policy. For both Gilman and Key, socialism ultimately means little more than improved working conditions and better wages for labor, enforced by government if necessary; taxation to provide social services to the poor; and collective but voluntary efforts of groups independent of government to ameliorate the worst effects of industrial capitalism.

This reconciliation of a very attenuated form of socialism with feminism in Gilman's and Key's work is enabled by the evolutionary functionalist frame of their arguments, especially its implicit teleology. Their concept of social evolution includes the teleological claim that change in social relations is generally in the direction of "the improvement of the race" and "progress," but it does not specify the content of such improvement or progress in any detail. Their concept of social evolution thus operates to guarantee that those activities in which individuals most want to engage are also those most likely to improve society and the human race. In *Women and Economics* Gilman frequently uses an analogy of the human body and the social body to illustrate this. For instance:

> The specialization of labor and exchange of product in a social body is identical in its nature with the specialization and exchange of function in an individual body. This process, on orderly lines of evolution, involves the gradual subordination of individual effort for individual good to the collective effort for the collective good—not from any so-called 'altruism,' but from the economic necessities of the case. . . . Social evolution tends to an increasing specialization in structure and function, and to an increasing inter-dependence of the component parts . . . and this is based absolutely on the advantage to the individual as well as to the social body. (1898: 102–3)

This analogy allows Gilman to argue that the improvement of human existence is inevitable because certain moral qualities, such as altruism, empathy, love, and service to others are "organically necessary" in modern life, given its "increasing economic inter-dependence of social relation" (1898: 324–25). But this reconceptualization of the social body in terms of the individual body disavows the specificity of the female body and positions men and women as subject to evolution in the same way. Thus, it suggests that liberal democratic capitalism can easily accommodate the changes in women's lives concerning mothering, paid work, and equal social and political participation that Gilman recommends.

On this basis Gilman argues that both feminism and socialism are inevitable and their effects are fundamentally the same. Women revolt against their economic dependence on men, and laborers against their working conditions, each group thinking only of improving its own situation. But both revolts lead to the improvement of society as a whole, because "with this higher growth of individual consciousness, and forming a part of it, comes the commensurate growth of social consciousness" (1898: 138–39). Furthermore, these changes can and will be attained with minimal change of basic economic and social structures because they are consistent with the general trend of social evolution. The vagueness of Gilman's concepts of improvement and progress makes it possible for her to argue that these feminist and socialist goals are fundamentally consistent with the material, social, and ideological conditions of liberal democratic capitalism in the United States. Thus, Gilman's teleological concept of evolution brings both socialism and feminism into line with individualism and obscures the radical structural changes that would be required and/or provoked by the reorganization of mothering that she proposes.

The way that evolutionary functionalism ultimately subordinates both socialism and feminism to individualism is even more prominent in Key's work. Key represents evolutionary functionalism as a religion; it replaces Christianity, which has outlived its evolutionary usefulness (1911: 6), and offers "the morality which sprang . . . from life and its needs"(1914: 20). Key appeals even more explicitly and more frequently than Gilman to ideas such as the enhancement of life and the improvement of the race, which mark the teleology implicit in evolutionary functionalism. For instance, she defines morals as having to do with "actions which possess a life-preserving and life-enhancing value, for individuals as for society" (1914: 4). Social evolution demands that humanity should make "its more immediate end the enhancement of all that is at present characteristic of humanity" in its "struggle for the strengthening of its position as humanity and its elevation to super-humanity" (1911: 52–53). On this basis, Key argues for the fundamental compatibility of socialism and feminism. She writes, "There is no more ethically promising aspect of woman's liberation than the role it plays in the great democratic revolution; that it coincides quite naturally with the increasingly individualised socialism and the increasingly socialised theory of evolution" (1914: 85; see also Nystrom-Hamilton 1913: 102-13). The circularity of Key's argument for a morality of life-enhancement and the enhancement of human nature that appeals to human nature itself and calls for the elevation of human nature to 'super-humanity' is an effect of its teleological presuppositions. These presuppositions, especially the view that, as a result of evolution, human nature is naturally tending in the direction of both the liberation of women and the resolution of the conflicts inherent in liberal democratic capitalism, bring both socialism and feminism into line with individualism.

The concept of social evolution, then, is doing significant ideological work in both Gilman's and Key's arguments. Its teleological conception of change in social relations, understood in terms of vague ends such as 'progress', 'the enhancement of life', and 'the improvement of the race' allows socialism and feminism to be articulated in terms that ultimately subordinate both to individualism and to the material, social, and ideological conditions of liberal democratic capitalism. As represented by Gilman and Key, neither feminism nor socialism constitutes a serious threat to industrial capitalist economic and political structures or to the individualist view of social change as requiring only the conscious, rational action of individual agents. Neither Gilman's nor Key's accounts of mothering generate a form of feminism that seriously challenges individualism in socialist terms. Gilman and Key underestimate both the degree and extent of change in other social structures, institutions, and

practices that their reorganizations of mothering would require and/or provoke and the likely opposition to the changes for which they argue. This suggests the failure of their arguments to consider the complex relationship of
women's economic dependence on men, women's primary responsibility for
mothering and the ongoing work of social reproduction, and the maintenance
of capitalist material conditions and social structures. The elements of individualism on which their arguments rely obscure this complexity. By emphasizing individual self-determination and by implying the instrumental rather
than constitutive relationship of subjectivity and its social contexts, Gilman's
and Key's evolutionary functionalist forms of feminism recuperate important
elements of individualism.

— the paradox of embodiment: women's freedom and women's sexuality —

Another important ideological moment in Gilman's and Key's analyses of
mothering occurs when their arguments for women's freedom encounter the
issue of women's sexuality. That women's sexuality is a problem for both of
their analyses of mothering is a function of the paradox of embodiment that
results from feminism's relationship to individualism. This is the difficulty of
explaining both women's experience of (human) embodiment and the specificity of women's embodied subjectivity in individualist terms. The interplay of
identity and difference characteristic of feminism in relationship to individualism is evident in Gilman's and Key's encounters with this paradox, and each of
their attempts to resolve this paradox recuperates certain elements of essential
motherhood. Gilman's human feminism makes an individualist argument for
women's economic, social, and political freedom, and in doing so participates
in the denial of the significance of embodiment characteristic of individualism
by denying the social significance of sexuality. But women's difference reap-
pears in Gilman's identity-based challenge to sexism and male dominance, for
the sexual morality she defends holds that women's sexual needs and interests
should be the standard for all sexual conduct. Gilman's explicit denial of the
social significance of sexuality combined with her implicit appeal to women's
difference in her argument for women's freedom work to blunt her individualist challenge to sexism and male dominance. And Gilman's denial of the significance for women of sexuality apart from mothering recuperates a crucial
element of essential motherhood.

Key's maternal feminism, on the other hand, explicitly appeals to women's
difference to argue for women's sexual freedom, but ultimately subordinates

women's sexual freedom to mothering. Key challenges the individualist denial of the significance of embodiment by insisting on the importance of sexuality in women's lives and on women's right to sexual satisfaction. But an appeal to identity is implicit in Key's argument for a sexual morality equally applicable to men and women and in her claim that both men and women should contribute to the good of society through parenthood. Here the combination of an explicit appeal to women's difference to argue for women's sexual freedom and an implicit appeal to identity to argue for men's and women's equal duty to contribute to society through parenthood works to undermine Key's difference-based challenge to individualism. Moreover, Key's view that women find their greatest self-development and fulfillment in mothering ultimately repudiates her demand for women's equal sexual freedom and recuperates important elements of essential motherhood. Thus, both Gilman's and Key's analyses of mothering point to the impossibility, within the terms of the conflicted relationship of feminism and individualism, of a social organization of mothering that includes both women's economic, social, and political freedom and women's sexual freedom. Gilman makes an identity-based argument for women's economic, social, and political freedom, but does so at the expense of women's sexual freedom, which reconsolidates an important element of essential motherhood. Key relies on a difference-based account of women's sexuality to advocate women's sexual freedom, thus challenging individualism. But she does so at the expense of women's restriction to mothering in the private home, mothers' exclusion from public life, and state supervision of mothering, which recuperates other important elements of essential motherhood.

Gilman's argument for women's economic, social, and political freedom rejects the concept of sex-specific 'natures' and holds that differences between men and women are the result of women's economic dependence on men. Not only women's excessive sex-distinction, but also "excessive sex-indulgence" results from the economic relationship of men and women (1898: 29–31). For Gilman, the purpose of sex is reproduction, and "a degree of indulgence which bears no relationship to the original needs of the organism . . . tends to pervert and exhaust desire as well as to injure reproduction" (1898: 31). This follows from Gilman's view that "[t]he sex-relation is primarily and finally individual. . . . [I]t does not become a social relation" (1898: 105). For this reason, human development, which is inherently social, is unrelated to sex. Gilman's 'human feminism' is explicitly premised on this view; it "holds that sex is a minor department of life; that the main lines of human development have nothing to do with sex, and that what women need most is the development of human characteristics" (1914b: 45). This account of sexuality and human development is quite clear in Gilman's position on birth control. She believes that population growth should be regulated because excessive population growth is an economic problem and frequent pregnancy is a health problem for women. But this should be achieved not through "artificial processes of prevention" but through "continence" (1914a: 261). She argues that men object to the woman movement because they fear "losing that service of woman . . . which in itself constitutes the biological base of woman's revolt—this exploitation of one sex for the pleasure of the other" (1913e: 146), and she is deeply suspicious of the "desire for 'safe' and free indulgence of the sex instinct without [its] natural consequence" (1915b: 177). She believes that it is men, not women, who desire women's greater sexual freedom. She writes: ". . . it remains generally true that, individual for individual, or sex for sex, the male claims more indulgence than the female is willing to give. . . . [T]he exclusive indulgence of the male is injurious and distasteful to the female. The slave female had to bear it . . . the free female will not" (1913e: 147). Women's freedom thus requires a sexual morality in keeping with what Gilman believes is the natural and appropriate place of sexuality in human existence. She argues that "in the normal relations of the sexes the female is the absolute arbiter. The male must adjust himself to her standard" (1913e: 145).

This account of women's sexuality is one basis of Gilman's critique of the traditional organization of mothering. Women's economic dependence and their resulting excessive sex-specialization have deformed women's natural sexuality and made them unfit for mothering. Good mothering requires the fullest development of women's human capacities, but women's excessive sex-specialization prevents this. "Small, weak, soft, ill-proportioned women do not tend to produce large, strong, sturdy, well-made men or women. . . . The female segregated to the uses of sex alone naturally deteriorates in racial development, and naturally transmits that deterioration to her offspring" (1898: 182). In addition, women's excessive sex-distinction, along with their restriction to the home and family, deprives women of the knowledge of the world and of social development that child rearing requires. Thus, Gilman's account of women's sexuality allows her to argue against the traditional view of good mothering as requiring women's sex-specific development. She shows that good mothering instead requires women's human development, women's economic independence, and women's participation in all humanly worthwhile activities.

But Gilman's view of sexuality denies its social significance by theorizing sexuality in terms of the view that the specificities of male and female embodiment are unrelated to human subjectivity. This recuperates individualism's mind/body dualism and its distinction of the natural and the social. At the same time, her claim that women's sexual needs and interests should be the standard for male sexuality implicitly appeals to women's difference and claims the significance of this difference, at least for sexual morality. This reappearance of women's difference, however, works not to challenge individualism in terms of difference, but rather to turn back Gilman's identity-based challenge to sexism and male dominance. For, within the constraints of the individualist framework of Gilman's analysis of mothering, the implicit appeal to women's difference recapitulates the nineteenth-century view of women as naturally asexual: uninterested in sexual pleasure and valuing sexuality only in relationship to mothering. In this way, Gilman's argument for women's social freedom implicitly recuperates an important element of essential motherhood.

Compared to that of Gilman, Key's concept of a specifically feminine form of self-development and fulfillment construes women's freedom as the freedom to experience the complete expression of their femininity in all areas of life. This allows her to argue for women's freedom from the constraints of traditional sexual morality. Key's emphasis on the importance of sexuality is consistent with her view that the enhancement of life through the self-development of the individual is the goal of social evolution. She argues that the best love, or "personal love," is a synthesis of the bodily and the spiritual that fosters the self-development of the lovers by leading to "an increasingly soulful sensuousness or . . . an increasingly sensuous soulfulness" (1911: 20). This account of love tries to envision self-development in terms of both body and soul and thus challenges the mind/body dualism and the denial of the significance of embodiment characteristic of individualism. Key further argues that this love generates its own moral standards—individual self-development and the enhancement of life—that are not necessarily those of traditional sexual morality. Any love that serves these goals is morally justified, whether or not it is legally or socially sanctioned, and sexual continence is valuable only to the extent that it serves these goals. While marital fidelity is generally required as a standard for most people, there does occur that love whose very greatness means that it does not require legal marriage or marital fidelity. For Key there should be no stigma attached to divorce and mothering out of wedlock when either leads to self-development and life-enhancement. Indeed, she argues that "when a pair of lovers have reached . . . full maturity, and their complete union can only further their own life-enhancement and that of the race, they commit a sin against themselves and the race if they do not enter into union" (1911: 123). It is these elements of Key's position on sexual morality that led many U.S. feminists to read her as offering a radical position on sexuality (Cott 1987: 46–48; see also Nystrom-Hamilton 1913: 106–7).

Key's difference-based argument for this "new morality of personal love," however, also incorporates an appeal to identity. Key's claim that women are as entitled as men to experience sexual satisfaction and to live according to the sexual morality she describes implies the identity of men's and women's interests with respect to sexuality. This is also evident in Key's further specification of what she means by the enhancement of life in this context. While individuals are entitled to choose lovers freely and to be happy in their sexual relationships, personal happiness and sexual pleasure alone are not sufficient moral justification of sexual relationships. Key condemns "soulless lust" and the "paltry desire for stimulation in new enjoyments" that may claim the status of great personal love (1914: 69–70). The ultimate moral justification of sexual relationships is "the improvement of the race," which for Key means healthy, educated parenthood based on the equal freedom and personal love of the parents. Key holds that ". . . when love is made the ethical norm for the relationship between men and women . . . these relationships . . . are governed by [an inflexible] law . . . that love implies a 'will to eternity' in the dual desire for faithfulness between husband and wife and for projected life in the new race" (1914: 82–83). This argument implies that parenthood is equally important for men's and women's self-development and fulfillment.

These challenges to sexism, however, are recuperated by the way in which Key ultimately bases her "new morality of personal love" on her view of women's nature as best fulfilled by mothering. The duty to contribute to the improvement of the race through parenthood ultimately falls more heavily on women, since motherliness is "the most essential attribute of their sex" and "the foremost essential quality of . . . womanhood" (1914: 115, 121). Key writes:

> Woman is happy to the extent that she can bestow her love upon a person closely connected with her. . . . The very fact that woman's strongest *primitive instinct* coincided with her greatest cultural *office* has been an essential factor in the harmony of her being. The modern, developed mother feels . . . a grateful joy in that she lives the most perfect life when she can contribute her developed human powers . . . to the establishment of a home and to the vocation of motherhood. These functions conceived and understood as social . . . give the new mother a richer opportunity to exercise her entire personality than she could find in modern commercial work. (1912a: 197, Key's emphasis)

Key thus clearly implies that mothering is more important to women's self-development and happiness than fatherhood is to men's self-development and happiness. This belief is also implicit in her proposal for state-sponsored education of young girls for mothering, with no corresponding education of boys for fatherhood (1914: 135–35, 154–67), and explicit in her recognition and acceptance of the greater likelihood of men abandoning or failing to support their children. Her solution to this problem, the state support of women and children not supported by husbands and/or fathers, implicitly accepts a traditional view of men as less committed to parenthood than women.

Key's argument that women are equally entitled to sexual freedom and fulfillment is thus implicitly contradicted by her view of women's nature and women's fulfillment as requiring mothering. And it is explicitly contradicted by the reorganization of mothering she recommends, which ultimately subjects mothering to state supervision and control. So, what many readers perceived as the radical elements of the sexual morality Key defends are contained within the ideological boundaries of essential motherhood. In this respect Key's account of mothering recuperates a crucial element of the sexism and male dominance that feminism means to challenge. Key's difference-based challenge to individualism's denial of embodiment, as well as her identity-based demand for women's sexual freedom and for men's equal commitment to parenthood, are undermined by the reconsolidation of essential motherhood's view that all women need to be mothers and are most fulfilled in mothering.

— the paradox of gender: failures of femininity —

Gilman's and Key's analyses of mothering are implicitly arguments for reconstructing gender, to the extent that they reconceptualize essential motherhood's view of the relationship of mothering and femininity. But the reconstructions of gender implicit in their arguments ultimately recuperate elements of the construction of femininity they mean to challenge. This recuperation is evidenced by several problematic female figures that occur in Gilman's and Key's accounts of mothering, namely the prostitute, the nonproductive but consuming woman, and the lesbian. These figures represent failures of femininity from the perspective of essential motherhood. They also embody fears concerning the effects of reorganizing mothering and reconstructing femininity as Gilman and Key recommend; most specifically, they represent cultural anxiety about detaching femininity from mothering. The occurrence of these figures in Gilman's and Key's texts, where they are also represented as threats to the reorganization of mothering, the family, and the social order that Gilman and Key advocate, shows that Gilman's and Key's proposals for reorganizing mothering are not entirely inconsistent with dominant conceptions of femininity. In both Gilman's and Key's work, these images of failures of femininity do the ideological work of marking the boundary between acceptable and unacceptable enactments of mothering and femininity, and in this way also contain the most radical elements of the social reorganization of mothering, and thus of femininity, for which Gilman and Key argue. These elements include the possibility of minimizing or even eradicating the significance of sexual difference and the possibility of female sexuality detached from mothering that are implicit in Gilman's identity-based challenge to sexism and male dominance, and the possibility of women's sexual self-determination implicit in Key's difference-based challenge to individualism. I argue that, in Gilman's work, the prostitute and the consuming but nonproductive woman work to recuperate essential motherhood's equation of femininity and the maternal, despite Gilman's explicit argument against this equation. In Key's work, on the other hand, the figures of the prostitute and the lesbian work to contain women's sexuality within mothering, despite Key's argument for women's sexual freedom. In addition, as these figures represent the boundaries of acceptable forms of mothering, they also raise the question of what exactly would remain to mothering were it reorganized as Gilman or Key recommends. I argue that Gilman's answer to this question naturalizes mothering in terms of female embodiment, while Key's answer mystifies mothering while also containing it in the private home.

The figure of the prostitute, the degraded opposite of the mother, occurs in both Gilman's and Key's work. For Gilman, prostitution is the logical result of women's economic dependence on men and women's excessive sex-distinction. These developments reduce women to "obtaining bread by the use of the sex functions" (1898: 96–97). Gilman is repulsed by the view of relations between the sexes as an exchange in which women trade sexual, housekeeping, and child rearing services in return for husbands' material support. She asks, "Are we willing to hold this ground, even in theory? Are we willing to consider motherhood . . . a form of commercial exchange? . . . It is revolting so to consider [it] . . . nothing could be more repugnant to human feeling . . . " (1898: 16–17). But Gilman also insists on the hypocrisy of distinguishing between "virtuous" and "vicious" women when all women are economically dependent on men. She writes:

> From the odalisque with the most bracelets to the debutante with the most bouquets, the relation . . . holds good—women's economic profit comes through the power of sex attraction. When we confront this fact . . . plainly in the open market of vice, we are sick with horror. When we see the same eco-

nomic relation made permanent, established by law . . . sanctified by religion
. . . covered by all accumulated sentimentality, we think it innocent, lovely
and right. (1898: 63)

Gilman states explicitly that the exchange of sex for material support is the
most offensive aspect of prostitution. But she also tends to equate prostitution
with "promiscuous and temporary sex-relations" (1898: 94) and to suggest that
women who participate in more blatant exchanges of sex for material support
are "females with inordinate sex-tendencies and inordinate greed for material
gain" (1898: 96). Thus, the prostitute resembles another problematic female
figure in Gilman's work, the "woman as a non-productive consumer" (1898:
116). While women have been denied opportunities for free, creative production, their powers of consumption are "inordinately increased by the showering
upon [them] of the 'unearned increment' of masculine gifts" and by the failure
to maintain any relationship between what a woman produces and what she
consumes (1898: 118). Gilman writes: "We have made for ourselves this end-
less array of 'horse-leech's daughters,' crying, 'Give! give!!' To consume food
. . . houses and furniture . . . decorations and ornamentations and amuse-
ments, to take and take forever—from one man if they are virtuous, from many
if they are vicious, but always to take and take and never think of giving anything in return except their womanhood—this is the enforced condition of the
mothers of the race" (1898: 118–19).

Gilman insists on the similarity of the economically dependent wife and the
prostitute as voracious, insatiable consumers. But this similarity depends on
the slippage of her argument from a focus on the economic exchange of sex
that defines prostitution to a focus on women's sexuality detached from reproduction and deviating from standards such as marital fidelity. This slippage
suggests that what is most threatening about both is women's desire out of
control. Gilman's equation of prostitution, "promiscuous and temporary sex-
relations," and the unproductive woman consumer reveals the frightening
prospect of women's desires unleashed from what essential motherhood determines to be their natural and appropriate ends. These figures thus also represent the impossibility of the combination of women's economic, social, and
political freedom and women's sexual freedom, and embody the way that
Gilman's argument opts for women's economic, social, and political freedom
at the cost of women's sexual freedom. While these figures support Gilman's
argument for women's economic, social, and political freedom, they do so by
reestablishing a specifically feminine asexuality consistent with an individualist denial of the significance of embodiment. And, by implying that women's

consumption is artificially increased as a result of sex-based inequality, these figures obscure the extent to which modern, industrialized capitalism requires the inordinate increase of powers of consumption, especially women's consumption.[4] Thus, they also contribute to the attenuation of socialism that, I have argued, occurs in Gilman's work.

The figure of the prostitute also appears in Key's work, and also serves in part to argue for women's economic independence. But Key distinguishes the prostitute from "the 'fallen' women, so named even when in true love they become mothers" (1914: 72, see also 38). Key equates prostitution not with female sexual promiscuity but with "coercive marriage"—loveless marriage in which a woman trades a "part of her person" for something else, whether her goal is luxury or mothering. Key's new morality of personal love also suggests that "there are many innocent victims among the prostitutes" (1914: 74). Consistent with her valorization of personal love, Key's objections to prostitution and coercive marriage focus less on the economic exchange of sex for material support and more on the immorality of sexual relationships and parenthood not based on personal love. Thus, the "fallen" woman who becomes a mother in true love, but outside of legal marriage, should not be condemned; she is living according to a higher morality than that which sanctions legal but loveless marriage.

In comparison to Gilman's view that prostitution unleashes women's desires through a combination of women's economic and sexual freedom, for Key the evil of prostitution is that it leads to the birth of children in circumstances where their mothers cannot care for them and their fathers are under no obligation to do so. In other words, prostitution leads to unhealthy forms of parenthood. Key's solution to this problem, the state support and supervision of mothers, does not entail a denial or repression of women's sexuality. But it does entail the continued economic dependence of women and the regulation of mothering by the state. It makes these mothers either indirectly dependent on the state to enforce fathers' support of their children, or directly dependent on the state itself for this support. And the direct state support of mothers and children also includes the detailed supervision and regulation of mothering by state authorities (1911: 368; 1914: 132, 157, 167). In other words, Key's argument does not require a denial of women's sexual freedom, but it requires that women's sexuality be subordinated to society's interest in proper mothering, ultimately defined and regulated by the state. Key's analysis of prostitution thus not only recuperates significant elements of essential motherhood, but also assigns to the state the power of enforcing it.

The containment of women's sexual freedom within the bounds of essential motherhood in Key's argument is also evident in considering the other problematic female figure in Key's work—the lesbian. The figure of the lesbian addresses a number of contradictions implicit in Key's difference-based challenge to individualism. By representing the failure of women's sexuality to develop in a "life-enhancing" direction, the figure of the lesbian represents the requirement of mothering for women's self-development and fulfillment and contributes to the containment of women's sexual freedom in mothering. But the figure of the lesbian also mediates a contradiction implicit in Key's work between women's satisfaction and fulfillment in mothering and the possibility of women's dissatisfaction in relationships with men. Key's concept of a specifically feminine form of self-development and fulfillment operates to require mothering of women. But it also raises the possibility that women's most satisfying and fulfilling social relations will not be relations with men, who, on the basis of Key's own account of women's difference, are less likely than women to find fulfillment in parenthood. As a representation of the failure of femininity, Key's image of the lesbian manages these contradictory implications of her appeal to difference by recognizing women's needs for friendships with other women but also subordinating these friendships to heterosexual relations.

While Key recognizes women's right to refuse marriage and mothering, she equates this with a failure of development. She writes, "[i]t lies in the individual sphere of woman's choice as of a man's choice not to choose marriage, or to desire it without parenthood . . . to isolate herself from what may be regarded as an obstacle to her individual development, or to her freedom of movement." But she also construes this as woman's "full right to allow herself to be turned into a third sex, the sex of the working bees, or the sexless ants, provided she finds in this her highest happiness" (1909: 69–70; see also 1912: 73, 93; 1914: 116). Women who do not become mothers may convince themselves that "they have had enough in their work, that many little joys can take the place of great happiness. And they believe this as truly as the infant believes he is satisfied when he sucks his own thumb" (1912a: 78). This portrayal of women's refusal of mothering represents it as a de-sexing of women that can provide only a narcissistic, self-absorbed pleasure that does not truly constitute fulfillment. This portrayal of women's refusal of mothering thus equates proper female self-development with the desire for and the experience of mothering.

Key's analysis of female friendship also supports essential motherhood by requiring women's heterosexuality. She argues that it is "the difference in the spiritual as well as the physical sex characteristics that makes love a fusion of two beings in a higher unity, where each finds the full deliverance and harmony of his being." Without sexual difference, the ideals of personal love are impossible, and, in friendships among women, "the human, individual difference instead of sexual difference forms the attraction" (1912a: 221). Key criticizes the "over-estimation of friendship" she sees in some forms of feminism:

> A passionate worship between persons of the same age—or of an elder by a younger member of the same sex—is among women as among men the customary and beautiful morning glow of love, which always pales after sunrise. ... Those who expect to find the complement of their being in friendship have therefore no greater prospect of attaining the essential in this sphere, and ... they run the risk of missing it in the sphere of love. ... The women of older times also cultivated friendship. But they did not content themselves with it in the place of love. (1911: 74–75)

Thus, women who seek fulfillment in friendship also represent a failure of feminine development. Seeking an outlet for their natural but unsatisfied desire for mothering, they "find in friendship for another woman a valve for their, in great part, unused feelings" (1912a: 79).

But Key's difference-based concept of women's specific self-development and fulfillment also implies that women are more likely to understand, empathize with, and support each other than men are likely to do for and with women, because parenthood has so much less to do with men's self-development and fulfillment. So Key must acknowledge that there is something specifically valuable for women in friendship with other women. But, she writes:

> I wish to emphasize that I speak here of entirely *natural spiritual conditions*. There is today much talk about "Sapphic" women; and it is even possible that they exist in that impure form which men imagine. I have never met them, presumably because we rarely meet in life those with whom no fibre of our being has any affinity. But I have often observed that the spiritually refined women of our time, just as formerly the spiritually refined men of Hellas, find more easily in their own sex the qualities which set their spiritual life in the finest vibration of admiration, inspiration, sympathy and adoration. (1912: 79, Key's emphasis)

Key implies that, while women are not likely to experience "admiration, inspiration, sympathy and adoration" from men, they are permitted to find these qualities in friendships with other women, as long as these friendships do not take the place of heterosexual relationships and mothering. Heterosexual relationships and mothering properly deprive women of the infantile self-gratification Key associates with the refusal of mothering, but women's friend-ships with other women, when properly subordinated to heterosexuality and mothering, compensate women for this loss. The defensive tone of Key's claim that she has never met any "Sapphic" women—she has never met any because she isn't one—and the evocation of lesbian eroticism (in the image of same sex friendship setting women's spiritual life in "the finest vibration") within her repudiation of lesbianism, however, indicate an unresolved ideological tension. This tension concerns the difficulty Key's conception of femininity faces in try-ing to theorize women's difference without also denaturalizing women's het-erosexuality and legitimating lesbianism.

In these ways the figure of the lesbian in Key's work also contains woman's desire within the bounds of mothering. Key's analysis of women's sexuality rec-ognizes and validates women's interest in and entitlement to sexual fulfill-ment, and even allows the detachment of women's sexuality from legal marriage and marital fidelity. But it ultimately cannot allow the detachment of women's sexuality from heterosexual mothering. The image of the lesbian rep-resents the unleashing of women's sexual desire from mothering as pathologi-cal both for women and for society. Like the prostitute and the nonproductive but consuming woman, the lesbian represents a limit to women's sexual free-dom. All of these figures effect the containment of women and feminine desire within the bounds of essential motherhood. They ensure that women, whether defined in terms of their human subjectivity or their specific femininity, remain in one way or another subject to mothering.

These problematic female figures represent impossible instances of feminin-ity, or reconstructions of femininity that are so unrelated to dominant concep-tions of femininity, understood in relationship to essential motherhood, as to be socially and culturally unacceptable and almost unimaginable. These images of the prostitute, the consuming woman, and the lesbian mark the lim-its of Gilman's and Key's attempts to reconstruct the connection of femininity and mothering. They do so by representing that which the dominant cultural imaginary cannot withstand in reconceptualizing mothering and femininity. The fact that Gilman's and Key's attempts to reorganize mothering and recon-struct femininity must bear some relationship to the dominant ideology that equates femininity and motherhood raises the question of what exactly moth-ering would entail if it were reorganized as Gilman or Key suggests. This ques-tion is particularly pressing in Gilman's case, since she argues for the socialization of housekeeping and mothering but also insists that she is not rec-ommending institutionalized child care or the abolition of mothering. But what will be distinct about being a mother, if much of the work of child rearing is done by persons other than children's mothers? Gilman's answer to this question makes several inconsistent claims that are also instances of the paradox of gender—the simultaneous detaching and reconnecting of sex, gender, and embodiment—that I have argued is a manifestation of the dilemma of difference in feminist theory.

On one hand, Gilman argues that the components of mothering valorized by the dominant nineteenth-century conception of womanhood can be conceptually disentangled and socially reassigned. This is especially clear in her argument that in earlier stages of evolution much of the work of mothering was actually done by men. The social evolution that led to the economic dependence of women on men also involved "the maternalizing of man" (1898: 127), since men, having reduced women to economic dependence, then had to care for both women and children. According to Gilman, "as the male . . . encroached upon the freedom of the female until she was reduced to . . . economic dependence, he thereby assumed the position of provider for this creature no longer able to provide for herself. He was not only compelled to serve her needs but to fulfill . . . the thwarted uses of maternity. He became, and has remained, a sort of man-mother" (1898: 125). In this account of the maternalizing of man, Gilman denaturalizes mothering, detaching it from female embodiment and femininity and showing that, under certain social conditions, it can be and has been an aspect of masculinity. The figure of the man-mother represents the possibilities for challenging essential motherhood and reconstructing gender that follow from an individualist account of subjectivity, by vividly suggesting the eradication of sexual difference at one of its most basic sites—mothering.

On the other hand, in describing the reorganization of mothering she recommends, Gilman writes, "The mother would not be excluded, but supplemented . . . the mother breast and mother arms there, of course, fulfilling the service which no other . . . could supervene" (1898: 287). She concludes that "while the mother keeps her beautiful prerogative of nursing, she need never fear that any other will be dearer to the little heart than she who is the blessed provider of his highest known good" (1898: 291). This aspect of Gilman's account of mothering naturalizes mothering, anchoring it even more firmly in the female body by reducing it to female arms and breasts. This naturalization of mothering has significant ideological effects. To reanchor mothering in the female body is to naturalize women's difference in terms of female embodiment. It is also to continue to link women and responsibility for child care, and to individualize mothering, both of which undermine Gilman's commitment to socialized mothering. Gilman's account of mothering recuperates crucial elements of essential motherhood and repudiates important aspects of the social reorganization of mothering that she recommends. This recuperation is evident in the paradox of a reconstruction of gender that both detaches mothering from femininity in the figure of the man-mother and naturalizes mothering in terms of female embodiment. This paradox results from the interplay of identity and difference typical of the relationship of feminism and individualism as this occurs in Gilman's account of mothering.

A different but also problematic specification of mothering occurs in Key's work. The particularity and specificity of a mother's love of her child, according to Key, is partly the result of their physical relationship and the child's physical relationship to the father. But mothering requires more than a love of the child based on the mother's having given birth to it and more than the mother's freedom from the demands of paid work and her devoted and ongoing observation of and interaction with her children. Equally important to mothering as Key envisions it is private, individualized, circumstances for child rearing; thus, her reorganization of mothering requires "a renaissance of the home" (1914: 132). A private home enables a mother to provide "that most essential education,—the indirect,—which radiates from the mother's own personality, from the spirit she creates in the home." Key writes, "[a] home atmosphere is not a condition which stays permanent of itself, one of those works of art which once created remain unchanged. The creating of a home is . . . a kind of art which has this in common with all art of life—that it demands the artist's continuous presence in body and soul" (1914: 133–34). Further, while some fathers may have a talent for education, "In the home, men cannot supplant the spirit and activities of women. . . . Can the heart in an organism be replaced by a pumping engine, however ingenious?" (1914: 136; see also Nystrom-Hamilton 1913: 114–18). That the kind of home Key has in mind here provides physical privacy for one family is clear from her criticism of "[t]he very worst suggestion . . . that of the family colony," which she takes to be Gilman's suggestion. Under these circumstances, Key argues, husband and wife have no privacy, children are subject to the conflicting demands of many adults, and the entire group experiences conflict and discord (1914: 146–47).

Key's image of the mother as artist, creating and maintaining in the private, one-family home what Key calls a "home spirit" or "home atmosphere," based on her "unceasing contribution of self," through which her personality "radiates" and indirectly educates her children (1914: 133–34) does significant ideological work in her argument. This image simultaneously supports essential motherhood's equation of mothering and femininity and mystifies mothering; its emphasis of a spirit or atmosphere that results from the radiation of a mother's personality throughout the home equates a woman's personality with her mothering. It obscures the ways in which mothering involves the work of meeting the concrete, material needs of children (as well as the ways in which homemaking involves physical labor aimed at meeting the material needs of household members). Thus, it effects an ideological containment of the feminine in mothering through a literal containment of the mother in the private home. And Key's emphasis on the privacy of the home relies on individualism's binary distinction of public and private. So Key's argument for the privacy of mothering is also implicitly an argument for the exclusion of mothering—and mothers—from the public sphere, which is another basic element of essential motherhood.

Gilman's and Key's attempts to specify the defining elements of mothering, reorganized as they recommend, thus also indicate the persistence of the dilemma of difference and its effects in their positions on mothering. In particular, the paradox of representation—the difficulty of representing women's experiences and situations in terms that are consistent with both what women actually experience and feminist social and political goals—is apparent here. In their attempts to represent mothering, Gilman and Key both have to rely on the exclusion and denigration of specific groups of women to support their valorizing definitions of mothering. And, in so doing, they both end up reestablishing an element of the traditional view of mothering that feminism means to challenge—the naturalization of women's mothering in terms of female embodiment in Gilman's case, and the containment of mothers in the private sphere in Key's case.

— the significance of gilman's and key's simultaneous influence —

The conflicting elements of Gilman's and Key's positions on mothering, as well as the contradictions that become evident in comparing their accounts of mothering, suggest the ideological significance of their simultaneous influence at the emergence of feminism. While the unity and cohesion of the suffrage movement did not persist after the ratification of the Nineteenth Amendment, the question of the proper status and place of women remained a very contentious issue in the United States. In the late 1920s and early 1930s, Cott argues, feminism was reconsolidated in largely individualist terms. Several conditions explain this reconsolidation of feminism at this time. These conditions include the lack of any one goal, such as the vote, to unite women nationally, and the culmination of the development of industrial capitalism, which solidified the sex-based division of labor that excluded women from the paid workforce and restricted them to the private, nuclear family. During this period feminism was also subject to persistent and conflicting criticism that it was undermining social order by making women too much like men and by uniting women in an unwarranted, sex-based antagonism to men. In response to these conditions, feminism emphasized women's equal individualist subjectivity, right to equal opportunity in education and employment, and the ideal of individual achievement (Cott 1987: 276–83). In other words, feminism responded to these conditions by rearticulating itself in terms more consistent with the dominant ideology.

In this context, the various elements of Gilman's and Key's positions on mothering can be disentangled and reassembled to create a tentative resolution of the conflicting tendencies of modern feminism, a resolution that would include an individualist position on mothering. Such a position would emphasize women's right to autonomy and choice with respect to mothering, such as the notion of voluntary motherhood advanced by birth control and family planning advocates, and women's right to combine mothering with paid work and/or active social and political participation. But it would also emphasize women's individual responsibility for their children, including their responsibility to look only to themselves and their immediate families for solutions to the problems they might encounter in trying to combine mothering with paid work and/or active social and political participation. In other words, such a position on mothering would include the equal freedom and entitlement to opportunity in paid work and social and political life for which Gilman argued, as well as women's equal freedom and entitlement to satisfaction in sexual life and the importance of private living arrangements for mothering that Key advocated. But it would include neither Gilman's ideas about the socialization of housekeeping and mothering, nor Key's ideas about widespread, government-provided support of mothers and children. Cott's analysis of the development of modern conceptions of marriage, the household, the family, and mothering, to which social science (especially psychology and home economics) and mass media (especially advertising) contributed, suggests an individualist conception of mothering along these lines (1987: 145–74).

At the same time, however, the ways in which Gilman's and Key's arguments recuperate different elements of essential motherhood raise the possibility of an almost complete recuperation of essential motherhood in an individualist ideological context, despite the best efforts of various versions of feminism to dislodge it. More specifically, the reinterpretation in modern psychological terms of women's sexuality as directed toward mothering and of the necessity of mothering for women's self-development and fulfillment preserves elements of both Gilman's and Key's views of women's sexuality. Such ideas about the relationship of women's sexuality and mothering, combined with an individualist deemphasis of social and economic reorganization of or support for mothering, very closely resemble the feminine mystique, the conception of femininity that became dominant after World War II and that the women's movement challenged later in the twentieth century. According to the feminine mystique, men and women should be equally educated, and women should work for pay prior to marriage and motherhood if they so choose. But women should also marry and become mothers, and once they do, they should occupy themselves entirely with housekeeping and mothering.

This is not to say that such a resolution of the contradictions evident in U.S. feminism early in the twentieth century directly caused the feminine mystique. An explanation of the causes of the feminine mystique would have to consider much more than just the ideological currents that came to dominate U.S. society and culture in the middle of the twentieth century. But the tentative resolution in individualist terms of the contradictions evident in feminism at its emergence, and the compatibility of a more individualist version of feminism with the feminine mystique, indicate the importance of the relationship of feminism and individualism for understanding the development of a variety of feminist analyses of mothering. Feminist analyses of mothering can vary greatly, depending on what elements of feminism and individualism they include and how they attempt to reconcile the conflicting implications of feminism and individualism. But in an ideological context characterized by the hegemony of individualism and essential motherhood, all feminist analyses of mothering will include contradictions. The difficulties that feminism encounters in its attempts to theorize mothering and resist essential motherhood in an individualist ideological context are well represented, but certainly not exhausted, by the debate between Gilman and Key. These difficulties persist in subsequent versions of feminism and feminist analyses of mothering.

MOTHERING AND
DIFFERENCE FEMINISM

the problem of embodiment

— mothering in contemporary feminist theory —

THE DIFFICULTIES OF theorizing mothering in an individualist ideological context are well illustrated by the turn of the century debate between Gilman and
Key. And these difficulties persist in contemporary feminist theory, given
the continued hegemony of individualism in U.S. society and culture. Like
Gilman and Key, contemporary feminist theorists have faced the challenge of
analyzing mothers' situations and experiences and theorizing the significance
of mothering in women's lives without recuperating essential motherhood.
This means that contemporary feminist theorists have encountered some version of the dilemma of difference and the paradoxes it produces, regardless of
how they approach the issue of mothering. Accounts of the resurgence, or "the
second wave," of the women's movement in the United States in the 1960s
often emphasize its multiple origins and the different kinds of feminism that
developed at this time, but a focus on the issue of mothering leads to a different account of this period of feminism. Historians have traced the origins of

contemporary feminism to the representatives of the women's rights movement that persisted in the twentieth century, such as the National Women's
Party (Rupp and Taylor 1987), and to the civil rights movement (Evans 1979),
the student left and the anti–Vietnam War movement (Evans 1979; Echols
1989). Historians of ideas, philosophers, and political theorists have identified
forms of feminist theory ranging from liberal, Marxist, and Marxist-socialist
feminisms to radical, cultural, psychoanalytic, and existential feminisms and
have stressed how different these forms of feminism are from each other
(Elshtain 1981; Jaggar 1983; Donovan 1985; Tong 1989).

A focus on the issue of mothering, however, yields a different picture. From
this perspective, second-wave feminist theory evidences two basic strategies for
avoiding essential motherhood while negotiating the dilemma of difference.
The first is to avoid essential motherhood by avoiding the issue of mothering as
much as possible, either by minimizing the significance of mothering in
women's lives or by analyzing mothering in overly simplistic, one-dimensional
terms. This approach to mothering often relies on important elements of individualism, whether they are directly stated or implied. This approach involves
feminist theory in all the difficulties of theorizing mothering in individualist
terms, and risks misrepresenting both mothers' situations and experiences and
the significance of mothering in women's lives. The second strategy is to deal
directly and explicitly with the issue of mothering, including all the aspects of
the dilemma of difference that this entails. This approach to feminist theory
usually requires a more or less explicit challenge to individualism. This second
strategy thus involves feminist theory in the difficulties of representing mothers' and women's experiences, situations, and interests in terms that are not
consistent with the dominant ideology, and risks the recuperation of elements
of essential motherhood.

In this chapter I consider the effects of the first of these strategies, that of
avoiding essential motherhood by minimizing the issue of mothering and/or
oversimplifying mothering, and begin a consideration of the effects of the second strategy. I argue that avoiding essential motherhood by minimizing or oversimplifying the issue of mothering has largely problematic results. It
misrepresents mothering, it fails to recognize how essential motherhood as an
ideological formation impinges on all women's lives and how the social organization of mothering is deeply interwoven with other social structures of liberal
democratic capitalism, and it leads to political practices that do not adequately
represent mothers or women. The second strategy, avoiding essential motherhood by theorizing mothering while also challenging individualism, however,
leads feminist theory into a wide-ranging search for alternative conceptions of

subjectivity. I will begin to address this issue in this chapter, with a consideration of the explicit challenge to individualism and the implicit account of
mothering that I see in the work of Jean Bethke Elshtain. But the question of
the effects of a variety of feminist attempts to theorize mothering while also
challenging individualism is a primary focus of the rest of this book. By bringing
together in this and the next chapter Elshtain's work and Simone de Beauvoir's
account of mothering and women's liberation in *The Second Sex*, I will consider
the difficulties of avoiding essential motherhood while also theorizing maternal
embodiment and the material aspects of mothering, and of challenging individualism while also relying on elements of the metaphysics of substance.

— minimizing and/or oversimplifying mothering —

The first of the strategies for avoiding essential motherhood that I have
described is more typical of early second-wave feminism. When the various
forms of feminist theory and practice that emerged in the 1960s and early
1970s are considered from the perspective of the issue of mothering, a striking
similarity becomes clear: all, to one extent or another, see mothering in overly
simplistic and largely negative terms. As Hester Eisenstein argues, "that feminism and motherhood were in diametric opposition had seemed almost
axiomatic in the early 1970s" (1983: 69). Consider, for example, three works
often taken to be emblematic of the varied theoretical origins of second-wave
feminist theory: Betty Friedan's *The Feminine Mystique* (1963), usually considered a classic of liberal feminism; Shulamith Firestone's *The Dialectic of Sex*
(1970), sometimes offered as an instance of Marxist or socialist feminism,
other times as an instance of radical feminism; and Mary Daly's *Gyn/Ecology*
(1978), often considered exemplary of radical or cultural feminism. While
these works attribute very different goals to the women's movement, and rely
on very different theoretical frameworks, their critiques of mothering are quite
similar and the solutions they offer for the problems presented by mothering
all depend in one way or another one elements of individualism.

Both the 'feminine mystique' described by Friedan and the 'myth of femininity' that Firestone identifies include versions of essential motherhood.
According to Friedan, the feminine mystique requires that women abandon all
activities except housekeeping and mothering and "live through their children"
(1963: 282, 288). Like Gilman, Friedan argues that this form of mothering is
harmful for both mothers and children. Women who devote all their time,
energy, and intelligence to mothering develop symbiotic relationships with
their children, unconsciously dominating or consciously doing everything for

their children; in either case keeping their children dependent on them. They satisfy their own otherwise unmet emotional and psychological needs and justify and extend their only socially valued function. Such mothers also perpetuate the feminine mystique itself, for this kind of mothering leads young men and women to marry early, looking for someone to care for them as their mothers did, and thus to become even less capable of raising self-reliant children (1963: 282–309). Friedan, like Gilman, argues that if women were to engage in other activities, especially paid work, that more appropriately engage their time, energy, and intelligence, and provide them with socially valued identities apart from their roles as housewives and mothers, they would also make better mothers (1963: 304–5, 343–44, 356–57). According to Friedan, women's paid work will end the feminine mystique and improve family and mothering with even less extensive changes in family living arrangements and in other social institutions such as schools and workplaces than even Gilman envisioned. Friedan implies that the problem of the feminine mystique can be solved by individual women making the choice to participate in other activities besides motherhood and housekeeping, a choice that will not seriously disrupt marriage, the family, or other social structures of liberal democratic capitalism. This conclusion is consistent with individualism's emphasis on the capacity for rational autonomy as definitive of human existence, and with its view of the relationship of subjectivity and social contexts as instrumental rather than constitutive.

Firestone rejects the claim that the liberation of women is compatible with traditional marriage and family life and argues for the complete elimination of what she calls the biological family. She envisions instead households consisting of a number of adults who agree to live together for a specific period of time, and who take equal responsibility for raising some socially regulated number of children, until these children are old enough to decide whether to remain members of that household or join another (1970: 229–34). This alternative is very different from the two wage-earner but otherwise traditional families Friedan recommends. But Firestone's analysis of women and children in the traditional family is quite similar to Friedan's, and includes a recognition, similar to Gilman's, of the effects of women's economic dependence on men. Firestone argues that the biological family is "an inherently unequal power distribution" (1970: 8) and this inequality is exaggerated in the modern nuclear family where the father has complete power over the mother by virtue of her economic dependence, and the mother has limited power over the children. Mothers are expected to give up all other activities, make mothering the center of their lives, and feel unconditional love for their children. Raising children becomes the substitute for all other activities from which mothers have been excluded, and the bond between the mother and child is based on their shared oppression and subjection to the father. According to Firestone, the contemporary myth of childhood intersects with the myth of femininity to produce a view of both women and children as charming but incapable of independent existence. This justifies male dominance and the creation of social institutions such as marriage and schools where women and children are ostensibly protected but actually controlled (1970: 91–104). Firestone's proposals for ending these oppressions include women's paid labor, the replacement of pregnancy and childbirth with technologies for reproduction apart from the female body, and the liberation of children to bargain for membership and care with groups of adults. These proposals call for far more radical changes in family living arrangements and other social institutions than Friedan or Gilman envision. But they are also individualist solutions in that they see not only women but also children as exercising rational, autonomous self-determination and agency through control of the body and free and autonomous choice of social relations.

Friedan's and Firestone's analyses of motherhood also implicitly comply with individualism's denial of the significance of embodiment. Friedan does so by minimizing the material aspects of mothering and homemaking—the extent to which this work involves providing bodily care and meeting the bodily needs of family members. Her failure to consider these aspects of mothering and homemaking as they are organized under capitalism allows her to minimize the material and social effects of women's entering the paid labor force in large numbers. It also allows her to recommend that women hire someone else to do this work for them, without considering the social and cultural effects this might have. Replacing the women and mothers who traditionally do this work in their own families for no direct remuneration with paid workers, most likely poorer women, subjects these paid workers to a version of the feminine mystique in their paid work. Paid housekeepers, babysitters, and day care workers would still be expected to demonstrate in their work the qualities and traits that essential motherhood requires of women. Firestone's recommendation that women employ technological interventions in reproduction in order to end women's bodily role in reproduction is even more consistent with individualism's denial of the significance of embodiment. Firestone assumes that women's experiences of pregnancy, childbirth, and lactation are entirely determined by their embodiment, without considering the possibility that these experiences could be different in different material and social contexts. She accepts individualism's denial of the significance of embodiment for subjectivity and its view of the instrumental relationship of subjectivity and social context. Her argument for replacing women's bodily role in reproduction with ex-utero gestation is consistent with individualism's view that the body should be subject to the rational, autonomous control of human agency.

In Daly's *Gyn/Ecology* there is a different, and more paradoxical, account of mothering. More so than Friedan and Firestone, Daly largely ignores the question of what have been actual women's situations and experiences of mothering in favor of an analysis of the cultural construction of the meaning of mothering in Western culture. But *Gyn/Ecology* contains almost no positive references to mothering other than to mother goddesses. Instead, Daly discusses how women are oppressed and exploited as mothers, sees mothers as "token torturers" of daughters in the service of patriarchy (1978: 139–41, 196–98, 277–78) and sees children injuring their mothers ("even before birth . . . and by the fact of being born we caused and experienced pain" [1978: 413]). Such images are much more frequent than Daly's very few references to mothers' satisfaction and happiness and/or love between mothers and children. Daly's analysis of male dominance and "the perverse patriarchal will for male motherhood" (1978: 245)—evident, for instance, in the appropriation of images of birth and mothering by male-dominated social institutions such as organized religion and American gynecological medicine—strongly suggests that women cannot experience mothering as anything other or more than oppressive and exploitive.

But Daly also argues that one of the worst effects of patriarchy is its severing of the bond between mothers and daughters. She argues that, while daughters rage at the powerlessness of their mothers, they also feel "the pull of the mother [that] is always there; the daughter seeks her everywhere" (1978: 346). For Daly, women's reclaiming the "given reality" of daughterhood is a reclaiming of self, "a Self-centering identity that makes female bonding possible," including a bonding that turns mothers and daughters into sisters and friends (1978: 347). The possibility of mother-daughter bonding, however, requires some sort of reconciliation of mother and daughter, given the painful and harmful aspects of their relationship that Daly describes. And the concept of reconciliation implies some participation of the mother in such a reconfiguring of their relationship. But Daly's account of the mother-daughter relationship is articulated entirely from the position of a daughter in a way that obscures the complexities of mothers' situations and experiences. Thus, Daly cannot explain what brings about their reconciliation. For in her account of the mother-daughter relationship, the subjectivity of the mother as a mother is almost entirely absent. Daly's suggestion that the reconciliation of mother and daughter depends on women's "reach[ing] the daughter within the mother" (1978: 347) also minimizes difference between mothers and daughters in a way consistent with individualism's denial of the significance of difference. It does so by reconfiguring the mother as a daughter, making her fundamentally the same as her daughter.

Daly's analysis of the mother-daughter relationship suggests the need for at least a more nuanced account of mothering. But *Gyn/Ecology* does not provide this. Instead Daly offers a vision of "Spinsters spinning out the Self's own integrity" (1978: 387). Despite what her intentions might be, Daly's insistent repetition of the word 'Self' evokes the individualist notion of a consciousness that is intact and accessible despite the specificities of its embodiment, social relations, and social contexts. Such individualism is also implicit in Daly's vision of women defining themselves without reference to men or children (1978: 3), discovering connections with other women making the same journey (1978: 366–72), and "cut[ting their] ties to the institution of patriarchal motherhood" (1978: 347). In these ways Daly implicitly envisions women's subjectivity in individualist terms, and women's freedom in opposition to mothering. Her account of women's liberation privileges self-determination, autonomy, and choice in a way consistent with individualist conceptions of subjectivity, and her account of women discovering or encountering others engaged in the same process of liberation is consistent with individualism's instrumental view of social relations. Daly's emphasis on the sameness of women denies differences among women, including women who are mothers and women who are not. At the same time, however, her insistence that all women have in common their oppression by men and/or patriarchy implicitly reinforces the concept of sexual difference. In both Daly's account of women's situation under patriarchy and her vision of women's liberation, the interplay of identity and difference typical of feminism's conflicted relationship to individualism is evident.

Friedan's, Firestone's, and Daly's accounts of mothering illustrate the pitfalls of trying to avoid essential motherhood by oversimplifying mothering or minimizing its significance. To the extent that these accounts of mothering are consistent with individualism, they do not avoid the implication that mothering is an obstacle to, rather than an exercise of, women's subjectivity. Each of these accounts of mothering in a different way implies that women should avoid mothering, or devote little time and attention to it, in order to exercise individualist subjectivity and find satisfaction in other activities. None of them recognizes the great variety of situations and experiences that women have in relationship to mothering or the complexities of the relationship of the social organization of mothering to other social structures and institutions. For this reason, they tend to suggest that women who do not want to avoid or minimize mothering in their lives are failing to attain the complete development of the capacities that define human subjectivity. They also fail to see that women may be located in material and social contexts that prevent them from exercising autonomy and choice in relationship to mothering. And they predict either that significant changes in women's personal and family lives will not affect social structures and public affairs, or that significant changes in social structures and public affairs can be attained simply by women's avoiding mothering.

While early second-wave feminist theories share this approach to and position on mothering, another form of modern feminism, difference feminism, which includes an alternative discourse of mothering, emerges later in second-wave feminism in the United States. Difference feminism produces a significantly different analysis of mothering because it adopts the second strategy I have described for theorizing mothering, directly and explicitly challenging individualism and the metaphysics of substance; thus, it encounters more directly the risks of difference. Some versions of difference feminism rely on theories of subjectivity that they see as viable alternatives to individualism, but insist on reinterpreting these theories in feminist terms. Difference feminism's reengagement with and reinterpretation of psychoanalysis along these lines is perhaps the most significant instance of this kind of reinterpretation. Other versions of difference feminism are committed to constructing theoretical frameworks based on women's own accounts of their situations and experiences. Feminist ethics of care and feminist standpoint epistemologies are examples of this second kind of difference feminism. Difference feminism is an explicit response to those aspects of individualist, identity-based challenges to sexism and male dominance that are problematic for theorizing situations and experiences more typical of women. It recognizes that an appeal to women's individualist subjectivity may produce an apparent gender neutrality that actually misconstrues important aspects of women's situations and experiences in theory and leads to disadvantages for women, or for some women, in practice. By appealing explicitly to women's difference, difference feminism hopes to represent women's situations and experiences more accurately. But difference feminism not only appeals to but tends to valorize women's difference. To avoid the risk of difference slipping into deviation, difference feminism argues that, although sexism and male dominance have very much shaped women's situations and experiences, it is nonetheless possible to theorize these situations and experiences apart from their oppressive contexts. Such accounts of women's situations and experiences provide the basis for positive accounts of women's subjectivity. Furthermore, such analyses of women's situations and experiences can be used as models or paradigms for reconceptualizing human subjectivity itself and thus for reorganizing material and social conditions so that both men and women can experience the greater realization of these positive aspects of human subjectivity.

While difference feminism offers a strenuous challenge to individualism, and to the elements of sexism and male dominance supported by it, it does not escape the dilemma of difference. Instead it encounters other risks of difference for feminist theory. These include overlooking or not adequately theorizing women's oppression and misrepresenting differences among women. Difference feminism's valorizing perspective strives to look at women's situations and experiences apart from the individualist presuppositions that render them deviations or failures to meet the standards for (individualist) subjectivity. Versions of difference feminism focused on women's psychological development, for instance, argue that the psychological capacities women may be more likely to develop than men, such as a capacity for empathy or a tendency to understand themselves in relation to rather than in isolation from others, are positive and valuable capacities for both men and women. This approach, however, may not consider the extent to which these aspects of women's difference are a function of sexism and male dominance. It may be that women are more likely than men to be empathetic or to understand themselves in relationship to others because their survival in male-dominated social contexts requires this of them. In other words, difference feminism's valorizing approach to theorizing women's difference risks reconsolidating elements of women's situations and experiences that feminism wants to challenge.

Difference feminism also encounters a version of the paradox of representation that I have argued is a function of feminism's conflicted relationship with individualism. Difference feminism appeals to accounts of women's situations and experiences from the perspective of women themselves, either indirectly in reinterpreting theories such as psychoanalysis from women's perspective, or directly in explaining how and why women experience and perceive the world as they do. But this appeal presupposes that there is some set of situations and experiences that are shared by all women, and/or that there is a women's perspective—a view of the world, or a mode of acquiring knowledge—shared by all women. This presupposition tends to minimize or overlook differences among women, and to obscure the extent to which it produces the commonality among all women that it claims to represent. Thus, difference feminism may not adequately represent the complexity and multiplicity of women's situations and experiences and may lead to the political misrepresentation of women's interests or the representation of some women's interests at the expense of others. Perhaps most significantly for theorizing mothering, difference feminism directly encounters the paradoxes of embodiment and gender that result from the dilemma of difference. To challenge individualism and the metaphysics of substance, difference feminist accounts of mothering need to challenge mind/ body dualism. This means that difference feminism must theorize the signifi- cance of embodiment and of gender for subjectivity without reconsolidating a view of gender that reduces gender to sexed embodiment. More specifically, dif- ference feminist accounts of mothering must recognize and theorize the signif- icance of maternal embodiment and the embodied aspects of mothering without reducing mothering entirely to a bodily process or bodily based instinct, which would reconsolidate essential motherhood's equation of the female body, femininity, and motherhood. The risk of recuperating this central element of essential motherhood is prominent in difference feminism.

Despite these difficulties, however, the difference feminism that emerged in the United States beginning in the middle of the 1970s is very important in relationship to mothering, since it allows for discourses on mothering other than the avoidance or depreciation of mothering that is more or less explicit in earlier second-wave feminist theory. Difference feminism's reconsideration of feminism's earlier rejection of psychoanalysis is particularly relevant to femi- nist theory's reconsideration of mothering in the late 1970s and 1980s. Friedan, Firestone, and Daly, for example, are all extremely critical of psycho- analysis. But Juliet Mitchell's *Psychoanalysis and Feminism* (1975), Gayle Rubin's influential essay "The Traffic in Women: Notes on the 'Political Economy' of Sex" (1975), and the work of feminist literary theorists like Jane Gallop (1982, 1985, 1988) all reengage with and reinterpret psychoanalysis, especially Lacanian psychoanalysis, and thus allow for more complex and nuanced approaches to the issue of mothering. A second development, also related to renewed interest in psychoanalysis, is the appearance of what came to be called French feminism in the United States, especially the 1980 Marks and Courtivron anthology *New French Feminism*, and the publication of trans- lations of Helene Cixous (1976, 1981, 1983, 1985), Luce Irigaray (1985a, 1985b), and Julia Kristeva (1980, 1982, 1984, 1986, 1987).[1] This work also pro- voked renewed interest among U.S. feminists in the representation of mother- ing, women's experiences of mothering, and psychoanalytic interpretations of mothering. Some of the accounts of mothering that I consider in subsequent chapters appeared at this time and are indicative of these trends. Nancy Chodorow's *The Reproduction of Mothering: Psychoanalysis and the Sociology of Gender* (1978) is an influential example of feminist theory's reconsideration of psychoanalysis, and Kristeva's "Stabat Mater," published in France in 1977 and in the United States in 1986, is a text that many U.S. feminists see as exemplary of French feminism.

This is not to say, however, that feminist theory's reconsideration of psycho-analysis and the appearance of French feminism are solely responsible for renewed interest in mothering among U.S. feminist theorists. For example, Adrienne Rich's *Of Woman Born* was published in 1976 and was widely read, well in advance of the appearance of French feminism in the United States, and Sara Ruddick's work on mothering (1980, 1984, 1987, 1989), like Rich's, owes little to either feminist psychoanalysis or French feminism. To the extent that discursive formations can provoke or include counter-discourses (Foucault 1980: 101–2; 1987: 134–164), and to the extent that feminism as a social movement was unlikely to move forward on any front as long as it was so far out of line with the dominant ideology of essential motherhood, one might argue that the relatively consistent avoidance or depreciation of motherhood in early second-wave feminist theory would have provoked its own reconsideration regardless of feminist reconsiderations of psychoanalysis and/or the appearance of French feminism. So it is clear that a number of factors came together in the mid-1970s to shift the focus and content of feminist theory on mothering.

To begin my analysis of feminist reassessments of mothering connected with difference feminism, I bring together in this and the next chapter the explicit challenge to individualism and the implicit account of mothering in the work of Jean Bethke Elshtain, and the account of mothering and women's liberation in Simone de Beauvoir's *The Second Sex*. Elshtain's *Public Man, Private Woman* (1981) is one of the first and most systematic attempts in the United States to criticize other feminist theories for their reliance on individ-ualism and their depreciation of mothering, and to use an appeal to women's difference as a paradigm for a feminist alternative to individualist social the-ory. Beauvoir's *The Second Sex* is both an important source and a site of con-tention for difference feminism, especially French feminism, and U.S. feminist interest in this text was renewed by the appearance in the United States of French feminism. I read Elshtain and Beauvoir in terms of the second of the two strategies for theorizing mothering and avoiding essential mother-hood that I have outlined. I emphasize certain common elements of Elshtain's and Beauvoir's approaches to theorizing mothering, commonalities that might not be immediately evident given their more obvious differences. Both Elshtain and Beauvoir explicitly challenge individualism, but they address in very different ways the paradoxes of embodiment and gender that this presents. Elshtain intends to develop a form of feminism that theorizes the importance and value of mothering in women's lives, but she avoids dealing with maternal embodiment and the material aspects of mothering. This yields an abstract and psychologistic account of mothering and recuperates significant elements of essential motherhood. Beauvoir deals directly with maternal embodiment, and addresses to some extent the material aspects of mothering. But her account of women's liberation nonetheless includes a contradictory analysis of the relationship and significance of embodiment and gender.

I argue that, while Elshtain and Beauvoir each offer a difference-based challenge to individualism, they also rely on one of the gendered binaries generated by the metaphysics of substance, so that elements of individualism complicate their difference-based challenges to individualism. Elshtain is explicitly committed to the public/private distinction, while Beauvoir implicitly retains a dualist analysis of embodiment and subjectivity. As a result, each of these analyses of mothering is characterized by contradictions resulting from the interplay of identity and difference in their theoretical frameworks. I locate the ideological moments in Elshtain's and Beauvoir's analyses of mothering that attempt to manage these contradictions, and show that significant elements of essential motherhood are reconsolidated in Elshtain's account of mothering, while major contradictions concerning mothering remain unresolved in Beauvoir's analysis of women's situations and experiences.

— jean bethke elshtain: family reconstructive feminism —

In *Public Man, Private Woman*, Elshtain criticizes feminist theories that rely on individualism and argues for a feminist theory based on an analysis of women's traditional activities and identities in the family. Her valorization of women in relation to "the family" is Elshtain's version of the appeal to women's difference that is characteristic of difference feminism. In Elshtain's analysis of women in relation to the family, however, her concept of "the family" is almost indistinguishable from her concept of mothering. Elshtain's analysis of women's difference thus risks the reconsolidation of essential motherhood's equation of the feminine and the maternal. Elshtain tries to avoid this risk by theorizing women's traditional identities and activities not explicitly in terms of mothering, but in terms of the public/private distinction. This approach, however, indirectly imports mind/body dualism into Elshtain's analysis of women in relationship to the family. For, in an individualist ideological context, the distinction of the private and the public is underwritten by the metaphysical distinction of mind and body. The importation of these elements of individualism significantly undermines Elshtain's difference-based challenge to individualism. The effects of individualism's public/private binary as it operates in a sexist and male-dominated context—the gendering of the private as feminine and the exclusion of the feminine from the public—persist in Elshtain's argument, despite her attempts to theorize the feminine as both private and public.

The ideological effects of Elshtain's concept of the family are a result of two slippages that occur in her argument for the form of feminism she advocates. Elshtain's analysis of the private sphere equates the private and the familial, and her account of the familial equates the familial with mothering. As a result of these slippages, Elshtain's valorizing analysis of women's private identities and activities yields an abstract, psychologistic account of the family and mothering. This is also a result of Elshtain's avoiding the issue of embodiment in mothering in an attempt to avoid the implications of essential motherhood. Elshtain considers neither the bodily elements of mothering, such as pregnancy and childbirth, nor the material aspects of the work traditionally done by women in the family. Avoiding these material aspects of mothering may appear to avoid essential motherhood's naturalization of mothering in terms of the female body. But Elshtain's use of the public/private distinction leaves in place a version of the relationship of the private, the bodily, and the feminine on which essential motherhood depends. Because of its implicit support of essential motherhood, Elshtain's attempt to ground a feminist ethical and political theory on an analysis of women's difference fails to accomplish its own goals. Regardless of what may be her intentions, Elshtain's account of mothering and the feminist theory based on it amount to a form of "family-values" conservatism, the most prominent form in which essential motherhood asserts itself in late-twentieth-century U.S. political culture (Stacey 1983; Young 1994; Elshtain 1994).

Elshtain first presents what I will call her family reconstructive feminism—adapting the term 'family reconstructive' that Elshtain uses for the mode of politics she favors (1981: 337)—in *Public Man, Private Woman*; she further develops it in later essays. Rejecting what she takes to be the dominant forms of modern feminism, Elshtain argues that feminism needs a communitarian theory of politics that includes the distinction of public and private. She also criticizes the theoretical foundations of other forms of modern feminism for their abstraction, especially their abstract account of women's private lives and activities. By abstract Elshtain seems to mean both too far removed from the material and historical specificities of human experience and overly general or universalizing. This abstraction is the source of the inadequate analysis of public and private Elshtain sees in other feminist theories. She argues that because these feminist theories do not adequately conceptualize the material and historical specificity of human existence and social relations, they do not see the importance of preserving a distinction of public and private in social and political arrangements and they misunderstand the value of women's traditionally private activities and identities. Instead, these feminist theories problematically assume "the superiority of a . . . public identity . . . tied to the public-political world revolving around the structures, institutions, values and ends of the state" (1982b: 46). But Elshtain questions whether " . . . any feminist political thinker . . . really want[s] to so relocate female subjects and reconstruct the matrix of their traditional identities by substituting the terms of universal, bureaucratic, socio-economic imperatives that, as women achieve a public identity, they lose this other world and the values embedded within it entirely" (1981: 305).

To avoid these problems, Elshtain offers a theory of participatory democratic citizenship, which includes her vision of the "ethical polity," a "communitarian ideal [that] involves a series of interrelated but autonomous social spheres" (1982b: 58). To foster participatory democratic citizenship, a political community must preserve those social relations that enhance the development of the capacities required for citizenship. It must also allow all persons to participate in political life without having to surrender their identities as members of more specific social groups. This requires reconceptualizing the private as the social location in which the capacities for citizenship are realized and nurtured. Elshtain holds that the distinction of public and private must be a feature of any participatory democratic political community, because this distinction is inherent in human social life (1981: 7–9, 317–22, 346–47, 351–52). She writes: " . . . on the basis of my recognition of the existence of limiting conditions and the inescapability of moral rules in fundamental areas of human existence, together with my presumptions concerning human sociality and the imperative to create meaning . . . I . . . treat the private . . . as a locus of human activity, moral reflection, social and historical relations, the creation of meaning, and the construction of identity having its own integrity" (1981: 331–32).

Instead of the devaluation of the private that she believes is common to liberal democratic capitalism and modern feminism, Elshtain argues for a "reconstructive ideal of the private" (1981: 322) based on the traditional values and practices of family life. This ideal suggests a mode of politics in which citizens act to preserve the private sphere from encroachment by public or political forces. By voicing private imperatives, duties, and values citizens challenge depersonalizing public power and create more humane public identities and policies (1982b: 55). They thus transform politics " . . . to affirm the protection of fragile and vulnerable human existence as the basis of a mode of political discourse, and to create the terms for its flourishing as a worthy political activity" (1982c: 621; 1981: 336). This transformation enables "a wider diffusion of what attentive love to all children is about" and shows "how it [this love] might become a wider social imperative" (1982b: 59). Elshtain also argues that this family reconstructive mode of politics is consistent with feminism; it need not entail the oppression of women. Instead, it resists the encroachment into the private sphere of public or political forces that do not respect the needs of children and dependent others and the value of women's identities and activities as mothers and family members. For "it is the isolation and debasement of women under the terms of male-dominated ideology and social structures that must be fought, not the activity, the humanizing imperative, of mothering, of being a parent itself" (1981: 333). Elshtain argues that preserving the integrity of the private sphere, reconceptualized as she recommends, will allow women to participate in public life without having to sacrifice their identities as mothers and family members.

Her claim that the family is the best model for reconceptualizing the private follows from Elshtain's view that the family is necessary for individual and social development. She argues that "some form of familial existence is a presuppositional feature of social existence" because "familial ties and modes of child-rearing are essential to establish the minimal foundation of human social existence" (1981: 322, 325–26). The argument that Elshtain makes here relies on her interpretation of psychoanalysis, which she offers in distinction to Juliet Mitchell's version of psychoanalysis and to what she identifies as 'psychoanalytic feminism', represented by Dorothy Dinnerstein's *The Mermaid and the Minotaur* (1976) and Chodorow's *The Reproduction of Mothering*. Elshtain's interpretation of psychoanalysis emphasizes children's need for ongoing, intense relationships with a limited number of caregivers. Elshtain's argument for the necessity of the family is also reminiscent of Key's view that children's proper development requires individualized attention to their specific needs. Like Key, Elshtain believes that the strength and intensity of the parent-child bond enables this individualized attention. According to Elshtain, family involves "attachments of a special kind—concrete, particular, and continuing," and provides children with "strong, early attachment to specific adult others." This intense and continuing love and attention makes possible the child's development of the capacity for basic trust. In such "powerful, eroticized relations with specific others, parents or their permanent not temporary surrogates," children's development is also structured so that they "internalize" these specific others and thus can later "identify with nonfamilial human beings." These developmental processes are the basis of conscience, empathy, pity, and compassion (1981: 328–29; 1990: 55–56). They are also the foundation of citizenship, which according to Elshtain requires that citizens empathize with each other and share a common identity based on mutual concerns (1982b: 446; 1990: 54–55).

Elshtain recognizes that familial authority appears to be at odds with democratic citizenship. Democratic citizenship presupposes the autonomy of citizens, who consent to be governed and who are equally capable and entitled to participate in self-government. Familial authority, however, presupposes the dependence of children on parents, the inability of children to govern themselves, and the greater power and authority of parents. But, Elshtain argues, since parental authority is limited and specific, aiming at children's development of the capacity for self-government and ending when this is achieved, it is part of the "constitutive background" of democracy (1990: 54–57). Elshtain also realizes that this "strong case" for the family is increasingly difficult to make in the contemporary American context, given the breakdown of a deep and widespread endorsement of family life. For Elshtain, however, this means a "softening" but not an abandonment of the privileging of family life in democratic political communities. Despite changes in the exercise of parental authority, changes in the interactions of other social authorities with families, and the development of other ways of living, democracy requires a normative endorsement of family over other modes of social existence (1990: 57–60).

— the private, the family, and mothering —

In light of Elshtain's critique of other forms of feminism, the abstract quality of her argument for family reconstructive feminism is striking (Dietz 1985, 1987; DiQuinzio 1995). Elshtain's critique of abstraction in feminist theory raises the expectation that her argument for family reconstructive feminism will be based on specific, detailed, and concrete accounts of women's experiences as mothers and family members. But this expectation is not met. While Elshtain continually alludes to the need for such accounts of women's experiences, she never offers this. In comparison, Friedan's and Firestone's accounts of family life, both major targets of Elshtain's critique, are full of specific, concretely described individuals and their experiences, drawn from interviews, personal observations, and written sources. As I see it, the abstraction of Elshtain's argument for family reconstructive feminism is a result of her failure to consider the material aspects of women's traditional activities in the family. By this I mean both the embodied aspects of human reproduction and the work of providing bodily care and meeting bodily needs that child rearing and family include.

One way in which Elshtain's account of women in the family overlooks the material aspects of family and child rearing is by overemphasizing their psychological and emotional aspects. Elshtain focuses on the emotional and psychological quality of the bonds and the processes of identification among family members, especially of children's development in relationship to parents. This focus implies that parenting is primarily an emotional or psychological response to children, and that the identities family members develop are primarily psychological or emotional dispositions. She says nothing about how parenting, especially the care of infants and small children, involves giving bodily care and meeting bodily needs. She does not consider the extent to which the work of meetings others' bodily needs is central to what she calls "women's traditional identities." Neither does she consider how the identities of family members and the bonds among them are established in the course of their doing together the mundane chores involved in maintaining day-to-day bodily existence and comfort. She gives no examples of specific family members engaged in any such activities, and no accounts of the thoughts and feelings that specific family members may have as a result of the material aspects of family life.

The effects of this abstraction are evident in Elshtain's conception of public and private and in her theory of citizenship. Just as Elshtain argues that certain human needs are "imbedded and answered, however imperfectly, within the traditional family" (1982b: 444), she also argues that the private and public "exude [their] own imperatives and values," have "their own intrinsic dignity and purpose" (1981: 305, 334, 351), and "generate their own imperatives" (1982b: 55). On this basis, she argues that familial feelings and values should be "diffused," "suffused," or "displaced" (1990: 56; 1982b: 59; 1981: 329) throughout the public sphere and that "attentive love to all children" should "become a wider social imperative" (1982b: 59). This argument for the political effectivity of private ideals, imperatives, and duties echoes Key's vision of motherhood as including the "radiation" of the mother's personality throughout the home. Elshtain seems to be envisioning a similar radiation of private ideals and values into the public sphere. She provides neither a detailed explanation of what she means by terms like "imbedded," "exude," "generate," "diffuse," "suffuse," and "displace," nor any examples of specific social policies that illustrate how familial values, duties, or imperatives or attentive love to all children become specifically political. These are particularly needed, however, given the tension between Elshtain's claim that social spheres exude or generate the values and institutions appropriate to them and her claim that the values and institutions of one sphere can and should become effective in the other. For if certain values, imperatives, or duties are inherently private and others inherently public, then it is at least unclear how private values, imperatives, and duties can be effective in the public sphere. Instead public and private values, imperatives, and duties seem to be opposed to each other rather than potentially effective in the other sphere.

Elshtain's abstract account of public and private leads to a contradictory account of citizenship. If persons are traditionally positioned in either the public or the private sphere, and if their identities and interests are a function of that positioning, then it seems that their positioning in one sphere locates them in opposition to the values, imperatives, and duties of the other. If these oppositions ultimately arise out of a distinction inherent in social existence, then it seems unlikely that they can ever be resolved. In other words, Elshtain wants to argue that men and women can be both public and private persons, and that the values, imperatives, and duties of one sphere can become effective in the other. But the abstract quality of public and private as she envisions them works against this. It suggests that not only values, imperatives, and duties, but also interests and identities are a function of either public or private, which are inherently distinct from and opposed to each other. This rules out the formation of political identities and interests itself as a political concern, and makes political life an interminable contest in which the private familial and the public political struggle for authority over each other (Dietz 1985, 1987).

Furthermore, this account of private and public leaves women with conflicting and contradictory alternatives for citizenship. Elshtain argues against women's capitulating to public pressure, either by accepting the public devaluation of their private identities and disempowering themselves politically, or by fleeing the private for a public identity and sacrificing their traditional, private identities. She argues that women should instead defend private, familial ideals and values in response to the public demands and pressures of politics. But this constitutes a contradictory political identity for women, especially in an individualist ideological context. Elshtain argues that women can be subjects of political agency and entitlement and have a public identity on the basis of their being mothers and family members. But, according to her own analysis of public and private, to be a mother and/or a family member is to have a private identity. If citizenship is public, but women's traditional identities and activities are private, then it remains unclear how women's difference can constitute the basis of women's citizenship.

These contradictory elements of Elshtain's theory of citizenship are effects of her attempt to theorize women's difference as a basis for citizenship in terms of the individualist distinction of private and public while also failing to address the issue of embodiment and the material aspects of family and mothering. In other words, Elshtain's attempt to theorize women as both public and private is undermined by her commitment to this distinction itself, given that she has not sufficiently considered how the public/private distinction presupposes the mind/body dualism characteristic of individualism and the metaphysics of substance. In the absence of an explicit alternative to individualism's dualist account of subjectivity and embodiment, Elshtain's argument for family reconstructive feminism is unable to counter the importation and reconsolidation of the other binaries—not only mind/body, but also social/natural and male/female—with which the distinction of private and public is entwined. Thus, her account of women's citizenship and her argument for family reconstructive feminism succumb to individualism's gendering of the natural, the body, and the private as feminine and its corresponding masculinization of the social, the mind, and the public.

Elshtain's attempt to theorize women's difference in terms of the public/private distinction while avoiding the issue of embodiment also depends on two slippages in her argument. These slippages ultimately equate the private with the family and the family with mothering. My analysis of these slippages, however, shows that they contribute to the reconsolidation of significant elements of essential motherhood in Elshtain's argument for family reconstructive feminism. While these equations attempt to valorize women's difference without renaturalizing the feminine in terms of embodiment, they do so only by recuperating essential motherhood's equation of the feminine and the maternal. A close reading of Elshtain's analysis of women in relation to the family shows how this analysis equates the family and the private. This ideological moment lays the groundwork for an equation of the family and mothering, and thus for an equation of women's (traditional, private) identities and mothering.

Elshtain establishes the equivalence of the private and the family in several ways. Sometimes she simply insists on it as an empirical matter, as in her claim that "to talk of an ideal of the private world within the context of contemporary American society is to talk about the family" (1981: 322). She also appeals to evolutionary history and archaeology to make this equation, and does so in ways that are inconsistent with her own critique of abstraction. For example, Elshtain considers a burial that took place approximately sixty thousand years ago, as it is described by paleontologists Richard E. Leakey and Roger Lewin. The survival and orderly placement of pollen grains at this site suggest that flowers were deliberately arranged around the body as part of the burial. In Leakey's and Lewin's description, "[i]t would appear that the man's family and friends, and perhaps members of his tribe had gone into the fields and brought back yarrow, cornflowers " Elshtain draws from this the conclusions that human beings "possess an inborn imperative . . . to find and to create meaning" and "have a need to live with and among others in relations of concrete particularity" (1981: 317–18).

Elshtain then construes these conclusions as establishing the necessity of the family by posing the following question: "[D]oes the fact that a particular social form, the family for example, is traceable to prehistory, all of recorded history, and is present in all known societies, constitute an important claim on us because it can be presumed to express something so fundamental about human beings that to reject it is either folly or madness?" She replies that "[t]his question cannot be answered abstractly. Rather one must take up evidence from the past, like the burial at Shandidar Cave, as clues to a vast and awesome mystery that embodies, at one end of a range of alternatives, authentic human imperatives . . . " (1981: 318–19). But her explicit statement that the question "cannot be answered abstractly" is followed by an abstract and even mystifying answer that construes the "evidence from the past" as "clues to a . . . mystery" that nonetheless "embodies . . . authentic human imperatives." But embodies is precisely what this statement does not do; it rather disembodies human existence by using abstract terms like "social forms" and "human imperatives" rather than considering the specificities of human embodiment and its social contexts. Elshtain's appeal to archaeological evidence thus establishes the necessity of the family on the basis of its endurance, but only by universalizing and dehistoricizing the family, a gesture that is fundamental to abstraction as she defines and criticizes it.

Similarly, Elshtain discusses "the wild boy of Aveyron," a young boy reportedly captured in southwest France in 1800 who appeared to have survived without human contact from about three years of age. The unsuccessful attempts of an abbé and a doctor to teach the boy indicate to Elshtain that "outside the bounds of human nurture . . . cut off from human society and language we could neither identify objects, not establish categories, nor engage in social relations." These conclusions are immediately connected to two of the feminist theories Elshtain criticizes. She writes that, while "no contemporary social critic ever advised that we return to a pre-social existence, ever advocated a new state of nature . . . " nonetheless "the past fifteen years have seen a number of visions of family-less, asocial existence celebrated." According to Elshtain, one such vision is presented by Firestone in *The Dialectic of Sex*, another "grew out of the counterculture commune movement in the 1960s" and "is reminiscent, though it is a far less coherent claim, of Chodorow's insistence that communal alternatives are *presumptively* preferable to private familial child-rearing" (1981: 323–26, Elshtain's emphasis).

This linkage of the boy of Aveyron with the ideas of Firestone and Chodorow solidifies the equation of the family and the private by setting up the opposite equation of the boy of Aveyron and feminist alternatives to "private familial child-rearing." This argument thus produces the necessity of the family by obscuring all distinctions among different alternatives to the family, reducing all such alternatives to leaving children in complete isolation to fend entirely for themselves. After all, if the accounts of his experiences are accurate, the boy of Aveyron was not only deprived of the family; he had no contact of any kind with any other humans for somewhere between seven to nine years. Thus, Elshtain's analysis of the boy of Aveyron supports the equation of the private and the family by reducing all possible alternatives to the private family to the complete abandonment of children. Her analysis of the boy of Aveyron also construes the family in binary terms; in Elshtain's account, there is only "the family" and "family-less, asocial existence," where the family is privileged in relationship to its opposite, which is defined as the lack or absence of the family. This account of the family and family-less, asocial existence further inscribes the binary logic of individualism that is at work in Elshtain's argument for family reconstructive feminism and that subtends the equation of the private and the familial.

An insistence on thinking about human existence in concrete and specific rather than abstract terms suggests two related problems with these arguments. First, the use of concepts such as "family" and "friends," which have quite specific meanings in modern social contexts, to explain the physical remains of events that occurred over sixty thousand years ago, or to interpret accounts of events of almost two hundred years ago, is highly questionable if material and historical specificity is a standard. At the very least, what these concepts mean in these specific historical circumstances must be explained. Otherwise, an appeal to archaeologically or historically specific evidence establishes the necessity of the family only by avoiding the very issues raised by the demand for specificity as opposed to abstraction. A second problem is that these arguments move from claims about human needs, considered abstractly, to the conclusion that a particular social institution is the best context for meeting such needs by appealing to the universality of that social institution. But even if the family, for example, occurs universally and remains in some basic way the same over time (that is, it has some unchanging characteristics that identify it as the social institution in question in very different historical circumstances), this alone proves nothing about the necessity, much less the comparative advantages, of the family. It proves only its endurance, and even the evidence for its endurance is produced by the abstract, ahistorical concept of the family with which the argument begins.

Finally, in Elshtain's early work, the vagueness of her definition of family contributes to the ideological equation of the family and the private. In *Public Man, Private Woman* she writes "I recognize that there is no such thing as 'the family' but that there are multiple variations on this theme. Nevertheless, in discussing the imperatives that must be infused within any familial form in order for it to serve the humanizing functions I explicate, it is more economical simply to speak of 'the family' " (1981: 322). In a later essay she says that by "family" she means "the widely accepted, popular understanding of the term as having its basis in marriage and kinship," insisting that this is the view of the family "that most Americans hold" (1982b: 443, 447). Elshtain says that she does not limit the family to the two-parent nuclear family of biological parents and children (1981: 322, 331–32). But she is not very clear about what alternatives to this sort of family she would count as family. She rejects the "tribal contrast model" she attributes to anthropologist Michelle Zimbalist Rosaldo (1974) as well as child rearing in the kibbutzim . . . the counterculture commune movement of the 1960's . . . [and] institutionalized forms of child care" (1981: 294–96, 326, 330, 338–39). Single parents and their children appear to count as families—at least when this is "required by the repressiveness of the welfare system" (1981: 332), but apparently not when it is chosen by these parents themselves. So it seems that for Elshtain the family refers to two adults and the children for whom they are primarily responsible.

In "The Family and Civic Life" Elshtain states this explicitly (1990: 48, 54–60). Making this definition of the family explicit, however, also indicates that Elshtain's concept of the family depends on certain exclusions. In this essay Elshtain accepts a "loosening but not a wholesale negation in our normative endorsement of intergenerational family life" (1990: 60). She explains that this is a response to a "radical criticism," namely that " . . . families in modernity coexist with those who live another way, whether heterosexual or homosexual unions that are by choice childless or by definition childless; communalists who diminish individual parental authority in favor of the preeminence of the group; and so on" (1990: 59). This explanation implies that a necessary condition of a group's being a family is the presence of children. But not all heterosexual unions that are childless are so by choice, and homosexual unions are not childless by definition; many gay men and lesbians are parents.

Elshtain's insistence that gay men and lesbians cannot participate in intergenerational family life as parents is relentless. In an argument against same-sex marriage, for example, Elshtain refuses to recognize that gay men and lesbians can and do take on parental responsibilities. She argues against same-sex marriage by insisting that "marriage . . . is and always has been about the possibility of generativity" and calls for the preservation of "the symbolism of

marriage-family as social regenesis" (1991: 686). But this argument makes the
case against same-sex marriage only by presupposing that gay men and lesbians
cannot participate in generativity. And the plausibility of this presupposition is
sustained in part by mind/body dualism's naturalization of the body as the
proper and unchangeable basis of human reproduction. Thus, marriage is only
for parents, and being a parent means being the genetic and/or biological
parent of a child. Similarly, Elshtain's argument for family reconstructive feminism equates marriage with the family (as in the formulation "marriage-
family") in order to solidify Elshtain's view of family as including children by
excluding from it those she sees as unwilling or incapable of producing and
rearing children. Elshtain's insistence on the presence of children in a family
further overlooks persons past typical child rearing age, who may live with adult
children or other family members, indeed who may be cared for by those with
whom they live. Such a group seems not to constitute a family, regardless of
ties of blood or marriage, living arrangements, and/or care given, unless
Elshtain's term "intergenerational family life" includes families with no children but with more than one generation of adults.

My analysis of Elshtain's concept of the family thus suggests that there are
three characteristics central to what she means by the family. These are the
presence of children, the presence of a limited number of heterosexual, male
and female adults (1981: 296), and a certain quality of feeling, an eroticized
intensity, that family members experience in relationship to each other. This
places her concept of family in historical context, for the family described here
is clearly the nuclear family typical of modern industrial capitalist societies. It
also indicates the ideological effects of the exclusions that generate this particular account of the family. By excluding from the category of family those cou-
ples or groups that do not consist of heterosexual adults and children,
Elshtain's argument for family reconstructive feminism produces the family
that it needs to sustain the claim that private values, duties, and imperatives
are essentially familial. Elshtain's presentation of this argument as if it were
based on an empirical description of the family obscures the extent to which
her argument for family reconstructive feminism prescribes a particular kind of
family. The exclusion of individuals or groups taken to be childless by choice or
definition ensures the heterosexual reproductivity of the family and reinforces
Elshtain's view that the defining aims of private, familial values, duties, and
imperatives are the protection and nurture of those unable or less able to care
for themselves.

The plausibility of Elshtain's equation of the family and the private and of
her view that the primary purpose of the family is nurturance is itself dependent on an implicit equation of the family and mothering. Elshtain uses

gender-neutral terms like "family" and "parenting" fairly consistently. She also claims as if it were an empirical matter that "[m]odern parental authority is shared by mother and father," which is evident because "[c]hildren . . . exhibit little doubt that their mothers are powerful and authoritative" (1990: 54). But her argument for family reconstructive feminism ultimately depends on connotations that are specifically maternal to secure the equation of the private and the familial. Elshtain's repeated claim that the protection and care of the fragile, the vulnerable, and the frail is the defining work of the private sphere evokes traditional aspects of mothering. Elshtain also frequently uses terms like "nurturing" and "preserving" to describe the traditional activities of the private sphere, which have not only a feminine, but a specifically maternal, connotation. And her use of terms such as "suffusion," "diffusion," and "displacement" to describe the reconstructed relationship of private and public she recommends evokes the indeterminacy of boundaries and identities attributed to mother and child in early infancy by certain versions of psychoanalysis.

The unacknowledged centrality of mothering to Elshtain's argument for family reconstructive feminism is also suggested by Elshtain's reserving some of her sharpest criticisms of other feminist theories for what she sees them saying or implying about mothering. Representing other feminist theories as hostile to or unable to adequately theorize mothering implies that family reconstructive feminism alone theorizes mothering adequately and recognizes its significance and value. For example, Elshtain is critical of both the appeal to matriarchy in radical feminism, which she sees as problematically ahistorical and utopian, and of radical feminism's failure to do justice to the value and importance of mothering in women's lives (1981: 214–17, 220). She criticizes liberal feminism's concept of roles because "this distorts the meaning of mothering" which "is *not* a 'role' on par with being a file clerk, a scientist . . . " (1981: 243, Elshtain's emphasis). Her argument against Marxist feminism's "narrow econometric model" is also phrased in terms of mothering. Elshtain writes, "[t]he most compelling example I can think of against Marxist feminism's infusion of econometric terms into the sphere of family ties and relationships would be to ask any mother whether she would accept 'producing the future commodity labor power' as an apt characterization of what she is doing" (1981: 265).

In addition to pointing out such flaws in other feminist theories, Elshtain substantiates her view that feminist theory has been inhospitable to mothering and solidifies her equation of the private, the familial, and the maternal by means of an anecdote, the only personal experience she describes in detail in *Public Man, Private Woman*. She relates that in the late 1960s she and a friend, "struggling with [their] identities as mothers and graduate students," attended the first meeting of a feminist group. When each person was asked to say why she was at the meeting, Elshtain's friend "began to speak of her conflict over public and private values, commitments and purposes" But "she was cut off abruptly and publicly shamed with this silencing declaration from the group's 'facilitator': 'We will have no diaper talk here. We're here to talk about women's liberation.'" Elshtain recounts how she and her friend left the meeting, for they "could not regard [their] children as abstractions, nuisances to be overcome, or evidence of [their] sad capitulation to . . . patriarchy" (1981: 334). In this anecdote, Elshtain conceptualizes herself and her friend in terms of public and private, mapping "mother" onto the private and "graduate student" onto the public. This reinforces the equation of the maternal and the private by implicitly invoking the individualist distinction of mind (graduate student/public) and body (mother/private). And, despite the fact that they later joined a feminist group with which they were satisfied (1981: 334), Elshtain presents this anecdote as if it stands for all of feminism. Her vehement tone, writing approximately ten to fifteen years after the incident, and her interpretation of it as a public shaming, represent all of feminist theory and practice as uniformly hostile not only to family, but specifically to mothering.

Most emblematic of this equation of the family and mothering, however, are Elshtain's very brief references in *Public Man, Private Woman* to the work of Carol Gilligan and Sara Ruddick, whose ideas, she suggests, are supportive of her own. She refers to Gilligan's 1977 essay, "In a Different Voice: Women's Conceptions of Self and Morality," the first appearance of the ideas presented more thoroughly in Gilligan's 1982 *In a Different Voice: Psychological Theory and Women's Development*. In a hesitant tone unlike that she usually employs, Elshtain writes:

> If it is the case that women have a distinct moral language, as Carol Gilligan has argued, one which emphasizes concern for others, responsibility, care, and obligation . . . then we must take care to preserve the sphere that makes such a morality of responsibility possible and extend its imperatives to men as well. If Gilligan . . . locates these qualities and capacities in women's involvement with families and the protection of human life, we must think about what would be lost if the private sphere erodes further or if we seek to alter our intimate relations entirely. (1981: 335–36)

This is immediately followed by a one-sentence reference to Ruddick: "One moral and political imperative that would unite rather than divide women, that would take what is already there but go on to redeem and transform it, would be a feminist commitment to a mode of public discourse imbedded within the values and ways of seeing that comprise what Sara Ruddick has called 'maternal thinking'" (1981: 336).[2] Here Elshtain represents Gilligan and Ruddick as making the same claim, namely, that mothering is a distinctive practice that gives rise to a distinctive moral outlook. But Gilligan's essay says little about what she takes to be the causes of the distinctive moral perspective her research detected among women; she briefly implies that women's—not mothers'—moral outlook is shaped by female socialization—not mothering. And Elshtain's claim that a commitment to maternal thinking would unite women presupposes that all women have mothering and/or maternal interests in common ("what is already there"). While female socialization and socialization for mothering are certainly related, especially under the hegemony of essential motherhood, it is this ideological formation that reduces one entirely to the other and refuses to recognize differences among women with respect to mothering. As I see it, Elshtain's reduction of one theorist's claims about women to another's claims about mothers reflects the way that Elshtain's claims about women are in effect claims about mothers. Elshtain's representation of Gilligan and Ruddick as making the same claims about motherhood is symptomatic of the way that her argument for family reconstructive feminism reconsolidates essential motherhood's equation of femininity and mothering.

— the risks of difference and the problem of maternal embodiment —

Elshtain's hesitant tone in referring to Gilligan and Ruddick, and the brevity of these references, also suggests an anxiety about appealing to feminist theorists whose work may support Elshtain's family reconstructive feminism, but also calls into question her representation of feminist theory as uniformly hostile to mothering. The lack of any references to Ruddick's later work on maternal thinking and practice, and the few, brief references to other feminist theorists' accounts of mothering, and to historical or sociological accounts of women's experiences of mothering in Elshtain's published work after *Public Man, Private Woman* further suggests that the account of mothering implicit in Elshtain's argument for family reconstructive feminism is operating ideologically to recuperate essential motherhood. In the hesitancy and brevity of these references to Gilligan and Ruddick and the paucity of references to other accounts and analyses of mothering in Elshtain's work I read an indirect recognition that mothering is more complex than Elshtain allows. I also see an indirect recognition that the concrete, specific, and detailed exploration of these complexities—called for by Elshtain's own critique of abstraction in feminist theory—would undermine Elshtain's argument for family reconstructive feminism by disrupting the equations of the private, the familial, and the maternal on which it depends.

A more direct confrontation with the complexities of mothering, especially the complexities of maternal embodiment and the material aspects of mothering and the family, would particularly problematize Elshtain's commitment to the public/private distinction. For this confrontation would require an analysis of the complex relationship of female embodiment, the social organization of mothering, sexism, male dominance, women's restriction to the private and exclusion from the public and political sphere, and the relationship of the social organization of mothering to material conditions and social structures of liberal democratic capitalism. But without addressing these issues, Elshtain's account of mothering, and the family reconstructive feminism based on it, does not avoid the risks of difference for feminist theory. By avoiding these issues, Elshtain's account of mothering may avoid directly renaturalizing women's difference in terms of female embodiment. But the account of mothering presupposed by Elshtain's argument for family reconstructive feminism effects this renaturalization indirectly, by theorizing women's difference, especially mothering, in terms of the private sphere.

Elshtain's account of mothering resembles in different ways those offered by Key and Gilman. Elshtain shares with Key a romanticizing and mystifying account of mothering that results in a containment of women. But, whereas Key more or less explicitly argues for the containment of mothers in the private home, the containment of women in the private, familial sphere is an unintended ideological effect of Elshtain's analysis of women in relation to the family. Like Gilman, Elshtain tries to theorize mothering as both natural and social, private and public. But, whereas Gilman cannot avoid the renaturalization of mothering in terms of female embodiment, Elshtain avoids directly renaturalizing mothering in terms of female embodiment, but at the cost of restricting mothering, and mothers, to the private sphere. And, given the relation of the public/private and mind/body binaries in an individualist ideological context, this indirectly renaturalizes mothering in terms of female embodiment.

As a version of difference feminism that attempts both to challenge individualism and to theorize mothering, Elshtain's argument for family reconstructive feminism clearly illustrates the risks of difference for feminist theory. Perhaps the most apparent and immediate of these risks in connection with mothering is the risk of reconsolidating essential motherhood by renaturalizing the relationship of the female body, femininity, and mothering. But my analysis of Elshtain's argument for family reconstructive feminism shows that avoiding the issue of embodiment does not guarantee that feminist theory will avoid reconsolidating elements of essential motherhood. For, even though she avoids the issues of embodiment relevant to mothering, Elshtain's difference-based challenge to individualism remains caught up in the gendered binaries of the metaphysics of substance. Her appeal to the distinction of public and private reinscribes the equation of the private, the bodily, and the feminine in the theoretical framework of her analysis of women in relation to the family. Thus, Elshtain's argument for family reconstructive feminism either relocates women in the family and the private, distinct from and opposed to the political and the public, or it fails to show what is specifically feminine about women's political agency and entitlement.

My reading of Elshtain's work illustrates the depth and difficulty of the dilemma of difference for feminist theory. Sexism and male dominance in an individualist ideological context rely on and perpetuate the naturalization of women's difference in terms of female embodiment, which is made possible by individualism's mind/body dualism and the binary logic of the metaphysics of substance. On the other hand, avoiding the issue of embodiment does not preclude the reconsolidation of essential motherhood. Thus, it seems that feminist theory, especially feminist accounts of mothering, must confront directly the issue of embodiment despite the risks that this poses. If this is so, then the question of how feminist theory confronts the issue of embodiment moves to the forefront of my analysis of feminist accounts of mothering. To begin to address this question, I turn in the next chapter to Simone de Beauvoir's account of mothering in *The Second Sex*.

ɩ

THE BODY AS SITUATION

implications for mothering

— essential motherhood and female embodiment —

AT THE CENTER of essential motherhood is the claim that what it means to be a woman is fundamentally a function of female embodiment. From this perspective, the fact that women play a specific role in the physical reproduction of the species means that to be a woman is to fulfill this role. The ideological elaboration of this claim further argues that, not only are women meant to become pregnant and give birth, but also that women are meant to do the work of child rearing. Women are expected not only to want to become pregnant and give birth but also to have a certain bond with or connection to the children to whom they give birth, perhaps as a function of experiencing pregnancy and childbirth or of a maternal instinct that all women possess. On either basis they are expected to love their children unconditionally, empathize completely with their children, meet their children's needs selflessly, and be completely fulfilled and satisfied by the experience of child rearing. I have argued that difference feminism, in its valorizing approach to theorizing women's difference, risks recuperating significant elements of essential motherhood. My reading of Elshtain's argument for family reconstructive feminism shows that her version

of difference feminism does not avoid the recuperation of essential motherhood by avoiding the issues of maternal embodiment and the material aspects
of the work of mothering. This conclusion about the importance of addressing
the material aspects of mothering is also supported by my analysis of Gilman's
and Key's debate about mothering. Key's difference-based challenge to individualism is like Elshtain's in recuperating elements of essential motherhood
by theorizing women's difference in terms of mothering while also psychologizing and dematerializing mothering. On the other hand, feminist identity-
based challenges to sexism and male dominance such as Gilman's do not
necessarily avoid renaturalizing mothering in terms of female embodiment
or failing to theorize the varied significance of mothering in women's lives.
Such analyses may also represent mothering as not requiring the exercise of
subjectivity, even as they argue for women's individualist subjectivity. Having
considered these accounts of mothering, I conclude that, despite the risks of
difference, such as problematizing women's (individualist) subjectivity and
recuperating elements of essential motherhood, feminist analyses of mothering
must confront as directly as possible the issues of maternal embodiment and
the material aspects of mothering.

With this conclusion in mind, I turn in this chapter and the next to Simone
de Beauvoir's account of mothering in *The Second Sex* and Sara Ruddick's work
on mothering. Beauvoir deals directly with the issue of female embodiment in
The Second Sex, and her analysis of mothering includes an in-depth analysis of
maternal embodiment, especially pregnancy. In the next chapter I consider
Sara Ruddick's work on mothering, which, I argue, directly confronts the issue
of the material aspects of mothering, as well as the issue of maternal embodiment. Both Beauvoir and Ruddick offer compelling analyses of mothering that
to a certain extent avoid essential motherhood's reduction of femininity and
motherhood to the female body. But other effects of the conflicted relationship
of feminism and individualism are evident in Beauvoir's and Ruddick's
accounts of mothering. I read Beauvoir's and Ruddick's work as examples of
difference feminism's strategy for avoiding essential motherhood by theorizing
mothering while also challenging individualism. I consider how and to what
extent each of these accounts of mothering negotiates the dilemma of difference, and what each offers toward a theory of subjectivity that significantly
resists individualism.

In *The Second Sex* Beauvoir sets out to explain women's oppression and
to argue for material and social changes that will end it. Whereas Elshtain
valorizes women's traditional identities and activities in order to reconstruct
the public and private, women's traditional identities and activities are for

Beauvoir precisely what must be changed in order to end women's oppression. Beauvoir attempts to theorize women's difference, especially women's experiences of embodiment, in terms that do not deny its significance but that also avoid explaining women's situations and experiences entirely as a function of female embodiment. She is particularly committed to avoiding conclusions that define women in terms of mothering, require mothering of women, or leave the current social organization of mothering intact. In my terms, Beauvoir's analysis of women's difference and female embodiment explicitly addresses the issue of maternal embodiment while also directly challenging essential motherhood. But the issue of mothering is nonetheless a point of ideological contention in *The Second Sex*. Like Elshtain's argument for family reconstructive feminism, Beauvoir's attempt to negotiate the dilemma of difference while also offering a difference-based challenge to individualism is undermined by elements of individualism that reappear in the theoretical framework she devises, and this is most evident in her account of mothering.

The most important elements of Beauvoir's theoretical framework for analyzing women's situations and experiences in *The Second Sex* are the distinction of immanence and transcendence she derives from Sartre's existentialist theory of subjectivity and the account of social relations she derives from Hegel's analysis of the oppositional relationship of self and other. These elements of her theoretical framework are intended to support a difference-based challenge to individualism. But, I argue, Sartre's distinction of immanence and transcendence incorporates elements of individualism's mind/body dualism, and the Hegelian account of the self/other relation is in some ways consistent with individualism's privileging of autonomy over interdependence in social relations. These elements of individualism complicate and undermine Beauvoir's challenge to it, and so Beauvoir's account of mothering, as well as her analysis of women's situations and experiences, are characterized by the paradoxes that result from the dilemma of difference in feminist theory.

Beauvoir clearly intends to challenge essential motherhood. Unlike Gilman, who accepts individualism's denial of the significance of embodiment and whose renaturalization of mothering in terms of female embodiment undermines her argument for women's individualist subjectivity, Beauvoir attempts to offer a theoretical alternative to individualism's dualist view of embodiment and subjectivity. To this extent her account of mothering resists the renaturalization of mothering in terms of female embodiment. But Beauvoir makes contradictory claims about pregnancy, childbirth, and child rearing, and these contradictions persist in her account of the life of an independent woman. These contradictions result from the individualist elements implicit in

Beauvoir's ostensibly difference-based theoretical framework. Beauvoir's contradictory claims about mothering, especially those concerning pregnancy, however, can be read not only as indicating contradictory elements of her theoretical framework, but also as suggesting the resistance of mothering to being theorized in the terms Beauvoir deploys. More specifically, these contradictions indicate the extent to which mothering cannot be adequately theorized in terms of the individualist implications of Sartre's distinction of immanence and transcendence and Hegel's account of the relationship of self and other. The ways in which Beauvoir's account of mothering resists the elements of individualism implicit in her theoretical framework also suggest certain elements of a theory of subjectivity implicit in Beauvoir's account of mothering that could operate as an alternative to individualism in feminist theory. I focus on the implications concerning embodiment, consciousness, and social relations that I see in the resistance of mothering, especially pregnancy and childbirth, to the individualist elements of Beauvoir's theoretical frame, and consider what these implications concerning embodiment, consciousness, and social relations contribute to a theory of subjectivity that resists individualism.

— the body in *The Second Sex* —

Many feminist theorists have addressed the question of Beauvoir's theory of embodiment and subjectivity, including the extent to which it is based on or includes one or more binary distinctions typical of individualism and the metaphysics of substance, whether it be mind/body, nature/culture, or self/other. Some have argued that Beauvoir's position is irredeemably dualist, while others have argued that her theory of embodiment and subjectivity avoids the dualism typical of individualism and the metaphysics of substance.[1] My theory of ideology and my conception of ideology critique, however, lead me to read Beauvoir in somewhat different terms. I do not set out to resolve the question of whether Beauvoir's theory of embodiment is dualist and/or individualist, or whether it can be interpreted as avoiding either or both. Instead, I argue that, given the interplay of identity and difference typical of feminist theory in an individualist ideological context, Beauvoir's theory of embodiment both resists and succumbs to individualism, and these contradictory impulses are most prominent in her analysis of mothering. My argument thus raises the question of whether it is possible to rearticulate those elements of Beauvoir's theory of embodiment and subjectivity that most strenuously resist individualism and, if so, how they might be deployed in feminist theory.

In *The Second Sex* Beauvoir first addresses the issue of embodiment by arguing against the view that female embodiment, especially women's reproductive capacities, determines women's appropriate social position and justifies men's power over women. She analyzes women's situation, arguing that this, rather than female embodiment, has so far determined women's character and experiences. In order to make this argument, Beauvoir adapts Sartre's distinction of immanence and transcendence and Hegel's account of the self/other relation. She argues that woman, like man, is a human existent who as a result of being embodied experiences immanence, "the 'en-soi' [the 'in-itself']—the brutish life of subjection to given conditions . . . constraint, contingence" (1989: xxxv). For Sartre, human existence also includes the possibility of the transcendence of immanence as a result of self-consciousness, or the 'pour-soi' (the 'for-itself'), that can envision alternatives to what exists and can act to realize them. Women, like men, desire to transcend immanence by engaging in freely chosen projects that enable them to justify their existence, reshape the world, and recreate themselves. But, according to Beauvoir, women's transcendence is complicated by the nature of the relation of self and other. Following Hegel, she argues: "we find in consciousness itself a fundamental hostility to every other consciousness; the subject can be posed only in being opposed—he sets himself up as the essential, as opposed to the other, the inessential, the object" (1989: xxiii). Men have constituted women as the Other—defined femininity in reference and in opposition to masculinity as that which it is not. In order to confirm their subjectivity and experience transcendence, men deny women the freedom appropriate to human self-consciousness. Men thus deny women all opportunities to experience transcendence and restrict women to immanence.

In this argument Beauvoir recognizes the specificity and significance of women's embodiment, but she also tries to avoid the determination of women's situations and experiences in terms of female embodiment. So she theorizes embodiment in terms of Sartre's distinction of immanence and transcendence to argue for the possibility of women's self-determination and transcendence. But according to Sartre's immanence/transcendence distinction, embodiment is the site of immanence and subjectivity is the locus of the possibility of transcendence. The immanence/transcendence distinction understands the embodied aspects of human existence in terms of facticity, or mere materiality, which is the basis of human finitude. Thus, embodiment is both a boundary and limit to self-consciousness or subjectivity, which is the basis of freedom and transcendence. In this way, however, the distinction of immanence and transcendence incorporates significant elements of individualism's mind/body dualism, and by relying on this distinction, Beauvoir incorporates these elements of individualism in her analysis of women's situation. Since individualism's denial of the significance of embodiment is directly at odds with Beauvoir's goal of explicating "the strange ambiguity of existence made body" (1989: 728), Beauvoir's reliance on Sartre's distinction of immanence and transcendence lays the groundwork for significant contradictions in her analysis of women's embodiment and situation.

This effect is evident in Beauvoir's discussion of the data of biology and women's oppression. While she intends to show that female embodiment does not determine the role or social position of women, her discussion of the data of biology has all the evaluative implications of mind/body dualism. The recurring image of women as "slave of the species" clearly implies that women's reproductive embodiment traps women in immanence. Furthermore, this relationship to immanence is specific to women; male embodiment does not have the same consequences for male subjectivity (1989: 22, 26). According to Beauvoir, "the individuality of the female is opposed to the interests of the species" (1989: 25) because women "have within them a hostile element—it is the species gnawing at their vitals" (1989: 30). Women's embodiment, as Beauvoir describes it, is alienating, a crisis of frailty and instability, and "the bondage of woman to the species" is only "*more or less* rigorous" depending on its social context (1989: 35, my emphasis). Only by way of menopause—itself a crisis—does woman "escape the iron grasp of the species . . . she is no longer the prey of overwhelming forces, she is herself, she and her body are one." But, Beauvoir also says, "it is sometimes said that women of a certain age constitute a 'third sex'; and in truth, while they are not males, they are no longer females"—they are "unsexed but complete" (1989: 31, 583). Whereas male embodiment and masculine subjectivity are relatively integrated, what Beauvoir calls women's "completeness" is at odds with women's reproductive embodiment (1989: 26).

Beauvoir's adoption of Hegel's account of the oppositional nature of the self/other relation similarly imports an element of individualism into her theoretical framework. Hegel's analysis of the self/other relation holds that consciousness is fundamentally oppositional—there is no self-consciousness or subjectivity without the positing of an other. For Beauvoir, this opposition also occurs at the level of groups: "no group ever sets itself up as the One without at once setting up the Other over against itself" (1989: xxiii). Beauvoir, like Hegel, argues that this opposition is reciprocal, that the consciousness that is objectified reciprocally objectifies the consciousness that objectifies it. According to Hegel, this reciprocal objectification establishes a dialectical struggle of consciousnesses. In this struggle there is the possibility that the absolute opposition of self and other can be transformed into a recognition of the self-consciousness of the other, or a reciprocity among consciousnesses. Regardless of how convincing is Hegel's argument for this possible outcome of the struggle of consciousnesses, in an individualist ideological context an analysis of social relations predicated on a fundamental opposition and hostility of subjects is consistent with individualism's view of social relations. Individualism sees subjects as fundamentally separated, as entering into social relations as a function of rational self-determination, and as seeking primarily to satisfy their own needs and desires and enhance their autonomy in social relations. Individualism does not appeal to the dialectic of consciousness that Hegel envisions; instead it tends to argue for social and political arrangements to manage the conflicts that it sees as inherent in social relations as a result of the opposition of individuals' interests. Beauvoir's reliance on Hegel's account of social relations imports the elements of individualism consistent with the Hegelian account into her analysis of women's situations.

On the other hand, Beauvoir argues that women are so far an exception to the dialectic of consciousness that Hegel describes; women have not so far objectified men as their other. For Beauvoir this raises the question of why women have not done so (1989: xxiii–xxvii). But the fact that women have not so far made men their other also implies the possibility that the hostile opposition of consciousness that she describes may persist among men and women, never coming to the resolution that Hegel envisions, or even the possibility that in the future women may make men their other. These possibilities are reinforced by the specific accounts of relationships between men and women, and mothers and children, that Beauvoir offers. Her accounts of these relationships often emphasize their opposition and hostility to such an extent that it becomes almost impossible to envision these relationships as other than oppositional. This further problematizes Beauvoir's argument that reciprocity and mutuality between men and women are possible, and her claim that greater freedom for women will bring this about.

In Beauvoir's explanation of why women have become other to men's one, rather than or in addition to men's becoming other to women, the contradictions that are effects of Beauvoir's implicit appeal to elements of individualism are also evident. To explain why women have become other to men Beauvoir looks first to female embodiment, arguing that biological as well as economic conditions in primitive societies explain women's becoming other for men. In these circumstances, "the support of life became for man an activity and a project through the invention of the tool; but in maternity woman remained closely bound to her body, like an animal" (1989: 65). But Beauvoir also argues that "the whole of feminine history has been man-made" (1989: 128); "[m]en have presumed to create a feminine domain—the kingdom of life, of immanence—only in order to lock up women therein" (1989: 65). In other words, Beauvoir argues both that women's role in reproduction traps them in immanence while men's role does not, and that men—not female embodiment—limit women to immanence.

To the extent that female embodiment traps women in immanence, women must somehow escape the trap of the body. But if women do this, they seem to become something other than women, as is also suggested by Beauvoir's account of menopause, after which, she says, women are "no longer females." In other words, Beauvoir's argument for the possibility of women's transcendence both distinguishes gender and the body and reduces gender to the (sexed) body in a way indicative of the paradox of gender that results from the dilemma of difference. Furthermore, to the extent that men trap women in immanence, women must oppose men in order to secure their opportunities for transcendence. But this undermines the possibility of reciprocity and mutuality in relations between men and women for which Beauvoir also argues. These contradictory implications of Beauvoir's account of women's embodiment and situation are an instance of the paradoxes of embodiment and gender, including their contradictory account of the body, sex, and gender, that are a manifestation of the dilemma of difference. Both the difficulty of theorizing women's difference without reducing it to the body, understood in terms of mind/body dualism, and the difficulty of theorizing gender in relationship to the sex of the body are evident in the inconsistent claims that Beauvoir makes about the role of female embodiment in determining women's experiences and situations.

Beauvoir's analysis of the body concludes that "the body is not a *thing*, it is a situation . . . the instrument of our grasp upon the world, a limiting factor for our projects," and that the facts of biology, while they cannot be denied, have in themselves no significance (1989: 34, Beauvoir's emphasis). Rather they acquire significance in relationship to specific material and social contexts. Women's embodiment alone does not explain women's oppression; rather, women's oppression is explained by the various material conditions and social relations that have characterized human history so far and what they have made of women's embodiment. Beauvoir argues that "the more women assert themselves as human beings, the more the marvelous quality of the Other will die out in them" (1989: 142). In making this argument, Beauvoir emphasizes women's possibilities, arguing that the facts of biology and history indicate only what women have been; neither proves that women cannot become other than what they have been (see also 1989: 597, 615, 624, 714). The concept of 'possibility', however, obscures the extent to which, on Beauvoir's own account, embodiment and history influence future possibilities. While Beauvoir argues that women's experiences are a function of their situation, not their embodiment, she also argues that the body is (at least an aspect of) one's situation. Thus, an ideological moment occurs with the deployment of the concept of possibility to reconcile the conflicting elements of Beauvoir's account of female embodiment and women's situation. This concept obscures the unresolved paradoxes of embodiment and gender in Beauvoir's analysis of female embodiment, women's situations, and women's possibilities, and these paradoxes persist in her account of mothering.

— mothering in *The Second Sex* —

Beauvoir directly challenges essential motherhood by arguing against its central claim that female embodiment determines women's mothering. Relying on her analysis of the body as situation, Beauvoir seeks to account for the significance of women's embodiment, including maternal embodiment, while also avoiding the renaturalization of mothering in terms of women's embodiment. The contradictory aspects of Beauvoir's account of mothering, however, indicate that her analysis does not entirely achieve these two goals. In order to reconcile her account of the significance of women's embodiment with her vision of women's transcendence, Beauvoir has to include an identity-based challenge to sexism and male dominance in her discussion of the independent woman. This undermines her difference-based challenge to individualism, reinforces the effects of the individualist elements of her theoretical framework, and brings her account of women's transcendence very close to individualism's implication that mothering is not an exercise of subjectivity.

Beauvoir's account of mothering begins with a discussion of contraception and abortion, including the hypocrisy of the then current practice of abortion. This rhetorical strategy forcefully removes mothering from the sole determination of biology and locates it as an object of choice and control and a site of struggle between men and women. It also foregrounds the possibility of transcendence in mothering by allowing Beauvoir to distinguish enforced maternity from maternity freely chosen (1989: 485, 492). Beauvoir recognizes that, at the moment at which she writes, mothering is determined in part voluntarily and in part by chance, since the availability of not only safe and legal contraception and abortion but also artificial insemination is required if women are to be free to become mothers only and if they choose. But she envisions a mothering that is entirely a function of women's free choices as an impending reality, arguing that "artificial insemination has not come into *common use at present*" (1989: 492, my emphasis). Beauvoir's analysis of abortion thus suggests that women's freedom with respect to mothering depends on control of the body. This conclusion supports her view of the possibility of women's transcendence in mothering. But it is also consistent with individualism's privileging of rational autonomy and self-determined control of the body, and with mind/body dualism's view of the body as a limit to self-determination.

But Beauvoir also considers the ambiguities of abortion. A woman seeking an abortion may be "divided against herself," experiencing a "natural tendency to have the baby" and feeling "uneasy about the dubious act she is engaged in" (1989: 490). According to Beauvoir, "the woman who has recourse to abortion is disowning feminine values, her values, and at the same time is in most radical fashion running counter to the ethics established by men." Despite these "ethics established by men," however, men contradict themselves with "careless cynicism," universally forbidding abortion but accepting it when it solves a problem for them, for instance, a man's arranging an abortion for a woman pregnant with his child out of wedlock. But "woman feels these contradictions in her wounded flesh" (1989: 491). This "wounded flesh" is also a source of knowledge; having experienced abortion, women "learn to believe no longer in what men say when they exalt woman or when they exalt man: the one thing that they are sure of is this rifled and bleeding womb, these shreds of crimson life, this child that is not there. It is at her first abortion that woman begins to 'know'" (1989: 492).

Beauvoir's analysis of abortion, like her account of female embodiment and women's oppression, makes contradictory claims about the body and gender. On one hand, Beauvoir argues that control of the body enhances women's freedom, which is consistent with the view that the body is an obstacle to transcendence. But her account of the ambiguities of abortion suggests that control of the body does not inevitably enhance women's freedom. In addition, Beauvoir's image of a woman feeling "these contradictions in her wounded flesh" represents women as coming to know something as a result of the bodily experience of abortion. This figures the body as a source of knowledge, indeed, of certainty, and confounds the representation of the body as an obstacle to transcendence. If the female body can be a source of knowledge, then women's embodiment can perhaps be a significant element of women's transcendence.

Beauvoir's discussion of "feminine values" and "the ethics established by men," especially her suggestion that a woman who has an abortion repudiates both, also problematizes gender. It suggests both a challenge to ethics that leaves gender intact and a forsaking of values that undermines the connection of gender and the body. The image of women challenging the ethics of men implies that these ethics, even if challenged by women, remain the ethics of men. But Beauvoir's representation of the woman who has an abortion as also forsaking feminine values undermines the connection of gender and the body. It places this woman outside of and in opposition to the femininity of these values, and raises the question of what it means for her to be a woman if she is forsaking some aspect of femininity. The distinction of a masculine and feminine ethics that mimics the distinction of men and women by insisting that men follow a masculine ethics while women practice a feminine ethics is consistent with a conception of gender as grounded in the (sexed) body. But the image of the woman who both challenges masculine ethics and repudiates feminine values detaches gender from (sexed) embodiment by separating the gender of the woman from the masculinity and femininity of the ethics and values she challenges. These contradictory implications of Beauvoir's account of abortion with respect to subjectivity, embodiment, and gender indicate the persistence here of the paradoxes of embodiment and gender that are effects of the dilemma of difference in feminist theory.

The account of mothering that follows Beauvoir's analysis of abortion is organized chronologically and includes two distinct analyses of pregnancy, a very brief account of childbirth, and discussions of the relationships of mother and infant and mother and older child. Beauvoir challenges essential motherhood by arguing that not all mothers desire to become mothers or enjoy mothering, by emphasizing the painful, difficult, and frustrating aspects of mothering, and by detailing the conflicts and tensions that can occur in the relationship of mother and child. In Beauvoir's account, there is nothing of Key's romantic mystification of mothering or of Elshtain's psychologizing and dematerializing of mothering. There are, however, two conflicting impulses at work in Beauvoir's account of mothering. One is an insistence on the constraints that limit women's choices and shape their experience of mothering, and a tendency to ground these constraints in female embodiment, which locates mothering in immanence. The other is a suggestion that the constraints of mothering and women's frustrations and dissatisfactions as mothers are not inherent in mothering but are a result of its social organization in sexist and male-dominant societies. This second impulse suggests the possibility of transcendence with respect to mothering, if it were socially reorganized.

As a result of these conflicting impulses, there is a pattern of contradiction in Beauvoir's account of mothering. It continually suggests a possibility of transcendence with respect to mothering, only to revoke that possibility and relocate mothering in immanence. Furthermore, these contradictions are mediated by several ideological moments of displacement. The contradictory aspects of pregnancy are displaced onto the fetus, the contradictory aspects of the mother-infant relationship are displaced onto the infant, and the contradictory aspects of the mother-child relationship are displaced onto the social context of their relationship. These displacements, particularly the last, denaturalize important aspects of mothering, thus supporting Beauvoir's challenge to essential motherhood and allowing her to argue for the social reorganization of mothering. But they also ensure that the contradictions implicit in her analysis of mothering remain unreconciled.

The pattern of suggesting and revoking the possibility of transcendence in mothering is most evident in Beauvoir's account of pregnancy. Beauvoir devotes considerable attention to pregnancy, and there is a repetitious quality to this discussion, which reads as if Beauvoir's analysis is struggling to impose the terms of immanence and transcendence and the Hegelian account of self and other on the experience of pregnancy, which resists being theorized in these terms. The distinction of immanence and transcendence presupposes the clear distinction of subjectivity and embodiment, and the oppositional account of self and other presupposes stable and unambiguous boundaries of subjectivity separating individuals from and opposing them to each other. But neither of these presuppositions is adequate to theorizing pregnancy, as indicated by Beauvoir's own account. For Beauvoir argues that in pregnancy the mother's subjectivity is dramatically affected by changes in her embodiment, and the boundary between mother and fetus is unstable and shifting, almost impossible to determine. The mother experiences the fetus as both a part of herself and a separate being, and the fetus both depends on the mother's body and develops so that it will be able to exist apart from the mother's body. Beauvoir's analysis of pregnancy thus problematizes the very terms on which she relies to develop her analysis.

For example, Beauvoir argues that pregnancy is both "an enrichment and an injury." The fetus is both part of the woman and a parasite; she possesses it but is also possessed by it. Since the fetus represents the future, the woman who carries it "feels as vast as the world," but its very significance annihilates her. Beauvoir writes: "[i]t is especially noteworthy that the pregnant woman feels the immanence of her body at just the time when it is in transcendence. . . . The transcendence of the artisan, of the man of action, contains the element of subjectivity; but in the mother-to-be the antithesis of subject and object ceases to exist . . . " (1989: 495). This statement evidences the pattern of simultaneously attributing transcendence to and revoking it from pregnancy that I have described. Beauvoir implies that the pregnant woman's body is truly in transcendence, but that she somehow cannot feel this. This problematizes the immanence/transcendence distinction in two ways. It implies that the body might be a site of transcendence, and it implies that the pregnant woman's body can somehow transcend itself apart from the woman whose body it is but who does not feel this transcendence. But, if the body can transcend itself apart from the woman whose body it is, then it seems that the woman is excluded from this transcendence.

The comparison to the artisan suggests the inferiority of pregnancy as an experience of transcendence, but it also claims that the antithesis of subject and object ceases in pregnancy, which hints at a remarkable instance of transcendence, the very overcoming of the subject/object antithesis. This suggestion, however, is revoked by the description of the pregnant woman that immediately follows: " . . . she and the child with which she is swollen make up together an equivocal pair overwhelmed by life. Ensnared by nature, the pregnant woman is plant and animal, a stock-pile of colloids, an incubator, an egg; she scares children proud of their young, straight bodies and makes young people titter contemptuously because she is a human being, a conscious and free individual, who has become life's passive instrument" (1989: 495). The rhetorical excesses of this statement—the pregnant woman swollen, overwhelmed, and ensnared; reduced to plant, animal, minute biological elements; the object of fear and amused contempt—return pregnancy to the boundaries of the immanence/transcendence distinction, insisting on its location in the realm of immanence.

The same pattern occurs several times in Beauvoir's statement that

> [o]rdinarily life is but a condition of existence; in gestation it appears as creative; but that is a strange kind of creation which is accomplished in a contingent and passive manner. . . . If the flesh is purely passive and inert, it cannot embody transcendence, even in a degraded form . . . but when the reproductive process begins, the flesh becomes root-stock, source, and blossom, it assumes transcendence, a stirring toward the future, the while [sic] it remains a gross and present reality. (1989: 495)

Here gestation appears to be creative, but this is repudiated by the view of the flesh as purely passive and inert. According to this view of the body, the body cannot be in transcendence, as Beauvoir earlier suggests. On the other hand, in reproduction perhaps the flesh is not purely passive and inert, if it becomes root-stock, source, and blossom, and stirs toward the future. But even in this case the flesh only assumes transcendence, which implies that transcendence is not its proper state.

Finally, Beauvoir writes:

> The fusion sought in masculine arms—and no sooner granted than withdrawn—is realized by the mother when she feels her child heavy within her or when she clasps it to her swelling breasts. She is no longer an object subservient to a subject; she is no longer a subject afflicted with the anxiety that accompanies liberty, she is one with that equivocal reality: life. Her body is at last her own, since it exists for the child who belongs to her. Society recognizes her right of possession and invests it, moreover, with a sacred character. . . . With her ego surrendered, alienated in her body and in her social dignity, the mother enjoys the comforting illusion of feeling that she is a human being *in herself*, a *value*. But this is only an illusion. (1989: 496, Beauvoir's emphasis)

The possibility of transcendence in pregnancy appears here in the claims that the pregnant woman is neither subject nor object and that her body is her own. But this possibility is undermined by the simultaneous claim that the pregnant woman's ego is surrendered and alienated in her body, and that her body exists for the child. The suggestion that the possibility of transcendence in pregnancy is a function of the pregnant woman's ownership of and unity with her body compounds the paradoxical quality of Beauvoir's representation of the woman's body. About menopause, Beauvoir argues that after menopause a woman and her body are one because the bodily functions that define her as anatomically and physiologically female have ceased. On the other hand, Beauvoir argues that in pregnancy it is these same bodily functions, rather than their cessation, that provide the possibility of bodily unity. Perhaps most paradoxically, Beauvoir asserts that in pregnancy the mother's body is her own, but this is so because her body exists for another, the child. Ultimately, however, the insistent repetition of the word illusion in this passage returns pregnancy to the realm of immanence.

The paradoxical elements of this representation of pregnancy are not resolved but rather are displaced onto the fetus. Beauvoir writes: "For she does not really make the baby, it makes itself within her . . . the child in the maternal body . . . is still only a gratuitous cellular growth, a brute fact of nature . . . she engenders him as a product of her generalized body, not of her individualized existence" (1989: 496). This image represents the fetus as active, making itself within its mother, which reinforces the immanence of pregnancy for the mother by figuring the mother as passive location or container of the fetus's self-creation. But it also represents the fetus as "only a gratuitous cellular growth, a brute fact of nature." This displacement of the paradoxical elements of maternal embodiment onto the fetus does the ideological work of restricting pregnancy to immanence, leaving the immanence/transcendence distinction in place. But this account of the fetus also resists and undermines the terms of the immanence/transcendence distinction as it applies to the fetus by representing the fetus as both an instance of the immanence of embodiment and as an active agent in its own creation. So the difficulties of theorizing embodiment and subjectivity in terms of the immanence/transcendence distinction remain unresolved in Beauvoir's first account of pregnancy.

Beauvoir's second account of pregnancy focuses on women's ambivalent attitudes and experiences of pregnancy through the stages of fetal development. When a woman first realizes that she is pregnant, "she knows that her body is destined to transcend itself; day after day a growth arising from her flesh but foreign to it is going to enlarge within her; she is the prey of the species . . . " (1989: 498). In the second stage, after the symptoms of early pregnancy have passed, the relationship of mother and fetus changes. The fetus is "firmly settled in the mother's womb; the two organisms are mutually adapted, and between them biological exchanges take place that enable the woman to regain her balance. She no longer feels herself possessed by the species; it is she who possesses the fruit of her body" (1989: 501). In this stage the mother experiences a contradictory validation of her identity and purpose: "[J]ustified by the presence of an other in her womb, she at last enjoys the privilege of being wholly herself" (1989: 501). In the final stage of pregnancy the temporary accommodation of mother and fetus is disturbed and the mother "is now in the possession not of the species in general but of this infant who is about to be born" (1989: 504).

This account of pregnancy is also marked by the contradictory pattern of a suggestion of the possibility of transcendence in pregnancy and the containment of pregnancy in immanence. The possibility of transcendence in pregnancy is attributed specifically to the body, as if the pregnant woman has no active role to play in this experience of transcendence. The pregnant woman is prey of both the species in general and the specific fetus she carries, and yet she possesses the fetus. She possesses the fetus and experiences union with it, but it is the otherness of the fetus that enables her to experience being herself. This account of pregnancy particularly complicates the Hegelian account of social relations that Beauvoir adopts. Beauvoir represents the first stage of pregnancy in terms of the opposition of the pregnant woman and "the species in general," and suggests that at least some accommodation of mother and fetus occurs as a result of the individuation of the fetus. But in the final stage of pregnancy the woman nonetheless remains "in the possession," not of "the species in general," but of "this infant." The image of the woman as possession of the fetus/infant revokes the subjectivity and agency attributed to the pregnant woman by the image of the pregnant woman as possessing and bringing forth the infant. It also suggests that the mutual adaptation of mother and fetus in the second stage of pregnancy is very tenuous, and is ultimately replaced, not by greater reciprocity and mutuality, but by a different kind of oppositional consciousness, at least on the part of the mother.

Finally, Beauvoir considers childbirth, which she describes as a crisis in which "women give expression to their fundamental attitude about the world in general and toward their own maternity in particular" (1989: 505). But Beauvoir says less about childbirth than she does about any other aspect of mothering. If childbirth—when the mother both does and does not contain the fetus and the fetus is and is not within the mother—is the moment at which the separate existence of mother and child is least decidable, then its absence in Beauvoir's account of mothering is significant. That childbirth is barely represented here suggests that this moment is least susceptible to being articulated in terms of the distinction of immanence and transcendence and the Hegelian account of self and other. As I see it, the minimal attention to childbirth in Beauvoir's account of pregnancy furthers the ideological work done by the displacement of the contradictory aspects of pregnancy onto the fetus. Both serve to manage and contain those elements of Beauvoir's account of pregnancy that would otherwise more directly undermine the immanence/transcendence distinction and the oppositional account of self and other in Beauvoir's theoretical framework.

Beauvoir's discussion of the relationship of the mother and child has a similar contradictory quality. Her representation of the mother-child relationship both appeals to and challenges the immanence/transcendence distinction and the Hegelian account of self and other. Beauvoir argues that the mother brings to the relationship with the infant all her previous experiences and expectations, but the infant takes no active part in this relationship; "its smiles, its babble, have no sense other than what the mother gives to them" (1989: 509). However, neither is the infant the penis equivalent of Freud's theory of women's penis envy. In refuting the Freudian account, Beauvoir attributes a kind of agency to the infant. She argues that the value of the penis for the adult male "lies in the desirable objects it enables him to possess," so "the adult woman envies the male the prey he takes possession of, not the instrument by which he takes it" (1989: 511). The "infant corresponds, for the woman, to the mistress whom she leaves to the male and whom he does not represent for her . . . the mother finds in her infant . . . what man seeks in woman: an other combining both nature and mind, who is to be both prey and *double*." The infant also returns the mother to her mother, for "[t]he infant's flesh has that softness, that warm elasticity, which the woman, when she was a little girl, coveted in her mother's flesh, and later, in things everywhere" (1989: 512, Beauvoir's emphasis).

Beauvoir's suggestions that there is an erotic element to the relationship of mother and infant, that the infant represents a feminine other, and that the infant establishes a further connection of its mother to her mother challenge several elements of essential motherhood. These include its claims that women's sexuality is necessarily and properly heterosexual, that sexual relationships with men that lead to motherhood are inevitably satisfying and fulfilling for women, and that the infant establishes further ties between its mother and father. At the same time, Beauvoir's attribution of a kind of agency to the infant challenges individualism's view of agency as rational autonomy. But while Beauvoir attributes this agency to the infant, she also insists that the infant is "a carnal plenitude" who "incarnates all nature" (1989: 512). Her analysis of the infant figures the infant as an agent while also representing the infant in terms of immanence, as flesh, carnality, and nature. Beauvoir's account of the infant in the mother-infant relationship thus makes contradictory claims about the infant. It implies the infant's subjectivity by attributing agency to it, and then revokes this implication and insists on the immanence and otherness of the infant. This revocation is an ideological moment that further contains the challenges to these distinctions implicit in Beauvoir's account of mothering.

Beauvoir's further discussion of the relationship of mother and child attempts to manage the contradictory qualities attributed to the infant at its initial appearance by displacing them onto the social context of mothering. But in doing so it also emphasizes the oppositional quality of the mother-child relation, making it difficult to see how this relation could ever be anything but the struggle of consciousnesses envisioned by the Hegelian account of the self/other relation. This is implicit in Beauvoir's image of the child as "an other combining both nature and mind" but "who is to be both prey and double." This image represents the contradictions of a relationship in which the responsibility for one human existent is almost entirely in the hands of another. The child is "a double, an *alter ego*, into whom the mother is sometimes tempted to project herself entirely, but he is an independent subject and therefore rebellious; he is intensely real today, but in imagination he is the adolescent and adult of the future" (1989: 512, Beauvoir's emphasis).

How the child is a potential double varies with the child's gender. The son can be imagined as a future great man whose accomplishments validate his mother's existence and care of him. The daughter, however, represents little possibility of transcendence. Some exceptional mothers can imagine their daughters overcoming the constraints of femininity and thus give their daughters "a man's education" (1989: 518). But most mothers demand that their daughters validate their mother's existence and care of them by accepting the same constraints that define their mother's existence. Either way, the mother's treating the child as a double amounts to preying on the child; the mother deprives the child of opportunities for transcendence in order to secure her own transcendence. Furthermore, this attempt at transcendence is futile. The child may grant a kind of necessity to the mother, but there is no reciprocity in their relationship and the child is still "a small, prattling soul, lost in a fragile and dependent body" (1989: 512). The dream of the son who becomes a great man is a contradictory one: "she would have him of unlimited power, yet held in the palm of her hand." But precisely by achieving greatness he escapes woman's power, and his mother will be able to console herself only with pride in having "engendered one of her conquerors" (1989: 517; see also 584–88). The daughter whom she insists remain her double nonetheless comes to be an other, and the mother will be "doubly jealous: of the world, which takes her daughter from her, and of her daughter, who in conquering a part of the world, robs her of it" (1989: 519; also 588–91).

Beauvoir ultimately attributes these elements of the mother-child relationship to a contradiction fundamental to the social organization of mothering in sexist and male-dominant societies, namely, that "the mother to whom it [the child] is confided in all its helplessness is almost always a discontented woman" (1989: 513). In this way Beauvoir displays the contradictory aspects of the mother-child relationship onto its social context. Beauvoir argues that given a relationship to the child's father in which she is sexually unsatisfied and socially inferior, and her lack of any freely chosen projects that enable her to experience transcendence apart from mothering, it is almost inevitable that the mother will succumb to the temptation to prey on her double/other child. Whether she makes the child her project or projects her frustrations onto her child, she reduces another human subjectivity to her means of escape from immanence.

This displacement of the contradictions of the mother-child relationship onto the social context of mothering further supports Beauvoir's challenge to essential motherhood and her argument for the social reorganization of mothering. But, because it does not resolve these contradictions, it also ensures that they will emerge elsewhere in her account of women's situations and experiences. And it preserves the individualist elements of her theoretical framework. Beauvoir's account of mothering thus concludes that mothering need not and should not involve the mother's pursuit of transcendence by means of her children. Rather, like Gilman, Beauvoir argues that mothering should be reorganized so that it is not an obstacle to women's pursuit of transcendence through more appropriate projects, specifically through work that makes women economically independent and through participation in cultural and political life, which will also improve family life (1989: 524–25). But, because the contradictions of her analysis of mothering have been managed and contained by the ideological moments of displacement I describe, these contradictions recur in Beauvoir's view of how to bring about the social reorganization of women's lives and of mothering she envisions.

— mothering and the independent woman —

In its concluding Part VII: Towards Liberation, *The Second Sex* says relatively little about mothering. Beauvoir repeats that mothering as it is currently organized is an obstacle to women's transcendence (1989: 696–97) and mentions that equality between men and women requires the availability of contraception and abortion, the same rights for women and children in and outside of marriage, and social support of mothering such as state-sponsored pregnancy leave and child care (1989: 724–25). This relative silence about mothering seems to suggest that "voluntary motherhood" (1989: 724) and the social reorganization of mothering Beauvoir recommends are easily accomplished. But Beauvoir also says that "[t]here is one feminine function that it is actually almost impossible to perform in complete liberty. It is maternity." Following this admission, Beauvoir summarizes the ways in which the independent woman is "torn between her professional interests and the problems of her sexual life" (1989: 696). She then discusses some of the professional activities in which women are most likely to have opportunities for transcendence and the conflicts women may encounter in pursuing them. But she never returns to the issue of mothering. That Beauvoir recognizes the impossibility of maternity in complete liberty and then fails to address this difficulty in her subsequent discussion of the lives of independent women implies that mothering remains inconsistent with women's freedom and transcendence. Thus, *The Second Sex* concludes with a detailed discussion of women's economic independence and equal participation in society and culture. Beauvoir confidently predicts that the liberation of women will lead to relations between men and women based on equality, reciprocity, and fraternity, and that sexual relations between men and women in particular will only be improved by these changes. But, as I see it, the confidence of these predictions is a function of Beauvoir's not having directly confronted the contradictions implicit in her account of mothering, including what she herself sees as the impossibility of mothering in complete freedom.

The persistence of these contradictions can be seen in the claims about embodiment that occur in Beauvoir's account of relations between independent women and men. In arguing for the possibility of equality, reciprocity, and mutuality between men and women, Beauvoir writes: "the fact that we are human beings is infinitely more important than all the peculiarities that distinguish human beings from one another. . . . In both sexes is played out the same drama of flesh and the spirit, of finitude and transcendence . . . they have the same essential need for one another; and they can gain from their liberty the same glory" (1989: 728). This identity-based argument for women's independence minimizes the significance of embodiment and women's difference in a way that is quite consistent with individualism. This argument, however, is contradicted by Beauvoir's own account of mothering, especially her account of pregnancy, which clearly denies that "the *same* drama of flesh and the spirit, of finitude and transcendence" (my emphasis) occurs for both sexes. On the other hand, in order to ensure that the liberation of women enhances sexual relations between men and women, Beauvoir must show that the independent woman will still be an other for man, as man will be for her. So she argues that women's liberation will not undo the significance of the bodily differences of men and women: " . . . her eroticism, and therefore her sexual world, have a special form of their own and therefore cannot fail to engender a sensuality, a sensitivity, of a special nature. . . . [H]er relation to her own body, to that of the male, to the child, will never be identical with those the male bears to his own body, to that of the female, and to the child" (1989: 731). This argument appeals to a difference-based account of women's embodiment, sexuality, and mothering that is directly at odds with the view of embodiment required by Beauvoir's argument for the possibility of equality, reciprocity, and mutuality between men and women. It also repudiates the challenge to essential motherhood's requirement of women's heterosexuality that is implicit in Beauvoir's analysis of the erotic elements of the mother-infant relationship.

The contradictory implications of Beauvoir's theory of embodiment undermine other elements of her analysis of the social relations of men and independent women. For instance, she argues that the source of the opposition and hostility of men and women is femininity, as this has traditionally been defined

(1989: 719). Completely voluntary mothering, women's economic independence, and the reorganization of child rearing based on greater social support
of mothering will reconstruct femininity and create the conditions in which
men and women can be truly equal. With respect to child rearing, Beauvoir
emphasizes that girls should have the same freedoms and face the same
demands as boys, so that they can be prepared for equality as adults. This reorganization of child rearing requires changing the relationship of parents.
Beauvoir writes: "Assuming on the same basis as the father the material and
moral responsibility of the couple, the mother would enjoy the same lasting
prestige; the child would perceive around her an androgynous world and not a
masculine world" (1989: 726).

The likelihood of such change in the relationship of parents, however, is
problematized by Beauvoir's claim that differences in male and female embodiment determine differences in their relationships to children (1989: 731). This
claim risks recuperating essential motherhood's view that mothers' relationships to children are determined by female embodiment, and thus undermines
Beauvoir's challenge to essential motherhood's assignment of primary responsibility for child rearing to women. And, while Beauvoir envisions mothers taking on material and moral responsibilities for the family on the same basis as
men have traditionally done, she does not envision fathers assuming any of the
family responsibilities traditionally assigned to mothers. But if women's liberation will not undo women's primary responsibility for child rearing, then the
traditional social organization of child rearing and its effects, including traditional femininity and opposition between men and women, are likely to persist.

In these ways, then, the interplay of identity and difference that marks the
dilemma of difference in feminist theory is clearly evident in the conflicting
claims that Beauvoir makes at the conclusion of *The Second Sex*. As Beauvoir
characterizes her own position, she rejects "the doubtful concept of 'equality
in inequality'" but accepts the possibility of "differences in equality" (1989:
722, 731). Beauvoir's attempt to recognize the significance of women's difference while also arguing for women's equality requires that she emphasize the
significance of difference to explain what has been women's situation in the
past, and then appeal to identity to argue that women can be men's equals,
experience a freedom and transcendence equal to that which men have known,
and experience mutuality and reciprocity in relationships with men. And, in a
way typical of the dilemma of difference, elements of individualism persist in
and undermine Beauvoir's difference-based challenge to individualism, while
the significance of difference persists in and undermines her identity-based
challenge to sexism and male dominance and her argument for women's liber-

ation and equality. The significance of women's difference persists in
Beauvoir's argument that women's independence will preserve the heterosexual eroticism that she sees as resulting from embodied sexual difference, and in
her implication that women's independence will not undo women's primary
responsibility for child rearing. At the same time, an appeal to identity is
implicit in Beauvoir's depiction of the independent woman, which represents
her as engaged in and experiencing transcendence through activities that are
not specific to women. But to the extent that these activities are actually those
in which men have traditionally engaged, Beauvoir's appeal to identity also
invokes individualism's implicit masculinization of subjectivity, agency, and
entitlement. This aspect of individualism is even implicit in Beauvoir's use of
the term "fraternity" to describe men and women's mutual freedom and
autonomy. While the slogan "liberty, equality, fraternity" is traditional in
French political culture since the Revolution, the repetition of the image of
fraternity in the conclusion of *The Second Sex* (1989: 716, 728, 732) points to
the implicit masculinity of the reciprocal and mutual subjectivity that
Beauvoir envisions men and women sharing. In this way too Beauvoir's account
of women's independence tries to avoid the significance of women's difference
that she herself has so thoroughly detailed in the rest of *The Second Sex*.

— reconceptualizing embodiment and subjectivity —

My reading of Beauvoir's account of mothering in *The Second Sex* stresses its
contradictory implications which, I have argued, are an effect of the dilemma
of difference in feminist theory. In order to theorize embodiment and subjectivity, Beauvoir relies to some extent on the individualist binary formulations
that she means to challenge, especially mind/body dualism. Thus, the alternatives to these binaries implicit in her work are only tenuously established. On
the other hand, my reading of Beauvoir's account of mothering emphasizes the
extent to which mothering, especially pregnancy and childbirth, resists the
terms that Beauvoir's analysis attempts to impose on it. I have argued that the
contradictions more or less implicit in Beauvoir's account of mothering indicate that the individualist elements of her theoretical framework are not adequate for theorizing mothering. Focusing on this resistance of mothering to
Beauvoir's theoretical framework, as well as highlighting Beauvoir's concept of
the body as situation and her view that embodied subjectivity is "strangely
ambiguous," have several implications for difference feminism's project of theorizing mothering while also challenging individualism and avoiding essential
motherhood.

That the analyses of mothering offered by Gilman, Key, Elshtain, and Beauvoir all to one extent or another make contradictory claims and/or have contradictory implications suggests that ambiguity, contradiction, and even incoherence may be more characteristic of mothering than any of these accounts directly acknowledges. That Beauvoir's account of mothering in particular suggests this is not surprising, for Beauvoir's theory of embodiment as situation indicates that the experience of embodied subjectivity itself is ambiguous and contradictory, especially when the relationship of embodied subjectivity and social contexts is taken into account. Beauvoir's theory of embodiment as situation implies that the body, by locating or positioning subjectivity in the world, brings embodied subjectivity into specific material and social contexts and into specific social relations. A theory of embodiment along these lines provides a basis for resisting individualism's decontextualizing account of embodied subjectivity. It implies understanding embodiment in terms of its contexts, and theorizing embodiment itself as a context, rather than container, of subjectivity. This conception of embodiment refigures the relationship of the body, subjectivity, and material and social contexts as more fluid and permeable. Such a theory of embodiment thus represents subjectivity as permeating embodiment and embodiment as permeating subjectivity. And it extends the fluidity and permeability of embodied subjectivity to the relationship of embodied subjectivity and its material and social contexts, so that the reciprocal permeability of embodiment and subjectivity is the basis for the social constitution of embodied subjectivity itself (Grosz 1994).

This account of embodied subjectivity deemphasizes the notion of social construction, a notion which suggests that sexed embodiment is distinct from but somehow made into gender or that sexed embodiment is a distinct and stable component or part of gender. Instead it suggests the notion of social constitution, which implies that sex and gender themselves are materialized and enacted as a function of the reciprocal permeability of embodiment and sex, gender, or subjectivity. The notions of fluidity and reciprocal permeability of embodiment and subjectivity further imply that the social constitution of embodied subjectivity does not necessarily produce a univocal, consistent, and coherent experience of subjectivity. The reciprocal permeability of subjectivity, embodiment, and their material, social, and ideological contexts means that the social constitution of embodied subjectivity is a process of overdetermination.[2] Processes of social constitution operate in several directions at once and a multiplicity of material and social factors plays a role in them. But no one element of this process ever totalizes—exhaustively, completely, and finally determines—embodied subjectivity. The elements of this process can be closely aligned, to produce a relatively stable and coherent experience of embodied subjectivity, but they can also be at odds with or work against each other. In this case, the process of over-determination produces an experience of embodied subjectivity that is relatively more ambiguous, contradictory, unstable, and even incoherent.

My reading of Beauvoir's account of mothering thus suggests that feminist theory should not presuppose the univocal coherence and stability of mothering. Resisting this presupposition would allow feminist theory to challenge essential motherhood's very notion of mother*hood* as a mother's univocal, stable, and coherent state of being. It would also undermine the views that mothering is essentially the same experience for all mothers in all social contexts and that mothering is an unequivocally and unambiguously satisfying experience for all mothers. It also suggests how feminist theory might resist versions of the sex/gender distinction consistent with individualism. According to certain versions of the sex/gender distinction, the social construction of gender operates on the sexed body, but does not determine the sex of the body itself. But reconceptualizing embodied subjectivity and its social contexts in terms of fluidity, permeability, and reciprocal over-determination implies that the sexed body itself is socially, though never exhaustively and totally, constituted. This allows much greater variability in the relationship of embodiment, subjectivity, and contexts, so that subjects' experiences of embodiment and of their material and social contexts can be more or less univocal, stable, and coherent, more or less ambiguous, fragmented, and contradictory (Riley 1988; Butler 1990, 1993).

In addition, precisely by identifying its contradictory determinations, Beauvoir's account of mothering suggests that pregnant embodiment itself might serve as a paradigm for a theory of embodiment, sex, gender, and subjectivity as over-determined and thus possibly ambiguous, unstable, and contradictory. As Beauvoir's account indicates, in pregnancy a woman's body is dramatically altered, and this has profound effects for her consciousness and experience and for others' perception of and reaction to her. Pregnancy thoroughly reconfigures not only a woman's embodiment and consciousness, but also her social relations and social contexts. But, at the same time, the pregnant woman remains herself even as she undergoes these changes (see also Young 1984; Zerilli 1992). As Beauvoir also shows, the ambiguity and contradictions of pregnancy are compounded by the way in which the changes experienced by the pregnant woman are also the conditions of the development of another subject. That the fetus's existence within and dependency on the body of its mother are a necessary condition for its coming to subjectivity further confounds the individualist view that subjectivity is a function of the containment of the self within a distinct and unified body. The further development of these implications for reconceptualizing embodied subjectivity, however, requires a further analysis of childbirth than Beauvoir offers. For, in an individualist ideological context, it is possible to see pregnancy in the terms I have elicited from Beauvoir's account of it and nonetheless argue that pregnancy is an aberration and that birth restores the mother and child to their individualist subjectivity.

These implications of Beauvoir's account of mothering also enable resistence to both the Hegelian account of oppositional consciousness and individualism's view of consciousness, agency, and social relations. The concept of reciprocal over-determination that is never total refigures consciousness in terms of connection to rather than separation from its social contexts. It suggests rethinking social relations as a locus of the constitution of subjectivity, or analyzing interactions with others as enabling subjectivity, as well as limiting or threatening it. It also implies reconceptualizing agency in terms of the reciprocal social constitution of agency, social relations, and their material, social, and ideological contexts. Furthermore, the representation of the relationship of mother and child in *The Second Sex* might serve as a model for these implications of Beauvoir's account of mothering. Beauvoir's account of the mother-child relationship shows that maternal consciousness is very much determined by its contexts, which include maternal embodiment, but that such contexts enable as well as restrict maternal agency. And, from the perspective of the mother-child relationship, agency also appears to be ambiguous and contradictory. For example, the mother's socially recognized responsibility for the child is one basis of her agency as a mother, but the particulars of the social organization of mothering can also greatly limit a mother's capacity to act. The nature of the embodiment of the infant or young child can be a limit to its agency, but the care of its body and the meeting of its bodily needs are a condition of its agency. How the child is cared for and how its needs are met very much determine its subjectivity, consciousness, and the extent and quality of its development of agency. And the child's dependency itself is one of the factors that determines its mother's responses to it. So the reciprocal but not total over-determination of maternal subjectivity and the subjectivity of the child are a condition as well as a limit of their consciousness and agency. Rethinking consciousness and agency in these terms suggests that the conflicts possible in the mother-child relation are perhaps a function of the contradictory elements of the processes of over-determination in which they participate. The further development of this approach to theorizing consciousness and agency requires a further analysis of the material aspects of mothering, or those ways in which mothering includes caring for the bodies and meeting the material needs of children, and of the relationship of this aspect of mothering to the determination of the subjectivity of child and mother. It also requires some explanation of how the reciprocal but not total over-determination of embodied subjectivity and its contexts enables agency and social relations, that is, of how subjects understood in terms of ambiguity, contradiction, or even incoherence are nonetheless capable of action. The further development of these implications of Beauvoir's account of mothering might lead to a theory of embodied subjectivity that more strenuously resists individualism than does Beauvoir's reliance on the immanence/transcendence distinction and the Hegelian account of social relations, and thus provides other approaches to negotiating the dilemma of difference and theorizing mothering in resistance to essential motherhood.

MATERNAL THINKING

practice and standpoint, experience and narrative

— mothering, subject positioning, and language —

MY READING OF Elshtain's argument for family reconstructive feminism indicates that feminist accounts of mothering that challenge individualism do not necessarily avoid essential motherhood by avoiding the issues of maternal embodiment and the material aspects of mothering. And because mind/body dualism is fundamental to both individualism and essential motherhood, feminist accounts of mothering must address the issues of maternal embodiment and the material aspects of mothering while also resisting mind/body dualism as strenuously as possible. My analysis of Beauvoir's account of mothering emphasizes a theory of embodied subjectivity implicit in it that may provide this sort of resistance to mind/body dualism. Beauvoir's view that embodied subjectivity is "strangely ambiguous," and the ways in which maternal embodiment in particular resists Beauvoir's attempts to analyze it in terms of the immanence/transcendence distinction suggest understanding embodied subjectivity in terms of the reciprocal permeability and over-determination of embodiment and subjectivity. A theory of embodied subjectivity along these lines indicates that the experience of embodied subjectivity can be ambiguous, contradictory, even incoherent. But does such a theory of embodied subjectivity enable feminist theory's resistance to essential motherhood? To address this question, I turn in this chapter to Sara Ruddick's work on mothering. One of the most influential theorists of mothering in contemporary U.S. feminism, Ruddick offers a very comprehensive account of mothering. She strives to include as many different aspects of mothering and as many different kinds of mothering as possible in her analysis. Ruddick's argument for a feminist, maternal peace politics is an instance of difference feminism's deployment of an analysis of women's difference as a paradigm for alternatives to individualism in social theory. So a consideration of Ruddick's work also allows further analysis of this aspect of difference feminism.

Ruddick has articulated what I take to be two relatively distinct accounts of mothering—a thoroughly developed account of maternal practice (1980, 1989) and a preliminary account of birthgiving (1994). These accounts of mothering attempt to negotiate the paradoxes of embodiment, gender, and representation that I have argued result from feminism's conflicted relationship to individualism. Ruddick addresses the paradoxes of embodiment and gender by striving to theorize female embodiment in a way that recognizes its significance for mothering, but does not reduce femininity and/or mothering to the female body. And she tries to represent mothering in terms that are consistent both with what women and mothers say about their experiences and with feminist social and political goals. Ruddick's commitment to negotiating these paradoxes in part explains her development of two relatively distinct accounts of mothering. But the difficulties and contradictions of her accounts of mothering indicate the persistence of these paradoxes, and thus of the dilemma of difference, in Ruddick's work.

Ruddick's account of maternal practice significantly resists individualism and essential motherhood while also negotiating the paradoxes of embodiment and gender. It theorizes the material aspects of mothering, and represents mothering in terms largely consistent with feminist social and political goals. But according to Ruddick, this account of mothering does not adequately represent what women and mothers have told her of their experiences of mothering, so it does not adequately negotiate the paradox of representation. This is the paradox feminism encounters in trying to represent both the interests and the experiences of women. To represent women's interests in an individualist ideological context, feminism must appeal to women's individualist subjectivity in order to claim women's political entitlement and agency. But to determine women as a group in need of political representation, and to represent women's experiences, feminism must appeal to difference to theorize women's shared political interests and the aspects of women's experiences that are more specific to women. Furthermore, because feminism analyzes the determination of women's experiences by sexism and male dominance, it may see women's interests and interpret women's experiences differently than do many women themselves. And in theorizing women's difference, feminism risks overlooking or minimizing differences among women, thus failing to represent the experiences and interests of at least some women.

Ruddick's account of birthgiving is an attempt to better represent women's and mothers' experiences. In analyzing birthgiving, Ruddick offers a theory of sexed, social/bodily subjectivity that resists individualism by directly challenging mind/body dualism. This theory of subjectivity is like Beauvoir's view of the body as ambiguously situating subjectivity in that it implies the reciprocal over-determination of embodiment and subjectivity and the possibility of partiality, ambiguity, contradiction, and incoherence in the experience of embodied subjectivity. But Ruddick's account of birthgiving also significantly risks the recuperation of essential motherhood because the theory of sexed, social/bodily subjectivity on which her account of birthgiving is based risks the reduction of mothering and femininity to the female body. To make this argument I analyze Ruddick's two accounts of mothering and their theoretical frameworks in terms of how they negotiate the dilemma of difference and its resulting paradoxes, emphasizing the difficulties of each account of mothering and the contradictions that emerge when they are brought together. In a way typical of the dilemma of difference, Ruddick's version of an appeal to difference to explain situations and experiences unique to or more typical of women undermines feminism's claim of women's individualist subjectivity and thus its political representation of women's interests in an individualist ideological context. But an insistence on women's individualist subjectivity undermines what are the strengths of Ruddick's analyses of mothering from the perspective of the issue of representation, including her analysis of women's difference and of differences among women and her representation of the specificity and variety of women's experiences and interests.

Having detailed these outcomes of Ruddick's accounts of mothering, I consider the concepts that are central to the theoretical frameworks on which Ruddick relies to develop these accounts of mothering. Whereas Ruddick's account of maternal practice relies on a practicalist approach to theorizing human action and a version of feminist standpoint theory, her account of birthgiving relies on the concepts of experience and narrative. I identify several moments at which these central concepts do the ideological work of mediating the contradictory implications of Ruddick's analyses of mothering. These ideological moments show the extent to which Ruddick's work on mothering remains caught within the terms of the dilemma of difference. But reading

Ruddick's work in this way also highlights several concepts that point feminist theory, especially feminist analysis of subjectivity, in the direction I have established in my analysis of Beauvoir's work. One of these concepts is the concept of subject positioning, which I use to further develop the concept of situation in Beauvoir's theory of embodiment. Ruddick's emphasis on the significance of persons being situated in specific material and social contexts, for instance, in her appeal to standpoint theory, implies thinking of subjectivity not as the possession of a set of characteristics, but as an ongoing, fluctuating process of positioning and repositioning. This is a further elaboration of the idea of the reciprocal, ongoing, but never total over-determination of embodiment and subjectivity that I have elicited from Beauvoir's account of mothering. Another of these concepts is the concept of the enabling conditions of knowledge and agency, which is suggested by both Beauvoir's concept of the body as situation and Ruddick's view of the relationship of subjectivity, practices, the contexts in which subjects engage in practices, and the knowledge and agency that result from engaging in a practice. If both embodiment and practices situate subjects, enabling them to acquire knowledge and to act, then knowledge is partial and limited, and different persons engaging in different practices will come to have different knowledge and different capacities for action. Further developing this concept of the enabling conditions of knowledge and agency requires an explanation of how being materially, socially, and ideologically situated enables knowledge and agency. It also requires an explanation of how being so situated enables shared knowledge and collective agency.

Finally, Ruddick's use of the concept of narrative in her account of birthgiving points to the possibility of theorizing subject positioning and the enabling conditions of knowledge and agency in relationship to language. I argue that theorizing subjectivity in discursive terms also indicates feminist theory's need to examine its own practice of representation in terms of the subject positioning of feminist theorists and the material, social, and ideological contexts of the production of feminist theory. In order to pursue this possibility of theorizing subjectivity in discursive terms and to consider the implications of this possibility for analyzing mothering, I consider in the next chapter Julia Kristeva's essay "Stabat Mater." While its psychoanalytic framework is problematic, Kristeva's account of mothering does offer a theory of embodied subjectivity that further develops the concepts I have elicited from Beauvoir's and Ruddick's accounts of mothering by arguing that embodied subjectivity is discursively constituted. Furthermore, an analysis of the issues raised by Ruddick's use of standpoint theory and the concept of narrative in light of Kristeva's theory of embodied subjectivity as discursively constituted suggests how feminist theory might examine its own practice of representation. Like standpoint theory, a theory of the discursive constitution of subjectivity implies that subjects cannot take up a position outside of the processes of subject constitution themselves. This raises the question of how knowledge of the discursive constitution of subjectivity is itself possible, and the question of the relationship of this knowledge to the context in which it is produced or the position from which it is articulated. Bringing these implications of Ruddick's and Kristeva's accounts of mothering together shows that feminist theory, including feminist accounts of mothering, cannot be operating outside of dominant ideological formations, so feminist theory must consider how it is operating within those formations. This means that it must consider the enabling conditions and ideological effects of its knowledge production, especially its representation of women. Feminist theory must consider what desires motivate its representations of women, mothers, and mothering, and how these desires might operate to obscure the enabling conditions and the ideological effects of feminist theory itself.

— maternal thinking and practice —

Ruddick's account of mothering as a practice argues that mothering includes complex modes of thought and action (1989: 13–17; 1987: 241; 1980: 214). A practice is a distinctively human activity in which persons respond to what they see as their material, emotional, psychological, and intellectual needs or interests, and those of others, in a coherent, socially organized way. For Ruddick, "the aims or goals that define a practice are so central or 'constitutive' of practices that in the absence of the goal you would not have that practice" (1989: 13–14). The goals of a practice suggest modes of perceiving, thinking, feeling, and acting—virtues—that contribute to their attainment, and constitute standards for evaluating the practice. Human needs and interests, including those of infants and children, are always experienced in specific material and social contexts (1989: 18–23; 1987: 243; 1980: 214–15). So practices and their goals and virtues are similarly specific, and the social context of a practice can foster or hinder the attainment of its goals. On this basis Ruddick argues that mothering is a practice. "The discipline of maternal thought . . . establishes criteria for determining failure and success, sets priorities and identifies virtues that the discipline requires" (1989: 24).

Maternal practice responds to children's demands for preservation, growth, and acceptability (1989: 17–23, 65, 123). Preserving children's lives requires controlling them, their environment, and other persons they encounter so that children survive. Fostering children's growth requires providing the material and social conditions needed for their physical growth and for their emotional, cognitive, and social development. Shaping acceptable children means "training a child to be the kind of person whom others accept and whom the mothers themselves can actively appreciate" (1989: 104). A variety of maternal actions contribute to attaining these goals. These include meeting children's bodily needs, presenting or welcoming challenges that enable children to acquire new skills and abilities, and adapting one's actions to children's changing needs and perceptions.

The virtues of maternal practice include a "metaphysical attitude" that prioritizes "keeping over acquiring . . . conserving the fragile . . . maintaining whatever is at hand and necessary to the child's life" (1989: 78–79; 1980: 217). An appreciation that the world and other persons, including children, are not entirely subject to one's control; a resilient, clear-sighted cheerfulness; and a willingness to work at preservation despite its limits are also virtues of maternal practice. In addition, maternal practice requires the ability to deal with complexity, tolerate ambiguity, and multiply options in order to respond concretely to specific problems (1989: 93); and an openness to children's development, especially the socially acceptable ways that they can come to be different from their mothers. While the demands of maternal practice are conceptually distinct, Ruddick recognizes that its various goal can be at odds with each other (1989: 122–23; 1980: 216–18, 221). Thus, a distinctive feature of maternal thought is the analysis of its conflicting goals in its specific material and social context to determine the action most likely to accomplish these goals to whatever extent possible in that context.

Ruddick's theory of maternal practice has distinct advantages compared to the accounts of mothering offered by Gilman, Key, Elshtain, and Beauvoir. Ruddick's theory of mothering as a practice is implicitly an identity-based challenge to sexism and male dominance, but it also to some extent resists individualism and theorizes women's difference. Understanding mothering as a practice implies that men and women are alike in that their consciousness and social relations are shaped by the practices in which they engage. It also indicates that mothering is an individually and socially significant practice in which both men and women can and should participate. In this way it undermines essential motherhood's claim that all women and only women should be mothers. At the same time, Ruddick's account of maternal practice more successfully resists the elements of individualism most consistent with essential motherhood than the accounts of mothering I have considered so far. It theorizes the material aspects of mothering, showing how maternal practice considers the specific, embodied needs of children and requires an engagement with bodies and the material world. The psychological processes in which mothers and children participate and the feelings they come to have are a function of children's embodied needs and interests and maternal practice's concrete and specific responses to them. In this way Ruddick resists the abstract and psychologistic account of mothering and family implicit in Elshtain's argument for family reconstructive feminism, and the romanticizing mystification of Key's view of the radiation of the mother's personality throughout the home. On the other hand, because she theorizes the cognitive and intellectual aspects of mothering, Ruddick also resists the naturalization of mothering in terms of embodiment that occurs in Gilman's account of mothering, and is an element of Beauvoir's analysis of mothering in terms of immanence.

Theorizing mothering as a practice also resists individualism's binary conception of public and private by distinguishing maternal practice from the family and the private sphere. Ruddick argues that maternal practice does not require a particular kind of family or social context, although different kinds of families and social contexts can be more or less supportive of or inconsistent with its goals. Ruddick's account of mothering allows for alternatives to the two-parent, heterosexual, nuclear family: "The work of mothering does not require a heterosexual or any other particular sexual commitment. . . . Nor does mothering require a particular household arrangement" (1994: 35; see also 1989: 49, 53–54, 207–8). But it also provides criteria—the goals of maternal practice—for evaluating such alternatives. In this way Ruddick's account of maternal practice also resists individualism's decontextualizing approach to subjectivity, social relations, and social contexts. Ruddick shows that the outcomes of maternal practice are very much a function of its social context. This further allows Ruddick to theorize differences among mothers' experiences as a function of their different social contexts, and to argue that a feminist account of mothering must allow for critical analysis and evaluation of its various social and institutional contexts.[1]

Ruddick's view of the relationship of practices and their social contexts thus leads to a more thorough analysis of how the social organization of mothering, especially as determined by essential motherhood, is related to other structures and practices of liberal democratic capitalism. It particularly addresses the question of how the social organization of mothering is related to other forms of social inequality. It denaturalizes women's private, unpaid mothering, which makes possible the analysis of how this particular social organization of mothering is related to women's economic dependence on men and women's social and political inequality. This denaturalization also enables the analysis of how different ways of socially organizing and engaging in mothering for different groups of people is related to forms of social inequality, such as those based on race, ethnicity, or socioeconomic class position. Understanding mothering as a practice very much determined by its social context raises the question of which social organization of mothering is most consistent with and supportive of freedom and equality for all women, and for all people. The extent to which an account of mothering as a practice enables critique of other social and political practices is also evident in Ruddick's own critique of militarism on the basis of her theory of maternal practice (1983, 1984, 1989). Ruddick's analysis of mothering as a practice can launch a better critique of the forms of inequality and oppression that can be present in liberal democratic capitalism than either Gilman's and Key's weak versions of socialism, or Elshtain's feminist communitarianism.

Ruddick's theory of maternal practice also resists the individualist view of the relationship of self and other that privileges separation, self-determination, and autonomy, and the Hegelian account of oppositional consciousness. Maternal practice represents mothers and children as active, engaged participants in a relationship of mutual self-constitution that transforms both. Autonomy is a valued outcome of maternal practice, but the concept of maternal practice allows for an understanding of autonomy in terms of mutuality and reciprocity. Fostering children's growth includes enabling them to become autonomous—less dependent on others and more able to meet their own needs. The goal of acceptability, however, means that autonomy must include an appreciation of persons' common interests and shared social contexts. Shaping acceptable children implies helping them become capable of reciprocal, mutually satisfying relationships with others, including relationships in which they themselves are caregivers (DiQuinzio 1995). Maternal practice represents subjects as fundamentally connected to and dependent on others and engaged in social relations as a result of dependency and mutual need, and it represents social relations as enriching as well as constraining. It sees subjects as capable of becoming more autonomous, including more capable of caring for others, without being completely separated from others or entirely disengaged from social relations. Children's desires and goals can be opposed to that which their mothers think is best for them, and to meet the goals of maternal practice mothers may have to oppose their children. But their relationship is not one of independent, rational agents who manage their conflicts by negotiating rights and responsibilities. Nor is it a relationship of oppositional consciousnesses, in which the selfhood of one requires the objectification of the other.

By resisting these elements of individualism, Ruddick's analysis of maternal practice more successfully resists essential motherhood and represents mothering in terms more consistent with feminist social and political goals than do the accounts of mothering proposed by Gilman, Key, Elshtain, and Beauvoir. Ruddick explicitly argues against essential motherhood's equation of female embodiment, femininity, and motherhood: "To claim a maternal identity is not to make an empirical generalization but to engage in a political act" (1989: 56). She shows that anyone, man or woman, can engage in maternal practice and develop its virtues by taking on its goals and acting to attain them (1989: 40–41; 1987: 241; 1980: 225–27), and she provides the basis for the argument that men should do so. Furthermore, to describe the virtues of maternal practice is not to claim that all mothers possess them or that a mother must fully realize these virtues to be a good mother. It is rather to describe an ideal that need not be entirely realized in order to inform the practice of mothering (1989: 24, 109–16; 1980: 214). Ruddick's use of the term "maternal" to name this practice recognizes the historical and cultural assignment of this work to women. It refuses the apparent gender neutrality of terms like "parenting," as they function, for example in Elshtain's work, to deny the complexity of the sex-based division of labor in child rearing and its social and cultural effects. But it does so without naturalizing women's mothering or valorizing mothers as inevitably virtuous. Thus, it enables the political demands for women's greater freedom with respect to mothering and men's greater participation in maternal practice.

Ruddick's account of maternal practice also foregrounds the needs of children, as these are determined by children's embodied subjectivity, social relations, and social contexts. This view of mothering as a response to children's needs further undermines the romanticizing or idealizing of mothers, by representing maternal virtues, not as emerging unbidden from maternal subjectivity or consciousness, but as at least partly elicited by children. By theorizing the needs of children, including the embodied basis of children's needs, Ruddick's account of maternal practice also resists romanticizing children and the work of caring for them. As Ruddick represents them, children make demands, often in tiresome, annoying, or enraging ways, and the work of keeping them clean, fed, clothed, healthy, and developing properly is usually quite concrete and mundane. In this way Ruddick's account of mothering counters both Key's mystification of mothering as the radiation of a mother's personality throughout her home and Elshtain's abstract and psychologizing account of mothering as the fulfillment of familial duties and imperatives based on emotionally intense attachments. Like Beauvoir, Ruddick recognizes the potential for conflict in the mother-child relationship and the vices of maternal practice, but she is also able to articulate the possibility for mutuality and reciprocity in this relationship. Ruddick's account of maternal practice is thus a less valorizing

and more critical analysis of mothering than that offered by Elshtain. By theorizing mothering as a practice, Ruddick is better able to distinguish the
elements of maternal practice that are determined by sexism and male dominance and those that are a response to the needs and demands of children.
This distinction is another way in which Ruddick's account of maternal practice provides a better basis for feminist critique of other social and political
structures than Elshtain's family reconstructive feminism.

Ruddick relies implicitly on a social constructivist theory of gender to support the detachment of female embodiment, femininity, and mothering that is
central to her analysis of maternal practice. She argues that in most social contexts women have been and are still more likely than men to engage in maternal practice and develop its characteristic modes of thought and action. But
this is a result of the relationship of the sex-based division of labor and the
social construction of gender: "given the social character of reason, the sexual
division of labor, the formative place of work in human lives, the processes of
identification that occur in families, we should expect women to develop a distinctive 'standpoint' comprised of metaphysical attitudes, epistemological
principles, cognitive styles, and values" (1987: 238). Modes of reasoning, feeling, and action are a function of the practices in which persons engage, but sex
is a basis on which societies and cultures determine who engages in which practices. Different practices and virtues thus come to be associated with masculinity and femininity. These practices and virtues are not naturally or
inevitably characteristic of men and women, however, and a reorganization of
the sex-based division of labor, such as a more equal participation of men and
women in maternal practice, would alter the social construction of masculinity
and femininity.

— rearticulating embodiment: natality and birthgiving —

Despite these advantages of her account of maternal practice, Ruddick considers whether it adequately addresses maternal embodiment and adequately represents mothering in terms of mothers' reports of their experiences of
mothering. She questions whether her argument against any necessary connection of maternal practice and female embodiment participates in individualism's denial of the significance of embodiment (1989: 188–98). She also
questions whether the concept of maternal practice adequately represents
mothers' experiences of pregnancy and childbirth. She takes seriously the
objection that she says she has heard from birth mothers, male mothers, and
adoptive mothers, "that, in disconnecting birthgiving from mothering [she]

failed to read the facts of birth and therefore got their experience quite wrong" (1994: 37). For these reasons, Ruddick turns her attention to maternal embodiment. She attempts to theorize maternal embodiment in a way that recognizes the significance of pregnancy and childbirth without defining women in terms of female reproductive capacities, and that is consistent with both feminist social and political goals and mothers' reports of their experiences of mothering.

Ruddick addresses the issue of embodiment in two ways. In *Maternal Thinking* (1989) she offers a theory of embodiment based on the concept of natality, which I argue is consistent with her account of mothering as a practice but does not theorize embodiment from the specific perspective of women giving birth. For this reason it fails to represent mothering in a way consistent with what Ruddick takes to be mothers' reports of their experiences. To reconceptualize embodiment in terms of natality, Ruddick argues that mothering begins in the bodily experiences of pregnancy and childbirth, and central to the care of infants and small children is the care of their bodies. Maternal practice includes processes that determine the meaningful organization of the child's body, the child's actualization of its bodily potentials, and the child's experience of embodiment. A reconceptualization of embodiment in terms of natality begins with a "welcoming and hopeful" perspective on birth, and shows how birth represents the "interwoven notions of beginning, action, difference, singularity, and promise."

Birth also constitutes a reciprocal relationship of birthgiver and infant, characterized by a dissolution of boundaries separating self and other that, from the perspective of individualism, is problematic. But, Ruddick argues, this dissolution is not a threat to subjectivity, rather it actualizes the possibility of subjectivity: "the entanglement of self and other in birth—physical union in metaphysical separateness—is a crystalizing symbol not of self-loss but of a kind of self-structuring." The birthing woman does not "lose" herself or experience herself as "dissolved" in childbirth; she experiences the singularity of pain and engages in a work that is hers alone. And her work achieves its aim only when the infant emerges as a separately embodied being able to exist apart from its mother's body. Rethinking the body in terms of natality thus figures embodiment as a basis of persons' separate existence, but sees this as made possible rather than threatened by natality (1989: 208–10).

Ruddick's analysis of natality more thoroughly considers the significance of maternal embodiment for mothering, thereby theorizing childbirth somewhat more specifically and resisting mind/body dualism somewhat more strenuously than does the concept of maternal practice. Ruddick's refusal of the concept of dissolution in favor of the concept of self-structuring for understanding birth in particular is consistent with rethinking embodiment and subjectivity in terms of their reciprocal permeability and mutual over-determination. But this rearticulation of embodiment in terms of natality does not enable the more adequate representation of the experience of mothering called for by Ruddick's reconsideration of her account of maternal practice. The problem is that Ruddick uses the concept of natality to refer both to being born and giving birth, which obscures how these experiences differ. But in rethinking embodiment on this basis, she actually theorizes birth more in terms of what it means to be born than in terms of what it means to give birth. Thus, an ideological moment occurs here, as Ruddick's account of natality fails to consider the position from which it is articulated. Her account of natality slips from theorizing the significance of embodiment for birthgiving women to theorizing the significance of the child's embodiment for its mother and for maternal practice, obscuring women's and mothers' situations, experiences, and perspectives on birthgiving in a way consistent with essential motherhood's tendency to see women's birthgiving as natural or necessary, and so not requiring analysis from women's and/or mothers' perspectives. This ideological moment indicates feminist theory's need for critical analysis of its own practice of representation, so that it can be more alert to such ideological moments and their effects.

To better represent mother's experiences of birthgiving embodiment, Ruddick offers, in "Thinking Mothers/Conceiving Birth" (1994), an account of embodiment from the specific perspective of birthgivers. In doing so she also argues for the possibility of a mode of thought—natal reflection—that originates in the experiences of pregnancy and birthgiving. Ruddick argues that an analysis of birthgiving that includes natal reflection requires a theory of the body as a site of knowledge. This means explicating both the primacy of the bodily roots of subjectivity and the fundamentality of sexual difference to embodiment. Freely adapting, as she characterizes it, the work of Rosi Braidotti (1989) and Luce Irigaray (1985a, 1985b, 1991), Ruddick begins by conceptualizing "the knowing self . . . as in the first instance, and to a degree always, as a bodily ego." Nothing persons experience can be 'only' or 'merely' bodily, rather all knowing is embodied and all aspects of embodiment have effects on knowing. Ruddick further argues that the bodily ego is social; "from the beginning it is constituted in and constructed by relationships in which 'the body' is held, touched, spoken to, heard, frightened, soothed, hurt, and comforted." This means that "potentially transformative physical experiences are imbued with meanings of past and future relationships and may therefore also be socially transformative" (1994: 41). In Ruddick's term for this, subjectivity is always "social/bodily." One of the social/bodily characteristics of subjectivity is that "the 'knowing self' is sexed when and insofar as it becomes a self." For Ruddick, "This means that the 'sexed,' exclusively female character of birthgiving and natal knowledge will not arise as a 'problem,' since ways of knowing will be intertwined with 'sexual difference' from the start." But Ruddick also argues that the sociality of sexed embodiment precludes the pre-suppositions that there are only two sexes or that sex is fixed for life. In most societies there are dominant conceptions of sexual difference, but "every body is sexed in ways that . . . can be related but never reduced to dominant concep-tions of male/female sexual differences." Thus, "to be sexed approximately 'female' is to encounter and . . . know the world in approximately 'female' ways" and birthgiving can be such an encounter (1994: 41).

This theory of sexed, social/bodily subjectivity does establish some connec-tion of birthgiving and maternal practice and does represent birthgiving and natal reflection from the perspective of birthgivers, and so it produces an account of birthgiving and natal reflection more consistent with what mothers have reported to Ruddick of their experiences of pregnancy and birth. It offers a difference-based challenge to those elements of individualism that make it difficult to theorize pregnancy and birthgiving. And it points to the reciprocal permeability and over-determination of subjectivity and embodiment that I have argued is implicit in Beauvoir's theory of embodiment. But Ruddick's the-ory of embodied subjectivity nonetheless has the contradictory implications that mark the persistence of the dilemma of difference, especially the simulta-neous detaching and reconnecting of the body, sex, and gender typical of the paradoxes of embodiment and gender. On one hand, Ruddick's theory of sexed, social/bodily subjectivity risks reconnecting the body, sex, and gender in a way consistent with essential motherhood. For example, Ruddick says that in theorizing birthgiving she is "respecting bodies as they are, metaphysically as well as socially, given us" (1994: 36). This is consistent with her claim that "the 'sexed,' exclusively female character of birthgiving and natal knowledge" is unproblematic if "ways of knowing are intertwined with 'sexual difference' from the start" (1994: 41). In these comments the concept of sex specifies the female body and female subjectivity in terms of the potential for pregnancy and birthgiving. As Ruddick also writes: "[t]o respect female bodies means respecting, even treasuring, the birthgiving vulnerabilities and procreative powers of females" (1994: 36).

Slippages that reconnect the body, sex, and gender in a way consistent with essential motherhood also occur in Ruddick's application of her theory of sexed, social/bodily subjectivity to birthgiving and natal reflection. Whereas Ruddick is fairly consistent in distinguishing being a woman and being a

mother in analyzing maternal practice, in her analysis of birthgiving she sometimes refers to women or the feminine where her argument allows only conclusions about mothers or the maternal. For example, Ruddick refers to "women
reflecting on birthgiving experiences" as grappling with the phenomenon of
chosen but unpredictable pain (1994: 42). This comment does not specify that
these women reflecting on birthgiving are themselves birthgivers. But it does
specify that these persons reflecting on birthgiving are women. This slippage
from birthgivers to women expands the category of those who can reflect on
birthgiving and develop the capacity for natal reflection to include women who
are not mothers, but not men. Thus, it equates women and mothers in a way
that is consistent with essential motherhood.

On the other hand, Ruddick's theory of sexed, social/bodily subjectivity
argues that the sociality of sexed embodiment means that there are not necessarily two sexes, and that sex is not necessarily fixed for life. These conclusions
imply that the determination of women's subjectivity by sex and/or gender is
less than total, which allows for the reciprocal permeability of embodiment and
subjectivity, and avoids theorizing sex as an aspect of the body understood in
dualist terms. But, while Ruddick insists that the sex of the body is social rather
than natural, she encounters significant difficulties in articulating this notion,
as indicated by her use of quotation marks for the terms "sexed," "sexual difference," and "female." These difficulties are a function of the extent to which she
has to rely on the individualist binaries natural/social and mind/body that her
analysis of the sociality of sexed embodiment means to challenge. Ruddick's
formulation social/bodily includes one half of the natural/social distinction and
one half of the mind/body distinction. Her concept of the social/bodily thus
brings into her theory of sexed, social/bodily subjectivity the implications of
these individualist binaries, including the feminization of the body and the natural. In this respect Ruddick's formulation social/bodily is like Beauvoir's imma-
nence/transcendence distinction in importing into Ruddick's theoretical
framework an element of individualism that undermines the theory of embodied subjectivity she is trying to articulate as an alternative to individualism.

Further inconsistent conclusions about sex, gender, and subjectivity result
from bringing together Ruddick's claim that sexed embodiment explains the
exclusively female character of birthgiving and natal knowledge and her claim
that the sociality of sexed embodiment precludes there being only two sexes
and sex's being fixed for life. Without explaining further why the sociality of
sexed embodiment rules out the binary fixity of sex, Ruddick refers to being
"sexed approximately 'female'" and acquiring knowledge in "approximately
'female'" ways. She also states that "[o]ne, but only one, of these [approxi-
mately female] encounters with the world occurs for some but certainly not all

females in birthgiving." I read this to mean that not all females who engage in birthgiving also engage in an "approximately female encounter with the world"—a reading supported by Ruddick's subsequent statement that a birthgiver "*may* acquire, and then through reflection articulate, distinctive . . . attitudes . . . capacities, and values" (1994: 41, Ruddick's emphasis). In this case the concept of sex seems to allow at least some variation in the ways that women are sexed and in the ways that birthgivers experience birthgiving and natal reflection. But, if "female" is an approximation of sexed subjectivity, then what does it mean to define female bodies in terms of their procreative potential, to insist that such bodies are "metaphysically given," and to claim that birthgiving and natal knowledge have an "exclusively female character"? What does it mean for an activity and the knowledge it generates to be both exclusively and approximately female? Ruddick's concept of an exclusive femininity articulated in terms of female reproductive capacities implies that women's subjectivity is determined by female embodiment. But the concept of an approximate femininity implies that women's subjectivity is not totally determined by female embodiment, nor by sex and/or gender.

If women's embodiment, or the sex and/or gender of the female body, cannot completely and exhaustively determine women's subjectivity, can the experience of birthgiving and natal reflection so determine maternal subjectivity? Ruddick's analysis of birthgiving sometimes suggests this. But the relationship of birthgiving, natal reflection, and subjectivity is problematized in her statement that "as birthgivers reflect upon the complexities of their experience it may be possible to imagine their acquiring cognitive and emotional capacities that they themselves trace to birthgiving experiences" (1994: 40). Instead of specifying how birthgivers' reflections on their experiences are, or give rise to, natal reflection, this statement represents someone else as imagining this. In this comment Ruddick avoids the conclusion that birthgiving determines maternal subjectivity. But she does so by hinting at the role of someone other than birthgivers in conceptualizing natal reflection which, problematizes the relationship of experiencing birthgiving and natal reflection and theorizing birthgiving and natal reflection. Must one experience birthgiving in order to engage in natal reflection? Must one experience both birthgiving and natal reflection in order to theorize their relationship? In this way Ruddick's account of maternal subjectivity raises the question of the relationship of subject positioning and knowledge, and points to the need for feminist theory to consider the subject positions from which it is articulated.

Ruddick does not resolve the inconsistent implications of her admittedly preliminary analysis of birthgiving and natal reflection in terms of sexed, social/bodily subjectivity. Indeed, in "Thinking Mothers/Conceiving Birth" she ultimately represents mothering in explicitly contradictory terms. This is most evident in the phrase "gender-full, gender-free" that Ruddick uses several times to describe mothering (1994: 35, 43, 44). But these inconsistencies also point to the difficulties of understanding mothering, especially pregnant embodiment and birthgiving, in individualist terms. In this way Ruddick's analysis of maternal embodied subjectivity resembles Beauvoir's account of mothering. Both simultaneously resist and are undermined by the elements of individualism implicit in the theoretical frameworks they deploy to analyze mothering. In addition to indicating the need to theorize embodied subjectivity and mothering in terms more strenuously resistant to individualism and essential motherhood, however, the inconsistencies of Ruddick's accounts of mothering also raise questions about what it means to represent and theorize experience. Thus, these inconsistencies imply the need for further analysis of the project of representing and theorizing mothering, an implication that emerges even more clearly from my consideration of the different theoretical frameworks of Ruddick's accounts of mothering.

— practice, standpoint, and knowledge —

Ruddick's arguments for maternal practice and for a feminist maternal peace politics rely on Nancy Hartsock's version of feminist standpoint theory (Hartsock 1985).[2] My analysis of Ruddick's use of standpoint theory shows that Hartsock's standpoint theory does support her account of maternal practice. But Ruddick's use of this standpoint theory in her argument for a feminist maternal peace politics is more problematic. Ruddick's account of maternal practice presupposes that persons come to have specific kinds of knowledge and take specific actions as a result of engaging in specific practices, a presupposition that is consistent with Hartsock's standpoint theory. But Ruddick's argument for a feminist maternal peace politics problematizes both what it means to be a mother and how to distinguish mothering from other, related practices. While Ruddick's account of maternal practice indicates that knowledge and agency are a function of being situated or positioned in a practice, her argument for a feminist maternal peace politics implies that knowledge and agency are a function of what distinct but related subject positions, associated with distinct but related practices, have in common or how they overlap. Ruddick's use of standpoint theory thus points to the complex relationship of practices and standpoints, the kinds of knowledge they generate or enable, and the agency they motivate or make possible, and, I argue, this complexity requires further analysis than Ruddick provides.

Ruddick's analysis of birthgiving replaces practicalism and standpoint theory with the concepts of experience and narrative, and this shift further foregrounds the questions that emerge from my analysis of Ruddick's use of standpoint theory. The theoretical framework of Ruddick's analysis of birthgiving raises questions about how persons come to be subjects of experience, how experience is related to knowledge, and whether engaging in a practice or having an experience is a condition of the possibility of understanding that practice or experience.[3] My analysis of the emergence of these issues in Ruddick's work on mothering shows that an explanation of the relationship of subjectivity to standpoints, practices, and/or experiences calls for the concept of overdetermination and thus precludes the complete and exhaustive determination of subjectivity by standpoints, practices, and/or experiences. In addition, Ruddick's concept of narrative suggests that theorizing subjectivity and knowledge in terms of subject positioning and explaining this less than total overdetermination of subjectivity must include some account of language and the practice of representation.

In *Maternal Thinking* Ruddick represents Hartsock as arguing that a feminist standpoint can emerge from "caring labor," of which maternal practice is an instance. Caregivers may come to understand themselves, their activities, social relations, and social contexts in terms of the goals of caring labor. They may also come to analyze the relations of power and domination that constitute the contexts of caring labor, including its social assignment to women. Ruddick sees Hartsock as arguing for the superiority of this feminist standpoint by comparing it to the "abstract masculinity" and the "fantasy of transcendence" presupposed by individualism. From a feminist standpoint, the abstraction of this concept of masculinity, the fantastical quality of its notion of transcendence, its disavowal of embodiment and dependence, and its harmful consequences for human existence become evident. Thus, a feminist standpoint is not simply an alternative to abstract masculinity; it is a better position from which to acquire knowledge. And, because it analyzes the power relations in which caring labor and caring laborers are enmeshed, a feminist standpoint facilitates both the critique of the conditions that oppress or subjugate caring labor and laborers and the development of a liberatory agenda for changing these conditions. It demands a reorganization of social structures, practices, and institutions consistent with the goals of caring labor and thus more consistent with human flourishing than abstract masculinity (1985: 232, 243–46).

While Ruddick says that she is drawn to the "critical power" of standpoint theory, she has reservations about claiming the epistemological and political superiority of a feminist standpoint. She retains what she calls "the practicalist belief that all reasons are tested by the practices from which they arise; hence justifications end in the commitments with which they begin." So she ultimately characterizes herself as a standpoint theorist who "does not take the final step that some appear to take of claiming for one standpoint a Truth that is exhaustive and absolute" (1989: 135). There are several problems, however, implicit in Ruddick's use of standpoint theory that her account of her relationship to standpoint theory fails to address. First, Ruddick's explication of standpoint theory tends to elide a caregiving or maternal standpoint and a feminist standpoint, which Hartsock distinguishes more clearly. By a feminist standpoint, Hartsock means a position from which one can analyze and evaluate the relationship of engaging in caregiving work and developing a caregiving standpoint. For Hartsock, the feminist element of a feminist standpoint is a materialist analysis of the power relations that determine caring labor, caregiving standpoints, and their material and social contexts. Hartsock does not argue for the superiority of a caregiving standpoint by comparing it to abstract masculinity; she makes this argument by evaluating both caregiving and masculine standpoints from the perspective of a feminist standpoint. Hartsock's standpoint theory distinguishes fairly clearly the issue of the relationship of a practice and its specific knowledge from the issue of the conditions that enable a feminist analysis of that relationship (Hartsock 1985: 245–46; see also Hartsock 1997a, 1997b).

This failure to appreciate fully what Hartsock means by a feminist standpoint leads Ruddick to her concern that standpoint theories require "claiming for one standpoint a Truth that is exhaustive and absolute." While this is certainly a possibility, Ruddick might have also considered further the possibility that standpoint theories can claim different kinds of truth for different kinds of standpoints. Standpoint theories can explain how different kinds of truth can be partial, fragmented, and unstable, because these truths are subject to change as the material, social, and ideological contexts of practices and their participants change. A consideration of standpoint theories in these terms points to a fundamental slippage that often occurs in their deployment. This is the tendency of the term 'standpoint' to slip between referring to specific locations or positions in specific social contexts and referring to a perspective or outlook available to persons so located or positioned. This slippage obscures rather than answers the question of just how subject positioning facilitates or determines one's perspective and knowledge. This slippage occurs in Ruddick's representation and use of standpoint theory, and it is consistent with her elision of caregiving, maternal, and feminist standpoints.

So, while Hartsock's standpoint theory may not solve all the problems involved in analyzing how subjects come to take up a feminist standpoint or to be positioned as feminist theorists, it does address the paradox of representation in an important way. Hartsock's standpoint theory allows an explanation of how subjects can be caregivers, mothers, and/or feminist theorists of caregiving and/or mothering by allowing a conception of subjects as multiply positioned and subject positions as overlapping. Hartsock argues that the experience of caregiving can contribute to the development of a feminist standpoint by raising questions about the social organization of caregiving. But she clearly indicates that answers to such questions emerge from a feminist standpoint—an account of practices and knowledge in terms of a political analysis of their material, social, and ideological context. She represents caregiving and feminist standpoints as distinct but also related, or, in my terms, overlapping. On the other hand, this concept of standpoints as overlapping does not fully address the problem of the tendency of the concept 'standpoint' in feminist standpoint theories to refer both to a location or position and an outlook or perspective. With this slippage, the deployment of standpoint theories tends to avoid the questions of how being positioned in a specific social location generates knowledge, and what kind of knowledge this is. The concept of standpoints as multiple and overlapping that I see implicit in Hartsock's standpoint theory begins to address these questions. But Ruddick's use of standpoint theory does more to obscure rather than address these questions. And Ruddick's reluctance to claim the epistemological or political superiority of any of these standpoints raises the further question of how she comes to have any critical perspective on women's reports of their experiences. If Ruddick cannot give some account of this, then she cannot analyze the determination of mothers' experiences, as well as of their reports of their experiences, by their sexist and oppressive contexts.[4] If so, her attempt to represent mothers' experiences in terms consistent with their reports will always be at odds to some extent with her attempt to represent mothers' experiences in terms of feminist social and political goals.

Ruddick's failure to appreciate fully the differences among caregiving, maternal, and feminist standpoints is thus an ideological moment that preserves what Ruddick sees as the close connections between mothering and the politics and practice of peace. But both the need for further analysis of subject positions such as 'mother', 'caregiver', and 'feminist theorist' and the suggestion that this analysis should focus on the multiple and overlapping quality of subject positioning are illustrated by Ruddick's argument for a feminist maternal peace politics. To make this argument, Ruddick analyzes women's politics of resistance and feminist politics and argues that bringing them into relationship with maternal practice leads to a feminist maternal peace politics. Her argument requires that the participants in these practices be specified fairly distinctly in terms of gender and their participation in mothering. But the subjectivities that Ruddick discusses resist such categorization. Instead they slip among the categories she deploys, so that her argument for a feminist maternal peace politics proliferates subject positions and problematizes the distinctions among them. These slippages especially fragment the subject position mother by blurring the boundaries that distinguish it from the other subject positions Ruddick describes.

Ruddick argues that three characteristics define a women's politics of resistance: "its participants are women, they explicitly invoke their culture's symbols of femininity, and their purpose is to resist certain practices or policies of their governors." In Ruddick's subsequent discussion of this politics, however, its participants become "women who take responsibility for caring labor" and women's resistance becomes "feminine resistance." The possibility of women's resistance is attributed to their social position, which "makes them inherently 'disloyal to the civilization,'" rather than to their being women. Ruddick refers to Kristeva's image of women's resistance—*woman* as "an eternal dissident in relation to social and political consensus, in exile from power . . . singular, fragmentary, demonic, a witch" (Kristeva 1987: 113). But in Ruddick's appropriation this image becomes an image of "the dissident *mother*." Ruddick offers as an example of this *women*'s politics of resistance the Madres of Argentina, emphasizing the "central *maternal* concepts" they exemplify. The Madres "translate the symbols of *mothering* into political speech," yet they "speak a '*women*'s language' of loyalty, love, and outrage" and they are "the *daughters* . . . of [Kathe] Kollwitz' *mater* dolorosa" (1989: 222–33, my emphasis).

The participants in feminist politics, on the other hand, are "partisans of women." While there can be tension between mothers and feminists, "*feminists* have proved many times over that, as partisans of *women*, they are sturdy allies of *mothers*." So, despite this tension, "many . . . *mothers* become *feminists*." *Feminists* examine critically women's social status and political relations, because these "exact from *mothers*—even those who are *men*—unnecessary and unacceptable sacrifices" (my emphasis). Mothers may also "become publically visible *as mothers* . . . [and] transform the meaning of motherhood" (Ruddick's emphasis). But when they do, *feminists* may not support them, because this form of politics "turns on *women*'s identities as *mothers, caretakers, kin workers,* and *shelterers*," which feminists want to critique rather than reinforce.

Nonetheless, feminism "actualizes the peacefulness latent in maternal practice" as a function of "its double origins in women's traditional work and feminist resistance to abuse against women." Thus, "insofar as *feminist mothers* are anti-militarist, so too is that part of the feminist movement . . . made up of *mothers* and *mother-identified men and women*." Ruddick concludes that these practices and political commitments can come together in "a single, womanly-manly work—a feminist, maternal politics of peace" (1989: 235–44, my emphasis).

Ruddick's argument for a feminist, maternal peace politics thus produces a variety of overlapping subject positions—women, mothers, daughters, feminists, women who take responsibility for caring labor, shelterers, kin workers, mothers who are men, feminist mothers, mother-identified men and women, partisans of women, allies of mothers—and a number of practices that stand in various relationships to gender and mothering. The beliefs and experiences that might lead persons to engage in feminist, maternal peace politics, the knowledge this engagement might lead them to, and the ways that their participation in this politics further determines their positions and consciousnesses are also multiple and overlapping. Ruddick's argument implies that the collective agency she envisions is made possible as much by the multiple and overlapping quality as by the specificity of the subject positions she describes. As I see it, this multiple and overlapping quality is a function of the fluidity and reciprocal permeability of subjectivity, embodiment, and contexts. In addition, Ruddick's phrase "womanly-manly work" to describe this peace politics echoes her description of mothering as "gender-full, gender-free." These phrases in effect recognize the multiple, overlapping, and therefore potentially contradictory quality of subject positioning, including the unstable boundaries marking off man and woman as subject positions, and the partiality and instability of the truths that emerge at these positions. Ruddick's argument for a feminist maternal peace politics is thus like her accounts of mothering in having inconsistent implications for mothering, gender, sex, and subjectivity. And, like her account of sexed, social/bodily subjectivity, one of these implications is that neither gender nor mothering completely and coherently determine subjectivity. This means that an analysis of subjectivity in terms of multiple and overlapping positionings must include the incomplete and potentially contradictory quality of the over-determination of subjectivity.

— experience, narrative, and knowledge —

Ruddick's use of the concepts of experience and narrative in her analysis of birthgiving and natal reflection suggests answering these questions about subject positioning, knowledge, and agency in terms of an account of language. Ruddick begins her analysis of birthgiving and natal reflection by surveying the development of her work on mothering so far, and she does so in terms of linguistic practices. She recounts that she rejected those feminist thinkers who "tended to speak as daughters trying to forge a daughter/self respecting connection to their mothers' lives." She rejects psychoanalytic approaches to mothering by comparing psychoanalytic tales and stories to mothers' tales and stories; to what mothers say when they "talk about themselves, when they appear as characters in their own maternal stories." Maternal narratives are also the basis for Ruddick's reconsideration of her account of maternal practice, for "mothers who have read *Maternal Thinking* tell [her] that . . . [she] got their experience quite wrong" (1994: 37), and "maternal conversations" are a context in which the distinction and connection of birthgiving and maternal practice are articulated (1994: 44).

Ruddick also represents her own theorizing in terms of both subject positioning and linguistic practices. She describes herself as "struggling to acquire and maintain a maternal perspective" while she read feminist theory and says that she read and discussed psychoanalysis "as a mother trying to discover a mother's voice" (1994: 30, 31). She also writes:

> I read both birthgiving and mothering with an explicitly feminist eye. I seek only representations of mothering that will undercut the subordination of women whether or not they are mothers and will enable those mothers who are women to take increasing control over and pleasure in their lives. . . . I will test emerging representations of birth by their ability to empower birthgivers (1994, 43).[5]

In these ways Ruddick implicitly recognizes her own multiple and overlapping subject positioning as a mother, a feminist, and a theorist. At the same time her representation of herself as "trying" and "struggling" to "acquire and maintain" a maternal perspective recognizes the incompleteness of the determination of subjectivity by mothering, a commitment to feminism, and/or the practice of feminist theory.

There are also slippages in Ruddick's account of herself as a mother, a feminist, and a theorist that similarly suggest theorizing subject positioning and knowledge in relationship to language. For example, Ruddick considers Alice Jardine's argument for "the demise of experience." By this Jardine means the demise of the view that experience (or "lived reality") contains or reflects its meaning; that its meaning is present and available to those whose experience it is and to others capable of reflecting on it, interpreting it, and understanding it. This view of experience represents theorists in particular as able to articulate and present to others—"read the facts of" (Ruddick 1994: 37)—the meaning of experience (Jardine 1985: 145–55). In response to Jardine's critique, Ruddick argues that "it is still those who thoughtfully reflect upon present and recent birthgiving, including the ways it is metaphorized and socially constructed, who will be best able to articulate emotional, social, and intellectual aspects of this particular labor." But Ruddick also characterizes herself as someone engaged in such reflection apart from the experience of birthgiving: "[s]ince I last gave birth twenty-five years ago, and since I went through birthgiving in a state of denial, I count myself as much a listener as mothers who have not given birth" (1994: 39).

Ruddick's response does not adequately address Jardine's argument against the self-evidence or unproblematic availability of the meaning of experience, since Jardine is asking precisely what sort of reflection on experience allows what kind of claims about its meaning. Ruddick's elision of "socially constructed" and "metaphorized" is symptomatic of the inadequacy of Ruddick's response to Jardine's critique, since these are not obviously the same things. Jardine's critique of experience calls precisely for consideration of the possibility, conditions, and effects of understanding a social process in terms of a linguistic operation. Ruddick's elision of socially constructed and metaphorized constitutes an ideological moment in which her response to Jardine's questions about representing the meaning of experience preserves the grounds of Ruddick's representation of maternal experience. At the same time, however, Ruddick problematizes both her own subject position and the relationship of her experience and her theorizing. She represents herself in terms of linguistic practices as reading, speaking, and theorizing as a mother and from a maternal perspective, but she also has to struggle to maintain this perspective and she counts herself as a listener who has not given birth. Ruddick's image of herself as a listener who has not given birth because she went through that experience "in a state of denial" implies that her being able to read, speak, and think as a mother and from a maternal perspective depends on her having articulated— put into words rather than denying—her experience of birthgiving. It implies that the experience of birthgiving and the articulation or representation of that experience are thoroughly intertwined. Thus, the possibility and meaning of subject positions such as 'mother' and 'feminist theorist' need further analysis in relationship to language and the practice of representation.

In this account of her subject position, however, Ruddick also problematizes the concept of experience that motivates her account of birthgiving and natal reflection in the first place. She develops an analysis of birthgiving and natal reflection in order to better represent what women and mothers report to her as their experience. But her appeal to the concept of narrative to do so undermines the view of the relationship of subjectivity and experience presupposed by her acceptance of women's reports of their experience as a basis for feminist theorizing. Ruddick's analyses of mothering not only destabilize and fragment the subject position 'mother'. They also destabilize and fragment the concept of the subject of experience—the concept of the subject fully and coherently constituted prior to experience, who engages in experience or to whom experience happens, and who is best positioned to report the meaning and significance of his or her experience.

— subject positioning and language —

According to my analysis of Ruddick's two accounts of mothering, then, her work raises important questions for feminist theory, even as it remains stuck within the terms of the dilemma of difference. Ruddick offers an account of mothering as a practice, which significantly resists essential motherhood, recognizes differences among women with respect to mothering, and serves feminist social and political goals, but minimizes the significance of maternal embodiment and does not adequately represent women's and mothers' reports of their experiences of mothering. She also offers an account of birthgiving and natal reflection that theorizes the significance of maternal embodiment and is more consistent with mothers' reports of their experience, but risks the recuperation of essential motherhood and to that extent does not adequately serve feminist social and political goals. The contradictions implicit in Ruddick's accounts of mothering, however, are like those in Beauvoir's work in also suggesting further approaches to rearticulating embodied subjectivity in resistance to individualism, especially mind/body dualism. So Ruddick's work contributes to the rearticulation of embodiment, subjectivity, and contexts I have argued is also implicit in Beauvoir's account of mothering. These contributions include rearticulating the relationship of embodiment and subjectivity, and the relationship of embodied subjectivity and its material, social, and ideological contexts, in terms of their reciprocal, less than total, and contradictory over-determination; rearticulating subjectivity as an ongoing process of positioning; and rearticulating the experience of subjectivity as partial, fragmented, unstable, and at least sometimes incoherent.

Reading Ruddick's work in light of the implications of Beauvoir's account of mothering especially highlights the importance of understanding subjectivity in terms of positioning.[6] This understanding of subjectivity raises questions about how subject positions are constituted or determined, how subjects come to be positioned and repositioned, and how the nature and quality of subjects' experiences are related to their specific positioning. My reading of Ruddick's work shows that developing a theory of subjectivity as positioning raises two additional questions concerning the enabling conditions of knowledge. One of these is the question of the relationship of subject positioning, knowledge, and agency, and the second is the question of how to analyze this relationship in terms of language. The first question asks, what is knowledge if subjectivity is understood in terms of positioning and how do subjects so understood acquire knowledge? What specific kinds of knowledge are made possible by specific subject positions, and what criteria for assessing knowledge claims are possible if subjectivity is reconceived in terms of positioning? Furthermore, what does agency mean if subjectivity is reconceptualized in terms of positioning, how does positioning enable agency, and what kind of agency is made possible by subject positioning? These questions are also applicable to common experiences, shared knowledge, and collective agency, such as those envisioned by Ruddick's argument for a feminist maternal peace politics. What do these mean and how are they made possible, if subjectivity is reconceptualized in terms of positioning?

These questions about subject positioning, knowledge, and agency are further complicated by taking into account the implication I have elicited from Beauvoir's and Ruddick's analyses of mothering that subjectivity is not necessarily or entirely univocal, consistent, stable, and coherent. If feminist theory pursues the possibility that the reciprocal but less than totalizing over-determination of embodiment, subjectivity, and contexts produces a subjectivity that is only more or less ambiguous, unstable, and contradictory, then how will it have to reconceptualize experience, knowledge, and agency as well as common experience, shared knowledge, and collective agency? My reading of Ruddick's work suggests approaching these issues by considering the ways in which subjects can be multiply positioned and the ways that subject positions can overlap. If relatively specific subject positions can be more or less clearly distinguished but the boundaries that distinguish subject positions are fluid and permeable, then elements of one position may also be elements of another. This overlapping of subject positions is part of what makes multiple positioning possible; it allows subjects to occupy more than one position at the same time, and to occupy their subject positions in various ways.

The concept of multiple and overlapping subject positioning explains how one might be, for example, a mother and a feminist theorist, how one's experiences as a mother might influence the feminist theory one produces, and how producing feminist theory might influence one's mothering. But it does not rule out others' being mothers and/or feminist theorists in a variety of other ways, nor does it assume that being either or both is necessarily an entirely univocal, stable, or coherent experience. Neither does it imply that being a mother is a necessary condition for theorizing mothering. This aspect of subject positioning also points to an explanation of the possibility of common experience, shared knowledge, and collective agency. If subject positions are multiple and overlapping, then it is possible that subjects will have some aspects of their experiences and knowledge in common. It is at least possible that there will be some basis for the constitution of an element of commonality in their social relations. And Ruddick's use of the concept of narrative in her account of birthgiving suggests that the constitution of this commonality will be a discursive process, such as the articulation and sharing of maternal narratives or participation in maternal conversations. This commonality may be sufficient to motivate and enable collective action that aims at goals whose commonality is similarly constituted. Like the concept of subject positioning on which it is based, this account of common experience, shared knowledge, and collective agency does not require the univocity, consistency, or coherence of subjectivity.

The second question foregrounded by my reading of Ruddick's work on mothering is how the relationship of subject positioning, knowledge, and agency might be understood in terms of language. This question emerges from my argument that Ruddick's use of the concepts of experience and narrative in her argument for sexed, social/bodily subjectivity and in her account of birthgiving and natal reflection suggests theorizing subject positioning in relationship to language and the practice of representation. This suggestion raises additional difficult questions for feminist theory. What theory of language would contribute to rearticulating subjectivity in terms of positioning and over-determination? Would such an account of language and subjectivity enable the resistance to individualism and essential motherhood that feminist theory requires, given their hegemony as ideological formations? What might it contribute to theorizing mothering, and to feminist theory's analysis of its own practice of representation? While these questions are very difficult, Ruddick's work suggests that they are unavoidable. For Ruddick's work shows that none of the elements of mothering that she represents—engaging in maternal practice, experiencing pregnancy, giving birth, thinking, reading, and speaking as a mother, struggling to take up and maintain a maternal perspective—is sufficient to completely and exhaustively determine any subject, including herself, to be a mother. And yet this recognition of the impossibility of motherhood, the impossibility of anyone's subjectivity being completely and

exhaustively determined entirely by motherhood, is made possible precisely by
the multiple and varied representations of mothering that Ruddick articulates.

This recognition of the impossibility of motherhood implicit in Ruddick's
work suggests that not only subjectivity, but also experience and the practice of
representation, are over-determined—they have multiple, overlapping, and
even contradictory causes, but they are not completely and exhaustively determined. If this is so, then Ruddick is right to insist that instances of subjectivity,
such as being a mother or being a woman, are both exclusive and approximate.
My reading of Ruddick's work on mothering thus suggests that in order to resist
both individualism and essential motherhood, feminist theory may have to
embrace a paradoxical account of subjectivity, experience, and representation
as both over-determined and never totally determined, that is, an account of
subjectivity, experience, and representation that is paradoxical from the perspective of individualism. For the way in which the subject position 'mother',
including Ruddick's own subject position, becomes problematic as Ruddick's
argument struggles to preserve her representation of mothering makes in-
escapable the following question: What is the relationship of subjectivity and
language such that experience and its representation are over-determined but
experience does not totalize subjectivity? Further development of the concept
of subjectivity as both over-determined and partial, fragmented, and unstable
that I have elicited from Beauvoir's and Ruddick's work on mothering must
include these questions. This is especially true if the further development of
this theory of subjectivity considers the relationship of subjectivity and language, which is also suggested by my reading of Ruddick's work on birthgiving.
With these questions in mind, then, I turn to the account of mothering and
the theory of the discursive constitution of embodied subjectivity represented
in Kristeva's "Stabat Mater."

c h a p t e r   s i x

EMBODIMENT
AND DISCOURSE

positioning maternal subjectivity in language

— embodied subjectivity, language, and psychoanalysis —

MY ANALYSIS OF Ruddick's work on mothering further develops the possibilities for rearticulating embodied subjectivity that I have derived from Beauvoir's account of mothering. The concepts of the reciprocal permeability of embodiment and subjectivity, subject positioning, and the over-determination of embodied subjectivity are suggested not only by Beauvoir's but also by Ruddick's account of mothering. My reading of Ruddick's work adds to these concepts the possibility of theorizing subject positioning in relationship to language. To consider further this possibility I offer in this chapter a reading of Julia Kristeva's essay "Stabat Mater." I argue that "Stabat Mater" presents the sort of theory of subjectivity in terms of language that is hinted at by Ruddick's use of the concept of narrative in her analysis of birthgiving and natal reflection. "Stabat Mater" also suggests that the figure of the mother is emblematic of subjectivity so understood. In these ways, Kristeva's account of mothering contributes to the resistance to both individualism and essential motherhood

that feminist theory needs, given the hegemony of these ideological formations. In addition, "Stabat Mater" offers the concept of a 'herethics', an ethical
theory and practice based on its discourse of the maternal and the feminine.
Kristeva's concept of a herethics is a version of difference feminism's project of
deploying analyses of women's difference as paradigms for social theories that
resist individualism. So a consideration of "Stabat Mater" also allows further
analysis of this aspect of difference feminism.

In considering Kristeva's concept of a herethics, however, I also show that
the account of mothering in "Stabat Mater" is itself not entirely consistent
with the terms of the herethics Kristeva proposes. In particular, certain aspects
of the representation of the child and the mother-child relationship in "Stabat
Mater" are not consistent with a herethics' demand for differentiation in sameness and the recognition of the discursively constituted subjectivity of the
other. About this I raise two questions: Is this inconsistency a function of the
psychoanalytic framework of "Stabat Mater," and can it be resolved? I argue
that the child and the mother-child relationship can be represented in ways
more consistent with a herethics by bringing Kristeva's account of mothering
into relationship with certain elements of Ruddick's account of maternal practice. But even so, questions about both the psychoanalytic framework of
"Stabat Mater" and the development of ethical and political theories based on
psychoanalytic accounts of women's difference persist. Most importantly,
do psychoanalytic accounts of women's difference risk the recuperation of
essential motherhood, given that some versions of psychoanalysis suggest that
women's becoming mothers is biologically determined, socially functional,
and/or required for women's maturity, self-development, and happiness?

My consideration in this and the next chapter of analyses of mothering
framed in psychoanalytic terms shows that the dilemma of difference persists
in this approach to theorizing mothering. Psychoanalysis, especially Lacanian
psychoanalysis, enables considerable resistance to individualism and the metaphysics of substance. But it also significantly risks the recuperation of elements
of essential motherhood. In "Stabat Mater" these risks are evident in its tendency to equate women and mothers and its attempt to satisfy the desire,
addressed to the mother and/or the child, for a unified and stable subjectivity,
a kind of subjectivity that, according to Lacanian psychoanalysis, is impossible.
To begin to address these concerns about psychoanalysis, I bring Ruddick's
criticisms of psychoanalysis to bear on the representation of mothering in
"Stabat Mater." In "Thinking Mothers/Conceiving Birth" Ruddick argues that
psychoanalysis misrepresents mothers and children and problematizes mater-

nal subjectivity (1994: 30-32). So, while "Stabat Mater" offers a compelling account of embodied subjectivity as discursive positioning, its psychoanalytic frame raises problems for both its representation of maternal subjectivity and for the development of a herethics. I discuss these problems after I present my reading of "Stabat Mater" and I continue this consideration of the risks and advantages of psychoanalysis for feminist analyses of mothering in the next chapter, where I discuss Nancy Chodorow's *The Reproduction of Mothering: Psychoanalysis and the Sociology of Gender*.

My reading of "Stabat Mater" is based on Kristeva's account of the function of the mother in the constitution of subjectivity. This is part of Kristeva's critique of structuralist theories of language (1984). Such theories, she argues, do not account for the relationship of embodiment and language because they presuppose a completely and exhaustively determined, disembodied subjectivity prior to language, which uses language to communicate meaning. These presuppositions are consistent with individualism's view that embodiment and material and social contexts do not fundamentally affect the operations of consciousness, such as language. Kristeva argues for a theory of language as the symbolic processes through which subjectivity is constituted, such that there is no subjectivity prior to and apart from language. Such a theory must take into account the effects of embodiment for language, which Kristeva theorizes as the semiotic. This theory of language requires an account of how the drives are at work in signifying processes, for which Kristeva appeals to Lacanian psychoanalysis. But she modifies the Lacanian account by focusing on the pre-Oedipal period to show how the structuration of the body and the regulation of the drives in relation to the mother that occur in this period are crucial elements of discursive subjectivity.

According to Lacan, the constitution of subjectivity begins in the mirror stage and culminates in the Oedipal complex. In the mirror stage the infant experiences a reflection or image of itself, in which it sees itself as separate from its mother—distinct, stable, and unified. But because the infant finds this distinction, stability, and unity represented outside of itself, in a reflection or image, this recognition of itself is also a misrecognition. The distinction, stability, and unity that the child perceives are characteristics of the image or reflection, not of the child's subjectivity. The mirror stage is thus the child's first experience of itself in relation to the gap between object and image, which prefigures the gap between signified and signifier on which language depends (Lacan 1977: 1–7). In addition to the mirror experience, the child becomes more aware of its separation from the mother, especially when its needs are not immediately met, which provokes the child's articulation of demands. With this awareness, the child experiences the relationship of lack or absence and signification. The lack or absence of that which the child needs and of the mother who could provide it (and from the child's perspective, should provide it) are a condition of the child's use of signifiers to name the thing needed and its address of these signifiers to another, the mother.

For Lacan, all demand includes the desire for something other than that which satisfies a specific need. This element of desire is the desire for the one-ness or fusion with the mother—in which there is no lack—that the child no longer experiences. This desire includes desire for what the child experiences as the exclusivity of this relation, or the mother's existing only for and in relation to the child. In Lacan's terms, the child ultimately desires to be the other to the mother, to be that which completely satisfies the mother's desire. But what Lacan calls this "something other" can never be provided because the child cannot reexperience the plenitude and completeness of the initial relationship with the mother. For this reason desire persists implicitly in the articulation of demand, and all demand is implicitly addressed in part to the omnipotent, phallic mother of infantile fantasy, imagined as the source of the plenitude and completeness that is the object of desire. Need and demand thus give rise to desire, which is also an experience of a gap—the gap between that which satisfies need and that which would satisfy desire if it were possible. This experience also prefigures the gap between signified and signifier. Desire always includes both a desire for a subjectivity that is complete, stable, and coherent, and an implicit recognition of the impossibility of such subjectivity (Lacan 1985: 75–85).

According to Lacan, the preliminary positioning of the child in relationship to signification that occurs in the mirror stage is completed in the Oedipal complex. The Oedipal complex is the installation or positioning of the child in the symbolic, the system of signifiers that is language. In the Oedipal complex, the Name of the Father, or the paternal function, represented by the phallus, intervenes in the mother-child relationship to prohibit the satisfaction of the child's desire for the mother and to repress that desire. The intervention of the paternal function provokes the child's recognition and acceptance of the mother's castration, and thus its recognition that all persons are positioned in relationship to the phallus, as either having or lacking it. The repression of the child's desire for the mother and the child's acceptance of the mother's castration position the child itself in relationship to the phallus and to sexual difference. The boy child is offered and accepts the future possibility of exclusive access to another woman as a function of his position in relation to the phallus, and the girl child is offered and accepts the future possibility of having access to the phallus by being the object of masculine desire. In this way, the child comes to occupy either a masculine or feminine subject position. The Oedipal complex also positions the child in relationship to the prohibition of incest, the law that founds culture. The child's taking up a position in relationship to the phallus and sexual difference locates the child in a cultural network that determines all persons as permissible or prohibited future erotic objects. This positioning also constitutes the child's initially polymorphous or undifferentiated drives as a socially and culturally acceptable sexuality.

Lacan argues that the Oedipal complex is fundamentally a linguistic process. In this process, the phallus operates as privileged signifier, representing the most basic organizing principles of human sociocultural existence, including an authority powerful enough to sunder the mother-child dyad. Culture is understood as a sign system of names, positions, statuses, and relationships, and the positioning of the child in a specific location in this sign system constitutes its subjectivity. The intervention of the paternal function transforms the child's experience of lack (of the mother, of the mother's desire, of the mother's phallus) into a position in the gap between signifier and signified in which enunciation occurs. The child comes to occupy a position in and from which it can say "I" and be so recognized by others. But because discourse presupposes a gap between signifier and signified, because the linkages of signifiers and signifieds in language are arbitrary, and because the determination of signified by signifier is always incomplete, subjectivity is itself divided—founded on and constituted by the gap between signifiers and signifieds that discourse requires. The child becomes a speaking subject as a result of the Oedipal complex, but this subjectivity is partial, fragmented, and unstable (Lacan 1977: 281–91; Kristeva 1984: 46–48).

While Kristeva accepts this Lacanian account of subjectivity, she revises it by looking to the pre-Oedipal period to explain the semiotic elements of language. She argues that in the pre-Oedipal period the drives are organized and regulated in the context of the child's relationship with the mother. The meaning of the body is established as the regulation of its initially polymorphous and objectless drives marks different parts of the body in relationship to the drives, organizing them as erotogenic zones. Because this regulation of the drives and organization of the body are pre-Oedipal, they are not subject to the paternal function. Rather they are mediated by the mother's body, in a process Kristeva calls "the maternal function." This regulating process is a function of the child's bodily dependence on the mother, and includes the mother's regulation of the child's bodily movements, especially its feeding and elimination, and her regulation of its access to her body. The maternal function preserves and transforms the polymorphous lack of differentiation and object attachment, or heterogeneity of the drives, thereby constituting the semiotic body. The semiotic includes this heterogeneity of the drives, which allows the semiotic to have disruptive effects in the symbolic (1984: 27). These processes are both obscured and taken up in subsequent stages of development, including the Oedipal complex. The semiotic persists in the Oedipal complex's discursive constitution of subjectivity as traces of the pre-Oedipal organization of the body and the regulation of the drives. The semiotic irrupts into language as its rhythmic, intonal, gestural, and melodic elements, and it enables linguistic operations such as metaphor, metonymy, and intertextuality. These operations also indicate that the position of the subject of enunciation is never self-identical, stable, complete, and exhaustive; it is rather plural, discontinuous, and labile (1984: 59–60).

One of the most important effects of Kristeva's theory of the semiotic is its putting subjectivity "on trial/in process."[1] Her analysis of language suggests that discursive practices strive to present representation itself as completely and exhaustively capturing and presenting the thing represented, and thus to unify and stabilize subjectivity. But discursive practices never successfully do either. All instances of representation implicitly reveal both the gap between signifier and signified and the tenuousness and instability of subjectivity. This aspect of subjectivity can also be understood in terms of Kristeva's concept of 'abjection'. Abjection is a psychic expulsion or banishment in which that which is abjected does not thereby become completely other to the self. Rather the abject remains at the borders of consciousness, simultaneously contributing to the integrity and revealing the precariousness of the subject who abjects it (1982). Discursive practices strive to abject the heterogeneity of the semiotic in order to unify and stabilize the position of the subject in the symbolic, shore up the symbolic's arbitrary linkages of signifier and signified, and impose uni-vocity on language. But this abjection itself indicates the tenuousness of the position of the subject in language and the incompleteness of representation. It does so by showing how subjectivity depends on the presence of this abjected heterogeneity at its borders, precisely to constitute its borders. Kristeva's theory of language significantly desubstantializes subjectivity; it refigures embodied subjectivity as a never complete and exhaustive process rather than the complete and stable possession of a set of defining attributes. This means that embodied subjectivity as a locus of enunciation is, in my terms, multiply, contradictorily, but not exhaustively over-determined, as a function of its discursive constitution.

— "Stabat Mater": maternal subjectivity —

Kristeva's account of the relationship of the semiotic and the symbolic, especially her claim that this relationship is enabled by the maternal function, suggests an approach to reading "Stabat Mater." I take the positioning of its two columns of text to represent visually the relationship of the semiotic and the symbolic. The first text, which frequently occupies the entire page, I call the dominant text to distinguish it from the bold-faced text. The dominant text offers an analysis of the image of the virgin maternal, an analysis that I read as a critique of essential motherhood. The dominant text shows how this image "tames the maternal" (1986: 162) and considers what elements of the feminine psyche are not adequately addressed by this image. The dominant text ends with Kristeva's call for a herethics, and the claim that this ethics requires a new discourse of and for the maternal and the feminine. I read the bold-faced text of "Stabat Mater" in terms of those aspects of the feminine and the maternal that, according to the dominant text, are no longer adequately addressed by the image of the virgin maternal. I ask whether, and if so how, these aspects of the feminine and the maternal are addressed in the bold-faced column.

"Stabat Mater" begins by explicitly framing the question of mothering and femininity in terms of difference: "If it is not possible to say of a *woman* what she is (without running the risk of abolishing her difference), would it perhaps be different concerning the *mother*, since that is the only function of the 'other sex' to which we can definitely attribute existence?" (1986: 161, Kristeva's emphasis). Saying what a mother is, though, is problematized by the dominant image of motherhood in Western culture, Christianity's image of the Virgin Mother of Christ, which represents femininity as completely determined by motherhood. For Kristeva, this representation is an idealization of primary narcissism—a fantasy that idealizes both the mother as she is for the infant, and their relationship. Compounding this difficulty is feminism's demand for a new representation of femininity. According to Kristeva, in rejecting the dominant representation of femininity in terms of mothering, feminism takes its fantasized image of mothering for "the real experience that fantasy overshadows" (1986: 161) and then rejects mothering entirely. The possibility of saying anything about mothering is now suspended between the uncritical, usually unconscious, acceptance of the dominant representation and the feminist rejection of mothering. So in the dominant text Kristeva postpones saying what a mother is in order to investigate the representation of femininity as virgin motherhood.

The image of the feminine and the maternal as virgin motherhood is an artifact of Western Christianity, especially Roman Catholicism. According to Kristeva, these images offer consolation and gratification, but they also domesticate, contain, subjugate, and/or deny the maternal and the feminine. For example, the image of the Mater Dolorosa, the mother (mater) who stands (stabat) at the foot of the cross on which Christ was crucified, locates the feminine and the maternal in a problematic relationship to language. The milk and the tears of the Mater Dolorosa are "metaphors of non-speech, of a 'semiotics' that linguistic communication does not account for." In this way "the Mother and her attributes . . . re-establish what is non-verbal and show up as the receptacle of a signifying disposition that is closer to so-called primary processes." But they also "find their outlet in the arts—painting and music— of which the Virgin necessarily becomes both patron saint and privileged object" (1986: 174). The Virgin Mother thus becomes "the parentheses of language. She adds to the Christian trinity and to the Word that delineates their coherence the heterogeneity they salvage" (1986: 174-75). The image of the Mater Dolorosa represents the abjected semiotic and the repressed maternal function and effects their return in representation. But it also figures the feminine and the maternal as that which enable representation (patron saint) and that which are represented (privileged object), but not as that which represent. By implying the impossibility of maternal speech, the image of the Mater Dolorosa evokes essential motherhood's view that motherhood is not an exercise of subjectivity.

Despite the consolations and gratifications offered by the virgin maternal, however, its effects for women's subjectivity have weakened its hold. The dominant text asks: "what are the aspects of the feminine psyche for which [this] representation of motherhood does not provide a solution or else provides one that is felt as too coercive by twentieth-century women?" (1986: 182). It answers this question in terms of four images that are absent or denied in the virgin maternal: images of the maternal body; birth, the war between mother and daughter; and the repudiation of the masculine. These images suggest an alternative representation of mothering, the discourse one might hear if one "listen[ed], more carefully than ever, to what mothers are saying today" (1986: 179). For example, in the dominant text's image of the maternal body, "a woman as mother would be . . . a strange fold that changes culture into nature, the speaking into biology." In its images of birth, pregnancy becomes "the threshold of culture and nature" and "the heterogeneity that cannot be subsumed in the signifier nevertheless explodes violently with pregnancy . . . and the child's arrival" (1986: 182–83; see also 1980: 238–41). These images reverse the relationship of culture and nature, discourse and biology, that is presupposed by the individualist concept of subjectivity. Individualism privileges culture and discourse over nature and biology, and sees subjectivity as the capacity to change nature into culture and biology into discourse. But these images of maternal embodiment and birth represent these transformations as also occurring in the opposite direction, with culture becoming nature and discourse becoming biology. These images thus suggest theorizing embodied subjectivity as a position at which these transformations of culture, nature, discourse, and biology continually occur, and they offer the maternal body as emblematic of embodied subjectivity so understood. They challenge the individualist view of the body as the material container and boundary of a disembodied consciousness and question whether individualism's ideal of rational, autonomous control of nature and the human body by subjectivity is even possible, and if possible, whether it is ever total. In this way these images of pregnancy and birth resemble elements of Beauvoir's account of pregnancy and Ruddick's account of natality and birthgiving. They represent the permeability and indeterminacy of bodily boundaries in pregnancy and birth, but without implying the loss or dissolution of (maternal) subjectivity.

The dominant text's image of birth also includes the "the self-sacrifice involved in becoming anonymous in order to pass on the social norm." In giving birth a woman subjects herself to the social norm, or what Lacan calls the Law of the Father, and to the responsibility of passing it on to her child: "One might repudiate [the social norm] for one's own sake," but "*one must* include the child [within it] in order to educate [the child] along the chain of generations" (Kristeva's emphasis). But "[f]eminine perversion . . . is coiled up in the desire for law as desire for reproduction and continuity, it promotes feminine masochism to the rank of structure stabilizer . . . " Kristeva wonders" to what extent" the "surge" of "the bio-symbolic latencies of motherhood . . . lays women open to the most fearsome manipulations" (1986: 182–83). This image of the mother and the social norm recognizes the risks of mothering for feminine subjectivity but implies that these risks are not inherent in mothering. Rather, they are a result of one possible response to the law's failure to totalize the chain of generations. The mother must serve as structure stabilizer, ensuring the totalization of the chain of generations—and the chain of signifiers— only if the law's failure to do so is a problem. But according to Kristeva's theory of language, the indeterminacy of the relationship of signifiers and signifieds is not a problem, rather it is a condition of the possibility of discourse itself. Furthermore, the image of the maternal body as the threshold of the intersection of biology and discourse implies a response to this dilemma of mothering and the law. A theory of embodied subjectivity that puts the subject in process/on trial, that theorizes subjectivity as the ongoing process of the discursive constitution of subject positioning, reconfigures the relationship of subjectivity and the law. Subjectivity is always a subjection to the law of the symbolic, but this subjection is never total and thus subjectivity is never totalized—completed and exhausted—by its subjection to the law. The image of the maternal body recognizes the indeterminacy of language and subjectivity. It does so by figuring the maternal body as a site at which the heterogeneity that the symbolic attempts to contain nevertheless explodes, a site at which continual transformations of culture, discourse, nature, and biology take place. This recognition weakens the seductive appeal of the role of structure stabilizer for mothering.

The image of the war between mother and daughter is emblematic of the question of the relation to the other woman that, according to Kristeva, is nowhere addressed in Western culture's dominant images of love and hatred. The dominant text states: " . . . a woman seldom (although not necessarily) experiences her passion (love and hatred) for another woman without having taken her own mother's place—without having herself become a mother, and especially without slowly learning to differentiate between same beings—as being face to face with her daughter forces her to do" (1986: 184). This image suggests several elements of an ethics that adequately addresses the relation to the other. It acknowledges the possibility of opposition and hostility in any relation to the other. But hostility is only one aspect of a passion that also includes love, and love is seldom possible without one woman's having taken up the place of another, specifically the place of the woman with whom she was at war—her mother. So hostility is not inevitable in the self/other relation, because there is the possibility of taking up the place of another, or, in my terms, the possibility of overlapping subject positions. For a mother is also daughter to her mother. In this way the concept of subject positioning allows the recognition of shared elements of subjectivity without denying the otherness of the other. This image of the mother-daughter relationship further suggests the application of the logic of this relationship—the logic of differentiation in sameness—to the relationship to the other woman. An ethical relationship to the other woman requires recognizing her difference without denying her sameness, which is possible if subject positions are overlapping in the ways that I have described.

The last of the images that are absent or denied in the virgin maternal is an adequate image of the repudiation of the masculine. While there is a repudiation of the masculine implicit in the virgin maternal, it amounts to an assertion in which "the Virgin assumes her feminine denial of the other sex (of man) but overcomes him by setting up a third person: *I* do not conceive with *you* but with *Him*" (1986: 180, Kristeva's emphasis). This image asserts women's difference and a feminine role in creation, but it does so by representing woman as conceiving and birthing the very being to whom she is subjected. On the other hand, a repudiation of the masculine that aims at "some understanding or other on the part of 'sexual partners' within the pre-established harmony of primal androgyny" denies women's difference. The dominant text calls instead for a repudiation of the masculine based on "counter-cathexes in strong values, in strong *equivalents of power*" (Kristeva's emphasis). Such an assertion of feminine values and feminine power avoids a denial of the feminine and theorizes women's difference, and so acknowledges "what is irreducible, of the irreconcilable interest of both sexes in asserting their differences" so that each can seek "an appropriate fulfillment" (1986: 184). This repudiation of the masculine is consistent with the logic of the mother-daughter relation. Relations between men and women include the potential for both a sameness that subsumes and denies difference and a hostile opposition that attempts to subjugate and negate the other. But preserving love and avoiding hostility requires a recognition of differentiation that does not deny sameness and a recognition of sameness that does not deny differentiation. This understanding of the self/other relation also applies to the relation of mother and child. An account of the mother-child relationship must represent the specificity of the child, but without deifying the child and subjecting the mother to the child, and without representing the mother entirely from the child's infantile, narcissistic point of view. These images of the war between mother and daughter and the repudiation of the masculine thus resist both individualism's view of the self/other relation and the Hegelian account of oppositional consciousness. And this reconceptualization of the self/other relation is also linked to theorizing subjectivity as discursive positioning. A recognition of the multiple and overlapping ways that subjects are positioned in language and of the partiality and instability of that positioning contributes to the differentiation within sameness that love requires.

In delineating these images of mothering that are absent in or denied by the virgin maternal, "Stabat Mater" begins a reconceptualization of mothering meant to avoid the effects of the virgin maternal for women's subjectivity. But a tendency to slip from theorizing mothering to theorizing femininity is also evident in these images. The image of the mother as structure stabilizer represents the possibility of *feminine* perversion in specifically *maternal* terms. The image of differentiation in sameness in the mother-daughter relation implies that *women's* herethical relations require their taking the place of their mother. And the new repudiation of the masculine that "Stabat Mater" envisions to replace that offered by the virgin maternal implies theorizing *women's* value(s) and power, and *women's* appropriate fulfillment in terms of *mothering*. Most explicitly, in "Stabat Mater" the call for a herethics includes this slippage from the feminine to the maternal: " . . . if ethics amounts to not avoiding the embarrassing and inevitable problematics of the law but giving it flesh, language and jouissance—in that case its reformulation demands the contribution of *women*. Of *women* who harbor the desire to reproduce (to have stability). Of *women* who are available so that our speaking species . . . might withstand death. Of *mothers*" (1986: 185, my emphasis). "Stabat Mater" rejects the virgin maternal because it subordinates the maternal and the feminine to the Christian god, to the Law of the Father, and to the masculine, and because it denies women's difference. But the images it offers in order to reconceptualize mothering significantly risk the recuperation of essential motherhood's equation of women and mothers.[2] This recuperation undermines "Stabat Mater's" attempt to articulate an alternative to the discourse of the virgin maternal.

"Stabat Mater's" images of "a motherhood that today remains without a discourse" suggest that Kristeva, like Ruddick, is concerned to open up the possibility of a discourse of the maternal that resists those elements of individualism and the metaphysics of substance that problematize the representation of mothering in an individualist ideological context. These images also suggest Kristeva's and Ruddick's common concern to develop an ethics that does not require an individualist theoretical frame. My analysis of these images that are absent from the virgin maternal extends the implication I have drawn from Ruddick's work that theorizing mothering and developing an ethical practice that includes mothering requires a theory of embodied subjectivity as discursive positioning. Thus, I turn to the bold-faced text of "Stabat Mater" to consider what it contributes to a theory of embodied subjectivity as discursive positioning and to a herethics. I argue that, like Ruddick's work on mothering, Kristeva's attempt to articulate this discourse of the maternal encounters the paradox of representation that results from the dilemma of difference in feminist theory. "Stabat Mater" does offer images of mothering that are absent from the virgin maternal, and in this way better represents women's and mothers' experiences than the virgin maternal. But the maternal discourse articulated in the bold-faced text of "Stabat Mater" is not entirely consistent with the herethics Kristeva proposes, and it also risks essential motherhood's equation of the feminine and maternal. In this way it undermines the resistance to essential motherhood also evident in "Stabat Mater."

— a discourse of the maternal —

The discourse of the maternal articulated in the bold-faced text of "Stabat Mater" offers a compelling image of embodied subjectivity as discursive positioning. But the bold-faced text of "Stabat Mater" also points to a problematic demand addressed to the mother in relation to language. What the bold-faced text calls "the weakness of language" gives rise to the demand that the mother guarantee the complete determination of the links between signifiers and signifieds in language and thus the unity and stability of subjectivity. At the very least, the weakness of language evokes the demand that the mother offer some consolation for the inevitable gap between signifiers and signifieds and for subjectivity's lack of stability, coherence, and completion. In either case, this demand looks to the mother to function outside of discourse as guarantee of or consolation for the weakness of language and subjectivity, thereby problematizing maternal subjectivity. The bold-faced text also implies two possible responses to this demand addressed to the mother. But neither of these responses is entirely consistent with a herethical relation to the other. I illustrate how these responses are inconsistent with a herethics by considering several problematic elements of the bold-faced text's representation of the child and the mother-child relation.

The interplay of the dominant and the bold-faced texts of "Stabat Mater" illustrates both the importance of dialogue in processes of acquiring knowledge and the inevitable possibility of contradiction and incoherence in these processes. The bold-faced column of "Stabat Mater" appears irregularly, thus representing visually Kristeva's claim that the semiotic irrupts into the symbolic. The bold-faced text often reads as an undercutting interruption of the dominant text, sometimes with a distinctly mocking tone. For example, the bold-faced text first appears when the dominant text offers a definition of mothering. The phrase "Let us call 'the maternal' . . . " is interrupted by a bold-faced passage beginning "FLASH," which asserts the difficulty of defining mothering: "[w]ords that are always too distant, too abstract for this underground swarming of seconds, folding in unimaginable spaces" (1986: 162; see also 1980: 268). This passage ends where the dominant text discusses male mystics who claim a maternal position in relation to God. This passage represents the semiotic as disrupting attempts at definition, and the maternal as

resisting containment within a definition. The cessation of this bold-faced passage shows that a masculine claim of a maternal subject position is a silencing
repression of the maternal. Another example of such an interruption occurs
when the bold-faced text reads "The immeasurable, unconfinable maternal
body" opposite the dominant text, which, under the heading "Alone of her
sex," refers to Freud collecting "countless statuettes representing mother goddesses." This juxtaposition represents the almost ridiculous futility of representations that reduce and confine the maternal, given that the maternal body
is immeasurable and unconfinable (even the number of Freud's statuettes cannot be counted). It also anticipates the dominant text's conclusion that, with
respect to the complexities of maternal experience, Freud offers "only a mas-
sive *nothing*" (1986: 177, 179, Kristeva's emphasis).

At other points the bold-faced text comments indirectly on the dominant
text, not so much mocking as complicating its claims. For example, the second
appearance of the bold-faced text occurs as the dominant text addresses "the
complex relationship between Christ and his Mother where relations of God to
mankind, man to woman, son to mother, etc. are hatched." The bold-faced
text opposite presents an image that hints at a mother holding an infant, especially in the phrase "Narcissus-like touching without eyes." But the subjectivities represented are indeterminate; not only is it unclear whose head, nape,
blood, hair, and fingers are meant, but the very boundaries of the human, the
animal, and the inanimate are called into question by references to "ebony . . .
nectar . . . wings of bees . . . silk, mercury, ductile copper . . . mane of beast,
squirrel, horse . . . " Where the dominant text figures the relationship of Christ
and his Mother as giving birth to further relations of domination and subordination, the bold-faced text suggests an indeterminacy of subject positions that
problematizes the separation and opposition presupposed by individualist
understandings of domination and subordination (1986: 166). These interactions of the dominant text and the bold-faced text issue a warning about the
difficulty of explicating subjectivity and experience in univocal and completely
consistent terms, and urge caution with respect to simplistic accounts of subjectivity that deny its partiality and instability.

Considered as a whole, apart from its relation to the dominant text, the bold-
faced text also enacts the emergence of a more specific voice, making more specific assertions, out of a more diffuse, less clearly identifiable voice offering
images and descriptions. In the earlier bold-faced sections, lists of noun phrases
without verbs are frequent. There are fewer uses of the first person—in the first
two sections of the bold-faced text there is no first person singular pronoun at
all—and the referents of the pronouns are often obscure. For example, in a

passage that begins with references to "my newborn" and "my body," the state-ment describing my body is followed by: "And yet, when its own joy, my child's, returns, its smile washes only my eyes" (1986: 167), leaving unclear whether the joy and the smile are my body's or my child's. In later bold-faced passages, how-ever, the first person is more frequent and the first-person voice more clearly enunciates claims or judgments. The bold-faced text thus enacts the process by which the subject comes to occupy a position in the symbolic, thereby enacting the constitution of embodied subjectivity as discursive positioning.

The images of embodiment and language that appear in the bold-faced text of "Stabat Mater" represent Kristeva's concept of embodied subjectivity as dis-cursively constituted and enable significant resistance to individualism's mind/body dualism. First, images of synesthesia, the interpenetration or confusion of sensory modalities, are pervasive in the bold-faced text. There are phrases such as "smooth darkness through her fingers . . . frozen light warmed under fin-gers," "the roar of a silence that hurts all over," and "[t]he wakeful tongue qui-etly remembers . . . " (1986: 166, 168, 172). These images undermine the distinctiveness of different organs or parts of the body on which the separation of sensory modalities depends. Synesthetic effects also frequently devalorize sight and highlight other senses. For example, the flash that occurs periodically is a "flash that bedazzles me" (1986: 179), a light that paradoxically makes it almost impossible to see. These synesthetic effects create an awareness of other senses, forcing a recognition of the elements of embodiment that are unacknowledged when sight is taken to be the only, or best, mode of percep-tion. A privileging of sight over other sensory modalities follows from the indi-vidualist view of the body as the container of subjectivity that figures consciousness as located in and looking out of the body through the eyes. So the devalorization of sight implicit in the synesthetic images of the bold-faced text in "Stabat Mater" also challenges mind/body dualism. In addition, these images participate in the effect of enactment that I have described. Attributing the effects and modalities of one sense to another confounds the reader's expectations, provoking the reader to consider what it might mean, for instance, to touch darkness and light or to taste memory.

Second, the bold-faced text frequently refers to bodily experiences that resist representation in terms of mind/body dualism, such as a shiver, a spasm, and vertigo. The image of vertigo is particularly significant, since it appears at moments when that which is expected or desired to unify and stabilize subjec-tivity instead gives way. For example, in trying to think through the "abyss" that separates mother and child, there is " . . . staggering vertigo. No identity holds up" (1986: 178–79). The earlier bold-faced passages, with their vivid but

confounding images and indeterminate positions of enunciation, also enact
this sort of vertigo. The reader attempting to sort out these images and positions in terms of the expectations of more conventional prose might also experience a vertigo in which no identity holds up. Third, images of the sea and
waves and of echoing and dissolving are significant in the bold-faced text of
"Stabat Mater." For example, in an image of a mother and infant "[a] wave
swells . . . when he goes to sleep, under my skin" (1986: 172). The "demented
jouissance" of mothering is "answered, by chance, by the nursling's laughter in
the sunny waters of the ocean . . . that overflowing laughter where one senses
the collapse of some ringing, subtle, fluid identity or other, softly buoyed by
the waves" (1986: 179–80). The community of women is located in the ocean
as a community of dolphins, and the languages of ancient matriarchal civilizations "take refuge in tones to recover an underwater, trans-verbal communication of bodies" (1986: 181, 182). Like the images of synesthesia and of bodily
experiences such as vertigo, these images represent the relationship of embodiment and subjectivity in terms of permeability and fluidity. They also represent the partiality and instability of subject positioning, not as a threat to or
failure of subjectivity, but as that which enables enunciation and allows movement among multiple and overlapping subject positions.

Most of these images of embodiment are closely connected to language in
ways that further explicate the discursive constitution of embodied subjectivity. In the images of fluidity, for example, there are also the answering laughter,
the dolphins, and the underwater communication of bodies. The image of vertigo is frequently conjoined with references to the weakness of language, especially with the lack or gap that language both requires and tries to cover over or
deny. In the bold-faced text, the body represented as fold, or as composed of
contradictory elements, is also figured as a border or crossroad in a way that
evokes the division or splitting that establishes the possibility of enunciation:
"[w]e live on that border, crossroads beings, crucified beings." This is especially
true of the mother, who is "a continuous separation, a division of the very flesh.
And consequently a division of language" (1986: 178). These images point
both to the gap on which signification depends and which splits subjectivity,
and to the transformation of nature, biology, culture, and discourse that occurs
at the site of the body, especially the maternal body. The reciprocal over-
determination of embodiment and language is also evident in an image of a
feminine see-saw: "Within this strange feminine see-saw that makes 'me'
swing from the unnameable community of women over to the war of individual singularities, it is unsettling to say 'I'" (1986: 182). This see-saw represents
two motions. There is first the see-sawing between an unnameable community

and a war, between a community that insists on sameness and denies the gap between self and other and between signifier and signified so that naming is neither possible nor necessary, and a hostility that denies any possibility of sameness. At each extreme, this motion misses the differentiation in sameness that herethics requires. But there is also the unsettling motion of saying "I." The discursive act which, more than any other, should stabilize subjectivity, instead unsettles it, because, literally, 'it' (das es, the id) is unsettling to say 'I' (Ich, Ego). Every saying "I" includes the repressed, unconscious drives, the pre-Oedipal structuration of the body, and the Oedipal complex's positioning of subject within the gap between signified and signifier, all of which divide and destabilize subjectivity. Saying "I" expresses both the desire for a settled 'I', a unified and stable subjectivity, and the impossibility of such subjectivity.

In these images, the bold-faced text of "Stabat Mater" provides a vivid account of embodied subjectivity as divided, partial, and unstable positioning in discourse. These images resist individualism's view of the body as a stable limit, boundary, or container of subjectivity. Their emphasis on the synesthetic elements of embodiment, on bodily experiences that resist symbolization in dualist terms, and on the fluidity and permeability of embodiment represents the body as thoroughly permeated by subjectivity and language. These images also imply that the body so understood situates subjectivity in specific social relations and contexts, and does so in a way that enables movement among multiple and overlapping discursive positions, a movement that is facilitated by the logic of differentiation in sameness. In its images of mothering, the bold-faced column of "Stabat Mater" resists the implication of individualism and essential motherhood that mothering is not an exercise of subjectivity. These images of mothering show instead that maternal subjectivity is exemplary of embodied subjectivity. What individualism sees as the highly problematic aspects of maternal subjectivity—its interpenetration by an other, its partiality and instability, and the multiple and overlapping positions occupied by the mother and child, especially in pregnancy and birth—are represented by the bold-faced text of "Stabat Mater" as characteristic of all embodied subjectivity.

In comparison, Beauvoir's account of pregnancy and birth struggles to artic-ulate these experiences in terms of a theoretical framework that ultimately refuses their significance while also recuperating significant elements of indi-vidualism and the metaphysics of substance. Ruddick's account of sexed, social/bodily subjectivity is better able than Beauvoir's immanence/transcen-dence distinction to theorize pregnancy and birth while also resisting individu-alism and the metaphysics of substance. But it still relies to some extent on the individualist binaries social/natural and mind/body. Kristeva's account of mothering theorizes pregnancy and birth while more strenuously undermining individualism and the metaphysics of substance than either Beauvoir's immanence/transcendence distinction or Ruddick's account of sex, social/bodily subjectivity. By theorizing embodied subjectivity, including maternal subjectivity, as discursively constituted, Kristeva is able to analyze the specificities of maternal embodied subjectivity without concluding that maternal embodiment completely and exhaustively determines maternal subjectivity. Kristeva's account of the "bio-symbolic latencies" of mothering better resists individualist binaries such as mind/body and social/natural than do Beauvoir's account of mothering and Ruddick's analysis of birthgiving and natal reflection.

— the weakness of language and the desire of/for the mother —

The bold-faced text of "Stabat Mater" also raises a problem for theorizing embodied subjectivity as discursive positioning. It suggests that, in the face of the weakness of language, there occurs the desire for completely and exhaustively determined, coherent, and stable subjectivity, and this desire is transformed into a belief in the mother: "If language is powerless to locate myself for and state myself to the other, I assume—I want to believe—that there is someone who makes up for that weakness. Someone of either sex, *before* the id speaks, before language, who might make me be by means of borders, separations, vertigos" (1986: 175–76, Kristeva's emphasis). And if the mother cannot make me be, then she is called upon to be compensation for the weakness of language by being "its [language's] permanent lining: the maternal receptacle." This "[a]rchaic maternal love would be an incorporation of my suffering that is unfailing, unlike what often happens with the lacunary network of signs" (1986: 176). While this someone may be of either sex, from an infantile perspective that someone who is there "before the id speaks, before language" is the mother. Furthermore, the function attributed to such a being in this passage is a traditionally maternal function, and, as Kristeva has argued, this is perhaps the preeminent function of the mother according to the image of the virgin maternal.

The bold-faced text of "Stabat Mater" also presents several images of the child that do not meet the terms of the herethics that Kristeva proposes. Specifically, these images are not consistent with the differentiation in sameness required for a herethical relation to the other. As I see it, these two problems—the desire for the mother to guarantee or console for language and subjectivity and these images of the child—are intertwined. In theorizing the weakness of language, "Stabat Mater" recognizes that partial, fragmented, and unstable subjectivity might look to the mother for a guarantee of or consolation for subjectivity and language. Its images of the child, however, also imply that the mother might look to the child, especially the infant, for a similar guarantee or consolation. In other words, the mother might look to the child to make her be. This aspect of the bold-faced text's image of the mother-child relationship represents the Lacanian view that the desire for completeness, stability, and coherence circulates in the mother-child relationship, and persists in subjectivity beyond the Oedipal complex. A herethical position in response to the desire for guarantee of or consolation for subjectivity would recognize but resist this desire. But the bold-faced text not only represents this desire, to some extent it also succumbs to it and posits its satisfaction. The bold-faced text of "Stabat Mater" does not sufficiently resist this desire, and, I argue, this is a function of its Lacanian psychoanalytic framework.

The bold-faced text thus problematizes maternal subjectivity even as it struggles to articulate a discourse of the maternal. To the extent that it calls on the mother to guarantee or console for the weakness of language and subjectivity, it positions the mother outside of discourse in a way similar to the virgin maternal's image of the mother as the "parentheses of language" that enable representation but do not represent. To the extent that it figures the mother as a daughter longing for and experiencing a return to her mother, the bold-faced text of "Stabat Mater" represents the mother as fleeing from or denying her divided, partial, and unstable subjectivity and posits the possibility of her enjoying an unconflicted reunion with her mother. In this image, the mother's mother is similarly positioned outside of discourse in a way that problematizes her subjectivity. But could the child and the mother-child relationship be represented in terms more consistent with a herethics? And, if so, would this representation resist the demand that the mother and/or the child guarantee language and subjectivity or console for the lack of this guarantee? In other words, might feminist theory take up in relationship to this desire a herethical position that recognizes but does not succumb to it?

Answering these questions requires a consideration of the three kinds of images of the child and the mother-child relation in the bold-faced text of "Stabat Mater," and of the conflicting impulses at work in them. These are images of unity or fusion, images of alterity, and images of hostility. The images of unity or fusion represent the mother-child relationship in terms of a prelinguistic, embodied reciprocity. For example: "Scent of milk, dewed greenery . . . recall of wind . . . it slides under the skin, does not remain in the mouth or nose but fondles the veins, detaches skin from bones, inflates me . . . and I hover with feet planted firmly on the ground . . . to carry him, sure, stable, ineradicable, while he dances in my neck, flutters with my hair . . . finally flies away on my navel in his dream carried by my hands. My son" (1986: 171). While the fetus is "this internal graft or fold" (1986: 178), the child is "without fold or shadow, neither being nor unborn, neither present not absent, but real, real inaccessible innocence, engaging weight and seraphic lightness" (1986: 172–73). In these images of unity and fusion, the child is rarely represented as speaking, although some form of communication between mother and child is implied. When the bold-faced text does hint at speech on the part of the infant, its significance to the mother is emphasized: the "childhood gentleness that awakes to meaning . . . causes me to soar in music, in dance" and "you speak without words, but your throat no longer gurgles—it harkens with me to the silence of your born meaning . . . " (1986: 173). The bold-faced text also suggests that these aspects of the mother-child relation enable the mother's return to her mother: "A wave swells again, when he goes to sleep, under my skin. . . . The wakeful tongue quietly remembers another withdrawal, mine: a blossoming heaviness in the middle of the bed. . . . Recovered childhood, dreamed peace restored . . . opaque joy that roots me in her bed, my mother's, and projects him, a son. . . . Alone: she, I, and he" (1986: 172; see also 1980: 239).

The bold-faced text also offers images of the radical alterity of the child, for example, images of the bodily separation of mother and child figured as gap or abyss: " . . . this other abyss that opens up between the body and what had been its inside. . . . What connection is there between myself, or even . . . between my body and this internal graft and fold, which, once the umbilical has been severed, is an inaccessible other? My body and him . . . no connection. . . . The child, whether *he* or *she*, is irremediably an other" (1986: 178–79, Kristeva's emphasis). Finally, there is in "Stabat Mater" one explicit image of hostility between mother and child, represented in terms of the failure to reciprocate the other's claim to subjectivity. This image is specific to a girl child, is voiced from the position of a daughter, and is directly connected to the possibility of hostility in women's relations with other women: "Concerning that stage of my childhood . . . I have only a spatial memory. No time at all. . . . Mummy. Almost no sight. . . . Almost no voice in her placid presence. Except, perhaps, and more belatedly, the echo of quarrels: her exasperation, her being fed up, her hatred." This hatred is held back, as if, even though the "unmanageable child deserved it . . . the daughter could not accept the mother's hatred—it was not meant for her. A hatred without recipient or rather whose recipient was no 'I' . . . " (1986: 180).

This hostility and lack of reciprocity is further perpetuated in women's relations with each other. While the community of women can be a community of dolphins, where there is "trans-verbal communication between bodies,"

when the other woman "posits herself as . . . singular and inevitably in opposition, 'I' am startled, so much so that 'I' no longer know what is going on"
(1986: 181). In these circumstances, the bold-faced text suggests, there are
two alternatives. Either I ignore the other woman, as a recipient not worthy of
my hatred, or, outraged by her stubbornness in believing herself singular, "I
unrelentingly let go at her claim to address me and find respite only in the
eternal return of power strokes, bursts of hatred . . . " (1986: 181). Either the
other woman's claim to differentiation is inconsequential and receives no
recognition, or it is intolerable and is met with hatred. In addition, it is this
hostility that locates the voice of the bold-faced text on the strange feminine
see-saw where it is unsettling to say "I." For this see-sawing is a "swing[ing]
from the unnameable community of women over to the war of individual singularities" (1986: 182). Thus, by putting subjectivity in this position where its
instability is evident, hostility is part of what gives rise to the desire for the
mother who guarantees or consoles for subjectivity and language. This is why
the daughter cannot accept the mother's hostility and remain an 'I'. To accept
the mother's hostility is to accept that there is no guarantee of or consolation
for language and subjectivity.

The bold-faced text's images of the newborn emphasize the prelinguistic,
embodied communication of mother and child, and suggest that such communication is possible among women. These images represent a mutually satisfying fusion of mother and child, and project the possibility of such
experiences among women. The implication that the newborn enables his or
her mother's unconflicted return to her mother ("recovered childhood,
dreamed peace restored") in particular extends the possibility of mutually satisfying fusion and uncomplicated communication to the mother's relation
with her mother. The bold-faced text expresses the mother's desire for someone to "make her be," and addresses this desire directly to the child, and indirectly, via the child, to the mother's mother. In these images the mother's
desire is a desire for both someone or something that completely and exhaustively determines her as a mother, and makes her movement among subject
positions (mother, daughter, other to the other woman) unproblematic and
unlimited. On the other hand, the images of the child as other and of the hostility of mother and daughter represent the mother-child relationship in terms
of difference so profound as to suggest that they will never have a relationship
of mutual differentiation in sameness.

What is not explicitly represented anywhere in "Stabat Mater" is the child's
installation in the symbolic, its becoming a speaking subject. While "Stabat
Mater" seems to resist Lacan's account of the child's installation in the sym-

bolic, however, it offers little in the way of an alternative image of the child's becoming a speaking subject. It is as if the bold-faced text of "Stabat Mater" can envision the child's installation in the symbolic only as a mother's complete surrender of the child to the Law of the Father, a surrender that entirely severs the child from the mother. So the bold-faced text refuses to make this surrender of the child and then cannot envision the child as speaking subject, except indirectly and in relation to the mother. But, more importantly, neither fusion with the other that denies differentiation nor an assertion of radical alterity that precludes sameness is consistent with the differentiation in sameness required by a herethics. The mother's desire for fusion with the child, her assertion of the radical difference of the child, her reliance on the child as a means to return to her mother, and her expression of hostility toward the daughter all tend to deny the child its own subjectivity, its divided, partial, and unstable discursive position as 'I'.

Taken together, these images of the child and the mother-child relationship can be read to suggest the complexity of this relationship. They show that this relationship includes fusion and separation, desire and hostility, and that mothers and children may experience conflicting desires and occupy contradictory positions in relation to each other. But without an account of the child's installation in the symbolic that preserves the possibility of mutual differentiation in sameness between mother and child, "Stabat Mater" risks denying the discursively constituted subjectivity of the child. Kristeva's concept of a herethics, however, suggests two possible responses to the desire of/for the mother for guarantee or consolation. The dominant text ends with the call for a herethics, phrased as a call to listen to the music, especially the music of the Stabat Mater, which "swallows up the goddesses and removes their necessity" (1986: 185). Phrased in this way, the call for a herethics suggests the response to the demand that the mother guarantee or console for subjectivity that the bold-faced texts refers to as "the artists' way." The bold-faced text also suggests a maternal recognition and acceptance of impossibility that can also be construed as a response to the demand that the mother guarantee or console for subjectivity.

The dominant text's call for a herethics implies that certain representations, such as the music of the Stabat Mater, release the mother from having to guarantee or console for subjectivity and language. In the bold-faced text, this artists' way is also represented as making up "for the vertigo of language weakness with the oversaturation of sign-systems . . . [that] renders belief in the mother useless." But it does so "by overwhelming the symbolic weakness where she takes refuge, withdrawn from history, with an overabundance of discourse" (1986: 177). On the other hand, as the dominant text opposite points out, the saint, the mystic, or the writer "succeeds in doing no better than to take apart the fiction of the mother as the mainstay of love, and to identify with love itself and what he is in fact—*a fire of tongues,* an exit from representation" (Kristeva's emphasis). This means that the artists' way might be "the implementation of that maternal love—a veil of death in death's very site and with full knowledge of the facts." But it might also be "[a] sublimated celebration of incest" (1986: 177). This artists' discourse suggests the possibility of representations that release the mother from the demand to guarantee or console for subjectivity and language. But it also suggests that these representations do so by somehow denying the mother; they remove the necessity of the goddesses, but do so by swallowing them up. The image of the artists' way as an overwhelming of the place where the mother takes refuge and a celebration of incest implies that the artist attempts to return to the maternal body, to renew his access to that body that has been denied to him by the Law of the Father, and in this way to deny that his position in the symbolic is founded on a gap or lack. Thus, the artists' way may not subject the mother to the demand that she guarantee language or console for the lack of such a guarantee. But neither does it fully recognize the discursive subjectivity of the mother. Rather, it denies the subjectivity of the mother in its attempts to occupy her place, or to return to the pre-Oedipal experience in which the child experiences no differentiation from the mother.

The final bold-faced passage, on the other hand, suggests a specifically maternal response to the desire of/for the mother. This passage represents the child, not as fused with the mother or as inaccessibly other, but as an impossibility that nonetheless is. From a maternal perspective, discontinuity, lack, and arbitrariness are not threatening, because "[f]or a mother . . . strangely so, the other as arbitrary (the child) is taken for granted. As far as she is concerned— impossible, that is just the way it is." For the mother the other is "natural, for such an other has come out of myself, which is yet not myself. . . ." Furthermore, "the other goes much without saying and without my saying that, at the limit, it does not exist for itself." This " 'just the same' of motherly peace of mind gnaws at the symbolic's allmightiness" and "constitutes the basis of the social bond in its generality." This discourse of an impossibility "that is just the way it is" refigures both the mother and the child as images of a recognition and acceptance of the impossibility of individualist subjectivity. This refiguration frees both from having to serve as guarantee of or consolation for subjectivity. But this maternal response to the demand that the mother or child serve as guarantee or consolation can also risk the denial of difference: "the leaden strap it can become, smothering any different individuality . . . it

can crush everything the other (the child) has that is specifically irreducible."
It is also like the artists' way in figuring the mother as a refuge: "it is there, too,
that the speaking being finds a refuge when his/her symbolic shell cracks and a
crest emerges where speech causes biology to show through: . . . the time of ill-
ness, of sexual-intellectual-physical passion, of death . . . " (1986: 185).

This image of the mother-child relation acknowledges several impossibilities—the impossibility of the otherness of the child, when the child is born of
oneself; the impossibility of the child's existence for itself when it is born of
another (oneself); the impossibility of a subjectivity that gives birth to another;
and the impossibility of speaking the other, of "saying other" when the other
"goes without saying." In this image, all of these impossibilities are nonetheless
"just the way it is." Such acknowledgment of impossibility resists the totalizing
impulses of the symbolic and enables a social bond based on differentiation
within sameness. It enables "our speaking species . . . [to] withstand death"
(1986: 185) because, having never posited the completeness, coherence, and
stability of subjectivity, it does not represent death as the undoing or dissolution of subjectivity so understood. But even in this discourse where subjectivity
is theorized in terms of impossibility, the mother can function as a threat to
the subjectivity of the other or can be called upon as a refuge for speaking subjectivity when "biology shows through." Compared to the artists' way, this
maternal recognition of impossibility is more consistent with a herethical position in relationship to the desire of/for the mother. It recognizes that both the
mother and the child experience the desire for a subjectivity that is impossible.
But it also figures the mother as a threat to the differentiation of the child, and
to this extent does not meet the terms of a herethics.

— the desire of/for the mother and
the contexts of mothering —

My reading of Kristeva's "Stabat Mater" further develops the concepts for theorizing subjectivity in resistance to individualism and the metaphysics of substance that I have elicited from Beauvoir's and Ruddick's accounts of
mothering. But it also shows that conflicting impulses are at work in Kristeva's
account of mothering as a result of its Lacanian psychoanalytic framework.
Kristeva's theory of subjectivity elaborates the concept of embodied subjectivity
as over-determined, fluctuating, and unstable discursive positioning that I have
argued is implicit in Beauvoir's and Ruddick's analyses of mothering. Kristeva's
theory of the discursive constitution of embodied subjectivity also further
develops Ruddick's use of the concept of narrative in theorizing mothering. It

thus more adequately negotiates the paradoxes of gender and embodiment by recognizing and accepting, rather than denying, the paradoxical elements of embodied subjectivity, especially maternal embodied subjectivity, as effects of its discursive constitution. In this way Kristeva's theory of subjectivity further develops Ruddick's notion of embodied subjectivity as both exclusive and approximate, elaborating what Beauvoir calls "the strange ambiguity of existence made body" (1989: 728).

Kristeva's theory of subjectivity thus challenges the elements of individualism that problematize the analysis of mothering for feminist theory. It especially challenges mind/body dualism more so than Beauvoir's immanence/transcendence distinction and Ruddick's theory of sexed, social/bodily subjectivity. Kristeva's analysis of the body in language undermines these binaries by figuring the body and subjectivity, as well as the natural and the social, in discursive terms as thoroughly and mutually permeating but never exhaustively constituting each other. Her theory of subjectivity also puts subjectivity in process/on trial; it significantly desubstantializes embodied subjectivity by representing it as an ongoing process of transforming nature, culture, biology, and discourse into each other. Kristeva also provides a compelling account of maternal subjectivity as exemplary of subjectivity in being divided, partial, unstable. In this way it resists individualism's tendency to see maternal embodied subjectivity as a deviation from its concept of subjectivity as rational autonomy. My analysis of Kristeva's theory of subjectivity thus suggests answers to the questions for feminist analyses of mothering that emerge from my argument that Ruddick's work implies an account of subjectivity as positioning. Kristeva's account of embodied subjectivity indicates that subject positioning is positioning in discourse. To be a subject is not to possess some set of disembodied capacities or characteristics, but to occupy—tentatively and unstably—an embodied location within a system of signifiers that enables one to speak. The process of coming to occupy a subject position is thoroughly intertwined with early childhood social relations, but, since subject positioning is never exhaustive, it is always in process. This allows for the multiple and overlapping quality of subject positioning that I have argued is implicit in Hartsock's version of standpoint theory, in Ruddick's account of a feminist maternal peace politics, and in Ruddick's representation of her own subject position.

Kristeva's theory of embodied subjectivity also addresses Ruddick's concerns about the tendency of standpoint theories to claim a standpoint that is exhaustive and absolute. An account of embodied subjectivity as discursively constituted is consistent with a theory of knowledge according to which knowledge is also partial and tentative but not for that reason without value or ineffective.

Kristeva's account of embodied subjectivity implies that what subjects can know is always a function of their discursive positioning. But it also implies that the process of acquiring knowledge is ongoing and subject to continual revision. It is likely to be fostered by collective discourse but also likely to lead to contradictory conclusions. I have shown that Ruddick struggles to take up and maintain a maternal standpoint in theorizing mothering, recognizes the partiality of her own accounts of mothering, participates in collective discursive acts to further theorize mothering, evaluates accounts of mothering in terms of their effects for women and mothers, and discovers elements of mothering that simply cannot be encompassed within a univocal and coherent theoretical framework. But, according to Kristeva's theory of embodied subjectivity, these aspects of Ruddick's theoretical practice are not some aberration specific to theorizing mothering, rather, they are typical of processes of acquiring knowledge.

Kristeva's argument for a herethics that recognizes the discursive constitution of embodied subjectivity and thus allows differentiation in sameness also addresses the questions about agency that I have raised in connection with the concept of subject positioning. The ongoing discursive constitution of embodied subjectivity means that subject positions and their contexts are mutually and reciprocally but not exhaustively over-determinative, so that subjectivity can act to affect its contexts. In other words, the discursive constitution of subjectivity includes the discursive constitution of contexts that enable agency. That subject positions are discursively constituted also means that they can overlap, which creates the conditions for the possibility of collective agency. Kristeva's account of the logic of differentiation in sameness allows a further development of standpoint theory's claim that standpoints are achieved or have to be constructed. To the extent that subjects can struggle to differentiate between same beings, as a herethics requires, subjects can find themselves placed in or participate in constructing discursive contexts and overlapping subject positions that enable them to act collectively without requiring that they share entirely a stable, coherent, and exhaustively determined identity.

These contributions of Kristeva's theory of embodied subjectivity to the resistance to individualism that feminist theory requires in an individualist ideological context, however, have to be considered in relation to the Lacanian psychoanalytic framework of "Stabat Mater" and Ruddick's criticisms of psychoanalysis. For feminist theory, especially feminist analyses of mothering, also requires resistance to essential motherhood. Ruddick's critique of psychoanalysis, however, implies that the risk of recuperating essential motherhood implicit in feminist theoretical appeals to psychoanalysis is deeply intertwined with the basic presuppositions of psychoanalysis itself. According to Ruddick, psychoanalysis overemphasizes infancy and early childhood, and in this way misrepresents mothers and children and problematizes maternal subjectivity. She argues that psychoanalysis theorizes mothering from the child's point of view; the mother's voice is absent from psychoanalytic accounts of children's experiences.[3] Ruddick particularly questions psychoanalysis' "dream of pleni-tude"—its image of the mother and child as a mutually desiring, mutually sat-isfying couple. Ruddick also argues that psychoanalysis slips from representing children's fantasies or projections of mothers to claiming that these fantasies or projections represent mothers as they truly are.[4] For example, the rhetorical elision represented by the term "pre-Oedipal mother" slips into the suggestion that mothers are somehow pre-Oedipal. This concern is particularly relevant to Lacanian psychoanalysis. For, if mothers are pre-Oedipal, then they somehow exist prior to the discursive constitution of embodied subjectivity, and their status as subjects in their own right is at least problematic. In addition, Ruddick writes, "The child hero of psychoanalysis is apt to remain as obsessed with gender and sexuality and as preoccupied with Mother, Father, and the pas-sions of family life as psychoanalysts themselves" (1994: 32). The child envi-sioned by psychoanalysis never grows up, so psychoanalysis provides no account of the variety of mother-child relationships consistent with good mothering, of the different kinds of complex thinking mothers do at later stages of children's development, of the different kinds of concerns and inter-ests that children can come to have as they grow, or of how children's thoughts, feelings, and actions contribute to the ongoing transformations of the mother-child relationship.

Ruddick argues that psychoanalysis also problematizes maternal subjectivity by requiring the absence or lack of the mother as a condition for subjectivity, language, and culture. This problem is also particularly relevant to Lacanian psychoanalysis. In Lacan's view of the function of the phallus in the constitu-tion of subjectivity, the phallus can be read as representing that which no one really has, namely, a complete, coherent, and stable subjectivity and the power that this might confer. But as long as the phallus bears some mimetic relation-ship to the penis, Lacan's theory does represent subjectivity in terms of what the mother, and all women, lack (Gallop, 1982: 95–100). Lacan's theory of sub-jectivity thus not only problematizes the position of the mother in relation to discourse, as the desire of/for the mother does. It also requires the lack or absence of the mother so that the child can come to be positioned in relation to the phallus and the Law of the Father, and thus come to occupy a position of enunciation. This account of subjectivity in which "the phallic mother" becomes "the castrated mother" not only disempowers mothers by theorizing them in terms of lack, but also locates mothers in a stage prior to discursive subjectivity. The alternatives phallic or castrated for the mother deny the complexity of maternal thought and action, especially the complexities of maternal power and powerlessness. To the extent that Lacanian psychoanalysis defines the subject positioning of mothers, and women, in terms of castration, mothers and women are not only required to accept the castration of the mother but also to accept their own castration in order to occupy even a highly problematic position in the symbolic. For Ruddick, this is perhaps the most serious way in which psychoanalysis problematizes maternal subjectivity (1994: 30–32).[5]

In "Stabat Mater," Kristeva reconceptualizes the mother in terms of the maternal function, representing the mother not simply as dephallicized, but also as an active subject in the constitution of the child's subjectivity. Kristeva also represents the mother in terms of the most disruptive elements of subjectivity—the semiotic—but, for Kristeva, this representation figures the mother as emblematic of subjectivity. In this representation of the mother, "Stabat Mater" revises Lacan's theory of subjectivity so that the mother's role in the discursive constitution of the child's subjectivity is not defined entirely in terms of lack or absence. But, as I have argued, this effect of "Stabat Mater" is at odds with its implication of the satisfaction of the desire of/for the mother, especially the satisfaction of the mother's desire for her mother enabled by the child. Kristeva's view that the mother is emblematic of subjectivity avoids to some extent Ruddick's criticism that psychoanalysis does not recognize maternal subjectivity. But to the extent that "Stabat Mater" not only represents but also succumbs to the desire for the mother as guarantee of or consolation for subjectivity and language, it does problematize maternal subjectivity. And to the extent that "Stabat Mater" not only represents but also succumbs to a maternal desire for the child as a guarantee of or consolation for subjectivity and language and/or as a means to a reunion with the mother's mother, it is susceptible to Ruddick's claim that psychoanalysis misrepresents children. In other words, Kristeva's account of mothering does dream "the dream of plenitude" that Ruddick attributes to psychoanalysis. This is one way in which "Stabat Mater" risks the recuperation of elements of essential motherhood. The implication that the mother and child can engage in a relationship in which each guarantees the subjectivity of the other problematizes both maternal subjectivity and the subjectivity of children by suggesting that they can somehow avoid the divided, partial, and unstable subjectivity "Stabat Mater" otherwise attributes to all subjects. The implication that mothers and children can be each other's consolation for the lack of any guarantee of subjectivity risks defining mothers and children entirely in relationship to each other and as entirely satisfying each other's desire. This implication contains women's desire within the bounds of mothering. It also denies the child any significant degree of differentiation in relationship to the mother, thereby denying the mother and child the possibility of a herethical relationship.

Moreover, in these images of the mother and child, the mother's desire of/for the child includes the demand that the child allow the mother's return to her mother: the "recovered childhood, dreamed peace restored" that the bold-faced text of "Stabat Mater" attributes to a woman's becoming a mother. This demand expresses the desire for unconflicted relations among women, implies the satisfaction of this desire, and suggests that the mother-child relation somehow makes possible such relations among women. Seeing that mothers are also daughters and that in becoming a mother a woman takes the place of her mother is consistent with differentiation in sameness to the extent that it recognizes the possibility of multiple and overlapping subject positioning. But representing women as daughters not only longing for but also experiencing reunion with their mothers implies that the daughter's partial, divided, and unstable subjectivity is problematic, and that the mother can either provide the completeness, coherence, and unity that the daughter lacks or console her for this lack. This image of the mother-daughter relationship also places mothers and daughters in a position prior to the discursive constitution of subjectivity, thus denying them the kind of subjectivity that Kristeva and Lacan otherwise attribute to all subjects. The suggestion that a woman's desire for reunion with her mother is satisfied in becoming a mother herself also minimizes the ways in which the overlapping of subject positions must be constructed or achieved in some way—an aspect of subject positioning that standpoint theory more clearly articulates. It implies an easy, unconflicted movement among subject positions that is at odds with the partiality, instability, and incoherence that Lacan and Kristeva attribute to subjectivity. This implication is another way in which psychoanalysis problematizes mothers' (and women's) subjectivity. So, as Ruddick's critique indicates, feminist theory should be wary of analyses of mothering, and of maternal ethical practices, that envision mothers almost entirely from an infantile perspective, and that position women, including those feminist theorists who are women, as daughters.

The conflicting implications of Kristeva's Lacanian theory of subjectivity undermine the possibility of mothers and children coming to have herethical relationships based on differentiation in sameness. But what might a herethics entail if it included not just the contributions of women, of mothers, but also of children; that is, if it included a representation of the discursive subjectivity of the child? I suspect that, if "Stabat Mater" also included images of the child's coming to be a speaking subject and of the transformations the mother-child relation undergoes as the child emerges into subjectivity and grows up, it would arrive at an image of the relationship of the older child and mother, and an ethics, not unlike those envisioned in Ruddick's account of maternal practice. Kristeva's herethics could be further developed by consideration of Ruddick's analysis of the goals and virtues of maternal practice, especially her analysis of the acceptance of differentiation as a virtue of the goal of shaping acceptable children. Such further development of Kristeva's concept of a herethics would be consistent with the implication of Kristeva's theory of subjectivity that subject constitution is an ongoing process and would allow a more adequate account of differentiation in sameness in the mother-child relationship than "Stabat Mater" provides.

This suggestion for elaborating Kristeva's account of the mother-child relationship may make it more consistent with a herethics. However, it does not entirely address the questions I have raised about the desire of/for the mother and/or the child to guarantee or console for language and subjectivity. Neither of the two responses to this desire represented in "Stabat Mater"—the artists' way and the maternal recognition and acceptance of impossibility—is entirely unproblematic. The artists' way, or the appeal to representations that console for the lack of any guarantee of language and subjectivity, risks the denial of maternal subjectivity. The maternal acceptance of impossibility risks the denial of the differentiation of the other. My suggestion for developing the images of the mother-child relationship in "Stabat Mater" along the lines of Ruddick's account of the goals and virtues of maternal practice, however, may minimize the risk of the denial of differentiation in the response of the maternal impossible to the desire of/for the mother. Ruddick shows that maternal practice's goal of shaping acceptable children includes the acceptance of a significant degree of differentiation on the part of the child. If the maternal recognition and acceptance of impossibility can include this goal—if it can recognize and accept that the child is born of oneself and yet is a subject in his or her own right as an impossibility that none the less is—then it may be a less risky response to the demand for a guarantee or consolation than the artists' way, which risks the denial of maternal subjectivity.

Feminist theory can draw several conclusions from the difficulty of articulating a satisfactory response to the desire of/for the mother. First, Kristeva's theory of embodied subjectivity indicates that this desire is inevitable in an ideological context defined by the individualism and essential motherhood. Kristeva argues that subjectivity is partial, divided, and unstable, and emerges from an experience with the mother in which there is no gap between need and its satisfaction. If this constitution of subjectivity occurs in an ideological context that promises the impossible—a complete, unified, and coherent experience of subjectivity as rational autonomy— then subjectivity will inevitably evoke a mournful recognition of the loss of that initial experience, and will inevitably include the desire to reexperience it. Furthermore, as long as all women are expected to become mothers and do all of the work of mothering, especially mothering newborns and infants, this demand for guarantee or consolation will also inevitably be addressed to mothers. For with this social organization of mothering, all subjects associate the completeness, unity, and coherence experienced in infancy with the mother. As long as women are expected to find complete happiness and fulfillment in mothering, mothers are also likely to address a similar demand to children, especially newborns and infants. And, given the continued hegemony of essential motherhood, which equates femininity with motherhood, the demand for guarantee of or consolation for language and subjectivity will be addressed not only to mothers but to all women.[6]

Second, the persistence of the desire of/for the mother, even in an account of embodied subjectivity like Kristeva's which insists on its instability and partiality, further supports the implication I have elicited from Ruddick's work on mothering that feminist theory requires a more thorough analysis of its own practice of representation. In the case of "Stabat Mater," the persistence of the desire of/for the mother indicates that theorizing mothering only in terms of the earliest stages of the mother-child relation, as psychoanalysis does, is not adequate for analyzing this desire. This means that feminist theory must look beyond the mother-child relation for the determinants of the persistence of this desire. If feminist theory's resistance to individualism includes resisting individualism's decontextualizing approach to subjectivity and its social contexts, then feminist theory must consider how the mother-child relationship is over-determined by its material, social, and ideological contexts. Theorizing how these contexts contribute to the persistence of the desire for guarantee of or consolation for subjectivity and language, and of its address to the mother and/or the child, requires a broader focus than Lacanian psychoanalysis and Kristeva's account of mothering provide. Considering the advantages of Kristeva's account of subjectivity in light of the representation of the desire of/for the mother in "Stabat Mater" and Ruddick's criticisms of psychoanalysis suggests several further questions. First, to what extent are the problematic aspects of the representation of the desire of/for the mother in "Stabat Mater" a function of the psychoanalytic frame of Kristeva's account of mothering?

Second, is it possible to theorize mothering in terms of Kristeva's theory of embodied subjectivity without implying that the mother and the child can satisfy each other's desire for a complete and exhaustively determined subjectivity? Is it possible to recognize the inevitability of this desire in terms that are consistent with differentiation in sameness? Is it possible to represent and analyze this desire without also succumbing to it? Third, what are the possibilities for analyzing this desire in terms of a broader context than the mother-child relation—terms that include the material, social, and ideological contexts of mothering? Can a psychoanalytic approach to mothering contextualize mothering in these terms? In other words, how might feminist theory consider the desire of/for the mother in terms of an analysis of the over-determination of subjectivity, experience, knowledge, and representation, that, I have argued, is also called for by Ruddick's use of the concepts of experience and narrative in theorizing mothering? To consider whether an account of mothering framed in psychoanalytic terms can proceed in these directions, I offer in the next chapter an analysis of Chodorow's *The Reproduction of Mothering*, which appeals to psychoanalysis to theorize mothering, but also includes an explanation of the over-determination of the mother-child relation in terms of its material, social, and ideological contexts.

chapter   s e v e n

MOTHERING
AND PSYCHOANALYSIS

the persistance of the dilemma of difference

— varieties of psychoanalysis —

KRISTEVA'S THEORY OF embodied subjectivity as discursive positioning has distinct advantages for theorizing mothering in resistance to individualism and the metaphysics of substance. But its psychoanalytic framework is problematic, as indicated by the relevance of Ruddick's critique of psychoanalysis to Kristeva's account of mothering. Kristeva's account of mothering also raises the question of whether a psychoanalytic approach to mothering can include an analysis of the material conditions, social arrangements, and ideological formations that over-determine both the experience of mothering and the representation of mothering. To address this question about psychoanalytic approaches to mothering, I focus in this chapter on Nancy Chodorow's *The Reproduction of Mothering: Psychoanalysis and the Sociology of Gender* (1978), one of the most influential accounts of mothering in U.S. feminist theory. Chodorow offers an explanation of the reproduction in women of the psychological capacities required by mothering and the desire to mother, as well as an account of the relationship of the reproduction of women's mothering and the material, social, and ideological circumstances of liberal democratic capitalism.

A close reading of *The Reproduction of Mothering* is a good way to consider further the risks of psychoanalysis for feminist analyses of mothering because Chodorow combines elements of three different versions of psychoanalysis in the theoretical framework she develops to explain women's mothering. She relies most explicitly on object relations theory, a version of psychoanalysis that focuses on pre-Oedipal development. But she also appeals to Gayle Rubin's concept of a sex/gender system (Rubin 1975), especially to explain the relationship of essential motherhood and the social structures and practices of liberal democratic capitalism. Rubin's analysis of the sex/gender system, however, is predicated on her interpretation of Lacan's account of the Oedipal complex as the process of positioning subjects in the kinship system that structures a society. So, by appealing to Rubin's analysis of the sex/gender system, Chodorow implicitly brings Lacanian psychoanalysis into her theoretical framework. Finally, Chodorow relies on traditional Freudian psychoanalysis for an explanation of women's heterosexuality, which is an important part of her explanation of women's mothering.

My reading of *The Reproduction of Mothering* emphasizes the contradictions that appear in Chodorow's account of mothering as a result of her attempt to combine different versions of psychoanalysis in her theoretical framework. I argue that, given this complex theoretical framework, Chodorow's account of mothering is susceptible to feminist theory's well-established critique of Freudian psychoanalysis for its complicity with essential motherhood, as well as to Ruddick's critique of Lacanian psychoanalysis for its problematic account of maternal subjectivity. In addition, I show that Chodorow's object relations theory recuperates significant elements of the individualist concept of subjectivity. These arguments indicate the persistence of the dilemma of difference in Chodorow's account of mothering. The interplay of identity and difference that results from feminism's conflicted relationship to individualism is evident in the theoretical framework of Chodorow's account of mothering and explains the contradictory conclusions about mothering that she draws. The persistence of the dilemma of difference in Chodorow's work supports my conclusions that psychoanalytic approaches to mothering include significant risks for feminist theory, and that psychoanalytic approaches alone are not sufficient for analyzing the material, social, and ideological over-determination of the experience and the representation of mothering.

Freud's theory of women's development can be read as a version of essential motherhood, and has been criticized in these terms by many feminist theorists in the United States. According to this reading, Freud argues that female embodiment determines women's psychic development in such a way that the completion of women's development, and women's experience of fulfillment, require mothering. More specifically, Freud's account of the girl's Oedipal complex yields his theory of penis envy, which says that women come to desire a child, especially a son, as substitute for the penis they do not have. From this perspective, women who do not want to be or do not enjoy being mothers are immature, maladjusted, or rebelling against femininity (Freud 1923, 1924, 1925, 1931). Feminist theory's critique of Freud's account of women's development particularly questions the role of teleology in traditional Freudian psychoanalysis. To what extent does Freud's theory of women's development conclude that women's development and fulfillment require mothering because it presupposes that women's mothering is required by human evolutionary development? I have argued that the teleological elements of Gilman's and Key's accounts of mothering subordinate the socialist elements of their arguments and their versions of feminism to individualism. The possibility of similar ideological effects of teleology in psychoanalytic accounts of mothering needs to be considered as well.

The question of the relationship of psychoanalysis, teleology, and essential motherhood is most directly relevant to traditional Freudian psychoanalysis. Ruddick's critique of psychoanalysis, however, is particularly relevant to Lacanian psychoanalysis, on which both Kristeva's account of mothering in "Stabat Mater" and Rubin's analysis of the sex/gender system rely. While Ruddick questions whether psychoanalysis represents the mother only from the child's perspective, I have shown that "Stabat Mater" also tends to represent the child from a particular maternal point of view. "Stabat Mater" figures both mother and child in terms of a desire for a guarantee of subjectivity and language and/or consolation for the lack of any such guarantee, and it not only represents this desire but to some extent enacts its satisfaction. Lacan's theory of subjectivity enables the resistance to individualism and the metaphysics of substance that feminist theory requires in order to theorize mothering, but it also risks the recuperation of essential motherhood in its tendency to problematize, if not deny, maternal subjectivity. A similar version of the dilemma of difference occurs in Chodorow's account of mothering. The Lacanian theory of subjectivity that Chodorow imports, via her appeal to Rubin's analysis of the sex/gender system, enables resistance to individualism and the metaphysics of substance. But Chodorow's object relations theory reconsolidates important elements of individualism, and her appeal to Freud for an explanation of women's heterosexuality recuperates an important element of essential motherhood. In Chodorow's case, the challenge offered by her account of mothering to the relationship of essential motherhood and liberal democratic capitalism is also undermined by this recuperation of elements of individualism and essential motherhood.

The inconsistencies that result from the combination of three versions of psychoanalysis in Chodorow's theoretical framework lead to three different contradictions in her account of mothering. Elements of her explanation of women's mothering contradict each other, the predictions she makes about the effects of shared parenting contradict each other, and elements of her explanation of women's mothering contradict some of the predictions she makes about the effects of shared parenting. I argue that the points in her argument at which Chodorow shifts from one version of psychoanalysis to another are ideological moments that attempt to mediate these contradictions. These ideological moments foreground the elements of Chodorow's theoretical framework that are most consistent with individualism, recuperate those elements of psychoanalysis that most strenuously resist essential motherhood, and contain those implications of her analysis of women's mothering that most seriously challenge the relationship of essential motherhood and liberal democratic capitalism.

The three versions of psychoanalysis at work in Chodorow's theoretical frame are at odds in two ways. First, the theory of the self presupposed by object relations theory is inconsistent with the Lacanian theory of subjectivity as discursive positioning presupposed by Rubin's analysis of the sex/gender system. Object relations theory argues that the self or the personal ego is established in the course of childhood social relations (Chodorow 1978: 48–54). In the context of these social relations, the self originates in "an inner physical experience of body integrity and a more internal 'core of the self'" and "through demarcation from the object world." These experiences lead to "ego boundaries (a sense of personal psychological division from the rest of the world) and a bounded ego (a sense of the permanence of physical separateness and of the predictable boundedness of the body)" (1978: 67–68). As a function of its earliest social relations, the infant experiences processes of identification, internalization, and introjection that establish "the continuity and core of self" (1978: 71). Object relations theory recognizes the role of unconscious processes in the formation of the self, and the persistence of unconscious psychic structures, processes, and motives in adulthood, but it emphasizes the stability and coherence of the core self. In this respect object relations theory's concept of the self is consistent with the individualist view of subjectivity as a stable and coherent identity, experienced as internal to and motivating of the subject.

Lacanian psychoanalysis, however, understands subjectivity as fundamentally divided, partial, and unstable. Because positions in the symbolic are arbitrarily fixed and therefore inherently unstable, because subjectivity begins in the experience of lack and is founded in the gap between signified and signifier, and because in the Oedipal complex desire is repressed but not obliterated, subjectivity is divided, unstable, and fragmented. Subjects' desires for unity, stability, integrity, and coherence are always undone by the unconscious and by desire. As Kristeva represents it, every "saying I" unsettles and destabilizes rather than unifies and stabilizes the subject of enunciation. In comparison to Lacanian psychoanalysis, object relations theory sees subjectivity as socially constructed but not as discursively constituted. According to Lacan, the stability and coherence of the self suggested by terms like 'integrity', 'continuity', and 'identity' as they occur in object relations theory and in the discourse of individualism and the metaphysics of substance are a fantasy.

Chodorow's object relations theory and Lacanian psychoanalysis also differ significantly with respect to the Oedipal complex. Object relations theory deemphasizes the importance of the Oedipal complex, especially the significance of castration, arguing that the Oedipal period is a stage in the development of the self that begins in the pre-Oedipal and includes the development of gender and sexuality. As a result, Chodorow's object relations theory represents the establishment of gender and sexual identity as begun pre-Oedipally. In Lacanian psychoanalysis, however, the Oedipal complex is the locus of both the discursive constitution of subjectivity as an unstable position in the symbolic, and the positioning of the subject in reference to the phallus and thus within the terms of sexual difference, and castration is crucial to both. For the child's recognition of the mother's castration provokes its placement in relationship to the phallus, and thus its entry into the symbolic. In Lacanian psychoanalysis, the constitution of gender and sexuality is completely intertwined with the constitution of subjectivity, and so, like subjectivity, gender and sexuality are partial, unstable, and fragmentary.

Chodorow attempts to combine object relations theory and Rubin's analysis of the sex/gender system to produce a framework for an account of women's mothering, but she does not address the contradictory account of the self, the Oedipal complex, and castration implicit in such a framework. As a result, Chodorow's theoretical frame produces contradictory conclusions about the possibility and the effects of reconstructing gender and sexuality, and about the effects of shared parenting. These contradictions are mediated in several ideological moments in Chodorow's analysis of women's mothering, ideological moments that recuperate the individualist elements of object relations theory's concept of the self. This recuperation largely rules out the conclusions about reconstructing gender and sexuality and about the effects of shared parenting that follow from Rubin's analysis of the sex/gender system. In this way Chodorow's argument for shared parenting also recuperates the heterosexual, nuclear family, and precludes the possibility that shared parenting will bring about significant changes in individual development or social structures.

The second contradiction implicit in Chodorow's theoretical framework is the inconsistency of the explanation of women's heterosexuality that follows from Rubin's analysis of the sex/gender system and Freud's explanation of women's heterosexuality. Rubin, like Lacan, argues that the constitution of subjectivity, gender, and sexuality are thoroughly intertwined and mutually over-determinative, and that subjectivity, gender, and sexuality are partial, divided, and unstable. According to Chodorow, however, traditional Freudian psychoanalysis not only argues that the constitution of subjectivity, gender, and sexuality are thoroughly intertwined. It also argues that, normally, gender and sexuality are completely, coherently, and more or less permanently established in the Oedipal complex. Chodorow argues that her appeal to Freud for an account of women's heterosexuality divests Freud's explanation of its teleological foundations. I argue, however, that teleological elements of Freud's account of gender and sexuality persist in Chodorow's explanation of women's heterosexuality. The persistence of teleology in Chodorow's explanation of women's heterosexuality obscures the extent to which this explanation of women's heterosexuality is at odds with that which follows from Rubin's analysis of the sex/gender system. Chodorow's attempt to bring Rubin's analysis of the sex/gender system together with Freud's explanation of women's heterosexuality produces contradictory conclusions about feminine and maternal heterosexuality. Chodorow's explanation of women's mothering challenges essential motherhood and its relationship to the social structures and practices of liberal democratic capitalism to some extent by denaturalizing women's mothering. But it also naturalizes mothers' heterosexuality, and thereby recuperates an important element of essential motherhood.

My consideration of the varieties of psychoanalysis that intersect in Chodorow's account of mothering further supports my view that psychoanalytic approaches to mothering include significant risks for feminist theory. Psychoanalysis risks the recuperation of essential motherhood and problematizes maternal subjectivity in several ways. At the same time, psychoanalysis does not necessarily resist individualism and the metaphysics of substance, and the version of psychoanalysis that does most strenuously resist individualism and the metaphysics of substance—Lacanian psychoanalysis—is also the version that most seriously problematizes maternal subjectivity. For these reasons, feminist theory, especially feminist analyses of mothering, must consider the advantages of psychoanalysis in relationship to these risks. This means that feminist theory must also ask what alternative approaches to mothering enable it to move beyond the mother-child relation, as psychoanalysis represents it, and consider the material, social, and ideological consequences that overdetermine both women's experiences of mothering and feminist theory's representation of mothering.

— nancy chodorow: the reproduction of mothering —

Chodorow's account of mothering begins by asking why it is that women mother. Why does the development of gender, at least in modern, Western, industrialized societies, result in women acquiring the psychological and emotional capacities needed to care adequately for infants and children as well as the desire to do so? Chodorow rejects several answers offered by feminist theory, such as social learning, cognitive developmental, and power differential theories. None of these can adequately explain women's mothering because mothering is not merely a set of behaviors or activities that someone can be trained or forced to perform. Mothering is "participation in an interpersonal, diffuse, affective relationship." It is "eminently a psychological role in a way that many other roles and activities are not" and "requires certain relational capacities which are embedded in personality and a sense of self-in-relationship." While other factors might contribute to women's mothering, none of them can lead or compel a woman to engage in a maternal relationship with an infant or child "unless she, *to some degree* and *on some unconscious or conscious level*, has the capacity and sense of self as maternal to do so" (1978: 33, Chodorow's emphasis).

Chodorow develops the complex theoretical framework I have described in order to explain the deep-seated and tenacious quality of the development of this capacity and sense of self in women. According to Chodorow, the persistence of women's mothering is a function of "social structurally induced psychological processes" (1978: 7). To explain these psychological processes, Chodorow follows object relations theory in focusing on the pre-Oedipal period, and theorizing the Oedipal complex in terms of the pre-Oedipal. According to object relations theory, identity development begins with the infant's pre-Oedipal experience of separation and individuation from its mother. The initial relationship of infant and mother is symbiotic from the infant's point of view; the infant experiences itself as fused with the mother, and does not recognize her separate existence as the source of its care and comfort. The mother's appropriate and reliable care of the infant enables it to experience frustration and dissatisfaction without overwhelming anxiety when its needs are not immediately met. This initiates the development of the infant's psychic sense of separateness from the mother on the basis of its sense of separate embodiment. The infant internalizes aspects of its primary care, which become the foundation for its ego. These experiences of infancy influence subsequent personality development and social relations, especially the infant's Oedipal experience.

Chodorow argues that, given the sex-based division of labor in which women rear children and fathers are physically absent from the family, the experiences of the pre-Oedipal period and the Oedipal complex are different for boys and girls. The gender difference of mother and son fosters the son's separation and differentiation from the mother and movement into the Oedipal period. The gender similarity of the daughter and the mother, on the other hand, fosters the continuation of their primary identification, which then persists into the Oedipal period. A boy's gender identity development is shaped by a preoccupation, established in the pre-Oedipal period, with resisting what is perceived as maternal omnipotence, establishing ego boundaries, and asserting a masculine sense of self. A girl's gender identity development, however, is shaped less by a need to differentiate herself from her mother and more by a concern with maintaining continuity in relationships and with establishing a sense of self in relation to others.

These differences in the pre-Oedipal mother-son and mother-daughter relationships determine children's and mothers' experiences of the Oedipal complex. The gender difference of mother and son fosters the mother's sexualized cathexis of the son, which moves the son out of the pre-Oedipal period earlier than the daughter and into an "oedipally toned relationship defined by its sexuality and gender distinction" (1978: 107). The Oedipal repression of the son's desire for the mother furthers the masculine gender identity development begun pre-Oedipally. Boys then pass through the Oedipal period without a specific, concrete male parent with whom to identify. So masculinity comes to be based on the repudiation of femininity, associated with the mother, and on a positional identification with an abstract understanding of masculinity as a result of the absence of the father. The gender sameness of mother and daughter, however, fosters the mother's continued narcissistic identification with the daughter, so that primary identification of mother and daughter is more intense and longer lasting. A girl's pre-Oedipal gender identity development is less influenced by a need to distinguish herself from her mother. Her subsequent experience of the Oedipal complex involves a concrete, personal, affective identification with her mother, so femininity comes to be characterized by a sense of self in relation and a capacity for empathy.

These gender differences in mother-son and mother-daughter relationships have significant effects on adult gender identity, especially on the development of the capacities required for child rearing. In comparison to women, men develop a more emphatic individuation, a greater capacity for autonomy, and a weaker capacity for empathy and intimacy. Given the lack of a concrete, personal, affective identification with the father, masculinity in men is less tightly secured than is femininity in women, so men feel a stronger need to assert a masculine identity. In comparison to men, women develop a sense of self as less differentiated and more continuous with others, a greater capacity for empathy and intimacy, and a weaker capacity for autonomy. A girl's separation from her mother is less complete than a boy's, so it is more likely that issues unresolved in the early mother-daughter relationship persist into the daughter's adulthood and affect her subsequent social relations. These effects of gender differences in the mother-son and mother-daughter relationships on adult development also explain women's mothering. The capacities that women are likely to develop and that men are likely to lack as a result of their different pre-Oedipal and Oedipal experiences are the same capacities for empathy and identification that nurturing requires. In addition, a woman is more likely than a man to desire to reexperience the mother-child relationship with a child of her own, given the persistence in her psyche of needs and desires unresolved in her relationship with her mother.

Chodorow further argues that women's mothering reproduces not only itself but also gender inequality and male dominance. By reproducing in girls the capacities and desires that lead them to become mothers, women's mothering reproduces the restriction of women to the private sphere of home and family and women's economic dependence on men. By reproducing men whose personalities make them unsuited to and uninterested in child rearing, and by relieving them of responsibility for it, women's mothering perpetuates male control of public resources and institutions, as well as men's control of the individual women and children who are economically dependent on them. Women's mothering also perpetuates male fears of women's omnipotence, and men's need to define themselves in opposition to the maternal and the feminine, which also contribute to male dominance and control of women. These outcomes of women's mothering thus sustain the defining features of the sex-based division of labor, as it occurs in modern forms of liberal democratic capitalism. These include the physical separation of workplace and home, which requires the presence of men in the workplace and women in the home, and the bureaucratic hierarchical organization of work and the competitive structures of capitalist market systems, which require and reward in men personality characteristics, such as aggressiveness and competitiveness, that are at odds with the demands of child rearing.

Chodorow argues that object relations theory, like Freudian psychoanalysis, takes for granted women's mothering, and so concludes that the effects of women's mothering on subjectivity and social structures are natural and inevitable. But she challenges this assumption by appealing to Rubin's argument that in modern societies, women's mothering is a function of the sex-based division of labor, which, when it is taken up by industrial capitalism, leads to the assignment of child rearing to women in the private sphere, and the absence of fathers from the family. Under these circumstances identity development in boy and girl children follows the different paths and has the different results that object relations theory predicts. But, Chodorow argues, these circumstances are not natural or inevitable, so neither are the gender differences they produce. Alternative child rearing arrangements would alter gender identity development. As Chodorow interprets it, then, Rubin's analysis of the sex/gender system "demonstrates that women's mothering is a central and defining feature of the social organization of gender and is implicated in the construction and reproduction of male dominance itself" (1978: 9).

— gayle rubin: gender and sexuality in the sex/gender system —

Rubin's analysis of the sex/gender system is part of her theory of women's oppression, which has two major components—an account of kinship systems based on the work of Levi-Strauss, and an account of the discursive constitution of subjectivity required for kinship systems to operate based on Lacanian psychoanalysis. Following Levi-Strauss, Rubin argues that in every human society some form of kinship system operates so as to structure social interaction and in this way organize the society itself. The operation of kinship systems can be understood in terms of the logic of the gift and the incest taboo. Marriage is a form of gift exchange in which women are exchanged among men, and the exchange of women establishes a kinship relation among those who participate in the exchange. Given the ordering function of kinship systems, the exchange of women is required for the perpetuation of a group's social structure. The need for the continued exchange of women explains the incest taboo, some form of which can be found in every society, but whose specific injunctions vary greatly. The incest taboo organizes all members of a society into two groups, those who may marry each other and those who may not, in order to ensure marriage, which forges social bonds among the men of those groups. The incest taboo "imposes the social aim of exogamy and alliance upon the biological events of sex and procreation" (1975: 173).

In addition to the incest taboo, kinship systems rely on a sex-based division of labor, which ensures marriage by ensuring that the smallest viable productive unit in a society consists of one man and one woman (1975: 178). Rubin's analysis of kinship systems, the incest taboo, and the sex-based division of labor indicates that "the social organization of sex rests upon gender, obligatory heterosexuality and the constraint of female sexuality" (1975: 179). The incest taboo and the sex-based division of labor themselves require two prior taboos, a taboo against the sameness of men and women and a taboo against homosexuality. The prohibition of the sameness of men and women, or the requirement of gender differences, perpetuates the sex-based division of labor by ensuring that men and women acquire different skills and become proficient at different activities. The requirement of gender differences ensures that men and women must marry in order to create sustainable productive social units, or families. Furthermore, since it not only prohibits some heterosexual unions but also requires that men and women unite in socially sanctioned marriages, the incest taboo presupposes a prohibition of all nonheterosexual unions. Thus, "Gender is not only an identification with one sex; it entails that sexual desire be directed toward the other sex" (1975: 180).

Rubin's account of these conditions for the operation of kinship systems raises the question of how kinship systems reproduce themselves. What prepares subjects to take up their position in the kinship system and fulfill the roles and functions it assigns to them? How do kinship systems produce gendered, heterosexual individuals who are predisposed to marry? To answer this question, Rubin appeals to Lacanian psychoanalysis. She reads Lacan's account of the discursive constitution of subjectivity through the installation of the subject in the symbolic as an account of the positioning of subjects in a kinship system. She develops a Lacanian interpretation of kinship systems as sign systems that denote statuses and relationships, thereby creating subject positions. Rubin thus theorizes subjectivity as the taking up of a position in a kinship system, and argues that Lacan's account of the Oedipal complex explains the structuring of the psyche that constitutes this positioning in a kinship system. For Rubin, "the Oedipal crisis occurs when a child learns of the sexual rules embedded in the terms for family and relatives . . . [it] begins when the child comprehends the system and his or her place in it; [it] is resolved when the

child accepts that place and accedes to it. . . . The Oedipal complex is an appa-
ratus for the production of sexual personality" (1975: 189).

In the Oedipal complex, children discover the significance of sexual difference and are confronted by the incest taboo, in the form of the prohibition of
their desire for the mother enforced by the paternal function. For the boy, the
threat of castration and the promise of the phallus induce him to repress his
desire for the mother so as to acquire the phallus, "the symbolic token that can
later be exchanged for a woman" (1975: 193). But the girl's encounter with the
incest taboo is coupled with her recognition of her castration. Thus, her repression of her desire for the mother includes her recognition of her position with
respect to the phallus. "Since the girl has no 'phallus,' she has no 'right' to love
her mother or another woman, since she herself is destined to some man"
(1975: 193–94). Accepting this destiny means accepting her position in the
kinship system as token to be exchanged, and coming to want the substitutes
for the phallus—the male sexual partner and the baby/son—that this position
offers. The internalization of the incest taboo is not merely the repression of
the child's desire for its mother; it is also the child's acceptance of its position
in a kinship system, including the orientation of its sexual desire toward those
deemed acceptable marriage partners by that kinship system.

According to Rubin's argument, then, the oppression of women is a function
of women's disempowered position as object of exchange in kinship systems.
Women are prepared to occupy this position by the constitution of their subjectivity in terms of femininity and heterosexuality and the repression of their
other sexual possibilities in the Oedipal period. Human cultures throughout
history have been organized in terms of kinship structures predicated on the
exchange of women, and such a sex/gender system persists in modern societies
even though other institutions have taken over the organizing function of kinship systems. So in modern societies, the sex-based division of labor, the incest
taboo, the taboo against the sameness of men and women, and the taboo
against homosexuality all persist, and exclusively female mothering and the
Oedipal complex endure as primary components of child rearing and the constitution of subjectivity. Rubin's explanation of women's oppression in modern
societies leads to two conclusions. Ending women's oppression requires reorganizing the sex/gender system, and reorganizing the sex/gender system will have
significant effects on all stages of individual development and on all other
aspects of culture and society.

Reorganization of the sex/gender system will have effects not only on gender
but also on sexual desire, for the sex/gender system's organization of gender is

dependent on its organization of sexual desire. While Rubin argues that "human sexual life will always be subject to convention and human intervention" and "the wild profusion of infantile sexuality will always be tamed" (1975: 199), she also insists that the sex/gender system that currently determines gender and sexuality can and must be consciously reorganized in order to liberate women. This means the end of gender, in the sense of socially obligatory feelings, behaviors, roles, and social positions for each sex. It also means the end of heterosexuality, in the sense of a structuring of sexual desire consistent with socially obligatory choice of a member of the opposite sex as a sexual partner. Rubin argues that "if the sexual division of labor were such that adults of both sexes cared for children equally, primary object choice would be bisexual" (1975: 199). By "bisexual" she means consistent with the labile, polymorphous eroticism, "the full range of libidinal attitudes, active and passive," characteristic of pre-Oedipal children (1975: 186). She also argues that "if heterosexuality were not obligatory, this early love [of the girl for the mother] would not have to be suppressed and the penis would not be overvalued." Finally, if the sex/gender system did not include men's property rights in women, that is, if there were no exchange of women, then "the entire Oedipal drama would be a relic" (1975: 199). Rubin concludes that "ultimately, a thorough-going feminist revolution would liberate . . . forms of sexual expression, and . . . liberate human personality from the straightjacket of gender" and that "the feminist movement must . . . dream of the elimination of obligatory sexualities and sex roles" (1975: 199–200, 204). Rubin envisions "an androgynous and genderless (though not sexless) society, in which one's sexual anatomy is irrelevant to who one is, what one does, and with whom one makes love" (1975: 204).

Chodorow's claim that child rearing can and should be reorganized follows from Rubin's analysis of the sex/gender system, in that Rubin explains how this system evolves historically. Appealing to the historicity of the sex/gender system allows Chodorow to identify two contradictions produced by the intersection of the sex-based division of labor and the social structures and practices of liberal democratic capitalism. These are the formation of masculine and feminine personalities whose emotional and psychological needs and interests are at odds with each other, and the changes in the family brought about by capitalism's recent demand for women in the paid workforce. Chodorow argues that these contradictions are currently making men and women increasingly dissatisfied with traditional gender roles and threatening the current arrangement of child rearing as women's responsibility. So feminism should confront these contradictions directly and use them as a basis for conscious intervention in the ongoing evolution of the sex/gender system. This leads her to the conclusion that "any strategy for change whose goal includes liberation from the constraints of an unequal social organization of gender must take account of the need for a fundamental reorganization of parenting, so that primary parenting is shared between men and women" (1978: 215).

— shared parenting, gender, and sexuality —

When Chodorow's version of object relations theory is considered in light of her appeal to Rubin's analysis of the sex/gender system, the implications of her explanation of women's mothering are ambiguous. Chodorow's appeal to Rubin's work imports its Lacanian presuppositions into her explanation of women's mothering. But Chodorow's commitment to object relations theory is at odds with a Lacanian theory of subjectivity as partial, divided, and unstable as a function of the nature of language, the unconscious, and desire. To the extent that Chodorow's explanation of women's mothering retains object relations theory's concept of the core self or personal ego, it represents gender and sexuality as coherent and stable attributes of the self. The ambiguity of Chodorow's conclusions about the effects of shared parenting for subjectivity and for social structures is the result of this tension between inconsistent theories of gender, sexuality, and subjectivity. Despite the contradictory aspects of Chodorow's predictions about these effects, however, her most explicit conclusion is that the social reorganization of child rearing will have relatively insignificant effects on subjectivity and social structures. This conclusion is not consistent with Chodorow's argument that the current social organization of mothering is crucially significant for the development of masculine and feminine personality. But this conclusion is consistent with object relations theory's concept of the self as a stable and coherent core of the self that is not fundamentally affected by its social contexts. Since its theory of the self is the element of object relations theory most consistent with individualism, I see Chodorow's predictions about the effects of shared parenting as the result of an ideological slippage between the Lacanian presuppositions of Rubin's work and object relations theory. In this ideological moment, Chodorow's explanation of women's mothering recuperates significant elements of individualism and repudiates those of its implications that most seriously challenge sexism and the oppression of women.

Since the primary goal of *The Reproduction of Mothering* is to explain the persistence of women's mothering, it is not surprising that Chodorow concludes with a call for shared parenting but does not go into much detail about it. The few comments she does make about shared parenting, however, are not consistent. These inconsistencies concern the effects of shared parenting on gender and sexual identity. On one hand, Chodorow suggests that shared parenting will reshape gender, but not eliminate gender as an element of identity. About the effects of shared parenting on sexuality, she says only that it will make sexual choices "more flexible, less desperate." She writes that "equal parenting would leave people of both genders with the positive capacities each has, but without the destructive extremes these currently tend toward" (1978: 218). Femininity would come to include a greater capacity for autonomy while retaining the capacities for nurturance, empathy, and love. Masculinity would come to include the capacities for nurturance, empathy, and love while retaining a capacity for autonomy based on differentiation, but this differentiation would be less defensive and reactive. And, although Chodorow does not say this explicitly, it is presumably these reshaped gender identities that make sexual choices more flexible and less desperate. If gender identities become more similar, then men's and women's needs and interests with respect to sexual relationships, love, and emotional commitment become more closely aligned. This reconstruction, rather than elimination, of gender seems to be what Chodorow has in mind when she asserts that "equal parenting would not threaten anyone's primary sense of gendered self" (1978: 218). While it is not clear how this reconstruction of gender manages to include only the positive aspects of traditional gender identities, Chodorow is confident that these reconstructed gender identities would be an improvement over the gender identities produced by women's mothering.

On the other hand, Chodorow says that "we do not know what this [gendered] self would be like in a nonsexist society." This conclusion is also implicit in her claim that if children experience close connection and identification with caretakers of both genders, they will "establish an individuated sense of self in relation to both." This would produce a child able to "choose those activities he or she desired, without feeling that such choices jeopardized their gender identity" (1978: 218). In relationship to caretakers of both genders, a child could internalize any combination of capacities and characteristics in the formation of his or her subjectivity, which implies radical change with respect to gender. If all sorts of combinations of capacities and characteristics are possible for persons, regardless of their sex, then it would be meaningless to distinguish persons in terms of the gender binary of masculine and feminine. The image of the choice of activities freed from the constraints of gender furthers this impression; it suggests persons choosing such varied combinations of activities that it would be meaningless to distinguish among the activities, or the persons, in terms of binary gender categories. In other words, if shared parenting would lead to identities based on capacities, characteristics, desires, and choices of activities that have little or no relationship to one's being male or female, then these cannot be gender identities. For according to Chodorow's object relations theory, 'gender' is the development of certain capacities, characteristics, desires, and choices on the basis of sex, for example, femininity's including a capacity for empathic identification and a desire to mother. In these claims about shared parenting, then, Chodorow suggests both that shared parenting will lead to minimal reshaping of gender identities, and that it will lead to change with respect to gender so significant that the binary distinction of masculine and feminine would be practically meaningless.

Chodorow also makes inconsistent suggestions about the effects of shared parenting on sexuality. Her comment that shared parenting would make sexual choices more flexible and less desperate is vague, but implies that shared parenting would have minimal effects on sexuality. In a comment about the different role of the father who is equally involved in parenting, however, Chodorow implies that significant change with respect to sexuality would result from shared parenting. She writes:

> Most commentators claim that children should spend some time with men. . . . Because they are concerned with children's adoption of appropriate gender roles, they assume a different role for the father. Fathers must be primarily masculine role models for boys, and heterosexual objects for girls, because traditional gender roles and sexual orientation are necessary and desirable. These roles have been functional, but for a sex/gender system founded on sexual inequality, and not for social survival or free human activity. (1978: 217–18)

This comment implies that not only traditional gender roles, but also traditional sexual orientation, would not persist, because they would not be functional, if shared parenting were established and the sex/gender system were reorganized to do away with inequality based on sex. Thus, in her discussion of the effects of shared parenting, Chodorow's few comments about the effects of shared parenting on sexuality also have contradictory implications.

Furthermore, to the extent that Chodorow says that shared parenting would have minimal effects, she contradicts the implications of her appeal to Rubin's analysis of the sex/gender system and of her own analysis of the role of women's mothering in perpetuating the social structures and practices of liberal democratic capitalism. Rubin's analysis of the sex/gender system presupposes that psychological processes of individual development are over-determined by the social and cultural contexts in which they occur. Rubin clearly recognizes the significance of women's mothering in her argument that the constitution of the child's gender and sexuality and its positioning in the kinship system are determined by the different cultural responses to boy and girl children's primary attachment to the mother. But for Rubin the significance of women's mothering goes beyond its effects on individual development, because the constitution of gender and sexuality are ultimately effects of the entire sex/gender system that sustains kinship. Rubin argues that the dominant sex/gender system includes not only women's mothering but also the limitation of gender to two possibilities and the requirement of heterosexual marriage, and Chodorow acknowledges this (1978: 9–10). Rubin's argument concludes that shared parenting will eliminate gender and obligatory heterosexuality, and thus fundamentally change the social structures, such as the heterosexual family, that depend on them. Chodorow follows Rubin's line of thought in her own analysis of how women's mothering sustains gender inequality. But Chodorow does not draw the conclusions about changes with respect to gender, sexuality, and social structures brought about by shared parenting that follow from both Rubin's analysis of the sex/gender system and Chodorow's own analysis of the effects of women's mothering.

While Chodorow says that "a system of parenting in which both men and women are responsible would be a tremendous social advance" (1978: 219), she says nothing about how shared parenting would alter social structures, not even how it would affect the family. She mentions "more collective child rearing situations," but argues only that such situations show that children growing up without exclusive mothering develop different but not undesirable personalities, and that children are better off when they have access to love from more than one person (1978: 217). She does not argue explicitly that shared parenting will lead to more collective child rearing situations. But if women's mothering is a crucial component of the sex/gender system in determining women's restriction to the private sphere, women's economic dependence on men, men's dominance over women and children, and men's control of social, economic, and political resources and institutions, then the reorganization of child rearing should have significant effects on all of these other social practices and structures. Chodorow's avoidance of this conclusion is not consistent with her appeal to Rubin's account of the sex/gender system. But it is consistent with the individualist aspects of object relations theory's concept of the self, which deemphasize the role of social structures and practices in determining subjectivity.

The contradictions I have identified in Chodorow's predictions about the effects of shared parenting raise a further question. Chodorow's reliance on

Rubin's analysis of the sex/gender system raises the expectation that Chodorow, like Rubin, will see shared parenting as undoing both gender and obligatory heterosexuality. So how is Chodorow able to argue, to the extent that she does, that shared parenting will reshape gender identities but minimally affect sexuality? How does Chodorow explain sexual identity, and what are the effects of this explanation on her conclusions about shared parenting? Answering these questions requires a closer analysis of Chodorow's explanation of women's heterosexuality.

— the reproduction of heterosexuality —

Chodorow argues that women's heterosexuality, like women's mothering, is not natural and inevitable, but is the result of socially induced psychological processes. To make this argument, Chodorow appeals to the traditional Freudian account of women's heterosexuality. But, she says, she reinterprets it by divesting it of its functionalist teleological presuppositions that the proper outcomes of individual development are determined by reproductive roles, and any development not consistent with reproduction is a deviation or failure of development. Chodorow argues that this reinterpretation allows her to explain women's heterosexuality as the usual outcome of the girl's Oedipal experience without naturalizing heterosexuality. But it also requires that she assume the heterosexuality of the parents, most importantly, of the mother. Chodorow expresses some concern about making this assumption. At the conclusion of her discussion of pre-Oedipal gender differences, she writes in a footnote: "I must admit to fudging here about the contributory effect in all of this of a mother's sexual orientation—whether she is heterosexual or lesbian. Given a female gender identity she is 'the same as' her daughter and 'different from' her son, but part of what I am talking about also presumes a different kind of cathexis of daughter and son deriving from her heterosexuality" (1978: 110). Despite these misgivings, however, Chodorow relies on the assumption of the mother's heterosexuality, and it persists in her explanation of women's heterosexuality and in her brief discussion of shared parenting. One reason why Chodorow's discussion of shared parenting is unable to envision the undoing of obligatory heterosexuality is that her explanation of women's heterosexuality is unable to envision a lesbian mother. In this way Chodorow's explanation of women's heterosexuality recuperates maternal heterosexuality, a crucial element of essential motherhood.

The question of women's heterosexuality is especially pertinent to Chodorow's account of women's development. Having emphasized the strength and persistence of the daughter's pre-Oedipal attachment to her mother, how does Chodorow explain the reorientation of the girl's desire from the mother to the father and then to other men? Chodorow argues that this is not a matter of explaining the origins of women's heterosexuality, but rather of interpreting its meaning and significance. She says that she accepts the traditional psychoanalytic view that women's heterosexuality results from the girl's turn to her father in the Oedipal period. But she argues that the girl's turn to the father can be explained without the teleological functionalism of Freudian psychoanalysis. To theorize women's heterosexuality apart from a teleological frame, Chodorow invokes her object relations account of gender differences in the pre-Oedipal and Oedipal stages. Because gender identity is initiated pre-Oedipally, the Oedipal complex is not the origin of gender, but rather a phase in its further development. The repression of the desire for the mother provoked by the father is different for boy and girl children because each has already undergone a different experience of separation and individuation in relationship to the mother. The entry of the father into the inner object relational world of the child makes possible new relational patterns and cathectic identifications. But these possibilities are limited by the gender differentiation of the child that is already in progress. According to Chodorow, this means that the girl develops her relationship with her father "while looking back at her mother" (1978: 126). Her primary relationship with the mother persists longer and is never as thoroughly repressed as the boy's relationship with the mother, so the girl tends to maintain both of her parents as love objects, and as rivals, through the Oedipal period. As a result the girl's Oedipal experience includes a "bisexual" (1978: 138, 140, 168) oscillation between attachment to the mother and attachment to the father, and the feminine psyche acquires a triangular object relational structure.

Given her rejection of teleological functionalism, Chodorow requires an alternative explanation of what motivates the girl's turn to the father in the Oedipal period. She argues that several aspects of the social organization of child rearing based on women's mothering determine this development. In general, she states, parental behavior and sexual orientation are crucial for the child's sexual orientation, as psychoanalysis' clinical findings indicate to her: ". . . a reading of cases, and the theory derived from them, suggests that sexual orientation and definition is enforced and constructed by parents. Parents are usually heterosexual and sexualize their relationship to children of either gender accordingly . . . " (1978: 113). In the case of the girl, the intense and overwhelming quality (from the girl's point of view) of the mother-daughter pre-Oedipal bond also motivates the daughter's turn to her father. The girl has ambivalent feelings about her relationship with her mother; she needs and wants to maintain their bond, but also feels trapped and overwhelmed by it. As the most available person, probably the only other adult in the nuclear family, the father symbolizes freedom from the dependence and merging of her relationship with her mother. For Chodorow, "This view places the narcissistic desire for the penis on the proper metaphoric level" by explaining that "the girl's wish to liberate herself from her mother engenders penis envy" (1978: 123). In addition, Chodorow argues that a father responds to his daughter with "seductive behavior" that reinforces her heterosexual behavior, citing empirical evidence that fathers tend more than mothers to sex-type their children. The father elicits and rewards his daughter's feminine heterosexual behavior, and provides her with a relationship representing her sexual specificity and independence, an alternative to the overwhelming relationship with her mother.

According to Chodorow's reinterpretation of the girl's Oedipal complex, heterosexuality means something different for men and women. For women, "There is a developmental distinction between the genesis of genital heterosexual impulses (or decision to engage in heterosexual erotic relationships) and heterosexual love as a psychological and emotional phenomenon that involves varieties of commitment, fantasy, and experiences of the other person" (1978: 168). While most women become heterosexual in the sense of desiring genital sexual relations with men, heterosexuality understood as a relational potential for emotional commitment to and love of someone of the opposite sex is less firmly established in women than in men. Women experience not only a greater need for relationships of close connection, intimacy, and empathy—relationships that recreate elements of the primary bond with the mother—than men, but also a need to impose on adult relationships what Chodorow calls the "bisexual triangle" that structures their inner object world. Men are less likely to need or want relationships that recreate these characteristics of the mother-child bond, and any such needs they do have are more likely to be met in sexual relationships with women, because these relationships more closely approximate for them the primary bond with the mother than sexual relationships with men do for women. For these reasons male heterosexuality is more likely to include both erotic object choice and emotional commitment. But women "have different and more complex relational needs in which an exclusive relationship with a man is not enough . . . they are encouraged by both men's difficulties with love and by their own relational history with their mothers to look elsewhere for love and emotional gratification" (1978: 199, 200).

This explanation of women's heterosexuality then dovetails with Chodorow's explanation of women's mothering. She argues that sexist and oppressive social structures determine that women solve the psychological and emotional dilemma that heterosexuality is for them by becoming mothers. Women may seek close personal relationships with other women through continued involvement with female relatives and/or affectively rich friendships with other women. But the organization of work and living arrangements under industrial capitalism, such as the nuclear family, are obstacles to this. In addition, in male-dominant societies, men have greater freedom than women to initiate sexual relationships, and women's lack of opportunities for economic independence means that they must enter into a relationship with a man to ensure their survival and that of their children. These social factors impinge on the internal structure of the feminine psyche and thus ensure that women become mothers. Chodorow writes:

> Women come to want and need primary relationships to children. These wants and needs result from wanting intense primary relationships, which men tend not to provide both because of their place in women's oedipal constellation and because of their difficulties with intimacy. Women's desires for intense primary relationships tend not to be with other women, both because of internal and external taboos on homosexuality, and because of women's isolation from their primary female kin (especially mothers) and other women. (1978: 203–4)

Becoming a mother allows a woman to recreate elements of the primary relation with the mother in her relation to the child and to impose on her relationship with the father of her child the triangular structure that the feminine psyche requires.

In this account of women's heterosexuality, I see three distinct contradictions, each of which has important ideological effects. First, Chodorow's explanation of women's heterosexuality differs much more from Freud's than she acknowledges. This is suggested by Chodorow's contradictory description of her approach to the issue of women's heterosexuality. About her reliance on traditional psychoanalysis, she writes, "There is no question that heterosexual orientation is a major outcome of the oedipal period for most girls, and that the traditional psychoanalytic account of the development of female sexuality and the growth of the girl's relationship to her father describes this. There is some question, however, about how we should read this outcome" (1978: 112). To avoid reading women's heterosexuality teleologically, Chodorow says, she focuses on "the continuing significance of a girl's relation to her mother throughout the oedipal period." This means that "sexual orientation is in the background" of her explanation of women's Oedipal experience and post-Oedipal development (1978: 114). She concludes that "the main importance

of the oedipus complex . . . is not primarily in the development of gender identity and socially appropriate heterosexual genitality, but in the constitution of
different forms of 'relational potential' in people of different genders" (1978:
166). But with this shift of focus, Chodorow's account of women's heterosexuality also comes to differ significantly from the traditional psychoanalytic
account, according to which the Oedipal complex is precisely the locus of the
development of gender identity and heterosexuality. As Chodorow herself
points out, in the traditional psychoanalytic account, "femininity *means* genital heterosexuality" (1978: 111, Chodorow's emphasis).

   In comparison to Freud, Chodorow also deemphasizes the importance of
castration and penis envy in the development of women's heterosexuality.
Freud argues that the girl recognizes her castration and blames this on her
mother, believing that, because her mother is also castrated, her mother could
not give her a penis. The girl thus devalues and rejects her mother and turns to
her father in hope of acquiring a penis. When the girl's desire for the father is
not reciprocated, however, this desire is transformed into a desire for substitutes for the penis—the male sexual partner and the baby/son. Thus, for
Freud, the girl's recognition of her castration and her subsequent anger at and
denigration of her mother motivate the turn to the father (Freud 1925, 1931).
Chodorow assumes the heterosexuality of the mother and emphasizes the
importance of the father's heterosexuality in the girl's Oedipal experience,
thereby significantly reconfiguring the Oedipal triad. For Freud's image of the
girl angrily rejecting her mother, the mother dephallicized, and the father
enforcing the repression of the girl's desire for the mother, Chodorow substitutes the girl torn between merging with the mother and escaping to the father,
the mother rejecting the girl as an erotic object, and the father welcoming the
girl's heterosexual behavior in relation to him. Chodorow represents Freud as
arguing that the girl's turn to the father is also accomplished by the girl's
"rejection as a sexual object by her heterosexual mother" (1978: 157). But
Freud emphasizes much more the mother's castration, the girl's castration, the
girl's anger at her mother, and the father's enforcement of the repression of the
child's desire for the mother, than he emphasizes any feelings or actions of the
mother. It certainly can be argued that Freudian psychoanalysis naturalizes
male and female heterosexuality in other ways, and that Freud never successfully revised his theory of the Oedipal complex to accommodate his belated
recognition of the significance of the pre-Oedipal period for women's development. But as it stands Freud's account of the girl's Oedipal complex does not
require the heterosexuality of the mother to the same extent that Chodorow's
account does.[1]

Chodorow's emphasis on the mother's rejection of the daughter in her explanation of women's heterosexuality is also inconsistent with her emphasis on the
persistence and intensity of the primary mother-daughter bond. This inconsistency is obscured by her appeal to learning in her explanation of women's heterosexuality. Chodorow sees girl's learning, either by imitation, instruction, or
choice of activities based on a recognition of essential motherhood's equation of
femininity with mothering, as relatively insignificant in women's mothering.
But she emphasizes the role of learning in explaining how children come to
identify with their same-sex parent, the identification on which heterosexuality
depends. She writes: "Both in clinical examples and in theoretical formulations
this identification is clearly a learning phenomenon: Children learn their gender
and then identify with and are encouraged to identify with the appropriate parent" (1978: 113). In addition, Chodorow recognizes that the girl's turn to the
father and the father's "heterosexual seductive" response occur in social contexts where there is little segregation and antagonism between the sexes, and so
girls interact with men after infancy and early childhood. But since women's
heterosexuality also predominates in social contexts in which men and women
are almost completely segregated in daily activities and living arrangements
and/or in which a high degree of antagonism between men and women is the
norm, there must be other factors that determine women's heterosexuality. In
these contexts, Chodorow states, women's heterosexuality may also result from
"self-convincing and learning of the appropriate role" (1978: 168). Chodorow's
appeal to the concept of learning to support her explanation of women's heterosexuality is an ideological moment that attempts to mediate an inconsistency of
this explanation and her explanation of women's mothering. Chodorow's explanation of women's heterosexuality represents the mother as rejecting the
daughter, while her explanation of women's mothering figures the mother as
deeply and intensely attached to the daughter.

Finally, Chodorow's explanation of women's heterosexuality is inconsistent
with her reliance on Rubin's analysis of the sex/gender system. Chodorow's
deemphasis of the significance of castration is one way in which her explanation of women's heterosexuality is inconsistent with Rubin's account of
women's heterosexuality. This inconsistency is also indicated by Rubin's and
Chodorow's different interpretations of the incest taboo. According to Rubin,
the creation and continuation of kinship structures requires exogamous
exchange of women, this exchange of women requires the incest taboo, and
the incest taboo requires the taboo on homosexuality. The Oedipal complex is
the inscription of these social and cultural constraints on the psyche; it is
the process that constitutes subjectivity, and constitutes it as gendered and
heterosexual. According to Chodorow, however, the incest taboo explains "the

difference in modes of masculine and feminine oedipal resolution" and operates as a taboo on nuclear family incest (1978: 132; also 157, 207). Chodorow
argues that "given the organization of parenting, mother-son and mother-
daughter incest [or 'relationships . . . sufficiently emotionally and libidinally
involved to keep son or daughter from forming nonfamilial sexual relationships'] are the major threats to the formation of new families, and not equiva-
lently mother-son and *father*-daughter incest" (1978: 132, Chodorow's
emphasis). This means that "the oedipus complex, as it emerges from the
asymmetrical organization of parenting, secures a psychological taboo on
parent-child incest and pushes boys and girls in the direction of extrafamilial
heterosexual relationships" (1978: 207). This second conclusion, however, is
not warranted by her analysis of the incest taboo unless female heterosexuality
is assumed. Indeed, on the basis of Chodorow's account of the intensity and
persistence of the mother-daughter bond, her analysis of the incest taboo
implies that this taboo is just as likely, if not more so, to push daughters into
extrafamilial relationships with women.

In a similar ideological moment, Chodorow simultaneously recognizes and
denies the significance of bisexuality. In her explanation of women's heterosexuality in social contexts where men and women have little contact or antago-
nistic relations, Chodorow mentions that, in addition to learning, "(something
like) constitutional bisexuality" may play a role in women's heterosexuality
(1978: 168). Chodorow, however, does not explain how bisexuality contributes
to women's heterosexuality in these social contexts, and this suggestion is not
really consistent with or supportive of Chodorow's explanation of women's
heterosexuality. This possibility of bisexuality rather problematizes women's
heterosexuality. It suggests another factor, in addition to the quality of the pre-
Oedipal mother-daughter relationship and the social organization of relations
between men and women, that would lead to female homosexuality. In order
to avoid this conclusion, Chodorow would have to appeal to Rubin's analysis of
how the incest taboo, obligatory heterosexuality, and the exchange of women
together sustain social structures regardless of the specific quality of other
social relations between men and women. But Chodorow's reinterpretation of
the incest taboo rules this out. By locating the incest taboo as operating within
the Oedipal family as she represents it, Chodorow weakens the links between
the constitution of gender and the constitution of heterosexuality, and
between obligatory heterosexuality and the social structures of modern societies, that are central to Rubin's analysis of the sex/gender system.

My analysis of the inconsistency of Chodorow's account of women's heterosexuality and Rubin's analysis of the sex/gender system suggests the ideological
significance of a brief argument in which Chodorow tries to show that Rubin's

explanation of the Oedipal girl's turn to the father is consistent with her own. Having argued that a girl's desire to liberate herself from her relationship with her mother motivates her turn to her father, Chodorow considers an alternative view. She mentions that Rubin, as well as Alice Balint, Ruth Brunswick, and Jeanne Lampl-de Groot, suggest that "love for the mother, rather than, or in addition to, hostility towards her, leads directly to penis envy." Chodorow notes that Rubin specifically "reminds us that a mother's heterosexuality is not an inevitable given" and that Rubin argues that it is the (socially obligatory but not natural) heterosexuality of the mother that leads the girl to devalue her own genitals and to desire and envy the penis. Chodorow quotes Rubin's statement that "if the pre-Oedipal lesbian were not confronted by the heterosexuality of her mother, she might draw different conclusions about the status of her genitals." But Chodorow then incorporates this statement into "the view of Balint, et al. [that] a girl turns to her father in defense, feeling angry, like a rejected lover." Chodorow concludes that these accounts are consistent with her own in stressing "that the intensity and ambivalence of her feelings cause a girl's turning from her mother" (1978: 124–25). Chodorow's summary of this alternative view of the girl's turn to the father recuperates Rubin's image of the daughter confronting a lesbian mother by incorporating it into Chodorow's view of the daughter as rejected lover. Chodorow contains Rubin's challenge to the assumption of the heterosexuality of the mother by subsuming it within precisely the view of the Oedipal girl that Rubin challenges.[2]

The contradictory elements of Chodorow's explanation of women's heterosexuality and the ideological moments that attempt to mediate these contradictions have two important effects. First, Chodorow's distinction of "relational capacity" and "genital sexuality" in her explanation of women's heterosexuality contains the potential that Lacan, Kristeva, and Rubin attribute to sexuality to disrupt, destabilize, and fragment subjectivity. Chodorow's view of sexuality is thus more consistent with the individualist view of sexuality as an accidental attribute of subjectivity than with the Lacanian view of subjectivity and sexuality that Kristeva and Rubin adopt. Chodorow's view particularly domesticates female sexuality, suggesting that, even if men come to share parenting equally with women, women's genital sexuality will still be heterosexual. But this implies that heterosexuality will still present a psychological and emotional dilemma for women, and that women will continue to solve this dilemma by becoming mothers. This containment of the disruptive potential of sexuality supports the implications of Chodorow's argument that shared parenting will have little effect on family structure and on the social structures that maintain women's inequality and oppression.

Second, Chodorow's explanation of women's heterosexuality naturalizes maternal heterosexuality. Despite her intention to denaturalize women's heterosexuality by explaining it in Freudian terms without relying on the teleological functionalism of Freudian psychoanalysis, the assumption of maternal heterosexuality persists in Chodorow's account of women's development. Chodorow's theoretical detour from object relations theory to Freudian psychoanalysis and back again hints at the possibility of lesbianism, including lesbian mothering. But it ultimately denies the possibility of lesbian mothering by arguing that the mother sexually rejects the daughter ("the girl's rejection as a sexual object by her heterosexual mother"). This denial of the possibility of lesbian mothering explains Chodorow's inability to envision, as Rubin does, that shared parenting would undo obligatory heterosexuality. So, by naturalizing maternal heterosexuality, Chodorow's account of mothering reconsolidates a crucial element of essential motherhood. And this weakens the challenge to women's mothering and to the relationship of essential motherhood and the social structures and practices of liberal democratic capitalism that Chodorow means to offer by appealing to Rubin's analysis of the sex/gender system.

— mothering, feminism, and psychoanalysis —

Several conclusions about the risks of psychoanalysis follow from my readings of Kristeva's and Chodorow's accounts of mothering. First, theorizing mothering in psychoanalytic terms significantly risks the recuperation of elements of essential motherhood. This risk might be worth taking, if psychoanalysis thoroughly and consistently resisted individualism and the metaphysics of substance, and thus undermined essential motherhood in other ways. But psychoanalysis does not necessarily do so, as my analysis of the ideological effects of object relations theory in Chodorow's account of mothering indicates. Furthermore, the resistance to individualism that is enabled by psychoanalytic theories of subjectivity is inextricably bound up with the ways in which such theories problematize maternal subjectivity. In a paradox typical of the dilemma of difference, the version of psychoanalysis that most strenuously resists individualism and the metaphysics of substance—Lacanian psychoanalysis—also most seriously problematizes maternal subjectivity. These conclusions do not deny the value of a theory of embodied subjectivity as discursive positioning for theorizing mothering. But they do suggest that the reconceptualization of subjectivity alone is not sufficient for resisting essential motherhood. Thus, as I argued in evaluating Kristeva's account of mothering in light of Ruddick's critique of psychoanalysis, feminist analyses of mothering need to go beyond the mother-child relation and theorize mothering in terms of the over-determination of mothering and the mother-child relation by its material, social, and ideological contexts.

Psychoanalytic approaches to mothering risk essential motherhood in several ways. One of the most problematic is their tendency to naturalize maternal heterosexuality. Moreover, this tendency is not exclusive to psychoanalytic approaches to mothering; several of the other accounts of mothering I have considered preclude the possibility of lesbian mothering, even as they recognize the possibility of lesbianism. Key's account of mothering, for example, represents what she considers "natural spiritual Sapphism" as an immature and unsatisfying substitute for mothering. Elshtain's account of mothering represents lesbians as "childless by definition." Chodorow recognizes that mothers are not necessarily heterosexual, but nonetheless assumes maternal heterosexuality in her explanation of women's mothering. What is more typical of psychoanalytic accounts of mothering is their tendency to recognize the possibility of eroticism among women but to desexualize it by theorizing it in terms of the mother-daughter relationship, as Beauvoir, Kristeva, and Chodorow all do. Even Rubin partly frames the possibility of lesbian mothering in mother-daughter terms, in her image of "the pre-Oedipal lesbian . . . not confronted by the heterosexuality of her mother" (1975: 187).

The persistence of the denial of the possibility of lesbian mothering in feminist analyses of mothering suggests that the naturalization of maternal heterosexuality is a crucial and deeply embedded element of essential motherhood. To secure its equation of female embodiment, femininity, and mothering, essential motherhood insists not only that all women want to be mothers and are fulfilled and satisfied by mothering, but also that all women are heterosexual. This presupposition pathologizes lesbianism as a deviation from "normal" femininity in two distinct ways. Lesbians are deviant, not only in their desire for women, but also in their refusal or inability to participate in mothering. Rubin's account of how the sex/gender system constitutes sexuality, however, suggests an analysis of essential motherhood's naturalization of women's heterosexuality. According to Rubin, because the sex/gender system requires that men and women unite in pairs to reproduce and rear children, bodily differences in reproductive capacities, or sex, must become gender, and gender must include women's sexual desire for men and men's sexual desire for women. In other words, that sex becomes gender is predicated on desire becoming heterosexual.

Rubin's account of the sex/gender system thus shows that social constructivist theories of gender can be predicated on a view of heterosexuality as normative. An explanation of how sex becomes gender that does not take into account the constitution of sexuality leaves the normalizing presumption of heterosexuality in place. This presumption then contains the detachment of sex and gender that is otherwise implied in social constructivist theories of gender. It settles the instability of the body, sex, and gender in these theories of gender by determining the alignment of gender and the reproductive differences of sexed bodies. The presumption of normative heterosexuality thus functions as a grid or matrix of intelligibility through which the body, sex, and gender come into a coherent and stable relationship. This heterosexual matrix determines that the body is intelligible only if it has a stable and coherent sex that is expressed as a stable and coherent gender identity, and if this gender identity includes sexual desire oriented to the "opposite" sex (Butler 1990: 6–25, 38–43, 72–75). In other words, the apparently natural stability and coherence of the relationship of the body, sex, and gender is produced by the oppositional privileging of heterosexuality, which not only construes other possibilities for sexuality as deviant, but also makes lesbian mothering impossible.

Thus, it seems to me that feminist accounts of mothering that rely on social constructivist theories of gender without questioning their presumption of normative heterosexuality offer an insufficient challenge to essential motherhood. They may challenge the view that bodily sex determines women's mothering by arguing that gender is socially constructed rather than biologically determined. But if they do not challenge the linkage of gender and normative heterosexuality through which essential motherhood connects bodily sex and women's mothering, traces of this connection will persist in these accounts of mothering. The insufficient challenge to the linkage of gender and normative heterosexuality in Chodorow's account of mothering is largely a function of her explanation of women's heterosexuality based on traditional Freudian psychoanalysis. Freud's teleological functionalism persists in Chodorow's explanation of women's heterosexuality, supporting her assumption of maternal heterosexuality and undermining her attempt to denaturalize women's heterosexuality. This conclusion reinforces my view, developed in my analysis of Gilman's and Key's accounts of mothering, that teleology operates in complicity with essential motherhood. The teleological element of Chodorow's theoretical framework also supports the recuperation of the individualist concept of subjectivity that is effected by object relations theory. Object relations theory's concept of subjectivity as identity—a stable and coherent core self resulting from the internalization of aspects of infantile social relations—underwrites an account of gender and sexuality as stable and coherent attributes of subjectivity. This concept of subjectivity also minimizes the disruption or undoing of subjectivity by the unconscious and by desire. It thus minimizes aspects of a Lacanian theory of subjectivity that, I have argued, might otherwise undermine essential motherhood's equation of female embodiment, gender, heterosexuality, and women's mothering. Object relations theory's concept of the self also obscures the complex relationship of individual development and social structures, as is evident in my comparison of Chodorow's and Rubin's analyses of the relationship of women's mothering and women's inequality and oppression. When Chodorow brings together object relations theory and Rubin's analysis of the sex/gender system, the elements of object relations theory that are most consistent with individualism undermine Rubin's challenge to the relationship of essential motherhood and women's inequality and oppression.

The containment of the possibility of eroticism among women within the mother-daughter relationship also contributes to the risk of recuperating essential motherhood, especially maternal heterosexuality, that I have traced in Beauvoir's, Kristeva's, and Chodorow's accounts of mothering. Representing eroticism among women in terms of the daughter's desire for reunion with her mother, satisfied by her becoming a mother herself, figures women's desire as best and most appropriately satisfied by mothering, thus containing women's desire within the bounds of mothering. In Beauvoir's case, this explains her inability to theorize a liberation of women that includes both equality in relationships with men and a significant social reorganization of mothering. In the case of Kristeva's account of mothering, figuring relations among women in terms of the mother-daughter relation problematizes the possibility of mutuality and reciprocity among women by overemphasizing sameness among women. Kristeva's herethics calls for differentiation within sameness in relation to the other woman, but it also represents this possibility in terms of the mother-daughter relation. If the desire of/for the mother is also effective in the mother-daughter relation, however, then this desire is at least an obstacle to the differentiation within sameness required for a herethical relation to the other woman.

Unlike Kristeva's "Stabat Mater," Chodorow's account of mothering does not focus exclusively on the earliest stages of the mother-child relationship. Chodorow's theoretical framework more clearly recognizes the importance of material, social, and ideological contexts for mothering than does "Stabat Mater." But Chodorow's account of mothering cannot adequately analyze these contexts of mothering, because of the ways in which her theoretical framework also tends to recuperate elements of individualism and essential motherhood. I have argued that individualism precludes the analysis of the over-determination of subjectivity, experience, knowledge, and representation in terms of their contexts because it insists that subjects are fully constituted as subjects regardless of their experiences and contexts. This argument indicates that an analysis of the over-determination of mothering is better facilitated by a theory of subjectivity, including maternal subjectivity, as tentative and unstable discursive positioning that produces a partial, divided, and fragmented subjectivity. But such a theory of subjectivity is ruled out by the combination of object relations theory and Freudian psychoanalysis, which recuperates elements of individualism and essential motherhood, that frames Chodorow's account of mothering. This aspect of Chodorow's theoretical framework also undermines her challenge to the relationship of essential motherhood, women's oppression, and liberal democratic capitalism, and her argument for a social reorganization of mothering.

It is thus clear that psychoanalytic accounts of mothering do not avoid the dilemma of difference. The interplay of identity and difference characteristic of feminist theory's difference-based challenge to individualism is evident in the various psychoanalytic approaches deployed by Kristeva and Chodorow. Their analyses of mothering also encounter the paradoxes of embodiment, gender, and representation generated by feminist theory's conflicted relationship to individualism and the metaphysics of substance. My consideration of Kristeva's and Chodorow's accounts of mothering thus indicates that there is considerable merit to Ruddick's critique of psychoanalysis, especially its implication that feminist analyses of mothering must move beyond the narrow focus on the earliest stages of the mother-child relationship that is typical of psychoanalysis. Of the analyses of mothering that I have considered so far, Ruddick's account most explicitly recognizes the possibility of lesbian mothering, most strenuously resists theorizing maternal subjectivity in terms of the mother-daughter relation, and most clearly represents the child's growth into adulthood including the transformations of the mother-child relationship this entails. Is this a result of Ruddick's resistance to psychoanalysis? If so, what elements of the theoretical framework of Ruddick's accounts of mothering enable this resistance? Furthermore, does rejecting psychoanalytic approaches to mothering mean that feminist theory must also relinquish the elements of psychoanalysis that resist individualism by destabilizing subjectivity? Can these elements of psychoanalysis be preserved in an account of mothering that better avoids recuperating essential motherhood than psychoanalysis does? Or is there some other way for feminist theory to include a theory of subjectivity as divided, partial, and fragmented, and thus resist individualism, while also theorizing mothering?

Ruddick's account of birthgiving and natal reflection insists on analyzing mothering in terms of women's reports of their experiences of mothering. How might the concept of women's experience be deployed in feminist analyses of mothering that do not rely on psychoanalytic theories of subjectivity? Does foregrounding women's experiences allow the analysis of mothering to go beyond the early stages of the mother-child relationship and to consider the material, social, and ideological contexts of mothering? What account of subjectivity, including maternal subjectivity, does it enable? With these questions in mind, I turn in the next chapter to two accounts of mothering that rely on the concept of women's experiences to consider how they encounter and negotiate the dilemma of difference.

MOTHERING AND
WOMEN'S EXPERIENCE

the desires of feminist theory

— the concept of experience in feminist theory —

MY ANALYSIS OF Ruddick's use of the concept of narrative in her account of birthgiving led to a consideration of Kristeva's account of mothering in "Stabat Mater," including Kristeva's theory of the discursive constitution of embodied subjectivity. I have argued that, while Kristeva's theory of subjectivity has distinct advantages for theorizing mothering in resistance to individualism and the metaphysics of substance, its psychoanalytic frame is problematic for resisting essential motherhood. Considering Kristeva's and Chodorow's accounts of mothering together shows that psychoanalytic approaches to mothering risk the recuperation of essential motherhood in several ways. These include their tendencies to articulate and enact the satisfaction of the desire of/for the mother, to naturalize women's mothering and maternal heterosexuality in teleological functionalist terms, to represent mothers almost entirely from children's point of view, and to represent children primarily as infants and very young children. As Ruddick argues, these tendencies of psychoanalysis significantly problematize maternal subjectivity and misrepresent the mother-child relationship.

With these concerns about psychoanalysis in mind, I return in this chapter to the concept of women's experience that Ruddick also relies on in theorizing mothering. Does the concept of experience provide leverage against the problematic aspects of psychoanalysis that I have detailed? If so, does it also adequately negotiate the dilemma of difference? Does the concept of women's experience enable the resistance to both individualism and essential motherhood that feminist analyses of mothering require in an individualist ideological context? The concept of women's experience may have certain advantages for theorizing mothering. But, as I have argued in connection with Ruddick's account of mothering, the use of this concept can also include the tendency to take women's reports of their experiences at face value. This tendency overlooks the ideological over-determination of both women's experiences and women's reports of their experiences. The appeal to the concept of women's experience can also be accommodated by individualism. Experience can be understood as that which happens to and is reported by, but does not determine, individualist subjects. Relying on the concept of experience to theorize mothering is thus not necessarily a challenge to individualism; it may recuperate elements of individualism that are consistent with essential motherhood. So my consideration of the concept of experience in feminist accounts of mothering asks what analysis of the over-determination of experience allows the deployment of this concept in a way that resists individualism and essential motherhood.

Since mothering has been a primary site at which the dominant ideology, especially essential motherhood, impinges on women, the desire to rearticulate women's experiences of mothering apart from this ideological frame and the hope that this rearticulation will provide a basis for resistance to essential motherhood are both understandable. Furthermore, in comparison to psychoanalysis, an account of mothering based on women's reports of their experiences has certain advantages. As I have argued, a psychoanalytic approach to mothering entails the difficulties of its teleological functionalism, its naturalization of women's mothering and maternal heterosexuality, its overemphasis on infancy and early childhood, its representation of mothering primarily from the child's point of view, and its decontextualizing approach to mothering. An account of mothering that begins by documenting and interpreting women's experiences of mothering avoids many of these difficulties. It allows a greater recognition of complexity and ambivalence in mothering, since, unlike psychoanalysis, it does not presuppose a singular and universal motive for women's becoming mothers or a singular and universal response on the part of women to mothering. It also allows a broader focus on the multiple and overlapping contexts of mothering and on how these contexts over-determine women's experiences of mothering. An account of mothering that begins with women's experiences also facilitates the representation of mothering from a maternal perspective, thereby offering a more nuanced account of maternal subjectivity that recognizes the complexities of maternal subjectivity.

The concept of experience as it operates in accounts of mothering that purport to present women's experiences, however, can also be complicit with individualism and essential motherhood, though in different ways than is psychoanalysis. To show this, I juxtapose in this chapter two accounts of mothering that rely on the concept of experience. These are Adrienne Rich's *Of Woman Born: Motherhood as Experience and Institution* and Patricia Hill Collins's discussion of black women and mothering in *Black Feminist Thought: Knowledge, Consciousness and the Politics of Empowerment*. Rich's *Of Woman Born* provides a detailed analysis of the history of mothering, consistently focusing on "what it was like for women" (1976: xviii). On the basis of her analysis of mothering, Rich concludes that male control of women's reproduction and of women's mothering is the primary foundation of patriarchy. Collins's account of black women's mothering is part of a longer work that represents many different aspects of black women's experiences. Collins addresses in detail the question of how best to theorize black women's experiences and black women's knowledge in order to analyze and contribute to black feminist thought.

Rich's and Collins's accounts of mothering are similar in several important ways, and they share most of these similarities with Ruddick's account of maternal practice. Like Ruddick, Collins and Rich devote considerable attention to children. Both represent children as embodied subjects expressing a variety of needs and demands to which mothers respond in varied and complex ways. They see children as complex and changeable beings who provoke many different cognitive, emotional, bodily, erotic, psychological, and spiritual reactions—reactions that are often contradictory—on the part of mothers. For example, Rich writes about her own experience of mothering: " . . . having borne three sons, I found myself living at the deepest levels of passion and confusion, with three small bodies, soon three persons, whose care I often felt was eating away at my life, but whose beauty, humor, and physical affection were amazing to me" (1976: 192, see also 17). Neither Rich nor Collins focuses primarily or exclusively on infants and small children; both present children of a variety of ages, including adult children reflecting on their experiences of being mothered, and mothers of adult children reflecting on their experiences of mothering. By emphasizing how mothers respond to the needs and demands of children and how children and mothers change over the course of their relationship, Rich and Collins are able to theorize the variety and complexity of mothering from a maternal perspective, but without reifying children as passive objects of maternal thought and passive recipients of maternal care.

Collins and Rich are also like Ruddick in emphasizing the intellectual and cognitive elements of mothering. Both reject the idea that mothering is natural or instinctual, and detail the complex processes of problem solving and decision making that mothering entails, especially for mothers in oppressive circumstances. Rich in particular argues that the view of mothering as natural or instinctual is an element of the institution of motherhood that serves the interests of men and contributes to maintaining patriarchy (1976: 24). Both Rich and Collins recognize that the demands faced by women mothering in oppressive circumstances are major obstacles to mothers' self-development, self-expression, and creativity as mothers and in other fields of endeavor. But both also show that the experience of mothering can be a powerful impetus to mothers' self-development and expression (Rich 1976: 6–8, 84–86; Collins, 1991: 118, 137). Collins and Rich also share with Ruddick a contextualizing approach to theorizing mothering that recognizes differences in women's experiences of mothering. Rich focuses on the complex history of mothering, as well as the significance of social and cultural differences in determining women's experiences of mothering. Collins theorizes in detail the many and overlapping social and institutional contexts that determine black women's experiences of mothering. She analyzes racism, racial segregation, and socioeconomic deprivation on the basis of race, and explains their economic, social, political, and cultural effects on black women's experiences of mothering. She writes: "[t]he institution of Black motherhood consists of a series of constantly renegotiated relationships that African-American women experience with one another, Black children, with the larger African-American community, and with self" (1991: 118).

According to Collins, African-Americans traditionally place a high value on black women's mothering, but understand mothering to include many different ways of caring for and nurturing children beyond arrangements in which biological mothers care only for their own children with little involvement of others. African-Americans have devised a wide variety of family forms in which fathers, grandparents, aunts, and other kin play important roles in child rearing. African-Americans also recognize a long tradition of "othermothering" in which those who are able to contribute to the care of children do so for children in need of care, regardless of kinship. Othermothers may care for children to whom they gave birth and also care for other children, or they may be women who never gave birth but contribute to the care of children, who may or may not be kin. Othermothering can range from informal babysitting to taking complete care of children for a temporary period to informal adoptions in which children who are not kin by blood or marriage become part of their othermothers' families. Othermothering can also include children's relationships with and dependence on othermothers in addition to their birth mothers. In this way it can help to "defuse the emotional intensity" of the mother-child relationship, especially the relationship of bloodmothers and daughters (1991: 128). Othermothering in African-American communities is also an important way of socializing young girls for mothering. Othermothering can generate networks of care that attempt to include all children needing care, and these networks can lead to more expansive and more consciously organized activities of care and nurture, such as political activism on behalf of all black children in a community. In othermothering networks, black women can experience considerable empowerment and enhancement of their social status in their communities.

One of the most striking aspects of Collins's and Rich's accounts of mothering is the extent to which they represent the ambiguity, ambivalence, and contradictory aspects of mothering. Like Ruddick's argument for maternal practice, Rich's and Collins's accounts of mothering recognize the extent to which women's experiences of mothering include suffering, sorrow, frustration, restriction, fear, doubt, sacrifice, anger, failure, and violence, as well as joy, love, satisfaction, and accomplishment. For example, Collins details the ambivalence and complexity of mothering for black women, especially the dilemmas black mothers face in mothering black daughters. She argues that black mothers want to protect and shelter their daughters from racism and sexism, and sometimes this means teaching them to conform to the demands of racism and sexism so as to avoid their worst sanctions. But black mothers also want to teach their daughters to challenge racism and sexism, even though this puts their daughters at risk. Black mothers want to pass on to their daughters the knowledge they have acquired in the course of their lives, including their knowledge of how to deal with racism and sexism. But they also want to prepare their daughters to live very different lives, as they work and hope for a future for their daughters that does not include racism and sexism. Collins analyzes the oppressive material and social circumstances in which, to one extent or another, black women mother as one factor determining the ambiguities of black women's experiences of mothering. She also argues that certain tendencies within the African-American community, such as a tendency to valorize the strong, suffering, black mother, can make black women's mothering more difficult. But Collins also shows that black women's experiences of mothering can be a foundation for political activism and a source of power. Thus, Collins shows that "Black motherhood is fundamentally a contradictory institution" (1991: 133).

Rich's discussion of maternal violence is also a powerful analysis of the contradictions of mothering, especially when mothering is done in social contexts that assign mothers complete responsibility for child rearing while providing little or no support for mothers and children. She argues that the development of the modern, nuclear family leads to the expectation that each mother will care only and entirely for her biological children, usually in isolation from other families and from other members of her extended family. This means that mothers are continually subject to the incessant demands of children and are held entirely responsible for the outcomes of child rearing. Rich envisions women "in the solitary confinement of a life at home enclosed with young children, or in the struggle to mother while providing for them single-handedly, or in the conflict of weighing her own personhood against the dogma that says she is a mother, first, last, and always." She argues that "if we could look into their fantasies . . . daydreams . . . imaginary experiences, we would see the embodiment of rage, of the overcharged energy of love, of inventive desperation . . . the machinery of institutional violence wrenching away at the experience of motherhood" (1976: 285).

Perhaps even more so than Ruddick, Collins and Rich represent mothering as a site of contestation and struggle. Rich figures this struggle in terms of patriarchal control of women's bodies: "[t]he woman's body is the terrain on which patriarchy is erected" (1976: 38). Rich argues that there is a "central ambiguity at the heart of patriarchy," namely "the ideas of the sacredness of motherhood and the redemptive power of woman . . . contrasted with the degradation of women in the order created by men. . . . Patriarchal man created . . . a system which turned against woman her own organic nature . . . [but] even safely caged in a single aspect of her being—the maternal—she remains an object of mistrust, suspicion, misogyny . . . " (1976: 69, 116). Collins emphasizes the ways in which black women's mothering is a site of struggle between systems of oppression and the attempts of oppressed peoples to define and control the social institutions and practices central to their communities. She explicates the " . . . ongoing tension . . . between efforts to mold the institution of Black motherhood to benefit systems of race, gender, and class oppression and efforts by African-American women to define and value our own experiences with motherhood" (1991: 118). Rich and Collins both recognize that in liberal democratic capitalist contexts (and, Rich would argue, beyond this context) women's experiences of mothering are complexly related to all the other social practices and structures that characterize these contexts. And both detail how women and/or mothers and/or feminists resist these aspects of mothering and in this way resist the liberal democratic capitalist social practices and structures that the social organization of mothering supports (Rich 1976: 66–67, 292; Collins 1991: 122–23).

In these respects Rich's and Collins's accounts of mothering resist and challenge individualism and essential motherhood. Their recognition of the complex changeability of children and of mothers' varied responses to children resists the individualist view of social relations that privileges rational autonomy and self-determination based on the separation and opposition of self and other. Like Ruddick, Rich and Collins see the relationship of mother and child as a relationship in which the subjectivity of each is continually constituted and transformed in relation to the other. Like Ruddick, they emphasize that reciprocity and mutuality are central to social relations and suggest that autonomy and self-determination should be rearticulated in terms of reciprocity and mutuality. Their recognition of the varied contexts of mothering also resists individualism's decontextualizing approach to the relationship of subjectivity, social relations, and social contexts. Rich's and Collins's accounts of mothering are like Ruddick's in seeing that women's experiences of mothering are very much a function of the social relations, institutions, and contexts in which specific mothers and children are situated. In thus recognizing differences among mothers, Rich and Collins resist essential motherhood's implication that mothering is essentially the same experience for all mothers. In theorizing the ambivalence and contradictions of mothering, Collins and Rich challenge essential motherhood's view that mothering is always and entirely an experience of joy and satisfaction for mothers. Both Rich's analysis of women's forced mothering as an effect of male dominance and Collins's analysis of the social organization of black women's mothering to serve the ends of racism, sexism, and capitalism resist essential motherhood's romanticizing of mothering and help to denaturalize the social organization of women's mothering. They show that the social organization of mothering is not a function of women's reproductive embodiment, but rather of the reciprocal over-determination of the social organization of mothering, women's oppression, racism, and liberal democratic capitalist structures and social relations.

Collins's and Rich's accounts of mothering also attempt to resist mind/body dualism. Each does so in a different way, but neither is entirely successful in challenging this element of individualism and the metaphysics of substance. Rich implicitly rejects mind/body dualism and the binary logic typical of individualism (1976: 46–48). But throughout *Of Woman Born* her attempts to articulate women's experience of embodied subjectivity, particularly the experiences of pregnancy and birth, in terms other than mind/body dualism are recuperated by the binary logic and the individualist discourse she tries to resist. Collins explicitly rejects mind/body dualism and the biological determinism it supports, particularly in theorizing black women's experiences of sexuality and sexual politics. She also clearly rejects biological determinist analyses of race, whose logic resembles that of biological determinist accounts of women's subjectivity. And throughout *Black Feminist Thought* she argues for a "both/and conceptual stance." When this is deployed, for instance, in analyzing black women's sexuality, it "encompasses the both/and nature of human existence," including the both/and nature of embodied subjectivity, and thus recognizes "the potential for a sexuality that simultaneously oppresses and empowers" (1991: 225–26, 166). But Collins devotes little attention to black women's experiences of pregnancy and, like Beauvoir in her account of mothering, she says almost nothing about black women's experiences of birthgiving. By avoiding black women's experiences of pregnancy and birth, Collins avoids the risk of reconnecting female embodiment, gender, and mothering, thereby avoiding the recuperation of essential motherhood. But by not analyzing pregnancy and birth she also avoids, rather than addresses, what individualism sees as the difficulties of theorizing maternal subjectivity and the subjectivity of the child that are raised by pregnancy and birth. So she does not offer any clear alternative to individualism's claim that the mother and child do not meet the criteria for individualist subjectivity because in pregnancy and birth they are not separately and distinctly embodied.

Thus, while Rich's and Collins's accounts of mothering resist individualism and essential motherhood in several ways, elements of individualism, especially mind/body dualism, persist in the theoretical frameworks of their accounts of mothering. As I see it, this is a function of their use of the concept of experience, which has much in common with Ruddick's use of this concept in her analyses of mothering. Theorizing mothering in terms of the concept of women's experience involves what Joan Scott calls the project of documenting and interpreting women's experience, according to which women's experience serves as evidence for the claims of feminist theory. Scott's critique of this deployment of the concept of experience is an elaboration of Alice Jardine's argument for "the demise of experience" that Ruddick considers in "Thinking Mothers/Conceiving Birth" (Scott 1991; see also Grant 1987; Mohanty 1992). Like Ruddick, Collins and Rich tend to deploy the concept of experience in a way that implies that their accounts of women's experiences represent the truth, meaning, and significance of women's experiences, which are obscured by accounts of women's experiences articulated from more privileged social positions. And, I argue, this use of the concept of experience is consistent with the individualist view of subjectivity. Furthermore, this recuperation of individualism in Collins's and Rich's difference-based accounts of mothering is evident in several ideological moments of slippage that mediate contradictions in their accounts of mothering. These contradictions are effects of the interplay of identity and difference in the theoretical frameworks of their analyses of mothering, and this interplay of identity and difference is typical of the dilemma of difference that feminist theory encounters in trying to theorize women's difference in an individualist ideological context.

In *Of Woman Born*, Rich relies on the distinction of experience and institution to represent women's experiences from a feminist perspective while also explicating the effects of institutions on them. But the experience/institution distinction yields contradictory conclusions about experience, works against a critical analysis of over-determination of women's experiences and their reports of their experiences, and recuperates certain elements of essential motherhood. I argue that Rich's claim to represent women's experience apart from its institutional contexts oversimplifies the relationship of subjectivity, experience, and social contexts. It also recuperates elements of the individualist view of subjects as fully constituted prior to and apart from experiences and social contexts. In Collins's analysis of black feminist thought, the concept of experience is part of a much more complex theoretical framework than Rich's distinction of experience and institution. Collins develops a version of standpoint theory to frame her account of black women's experiences and knowledge. A close analysis of Collins's standpoint theory, however, shows that the concept of experience also has certain ideological effects in her work. Several slippages occur in Collins's analysis of the relationship of subjectivity, experience, consciousness, standpoint, and knowledge. Collins's standpoint theory includes the tendency I have identified in connection with Ruddick's use of Hartsock's version of standpoint theory for the concept of standpoint to slip between referring to a situation or location and referring to an outlook or perspective.

In both Rich's and Collins's claims to present women's experiences apart from their institutional and/or ideological contexts I read the desire for a unified, stable, and coherent subjectivity and for unity among women. This is a version of the problematic desire of/for the mother that, I have argued, is expressed in Kristeva's "Stabat Mater." I make this argument by analyzing the autobiographical elements of *Of Woman Born* in light of its failure to include any representation of Rich's experience of lesbian mothering, and by analyzing the presuppositions of Collins's argument for an Afrocentric feminist stand-point epistemology. Bringing this argument together with the recuperation of elements of individualism and essential motherhood in Rich's and Collins's accounts of mothering shows how the dilemma of difference emerges in accounts of mothering based on the concept of women's experience. More specifically, the paradox of representation that is an effect of the dilemma of difference is particularly difficult for accounts of mothering based on the con-cept of women's experience. This is the paradox that feminist theory encoun-ters when it attempts both to represent women's interests, which requires an identity-based account of women's subjectivity consistent with individualism, and to represent the specificity of women's experiences, which requires a difference-based account of women's subjectivity. An identity-based account of women's subjectivity does not adequately represent the specificity of women's experiences, and a difference-based account of women's subjectivity does not adequately represent women's political entitlement and agency. One conclusion that follows from my analysis of the paradox of representation in accounts of mothering based on the concept of women's experience is that feminist theory must examine more closely its own practice of representation, especially the circulation of the desire of/for the mother in its representation of women's experiences. Like Kristeva's "Stabat Mater," such accounts of mother-ing raise the question of whether it is possible to represent and analyze this desire without entirely succumbing to it. In other words, is it possible to theo-rize some degree of commonality in women's experiences without positing either the unity, stability, and coherence of women's subjectivity or the uncon-flicted unity among all women?

— adrienne rich: experience and institution —

Rich analyzes mothering in terms of the distinction of experiences and their institutional contexts. In the foreword to *Of Woman Born* she writes: "[t]hroughout this book I try to distinguish between two meanings of mother-hood, one superimposed upon the other: the potential relationship of any woman to her powers of reproduction and to children; and the institution, which aims at ensuring that that potential—and all women—shall remain under male control" (1976: xv). The distinction of experience and institution facilitates Rich's analysis of mothering in several ways. It allows her to argue that the institution of motherhood oppresses women by subjecting the experi-ence of mothering to male control. It also allows her to argue that the experi-ence of mothering is not inherently oppressive of women, and to show that even when women's experiences of mothering are controlled by men to serve men's interests, women can also experience joy, love, satisfaction, and accomplishment as mothers. Rich's distinction of experience and institution thus allows her to argue that the institution of motherhood can and should be reorganized so that it is controlled by women, serves the interests of women and children, and advances the goals of feminism.

By distinguishing experience and institution, Rich means to develop a difference-based challenge to sexism and male dominance as they are manifest at the site of mothering. Rich's experience/institution distinction, however, does not adequately negotiate the dilemma of difference, because it includes a number of slippages that recuperate important elements of individualism. The experience/institution distinction tends to slip into a representation of women as individualist subjects of experience, complete and unified in their possession of the capacities that define subjectivity prior to their experiences and apart from the institutional contexts of their experiences. This slippage implies that subjects are the privileged interpreters of their experiences, figuring the person whose experience it is as the subject best positioned to present, explain, or interpret the meaning of an experience. It also implies that institutions are either instrumental or opposed to subjects, thus participating in individualism's decontextualizing approach to the relationship of subjectivity, social relations, and social contexts. As a result, Rich's explication of the experience of mothering and the institution of motherhood makes contradictory claims about the relationship of experiences and institutions, especially the experience of embodiment and its contexts, and about the possibilities for knowledge of experiences, institutions, and their relationship. These contradictions indicate the complexity of the relationship of experiences and institutional contexts that is not adequately theorized by Rich's distinction of experience and institution.

For example, in distinguishing the experience and the institution of motherhood, Rich explicates the institution of motherhood in terms of agency and intentionality; she describes it as having both an aim and effects. The institution of motherhood "has been a keystone . . . of social and political systems," it "has withheld [women] from decisions affecting their lives," it "exonerates men from fatherhood," it "creates the . . . schism between 'private' and 'public' life," it "calcifies . . . choices and potentialities," it "has ghettoized and degraded female potentialities" (1976: xv). That the institution of motherhood has been "superimposed upon" the experience of mothering also attributes agency to the institution, since "superimposed" can mean both "placed or laid upon or over" and "caused to co-exist." The notion of superimposition thus implies that the institution of motherhood determines the nature and quality of women's experience of mothering. In comparison, Rich describes the experience of mothering as "the potential relationship of any woman to her powers of reproduction and to children" (1976: xv). In referring to the experience of mothering, she uses terms such as "potentialities," "power," "capacity," and "possibility" (1976: xv). Rich's claim that the institution of motherhood is superimposed upon the experience of mothering, and her frequent use of "under" in connection with the experience of mothering, as in "under male control" and "under patriarchy," also link mothering as experience to the concept of potential. These claims represent the experience of mothering as persisting beneath and deriving its shape or form from the institution of motherhood. Furthermore, Rich represents the experience of mothering not only as a potential, but as a potential relationship (to powers of reproduction and to children). The notions of a potential relationship and a (potential) relationship to reproduction and children further attenuate the experience of mothering. They suggest that the experience of mothering is almost nothing in itself; it has a potential existence, and it has that only in relationship to a process that reproduces something else, namely, children. Rich's account of how she distinguishes the experience of mothering from the institution of motherhood implies that the experience of mothering has little to do with agency and intentionality.

Eliciting these implications of Rich's distinction of institution and experience assumes that by "motherhood" Rich means "being a mother." But when Rich explicitly discusses the experience of being mothered or specifically indicates that she means "motherhood" to include "being mothered," different presuppositions about experience are at work. *Of Woman Born* begins with this statement: "All human life on the planet is born of woman. The one unifying and incontrovertible experience shared by all women and men is that monthslong period we spent unfolding inside a woman's body" (1976: xiii). About this experience Rich says, "[w]e carry the imprint of this experience for life, even into our dying. Yet there has been a strange lack of material to help us understand and use it" (1976: xiii). In introducing the autobiographical element of *Of Woman Born*, Rich writes: "I told myself that I wanted to write a book on motherhood because it was a crucial, still relatively unexplored, area for feminist theory." But, she continues, "I did not choose this subject, it had long ago chosen me" (1976: xvii). In these comments, Rich describes the experience of being mothered as both a subject and an agent. It unifies men and women, rules itself out as a site of controversy, and imprints itself on all subjects. It even makes choices. In addition, the experience of being mothered is a distinct entity unto itself; it is not explicitly distinguished from a corresponding institution superimposed on it.

Having introduced the experience/institution distinction, Rich struggles to further specify the relationship of the experience of mothering and the institution of motherhood. For instance, she argues that "[t]he institution of motherhood is not identical with bearing and caring for children." But it "creates the prescriptions and the conditions in which choices are made or blocked." It is "not 'reality' but" it has "shaped the circumstances of our lives . . . the social institutions and prescriptions for behavior created by men have not necessarily accounted for the real lives of women. Yet any institution which expresses itself so universally ends by profoundly affecting our experience, even the language we use to describe it" (1976: 24). In these comments Rich also suggests the agency of the institution of motherhood and implies that the institution thoroughly determines the experience of mothering. But she also implies that the experience of mothering, as part of women's reality and the real lives of women, is clearly distinguishable from the institution of motherhood.

Rich's distinction of experience and institution thus has several conflicting implications. It suggests that the institution of motherhood is active, while the experience is passive and unformed. But it also suggests that the experience of mothering, especially the experience of being mothered, is active, having a distinct existence and effects apart from any determining institution. Rich also implies both that the institution of motherhood thoroughly determines the experience of mothering and that at least some elements of the experience are not subject to the determining effects of the institution. Thus, she implies both the possibility of experiencing mothering without experiencing the institution of motherhood, and the impossibility of experiencing mothering apart from the institution of motherhood. The distinction of experience and institution also implies that the experience of mothering is directly accessible to description, analysis, and interpretation. But Rich's suggestion that the institution of motherhood thoroughly determines the experience implies that there is little or no knowledge of the experience of mothering apart from the institution of motherhood. Furthermore, the distinction of experience and institution leaves unclear whether knowledge of either the experience of mothering or the institution of motherhood is possible apart from any experience of either or both.

The contradictory implications of Rich's experience/institution distinction are also implicit in Rich's discussion of how women might begin to challenge the institution of motherhood, where these contradictory implications become intertwined with the problem of theorizing women's embodied subjectivity

while also resisting mind/body dualism. Rich argues that challenging the institution of motherhood requires recognition of "the full complexity and political
significance of the woman's body . . . of which motherhood is simply one—
though a crucial—part." She realizes that "it can be dangerously simplistic to
fix upon 'nurturance' as a special strength of women" and that patriarchal control of female embodiment subjects women to a crippling dilemma: "[w]e have
tended either to *become* our bodies . . . or to exist in spite of them" (1976: 289,
290, Rich's emphasis). But she also envisions "ways of thinking we don't yet
know about" in which thinking is "an active, fluid, expanding process." She asks
"whether women cannot begin, at last, to think through the body, to connect
what has been so cruelly disorganized—our great mental capacities, hardly
used; our highly developed tactile sense; our genius for close observation; our
complicated, pain-enduring, multipleasured physicality" (1976: 290). Rich
argues that there is "a possibility of converting our physicality into both knowledge and power" and concludes that "[t]he repossession by women of our bodies will bring far more essential change to human society than the seizing of the
means of production by workers. . . . [W]e need to imagine a world in which
every woman is the presiding genius of her own body" (1976: 290, 292).

These comments indicate several ways in which Rich's attempt to distinguish the experience of mothering and the institution motherhood and explicate the experience apart from the institution leads to a problematic theory of
women's embodiment. Rich's attempt to reconceptualize embodiment resembles Ruddick's struggle to articulate a theory of embodied subjectivity as social/
bodily. The paradoxical quality of these analyses of embodiment is typical of
the paradox of embodiment and gender generated by the dilemma of difference. On one hand, Rich's image of "thinking through the body" and her claim
that the body has social and political significance resist mind/body dualism by
arguing for the reciprocal over-determination of embodiment, consciousness,
and subjectivity.[1] But her account of women's embodiment also reifies the
body as something that can be possessed, and her image of women as "presiding geniuses" of their bodies is consistent with mind/body dualism in representing women's subjectivity in terms of disembodied consciousness located
within a material container. Rich argues for transforming women's embodiment into power and knowledge, but her discussion of this possibility continually slips into theorizing the female body apart from women's subjectivity.
This is evident in her references to "the actual—as opposed to culturally
warped—power inherent in female biology," the womb as "the ultimate source
of [maternal] power," and "the kind of inwardness that women have come
by organically" (1976: 22, 52, 92). Rich's call for a new understanding of the

relationship of thought and embodiment is thus undermined by a dualist concept of embodied subjectivity according to which the body, the organic, and biology are distinct from and opposed to the mind, the social, and the cultural.

Rich's theory of embodiment is also characterized by the instability of the body, sex, and gender that is typical of the paradoxes of gender and embodiment. By theorizing the meaning of the female body in terms of the power inherent in it or the inwardness that it bestows, Rich locates gender in the female body and naturalizes gender as an attribute of the individual. This aligns gender with the sex of the body. At the same time, however, Rich's call for women's repossession of their bodies and her image of women as presiding geniuses of their bodies figures gender as a dematerialized attribute of consciousness or subjectivity, understood apart from the body. This aligns gender with women's subjectivity and obscures the significance of the sexed body. Furthermore, to the extent that Rich's rearticulation of embodied subjectivity reconnects female embodiment, femininity, and mothering, risks the recuperation of a central element of essential motherhood. While she insists that mothering is only one part of the "significance of the woman's body," many of the "disorganized" elements of the body that Rich wants to "connect" have maternal connotations, such as the "genius for close observation" and the "pain-enduring physicality" that Rich attributes to women. The comparison of women's repossession of their bodies to the seizure of the means of production by workers also figures the female body as a reproductive body. This instability of the body, sex, and gender and this representation of the female body as a reproductive body in Rich's reconceptualization of embodied subjectivity indicate the persistence of elements of individualism that problematize feminist theory's attempts to theorize women's difference.

In addition to having these contradictory implications, Rich's account of mothering does not provide what it claims to offer—an account of the experience of mothering apart from the institution of motherhood. The claim to have access to women's experiences apart from their material, social, and ideological contexts presupposes either that women's reports of their experiences are the most reliable accounts of these experiences or that the feminist theorist has some direct access to these experiences and their meaning. The first of these presuppositions is predicated on the individualist view of subjects as constituted prior to and apart from their experiences. The second is predicated on the individualist view of disembodied, knowing subjectivity as capable in principle of knowledge of any and everything because it can unproblematically take up any subject position. Rich's use of the term "motherhood" to refer both to being a mother and being mothered is symptomatic of this problem in that it obscures the ways in which being a mother and being mothered are different subject positions. Her argument thus accommodates considerable slippage from one of these positions to the other, without directly addressing how they are different positions, what enables movement between them, and how it is possible to have knowledge of them. So, like Ruddick's analysis of mothering in terms of women's experiences, Rich's attempt to specify the distinction of experience and institution with respect to mothering suggests the need for a theory of subjectivity as positioning and raises the question of the conditions of the possibility of knowledge if subjectivity is thus reconceptualized.

The failure of Rich's account of mothering to present women's experiences of mothering apart from the institution is most evident in considering the autobiographical thread that runs through *Of Woman Born*. This autobiographical thread is emblematic of the problematic account of the relationship of subjectivity, experience, and knowledge implicit in Rich's distinction of experience and institution. Autobiography positions its subject simultaneously at the center of his or her experience and outside of it as an observer who reports it. Rich claims to present her own experience of mothering, but in doing so she leaves her own subject position as a theorist of mothering unanalyzed. From what position(s) is her account of mothering articulated? What position(s) enable her knowledge of mothering? This ideological effect of autobiography contributes to the recuperation of elements of individualism consistent with essential motherhood, and obscures the desires that circulate in Rich's account of mothering. But, if the claim to represent women's experiences of mothering does not provide the account of women's experiences that it promises, what does it provide instead? To answer this question I consider what I see as one of the most significant contradictions in Rich's account of mothering. Rich's autobiographical claim that she presents her own experience in *Of Woman Born* is contradicted by her failure to discuss her experience of lesbian mothering. In *Of Woman Born* Rich frequently discusses her experiences of mothering, and she gives a detailed analysis of the experience of being a lesbian daughter. But, despite Rich's oblique references to herself as a lesbian (1976: 47, 206), *Of Woman Born* nowhere presents Rich's experience of lesbian mothering; indeed, it includes almost no consideration of lesbian mothering at all.[2]

— the lesbian mother and the lesbian's mother —

In the foreword to *Of Woman Born*, Rich describes what she presents in this text as "rooted in my own past, tangled with parts of my life which had stayed buried. " This "journey into the past is complicated by . . . false namings of real events" and being a mother is "a ground which seemed to me the most painful, incomprehensible, and ambiguous I had ever traveled, . . . hedged by taboos, mined with false namings" (1976: xvii). These comments indicate that the inconsistencies resulting from the experience/institution distinction persist in Rich's claim to present her own experience. Rich says that her experience is incomprehensible and ambiguous, but also says that it can be understood in terms of truth and falsity, since the "false namings" can be distinguished from the "real events." Despite these inconsistencies, Rich's claim to present her own experience generates the expectation that *Of Woman Born* will include some account of Rich's own experience of lesbian mothering. This expectation, however, is not fulfilled, and the way the text avoids doing so is suggestive of both what desires and interests might motivate the attempt to represent women's experiences, and what the effects of this attempt might be. Rather than representing Rich's, or anyone's, experience of lesbian mothering, *Of Woman Born* figures the lesbian almost entirely as a daughter, and attributes to this daughter a desire for reunion with her mother very similar to that hinted at in Beauvoir's account of mothering in *The Second Sex* and expressed in Kristeva's "Stabat Mater." The lack of any representation of lesbian mothering in *Of Woman Born* suggests to me that the claim to represent women's experiences does not and cannot provide what it promises. Instead this claim expresses a desire for those elements of the individualist concept of subjectivity that purport to unify and stabilize subjectivity and thus to ground the meaning and significance of women as subjects of experience, and it expresses this desire as the desire of/for the mother.

What little Rich says about lesbianism and mothering occurs in her discussion of daughterhood and mothering. She argues that feminist visions of sisterhood are predicated on "the knowledge—transitory and fragmented, perhaps, but original and crucial—of mother-and-daughterhood" (1976: 226), and she illustrates this with examples from the works and lives of women authors, including Virginia Woolf, Sylvia Plath, Emily Dickinson, and Radclyffe Hall. Rich's discussion of the mother-daughter relation is in many respects similar to that Mary Daly offers in *Gyn/Ecology*. Both represent mothers and daughters as divided from each other by their subjection to male dominance, but also represent daughters as longing for reconnection with their mothers. Many of the images of the mother-daughter relationship that Rich cites express this longing for reconnection with the mother in terms of shared emotions or physical sensations. For instance, in commenting on *The Well of Loneliness*, Rich focuses on a passage that represents Stephen's longing for a reconnection with her mother and figures the possibility of this reconnection in terms of their shared experience of the fragrance of meadow flowers (1976: 233). She also quotes a letter in which Emily Dickinson writes that on the night before her mother died, her mother "was happy and hungry and ate a little supper I made her with so much enthusiasm, I laughed with delight" (1976: 230). Given its position in the sentence, the phrase "with so much enthusiasm" ambiguously refers both to Dickinson making the supper and her mother eating it. These images suggest a bond between mother and daughter that allows them to share experiences and understand each other, and imply that this bond is a result of the sameness of their experience of (female) embodiment.

Like these two images, Rich's discussion of the mother-daughter relationship is voiced almost entirely from the position of a daughter. Even when Rich directly poses the question of what is required to mother daughters, she answers in terms of what "we wish we had, or could have, as daughters" (1976: 249). Rich also gives an analysis of "childless" women that subsumes their experiences under the terms of the mother-daughter relation, even as she is trying to resist the categorization of women in terms of whether they are mothers. She concludes not only that the institution of motherhood affects all women, whether or not they are mothers, but also that "we are none of us 'either' mothers or daughters . . . we are both" (1976: 257), thus denying the different ways that the institution of motherhood affects those women who are daughters but are not mothers. And in the last section of her discussion of mothering and daughterhood Rich portrays herself as the daughter of both a white and a black mother, referring to the black woman employed by her family to care for her until she was four years old. Rich represents the retrieval of her memories of her black mother as a resistance to the "double silence of sexism and racism" according to which her black mother "was meant to be utterly annihilated" (1976: 258–59). But the effect of her use of the terms "white mother" and "black mother" is problematic. While her intention clearly seems to be to honor the woman she calls her "black mother," this phrase obscures the very significant social differences between these two women Rich calls mother. Her discussion of the mother-daughter relation concludes that "[w]omen are made taboo to other women. . . . In breaking this taboo, we are reuniting with our mothers; in reuniting with our mothers we are breaking this taboo" (1976: 259). With these images of mothering that are voiced from the perspective of a daughter, Rich's discussion of the mother-daughter relationship is open to Ruddick's criticism that feminist accounts of mothering that speak from the position of a daughter problematize maternal subjectivity. None of these images of the mother-daughter relationship represents the mother's point of view on the situations Rich describes or articulates the mother's experience of mothering a daughter.

On the basis of this analysis of the mother-daughter relation, Rich draws the following conclusion about the relationship of the lesbian daughter and her mother:

> A woman who feels an unbridgeable gulf between her mother and herself may be forced to assume that her mother . . . could never accept her sexuality. But, despite . . . popular ignorance and bigotry, and the fear that she may have damaged her daughter . . . the mother may at some level . . . want to confirm her daughter in her love for women. Mothers who have led . . . traditional, heterosexual lives have welcomed their daughters' women lovers and supported their domestic arrangements, though often denying, if asked, the nature of the relationship. A woman who fully and gladly accepts her love for another woman is likely to create an atmosphere in which her mother will not reject her. (1976: 244, Rich's emphasis)

This passage is followed by what I see as the closest Rich comes in *Of Woman Born* to identifying herself as a lesbian mother, the statement that "for those of us who had children, and later came to recognize and act upon the breadth and depth of our feelings for women, a complex new bond with our mothers is possible." This statement is followed by a long citation from the poet Sue Silvermarie, which says, in part:

> I find now, instead of a contradiction between lesbian and mother, there is an overlapping. What is the same between my lover and me, my mother and me, and my son and me is the motherbond. . . . In loving another women, I discovered the deep urge to both be a mother and find a mother in my lover . . . the drama between two loving women, in which each can become mother and each child.
>
> When I kiss and stroke and enter my lover I am also a child re-entering my mother. I want to return to the womb-state of harmony, and also to the ancient world . . . return to the mystery of my mother, and of the world as it must have been when the motherbond was exalted.
>
> Now I am ready to go back and understand the one whose body actually carried me. . . . I could never want her until I myself had been wanted. By a woman. Now that I know, I can return to her . . . and I can hope that she is ready for me. (1976: 234–35)

This image of lesbianism represents the lesbian as a daughter, and like other daughters in longing for reconnection with her mother. The overlapping of lesbian and mother that Silvermarie describes immediately slips into a sameness of her lover, her mother, her son, and herself. Silvermarie's image of lesbianism is like the images of the mother-daughter relationship that Rich cites from Hall and Dickinson in grounding this sameness in the female body, specifically the body of her lover and the body of her mother. Silvermarie's image also figures the lesbian as desiring her mother's acceptance and validation of her lesbianism, and as better positioned than a heterosexual woman to experience reconnection with her mother, as a function of her relationship with a woman lover. Thus, like Rich's account of the lesbian daughter, Silvermarie's image contradictorily represents the lesbian as both an abject daughter and a powerful daughter. In this image the lesbian idesires and recieves confirmation from her mother; her mother welcomes her woman lover and "supports their domestic arrangements" but "denies . . . the nature of their relationship." But the lesbian is also a powerful daughter who "creates an atmosphere in which her mother will not reject her."

Silvermarie's account of her experience of lesbianism and mothering is particularly problematic as a representation of lesbian mothering. Silvermarie represents her relationship with her lover as the source of both her desire to be a mother and her desire to find a mother. She represents herself and her lover as both mother and child to each other, and indicates that her relationship with her lover connects her via "the motherbond" to her mother and to her son. But other than mentioning this motherbond connection to him, Silvermarie says nothing else about her son. Rather she discusses at length how her lover's desire for her enables her return to, understand, and forgive her mother, and, perhaps, find that her mother is ready for her. The motherbond thus enables an unproblematic shifting among subject positions and a movement among temporalities, including a return to "the womb-state of harmony" and to the ancient world where this bond was exalted. Despite references to the overlapping of her experiences as a lesbian and as a mother, Silvermarie's account of her experiences says almost nothing about her being a mother. Like Rich's claim to present her own experience in *Of Woman Born*, it promises the representation of lesbian mothering but effects its erasure by instead presenting the lesbian daughter.

Furthermore, Rich's turning to another woman poet for this account of lesbian mothering is significant when considered in light of her claim to represent her own experience. In the foreword to *Of Woman Born*, Rich writes, "I cannot imagine having written this book without the presence in my life of my mother, who offers a continuing example of transformation and rebirth, and of my sister, with and from whom I go on learning about sisterhood, daughterhood, motherhood . . . " (1976: xxi–xxii). This image of relationships among women fostering knowledge of women's experience is like Silvermarie's suggestion that her relationship with a woman lover furthered her understanding of her mother, son, and their relationships. But Rich's reliance on Silvermarie's account of her experience also implies an unproblematic substitutability of one woman's experiences for another's that is consistent with Silvermarie's vision of the unproblematic shifting of subject positions among women lovers made possible by lesbianism, understood in terms of the sameness of women lovers. This implication represents the fundamental sameness of all women that is also indicated by Rich's claim that all women are both mothers and daughters. It also reinforces the denial of difference that is evident in Rich's inclusion of women without children in her claim that all women are mothers and daughters, and in Rich's equation of the position of her white mother with the position of the black woman who cared for her as a child. From the perspective of a Kristevan herethics, these erasures of sexual and racial difference fail to meet the terms of differentiation in sameness that an ethical relation to the other requires.

On the basis of this reading of Rich's failure to present what the autobiographical thread of *Of Woman Born* promises, I conclude that the claim to represent women's experiences enacts a desire of/for the mother similar to that which, according to Kristeva, is provoked by the weakness of language and the instability of subjectivity. But unlike "Stabat Mater," which recognizes that this desire is problematic even as it succumbs to it, Rich's representation of lesbian mothering much more clearly enacts the fulfillment of this desire as unproblematic. It grants in a very literal way the child's Oedipal wish for reunion with the mother ("I am a child . . . re-entering my mother") and it offers the possibility of an easy shifting among subject positions predicated on sameness rather than on a recognition of difference. This insistence on sameness among mothers and daughters also recuperates the heterosexual and lesbian difference, positioning all women as daughters longing for mothers, and obscuring the specificity of lesbian mothering. Rich's discussion of mother-daughter relationships opens up the possibility of differences among women, but then denies it in order to reinstate the stability and coherence of the identity 'woman' and the unity of the group 'women'. Whatever Rich's intentions, then, her account of women's experiences is complicit with the heterosexual matrix that supports the coherence and stability of female subjectivity and unity or commonality among women by equating maternal subjectivity with heterosexuality. Lesbian mothering remains impossible within the terms of this account of lesbianism. Rich's analysis of the mother-daughter relation thus recuperates a crucial element of essential motherhood while also sustaining individualism's promise of a completely and exhaustively determined subjectivity that is capable of being everywhere, of unproblematically taking up any subject position, and thus capable in principle of knowing everything.

The absence of any account of Rich's own experience of lesbian mothering in *Of Woman Born* also indicates that autobiography can recuperate significant elements of individualism. As an appeal to the author's own experience, autobiography participates in the ideological work of the concept of experience in several ways (Fuss 1989: 113–18; Scott 1991: 777, 786–87). Since it suggests that what the author presents is not an interpretation, but simply a truthful report, it deflects questions about the over-determination of the experience, of its subject, and of its subject's report of his or her experience. Autobiography may tend to imply that it is not open to critical analysis because it is a report of the author's own experience. In an individualist ideological context, autobiography may certainly be read in these terms. That the lack of any account of Rich's experience of lesbian mothering in *Of Woman Born* also participates in the denial of difference is another way in which autobiography may reconsolidate the individualist subject. Like the concept of women's experience, autobiography can also presuppose the individualist subject—the subject fully and exhaustively constituted by the possession of the capacity for rational autonomy, the subject to whom experience happens and who is the privileged reporter and/or interpreter of his or her experience. With respect to the paradox of representation, this analysis of the ideological effects of autobiography suggests that taking women's reports of their experiences uncritically, without considering their material, social, and ideological over-determination, does not sufficiently resist individualism and the metaphysics of substance and thus does not adequately negotiate the paradox of representation.

The appearance of the lesbian's mother in place of the lesbian mother promised by the autobiographical thread of *Of Woman Born* is also suggestive of what interests and desires might be at work in feminist theory's claim to represent women's experience. This claim is motivated at least in part by a desire for women, and a desire for unity and understanding among women, especially among mothers and daughters. Claims about women's experience, then, may express, not the reality of a coherent and stable female subjectivity and a commonality and unity among women, but the desire for them. The claim to represent women's experience insists on the presence of women, but it also implicitly recognizes an absence with respect to women. When the experience in question is the experience of being mothered, this lack is specifically a lack of the mother—for instance, in Rich's statement about the experience of being mothered that there is a strange lack of material (a word whose root is the Latin "mater," or mother) to help us understand it (1976: xiii). The impulse to fill with the lesbian's mother the gap where the lesbian mother is promised but does not appear suggests that the claim to represent women's experience expresses and enacts the satisfaction of the desire for a coherent and stable experience of subjectivity and for unity among women. By suggesting the possibility of a unified, stable, and complete subjectivity, the claim to represent women's experience denies both that difference is effective in subjectivity and that there are differences among women.

— patricia hill collins: experience, consciousness, and standpoint —

In comparison to Rich's account of mothering, Collins's account does not require sameness among women, or among black women, in order to articulate the specificity of black women's mothering, and recognizes differences among black mothers, including black lesbian mothers (1991: 128–29). On the other hand, Collins's discussion of relationships between black mothers and daughters is idealizing in its tendency to deny the existence of any conflicts between black mothers and daughters. While Collins theorizes the difficult dilemmas that black mothers face and the conflicting impulses black mothers experience, she attributes to black daughters a uniformly positive experience of their mothers and a complete understanding and acceptance of their mothers. The "many . . . contradictions in Black mother-daughter relationships" are only "apparent" because understanding black mothers' goal of balancing the need to ensure their daughters' survival and the desire to encourage their daughters to exceed the boundaries they face explains these contradictions (1991: 125). While some of the black women Collins describes and/or cites in this discussion resented, disliked, or rejected their mothers in their youth, all of them, according to Collins, came as adults to recognize that their mothers raised them well. None of them have anything critical to say about their mothers. They, and Collins, especially attribute to their mothers their adult qualities of self-reliance, assertiveness, and sense of their unique self-worth. For example, in referring to Cheryl West's account of growing up with her lesbian mother and her mother's lover, Jan, Collins mentions West's comment that Jan "could be a rigid disciplinarian." But she emphasizes West's description of Jan as "loving, gentle, . . . involved, nurturing." Jan is more the mother of essential motherhood than is West's birth mother, who worked two jobs while Jan "braided [West's] hair in the morning . . . and tucked [West] in at night." Collins understands even Renita Weems's account of being deserted by her alcoholic mother as Weems's effort to understand her mother, rather than or also as Weems's criticism of her mother. According to Collins, this effort leads to Weems's acceptance of her mother, and to her recognition that her mother loved her. But, in words that echo Kristeva's description of the belief in the mother who "makes me be," Weems writes, "My mother loved us. I must believe that" (1984: 26). Weems's claim that she must believe in her mother's love suggests that this belief is significant, not because it states a fact, but because of what it enables. This belief sustains Weems's sense of her self and her origins, explaining how she came to be who she is and allowing her to go on with her life by rooting her sense of her self and her origins in her mother and her mother's love for her. But such a belief in a mother's love also enables a denial of any division, partiality, or instability of subjectivity, thus supporting an individualist concept of subjectivity.

Like Rich's image of the lesbian daughter who creates the conditions in which her mother accepts her, Collins's discussion of black mother-daughter relationships insistently portrays an unambiguously and exhaustively strong and loving mother who brings into existence and guarantees the daughter's subjectivity. Despite Collins's warning about the effects of the stereotype of the strong, suffering black mother, her account of black mothers and daughters cannot entirely resist this vision. This version of the desire of/for the mother expressed in Collins's account of black mother-daughter relationships does not preclude differences among mothers, and among women, as the figure of the lesbian's mother does in Rich's analysis of mother-daughter relationships. On the other hand, a close reading of Collins's argument that black feminist thought is predicated on an Afrocentric feminist standpoint epistemology shows that this argument does tend to require sameness and unity among black people. Collins's argument for an Afrocentric feminist standpoint epistemology displaces the desire for a coherent and stable subjectivity, articulating this desire not in terms of the mother, but in terms of the African origin of the standpoint that unifies black consciousness.

How, then, do the concepts of experience, standpoint, and consciousness operate in the theoretical framework of Collins's account of black feminist thought? In specifying what counts as black feminist thought and what is entailed in being a black feminist thinker, Collins rejects biological determinist criteria for race. She also insists that a definition of black feminist thought must avoid both "the materialist position that being Black and/or female generates certain experiences that automatically determine variants of a Black and/or feminist consciousness" and "the idealist position that ideas can be evaluated in isolation from the groups that create them" (1991: 20). By positioning her account of black feminist thought between these alternatives, Collins expresses the conflicting impulses at work in standpoint theory. On one hand, Collins asserts that "black women" is a socially meaningful group of persons who have distinctive experiences and ideas, partly as a function of the racist, as well as sexist, social and institutional contexts of their experiences, and partly as a function of their African cultural heritage. This assertion is the basis of her insistence on the centrality of black women's experiences and ideas as the content of black feminist thought, and the centrality of black women in the production of black feminist thought. On the other hand, Collins wants to recognize differences among black women and to avoid valorizing the oppressive social and institutional contexts of black women's experiences and knowledge production. So her account of black feminist thought must also avoid universalizing black female subjectivity and must provide adequate grounds for critique of the oppressive social contexts of black women's experiences.

I see Collins's argument for an Afrocentric feminist standpoint epistemology as an attempt to address the questions about subject positioning and knowledge that I have argued are raised by Ruddick's account of mothering. My reading of Collins's account of black feminist thought and her Afrocentric feminist standpoint epistemology traces the ways in which this account of black women's subjectivity disentangles and reconnects standpoint, experience, and consciousness in relationship to knowledge and epistemology. I show how Collins analyzes different kinds of knowledge in terms of the subject positions from which such knowledge is likely to emerge and I consider the advantages of her version of standpoint theory for negotiating the paradox of representation. I argue that, despite these advantages, the concept of experience is doing significant ideological work in Collins's argument for an Afrocentric feminist standpoint epistemology. In Collins's theoretical frame, the concept of experience mediates this argument's contradictory implications for theorizing subjectivity.

Collins's standpoint theory distinguishes three specific subject positions, and theorizes each of them as a location from which subjects focus on a distinct object of understanding and develop a specific kind of knowledge. These three positions are a black women's standpoint, the position of black women intellectuals, and an Afrocentric feminist standpoint. According to Collins, the black women's standpoint is constituted by the oppressive situation of black women determined by the intersection of race, gender, and class oppression (1991: 10). These intersecting oppressions create what Collins calls an "outsider-within stance" that enables black women to acquire an everyday knowledge or common sense about their experiences of sexuality, family, work, other social relations, and the social contexts of these experiences. These intersecting oppressions also determine that black women's everyday knowledge will often highlight the contradictions between the claims of dominant ideological formations and black women's self-understandings. As black women discuss and analyze each other's experiences and share their everyday knowledge, they participate in the formation of a distinctive black women's consciousness. Collins emphasizes that black women's consciousness is an achievement, a collective creation, rather than an inevitable outcome determined solely by the black women's standpoint. The multiple and overlapping determination of the black women's standpoint enables a recognition of differences among black women and different understandings of themselves and their social contexts. When black women discuss and analyze their differences and share their different understandings of themselves and their different social contexts, black women's consciousness comes to recognize differences among black women. Thus, the first subject position that Collins distinguishes, the black women's standpoint, is a complex, over-determined position from which black women develop a complex understanding of their experiences that recognizes both commonality and difference of experiences and beliefs.

Collins argues that the best way to understand the subject position of black women intellectuals and the black feminist thought they produce is "to specify the relationship between a black women's standpoint—those experiences and ideas shared by African-American women that provide a unique angle of vision on self, community, and society—and theories that interpret those experiences" (1991: 22). The subject position of black women intellectuals enables a distinct knowledge, black feminist thought. Black women intellectuals can be positioned in traditional sites of knowledge production, such as universities, literature and publishing, and other dominant or elite art forms. In these contexts black women intellectuals also occupy an outsider-within stance, which gives them a distinctive perspective on the production of knowledge in these locations. Given the history of the exclusion of black women from traditional sites of knowledge production, however, black women intellectuals are also likely to be positioned in other locations, many of them more specific to African-American communities, such as black churches and gospel and blues music. From these positions, black women intellectuals further the rearticulation of black women's experiences that is made possible by a black women's standpoint, and thus further the development of black women's consciousness. But what distinguishes black women intellectuals is that they develop theories that interpret the black women's standpoint and black women's consciousness. In other words, black women's standpoint and consciousness together become the objects of the specific knowledge that black women intellectuals produce.

Collins's distinction of black women's experience, standpoint, and consciousness from the position of black women intellectuals and black feminist thought can be illustrated in relationship to mothering. Black women may articulate, share, and discuss their experiences of mothering, which are shaped by their standpoint, and thus may create a collective consciousness of the meaning and significance of black women's mothering. Like Ruddick, Collins argues that maternal stories and conversations are a crucial locus of the development of a maternal standpoint. Stories such as those Collins recounts from blues songs, oral histories, and black women's fiction and autobiography embody this knowledge, and the telling of these stories is central to the creation of black women's everyday knowledge or consciousness of mothering. Collins's conception of black women's standpoint, experiences, and consciousness of mothering can be described in Ruddick's terms as an everyday knowledge of how to achieve the goals of maternal practice in black women's specific social contexts and of why it is important to do so. But claims such as "[h]istorically, community-based child care and the relationships among bloodmothers and othermothers in women-centered networks have taken diverse institutional forms" and "Black women's experiences as othermothers provide a foundation for Black women's political activism" (1991: 121, 129) are typical of black feminist thought, rather than black women's consciousness. Such claims are articulated from the position of black women intellectuals, theorizing the meaning and significance of black women's experiences, standpoint, and consciousness with respect to mothering.

In analyzing the epistemological foundations of black feminist thought, Collins specifies a third subject position and another object of knowledge. According to Collins, the criteria of adequacy that justify the claims of black feminist thought constitute an Afrocentric feminist epistemology, which is possible because black women have access to both Afrocentric and feminist standpoints. She argues that, despite varying histories, black societies reflect elements of "a core African value system that existed prior to and independently of racial oppression." In addition, " . . . as a result of . . . systems of racial domination, Black people share a common experience of oppression. These two factors foster shared Afrocentric values" that are expressed in the social relations and structures of black communities in Africa, the Caribbean, and the Americas. Collins concludes: "[t]his Afrocentric consciousness permeates the shared history of people of African descent through the framework of a distinctive Afrocentric epistemology" (1991: 206). She comments on the "remarkable resemblance" of Afrocentric ideas and values and to "similar ideas claimed by feminist scholars as characteristically 'female'" (1991: 207) and argues that such a feminist standpoint is also available to black women, given their experiences of gender oppression.

Thus, Collins argues for a distinctive Afrocentric feminist standpoint that offers four criteria for assessing knowledge claims. These include the use of concrete experience as a criterion of meaning and credibility, the use of dialogue in assessing knowledge claims, an ethic of caring, and an ethic of personal accountability (1991: 210–18). Collins emphasizes the African roots of the Afrocentric feminist epistemology she outlines, as is evident in her account of the African roots of the four criteria of this Afrocentric feminist epistemology. She argues that "every culture has a worldview that it uses to order and evaluate its own experiences. For African-Americans this worldview originates in the Afrocentric ideas of classical African civilizations, ideas sustained by the cultures and institutions of diverse West African ethnic groups" (1991: 10). An Afrocentric consciousness recognizes "longstanding belief systems among African peoples" and "being Black encompasses *both* experiencing white domination *and* individual and group valuation of a long-standing Afrocentric consciousness" (1991: 27, Collins's emphasis). The exclusion of African-Americans from the dominant social and institutional contexts of white American society has allowed them to pass on from one generation to the next this Afrocentric worldview. According to Collins, "Black women fashioned an independent standpoint about the meaning of Black womanhood" by using "African-derived conceptions of self and community" to resist their devaluation by white people on the basis of the ideals and standards of white-dominant societies. Thus, their "grounding in traditional African-American culture fostered the development of a distinctive Afrocentric women's culture" (1991: 11). In addition, given their roles as mothers, othermothers, teachers, and activists, black women have been especially important in maintaining, transforming, and passing on this Afrocentric worldview in black communities.

Collins notes the similarity of her specification of 'Black' in terms of an Afrocentric worldview and the specification of 'feminist' in feminist standpoint theories. Collins's account of black feminist thought stresses the extent to which a standpoint is achieved, not given simply as a function of subject positioning, in a way that is similar to Hartsock's feminist standpoint theory. Like Hartsock, Collins argues that the articulation of a standpoint requires "struggling to develop new interpretations of familiar realities," although the processes of reinterpretation in the cases of feminist and Afrocentric feminist standpoints are different. Collins argues that "constructions of gender rest on clearer biological criteria than do constructions of race," whereas racially and ethnically identified groups share "distinct histories, geographic origins, culture and social institutions." Nonetheless, just as women share common experiences, especially the experience of oppression on the basis of sex, that can lead them to "struggle . . . to reject patriarchal perceptions of women and to value women's ideas and actions," so too "African-American women draw on [the] Afrocentric worldview to cope with racial oppression," even when this worldview "remains unarticulated and not fully developed into a self-defined standpoint" (1991: 27).

As a theoretical framework, Collins's version of standpoint theories has several advantages for negotiating the paradox of representation in feminist theory. It represents black women as occupying multiple and overlapping subject positions, and recognizes that the complexity of subject positioning rules out any easy and unproblematic shifting among subject positions. Thus, it also recognizes the complexity of relations among women, which can include both commonality and difference. Collins distinguishes a black women's standpoint from an Afrocentric feminist standpoint, just as Hartsock distinguishes a caregiving standpoint from a feminist standpoint. Collins's Afrocentric feminist standpoint includes a political analysis of the conditions that determine black women's experiences, just as Hartsock's feminist standpoint includes a materialist analysis of the conditions that determine the experiences of caregivers. By defining the black women's standpoint in terms of racial and gender oppression, Collins's theoretical frame recognizes the over-determination of black women's experiences by racist and sexist social institutions and practices. It does not take black women's reports of their experiences at face value or uncritically. Instead it represents black women's reports of their experiences as themselves the results of processes of analysis and dialogue, and it distinguishes the standpoint that shapes black women's experiences from the position that fosters the analysis and critical interpretation of both their experiences and black women's reports of their experience.

Collins's version of standpoint theory is also like Hartsock's in being informed by a liberatory agenda for changing the oppressive conditions that determine black women's experiences. This not only facilitates critical analysis of black women's experiences, but also suggests concrete strategies for representing the social and political interests of black women by acting to change the social contexts that shape their experiences. With respect to black women's experiences of mothering, Collins's version of standpoint theory indicates that black women's reports of their experiences of mothering are the starting point for an Afrocentric feminist analysis of black women's mothering. Black feminist thought considers these reports in terms of the standpoints and social contexts that shape them, taking into consideration black women's understandings of the relationship of their experiences of mothering and their social contexts. But the more fully articulated understanding of this relationship produced by black feminist thought furthers the development of black women's consciousness of mothering and connects black feminist thought's analysis of black women's mothering to its liberatory agenda.

Despite these advantages of Collins's theoretical framework, however, the concept of experience is doing significant ideological work in her argument for an Afrocentric feminist standpoint epistemology. The concept of experience mediates several tensions implicit in Collins's account of an Afrocentric feminist standpoint epistemology, which has the effect of unifying and stabilizing the concept of subjectivity implicit in her standpoint theory. It also obscures the extent to which her argument for an Afrocentric feminist standpoint epistemology universalizes and decontextualizes West Africa as the foundation of a cultural heritage shared by black people in other parts of the world. One of the tensions in Collins's argument for her version of standpoint theory is the tension between her account of a black women's standpoint and her account of differences among black women. Collins's argument, like Ruddick's account of the possibility but not inevitability of natal reflection among birthgivers, suggests that black women tend to have certain ideas and values in common because they tend to have certain experiences, and the social contexts that shape those experiences, in common. She argues that "the material conditions of race, class, and gender oppression can vary dramatically and yet produce some uniformity in the epistemologies of subordinate groups" (1991: 207). But Collins also argues that African-American women do not necessarily respond in the same way to the black women's standpoint, because "diversity among Black women produces different concrete experiences that in turn shape various reactions to the core themes" (1991: 23). Factors such as social class, sexual orientation, ethnicity, geographic region, urbanization, and age "combine to produce a web of experiences shaping diversity among African-American women" (1991: 24). Collins concludes that "being Black and female may expose African-American women to certain common experiences, which in turn may predispose us to a distinctive group consciousness, but it in no way guarantees that such a consciousness will develop" (1991: 25).

In Collins's analysis of the relationship of standpoint, experience, and consciousness, there is considerable slippage of the concept of experience. Sometimes her analysis of these relationships closely links the concepts of experience and standpoint, arguing that black women's standpoint and experience operate together to determine black women's consciousness. But at other points Collins's analysis of the relationship of standpoint, experience, and consciousness closely links the concepts of experience and consciousness, implying that a black women's standpoint has a considerably less direct effect on black women's experience and consciousness. This slippage of the concept of experience is also indicated by Collins's need to appeal to other factors, such as social class, sexual orientation, ethnicity, geographic region, urbanization, and age, that "combine to produce a web of experiences" in her discussion of differences among black women. Collins appeals to these factors at those points where her analysis of the relationship of standpoint, experience, and consciousness closely links the concepts of experience and consciousness. In this case, these other factors do the work of linking the black women's standpoint to black women's experience and consciousness. This slippage of the concept of experience in Collins's standpoint theory is a version of the slippage between two senses of the term standpoint that I see in Ruddick's and Hartsock's use of the term, namely the sense in which standpoint means a position or location and the sense in which standpoint means a perspective or outlook. This slippage of the concept of experience obscures rather than addresses the questions about the relationship of subject positioning and, knowledge that, I have argued, are raised by reconceptualizing embodied subjectivity as subject positioning.

The concept of experience also mediates a tension in Collins's account of the relationship of black women and black women intellectuals. In her account of black women's consciousness, Collins emphasizes the potential role of all black women in articulating and furthering the development of this consciousness. She argues that although black women have "varying types of consciousnesses regarding our shared angle of vision," they also have the "ability to forge these individual, unarticulated, yet potentially powerful expressions of everyday consciousness into an articulated, self-defined, collective standpoint" (1991: 26). This argument is consistent with those aspects of Collins's account of a black women's standpoint that closely link the concepts of experience and standpoint and argue that experience and standpoint determine consciousness. But her account of black feminist thought emphasizes the distinctive role of black women intellectuals in articulating and furthering the development of black women's consciousness. Collins argues that black women intellectuals produce black feminist thought through a process of rearticulation, "taking the core themes of a Black women's standpoint and infusing them with new meaning." Black women intellectuals produce "theories clarifying a Black women's standpoint" and these theories "form the specialized knowledge of Black feminist thought." Black feminist thought "consists of theories or specialized thought produced by African-American women intellectuals designed to express a Black women's standpoint" (1991: 30–32). This argument for the unique role of black women intellectuals in the production of black feminist thought is consistent with those aspects of Collins's account of a black women's standpoint that closely link the concepts of experience and consciousness and imply that the black women's standpoint does not inevitably and univocally determine experience and consciousness. This linkage of the concepts of experience and consciousness weakens the effects of a standpoint on experience and consciousness, thereby creating the need for black women intellectuals to articulate the relationship of standpoint to experience and consciousness. While Collins argues that all black women play a role in the articulation of black women's consciousness, she also implies that only certain women, namely black women intellectuals, complete this articulation of black women's consciousness.

These slippages of the concept of experience allow Collins's argument for a black women's standpoint and an Afrocentric feminist standpoint epistemology to preserve a theory of subjectivity consistent in many ways with individualism. Collins argues that oppressive situations are "inherently unstable," producing not only subjugation but also resistance (1991: 10), but she does not extend this inherent instability to subject positioning itself. While Collins's standpoint theory envisions black women as occupying multiple and overlapping subject positions, it also suggests that each of these subject positions is a unified and stable position in which individuals experience a unified, stable, and coherent subjectivity. Thus, while she envisions the production of knowledge as a collective endeavor to which many subjects make varying contributions, she also envisions knowledge production as ultimately yielding a unified, stable, coherent, and complete account of black women's subjectivity. Although no one black woman has a complete and exhaustive angle of vision on black women's subjectivity, black women together can, in principle, arrive at a complete and exhaustive account of black women's experience and subjectivity.

The persistence of these elements of individualism is also enabled by Collins's conception of West Africa as the origin and source of a cultural heritage shared by black people in other parts of the world, and passed on relatively intact from generation to generation. Collins's account of this African cultural heritage emphasizes its unity, stability, and coherence. She argues that "the Afrocentric ideas of classical African civilizations" are unified enough to be so identified, even though these ideas are sustained by a variety of "cultures and institutions of diverse West African ethnic groups." Thus, despite Collins's assertion of differences among black women, she also envisions all black women as having access to a unified, stable, and coherent set of ideas and values—"African-derived conceptions of self and community"—that is stable and coherent enough to be so identified through the process of being passed on from generation to generation. But, while Collins attempts a nuanced

account of this cultural heritage, I see in her argument for an Afrocentric feminist standpoint epistemology an expression of the desire for such unity and
stability of experience and standpoint among black people. Collins's appeal to
West Africa as the source of a cultural heritage that unifies black people and
stabilizes their standpoint is, like Rich's offering of the lesbian's mother in
place of the lesbian mother, the expression of a desire rather than the representation of a fact. Furthermore, as Collins indicates, the position of black women
intellectuals in particular would be unified and stabilized by the existence of
an African cultural heritage in the form Collins describes it, since black women
intellectuals in particular face the "danger [of] the potential isolation from the
types of experiences that stimulate an Afrocentric feminist consciousness"
(1991: 34). Her argument for an Afrocentric feminist standpoint voices the
desire for a unified, coherent, and stable subjectivity, and does so in a way that
obscures the over-determination of subject positions, especially the subject
position of a theorist of black feminist thought. Like Rich's subject position in
her autobiographical account of her experiences of mothering, Collins's subject position as a theorist of women's experiences is not adequately analyzed in
her argument for an Afrocentric feminist standpoint epistemology.

— the desires of feminist theory —

My analysis of Rich's and Collins's accounts of mothering leads to several conclusions about the project of theorizing mothering in terms of the concept of
women's experience. Some of these conclusions indicate that the problems I
have raised in connection with psychoanalytic approaches to mothering are
not unique to psychoanalysis. For instance, Rich's account of mothering naturalizes maternal heterosexuality to the extent that it cannot envision a lesbian
mother, and versions of the desire of/for the mother, voiced from the position
of a daughter, persist in Rich's and Collins's analyses of mothering. That these
two problems occur in accounts of mothering that are not framed in psychoanalytic terms supports my view that these problems have as much to do with
the ideological intersection of essential motherhood and individualism as they
do with psychoanalysis. In this ideological context, the naturalization of
maternal heterosexuality preserves the heterosexual matrix, which supports
the linkage of sex and gender on which both individualism and essential motherhood depend. The naturalization of maternal heterosexuality supports
essential motherhood by sustaining the connection of female bodily sex, femininity, and mothering, thereby perpetuating sexism and male dominance. The
naturalization of maternal heterosexuality ensures that mothering, and

women, must be positioned in relationship to men and rules out alternative social organizations of mothering in which men might have little or no power. The naturalization of maternal heterosexuality also supports individualism by deploying gender to link the (male or female) body and (masculine or feminine) subjectivity, thus unifying and stabilizing subjectivity. I have argued that the material and social conditions of liberal democratic capitalism that individualism rationalizes are not likely to produce the experience of subjectivity, understood as rational autonomy, for most persons. But the failure of these conditions rationalized by individualism to provide the experience of the kind of subjectivity that individualism promises is obscured by the way in which the heterosexual matrix naturalizes gender and thus secures the appearance of subjectivity as unified and stabilized by gender.

The expression of the desire of/for the mother that occurs in both Rich's and Collins's accounts of mothering also supports my reading of this desire in relationship to individualism as a hegemonic ideological formation. My analysis of the desire of/for the mother shows how the intersection of individualism and essential motherhood as dominant ideological formations explains both the persistence of the desire for a complete, coherent, and stable subjectivity and the address of this desire to mothers, and, via essential motherhood, to all women. Given the hegemony of essential motherhood and the social organization of mothering that it supports, this desire for individualist subjectivity is likely to be articulated in terms of infantile and early childhood experiences of being mothered and thereby projected onto all women. Moreover, the articulation of the desire for subjectivity as the desire of/for the mother deflects criticisms of individualism and of the material and social circumstances of liberal democratic capitalism. Instead of looking to these circumstances to explain the impossibility of individualist subjectivity, persons in these circumstances can pursue and engage in relationships with women in the hope that such relationships will eventually provide the kind of subjectivity that individualism promises. Alternatively, they can convince themselves that they have experienced and continue to experience individualist subjectivity by persisting in the belief that as children they experienced the kind of mothering that essential motherhood promises. Or they can blame mothers, and women, rather than the material and social circumstances of liberal democratic capitalism, for not providing this experience of subjectivity.

The persistence of the desire for individualist subjectivity, in the form of the desire of/for the mother, in feminist accounts of mothering that more or less explicitly oppose essential motherhood also shows how thoroughly essential motherhood and individualism are intertwined. The desire for a complete, unified, and coherent subjectivity is not limited to individualism, where it is implicit in the denial of the instability and partiality of subjectivity, or to psychoanalysis, where it is implicit in its account of the mother-child relation in which each satisfies the desire of/for the other. This desire for someone— mother or child—to guarantee language and subjectivity or to console for the lack of this guarantee can also circulate in difference feminist projects of using an account of women's difference as a paradigm for social theory and practice, such as Elshtain's feminist communitarianism, Ruddick's feminist maternal peace politics, and Kristeva's herethics. To the extent that such projects imply the stability and coherence of the categories 'woman' and/or 'mother' as a foundation for social theory and ethical and political practice or as a presence outside of the constitution of subjectivity, they can also be an attempt to satisfy the desire for someone—in this case, women and/or mothers—to guarantee the stability and coherence of subjectivity and thus ground the possibility of ethical and political relationships.

The expression of the desire of/for the mother in feminist theory has a number of effects that are problematic for theorizing mothering. It deflects the analysis of the over-determination of subjectivity, experience, and knowledge that, I have argued, feminist accounts of mothering require in an individualist ideological context. While Ruddick, Rich, and Collins all take a contextualizing approach to mothering, their analyses stop short of considering the complexities of the over-determination of experience when it comes to some aspect of women's experience of mothering. All preserve some aspect of women's experience of mothering and/or the experience of being mothered that is unproblematically accessible to documentation and interpretation by feminist theory and thus can serve as a foundation for analysis of other aspects of women's experience. This expresses and to some extent satisfies the desire for an easy, unproblematic movement among subject positions that I have traced in the expression in "Stabat Mater" of the daughter's desire for reunion with her mother as well as in Rich's and Silverman's account of lesbian daughterhood and in Collins's account of black women's experiences. Such an account of movement among subject positions obscures the possibility of conflict in social relations, especially in relationships among women, while also denying the difficulties of the differentiation in sameness that Kristeva describes. That this effect occurs in connection with mothering and being mothered links this desire for unproblematic movement among subject positions to the desire of/for the mother. Thus, as I see it, the feminist project of documenting and interpreting women's experiences expresses the desire for a subjectivity that is both coherent, unified, and stable and capable in principle of occupying any subject position. In other words, the "dream of plenitude" that Ruddick attributes to psychoanalysis is not unique to psychoanalysis. Rather, it is the individualist concept of a subjectivity capable of being everywhere and knowing everything that dreams this dream. And, given the intertwining of individualism and essential motherhood, individualism dreams this dream, expresses this desire for subjectivity, in terms of the mother by demanding that the mother satisfy this desire and/or console for the impossibility of its satisfaction.

My analysis of the persistence of the desire of/for the mother in feminist accounts of mothering also has several implications for difference feminism's use of accounts of women's difference as a basis for social theories that resist individualism. I have argued that psychoanalytic accounts of women's difference risk the recuperation of essential motherhood when they are deployed in this way. Accounts of women's difference that theorize some aspect of mothering as unproblematically accessible to documentation and interpretation and thus available as a basis for political and social theory also risk the recuperation of essential motherhood in several ways. To the extent that such accounts of mothering position women, mothers, and/or feminist theorists as daughters longing for and/or experiencing reunion with the mother, they risk reconsolidating essential motherhood's view of mothering as limitless, self-sacrificing availability. To the extent that these accounts of mothering rely on such a view of the mother-daughter relation to theorize relationships among women, they call on the mother to make ethical relations possible by guaranteeing the stability, unity, and coherence of the subject of ethical practice. They thus problematize maternal subjectivity by representing the mother not as a subject in her own right, but as a guarantee of subjectivity.

My reading of Rich's and Collins's accounts of mothering shows that the desire of/for the mother and the desire for individualist subjectivity are deeply intertwined in the project of documenting and interpreting women's experience and deploying accounts of women's experiences as a foundation for political and social theory. This supports the conclusion of my evaluation of psychoanalytic accounts of women's difference that feminist theory, especially feminist analyses of mothering, requires a theory of subjectivity that more adequately theorizes the complexities of the constitution of subjectivity and its material, social, and ideological contexts. An explanation of the reciprocal over-determination of subjectivity and its contexts needs to show how these contexts are effective in determining subjectivity, and how subjectivity is effective in determining its contexts while neither exhaustively, completely, and coherently determines the other. I have argued that a theory of the discursive constitution of embodied subjectivity such as Kristeva's would be more effective in analyzing the over-determination of subjectivity and its contexts, because it would do so in terms of the indeterminacy of language. Such a theory of subjectivity would destabilize rather than reconsolidate the individualist subject of experience, so it would undermine rather than recuperate the over-determination of subjectivity by individualism and essential motherhood. This would enable feminist analyses of mothering to more strenuously resist the desire for individualist subjectivity articulated as the desire of/for the mother and to examine more critically the conditions and effects of its representations of mothering.

Feminist analyses of mothering based on a theory of the discursive constitution of embodied subjectivity such as Kristeva's, however, must also resist the problems that arise from the psychoanalytic elements of such theories of subjectivity. The most difficult of these problems is the tendency to problematize maternal subjectivity by representing it as outside of or prior to the discursive constitution of embodied subjectivity and/or to represent the mother as the guarantee of subjectivity or the consolation for the instability and partiality of subjectivity. I have argued that Kristeva's theory of subjectivity undermines the individualist subject of experience, guaranteed by the mother, such as that which is presupposed by the concept of women's experience in Ruddick's, Rich's, and Collins's accounts of mothering. But Kristeva's theory of subjectivity also tends to problematize maternal subjectivity in just the way that Ruddick, Rich, and Collins try to avoid by relying on the concept of women's experience to theorize mothering. Thus, it is clear that the dilemma of difference is a persistent problem in analyzing mothering, whether such analyses rely on psychoanalytic approaches to theorizing subjectivity or on the concept of women's experience. Psychoanalytic approaches to theorizing subjectivity, especially Lacanian psychoanalysis, strenuously resist individualism, but they seriously problematize maternal subjectivity, and thus significantly risk essential motherhood. Analyses of mothering based on the concept of women's experience significantly resist essential motherhood by representing maternal subjectivity in terms of the complexity, ambiguity, and incoherence of mothering more adequately than does psychoanalysis. But they also recuperate significant elements of individualism, thus risking individualism's implications that being a mother is neither a significant element of a mother's experiences and situations nor an exercise of subjectivity. Perhaps most problematically for feminist theory, in an ideological context defined by individualism and essential motherhood, theorizing mothering in terms of psychoanalytic approaches to subjectivity and theorizing mothering in terms of the concept of women's experience both express the desire of/for the mother in a way that makes more difficult critique of the ideological formations of individualism and essential motherhood themselves.

c o n c l u s i o n

THE IMPOSSIBILITY
OF MOTHERHOOD

a paradoxical politics of mothering

— the impossibility of motherhood —

MY READINGS OF the wide variety of feminist accounts of mothering that I have considered clearly establish that mothering is a site of contention not only in U.S. political culture but also in modern feminist theory. Disputes about mothering in U.S. political culture overlap with and influence disputes in feminist theory, so it is not surprising that issues related to mothering are currently debated in law and social policy, in business and workplace settings, in popular culture, in (all the different kinds of) families in the United States, among women, and in the minds of women, as well as among and in the minds of feminist theorists. Nor is it surprising that there should be less rather than more consensus about mothering in U.S. political culture and among feminist theorists at this time. More options with respect to mothering are possible for more women than ever before, largely as a result of the women's movement. But many women are still confused and beleaguered in their choices about mothering. At least partly as a result of a backlash against feminism, women are beset

242

on all sides by contradictory pressures about whether and how to be mothers. And, because many women are not in a position realistically and practically to avail themselves of the options with respect to mothering that are currently available, mothering perhaps does more to create conflicting interests among women than to unite them. At the same time, the variety of approaches that feminist theorists have adopted or devised for theorizing mothering have generated more disagreement than consensus among feminist theorists about mothering, as well as about the central concepts and the implications of these approaches to mothering.

My readings of these feminist accounts of mothering thus confirm that, at least in relationship to mothering, feminism in an individualist ideological context has "only paradoxes to offer" (Scott 1996). The feminist accounts of mothering that I have considered are framed in different theoretical terms, make different assumptions about what defines or constitutes mothering, emphasize different aspects of women's situations as mothers and their experiences of mothering, and draw different conclusions about the meaning and significance of mothering in women's lives and the social reorganization of mothering. Moreover, most of these accounts of mothering position themselves, to one extent or another, in resistance to essential motherhood. But all of them encounter, in one way or another, the dilemma of difference, including the paradoxes of embodiment, gender, and representation, that is an effect of the conflicted relationship of feminism and individualism. Feminist theory has been struggling with these paradoxes in connection with mothering since the emergence of feminism, and has offered a variety of attempts to resolve them. But none of the accounts of mothering that I consider entirely resolves the dilemma of difference and its resulting paradoxes. None successfully resists essential motherhood without also recuperating elements of individualism that problematize the analysis of mothering, and none successfully resists individualism without also recuperating elements of essential motherhood.

My analysis of feminist theory's struggles with the issue of mothering further suggests the need for reconceptualizing the goals of feminist theory itself as resistance to individualism and essential motherhood rather than resolution of the problem of mothering. Given the hegemony of individualism and essential motherhood, mothers' (and women's) identities, situations, and experiences themselves are contradictorily over-determined. So, in order to recognize, theorize, and negotiate these contradictions, feminist theory will have to abandon the goal of developing a unitary and totalizing account of motherhood. For this is the sort of goal taken up by the individualist subject, who is thought to be

THE IMPOSSIBILITY OF MOTHERHOOD

capable in principle of producing a complete, coherent, and exhaustive account of anything because he is able in principle to take up an unlimited, objective perspective on everything. Instead feminist theory will have to focus on specific instances of mothering in specific contexts in order to analyze in detail the complex processes of over-determination that differently constitute mothering in different material, social, and ideological contexts. Feminist theory will also have to theorize the ways in which the subject position 'mother' is variously and contradictorily constituted, so that the experience of being a mother is more or less partial, divided, fragmented, and even incoherent. Perhaps most importantly, feminist theory will have to be critically vigilant about its conflicted relationship to individualism and about its own desires for the experience of the complete and coherent subjectivity that individualism promises but never provides.

My readings of the accounts of mothering that I have considered also point to some of the more specific issues that feminist theory will face if its goals are reconceptualized along the lines I suggest. First, how can feminist theory preserve those elements of individualism required to sustain its claim of women's equal political agency and entitlement? How can feminist theory retain the advantages of an identity-based challenge to sexism and male dominance without recuperating those elements of individualism that problematize the analysis and representation of women's experience, situations, and interests? As paradoxical as it may seem, preserving these elements and advantages of an identity-based challenge to sexism and male dominance may require a more thorough challenge to individualism and the individualist foundations of dominant conceptions of subjectivity, agency, and entitlement than feminist theory has yet sustained. Feminist theory must insist that individualism is an inadequate account of subjectivity—of masculine as well as feminine and maternal subjectivity. For as long as feminist theory remains in thrall to the view that men or masculinity somehow better exemplify subjectivity as individualism defines it and thus better qualify for political agency and entitlement than women or femininity do, feminist theory itself will contribute to the double bind for women, and especially for mothers, constituted by the intersection of individualism and essential motherhood. An account of masculine—and paternal—subjectivity as contradictorily over-determined and therefore partial, divided, fragmented, and even incoherent would do more to advance the claim for women's equality than an argument for women's equal individualist subjectivity.[1] In other words, preserving what feminist theory has seen as the advantages of individualism may actually be better accomplished by a more thorough difference-based challenge to individualism.

I have argued that at the center of feminism's difference-based challenge to individualism is the question of how best to theorize embodied subjectivity. A persistent implication of the accounts of mothering I have considered is the importance of resisting as strenuously as possible the major elements of an individualist account of embodied subjectivity, especially mind/body dualism and the theories of knowledge, agency, and social relations that this dualism supports. My readings of these accounts of mothering further suggest that understanding embodied subjectivity in terms of the concept of subject positioning is a promising alternative to individualism for feminist theory. This approach to theorizing embodied subjectivity posits the reciprocal permeability of embodiment and subjectivity, the partiality and instability of subjectivity, the overlapping quality of subject positions, and the significance of reciprocity and mutuality in social relations including social relations in which subjects acquire knowledge and exercise agency. I have suggested that an understanding of embodied subjectivity along these lines can better account for the fragmented, divided, contradictory, and sometimes even incoherent subjectivity that persons experience as a result of the contradictory ideological over-determination of subjectivity, experience, and knowledge that occurs in liberal democratic capitalist material and social contexts. One of the advantages of such an account of embodied subjectivity, from the perspective of the project of theorizing mothering, is that it represents maternal embodied subjectivity, not as a deviant or failed subjectivity, but as a paradigmatically human subjectivity. It rejects individualism's view that pregnancy and childbirth are strange, frightening, almost inexplicable departures from the rational, autonomous, and separately embodied existence of human subjects. Instead it represents pregnancy as a crucially important instance of the embodied processes of subject constitution in which all subjects continually participate, and birth as the basis of all other processes of subject constitution. Another advantage is that it represents the mother-child relationship, in which a mutual, reciprocal, and ongoing constitution of subjectivity occurs, as a paradigmatically human relationship.

My readings of Ruddick's and Kristeva's accounts of mothering in particular suggest the further elaboration of this account of subject positioning in discursive terms. Ruddick's emphasis of the concept of narrative in her account of mothering implies the need to theorize embodied subjectivity in relationship to language, and Kristeva's theory of the discursive constitution of embodied subjectivity explicitly provides such a theory. Theorizing subject constitution as a discursive process also indicates the importance for feminist theory of taking seriously women's accounts of their experiences, but also of critically analyzing the material, social, and ideological conditions that over-determine women's account of their experiences.

But, as my readings of difference feminist accounts of mothering indicate, feminism's difference-based challenge to individualism presents other problems, particularly the risk of recuperating crucial elements of essential motherhood. So, can feminist theory preserve the advantages of a difference-based challenge to individualism while also minimizing these risks? The difference feminist accounts of mothering I have considered tend to rely on either psychoanalysis or feminist standpoint theory and the concept of women's experience to theorize women's difference. But, I have argued, psychoanalytic approaches to women's difference can yield a problematic account of maternal subjectivity, while feminist standpoint theory's presuppositions about women's experience may recuperate the individualist subject, understood as the subject of experience. In addition, both psychoanalytic approaches to women's difference and the concept of women's experience can include the desire of/for the mother, which I have interpreted as a desire for the complete and coherent subjectivity promised by individualism, including the demand that the mother make this experience of subjectivity possible or console for its impossibility. The advantages of these two approaches to theorizing women's difference for resisting individualism, however, also raise the question of whether it is possible to bring them together in some way that preserves their advantages while minimizing their risks. For instance, is it possible to reconceptualize the concept of a standpoint in feminist standpoint theories in terms of the discursive constitution of subjectivity? Is Lacanian psychoanalysis the best approach for reconceptualizing the concept of a standpoint in discursive terms? Or are there other accounts of the discursive constitution of subjectivity that feminist theory might adopt or develop for this purpose?[2] Furthermore, would a reconceptualization of the concept of a standpoint in discursive terms address the problem of the concept of a standpoint slipping between two meanings, namely, a standpoint understood as a position or location and a standpoint understood as a perspective or an outlook? Would it address this problem more adequately than do Ruddick's, Rich's, and Collins's uses of the concept of women's experience? On the other hand, is it possible to theorize the discursive constitution of subjectivity without positioning the mother as prediscursive and thus problematizing maternal subjectivity, as I have argued occurs in Lacanian psychoanalysis and in Kristeva's account of mothering? Can the concept of subject positioning that I have elicited from Beauvoir's, Ruddick's, and Kristeva's accounts of mothering include a theory of the discursive constitu-

tion of women's, mothers', and/or feminist standpoints that avoids the problem of positioning the mother as prediscursive? While none of these questions
is easy to answer—and I don't propose to answer them here—it seems to me
that an ongoing engagement with the issue of mothering brings these and
other, related questions to the forefront of feminist theory's continuing efforts
to reconceptualize embodied subjectivity.

In other words, my readings of these feminist accounts of mothering show
that representing and analyzing mothering inevitably includes the project of
reconceptualizing embodied subjectivity. This is perhaps most evident in my
consideration of Beauvoir's struggles to theorize pregnancy and childbirth,
but individualism's conception of subjectivity is at least called into question
by all of the accounts of mothering that I have examined. Furthermore, my
readings of these accounts of mothering establish not only the impossibility of
motherhood, but also the impossibility of individualist subjectivity. Feminist
theory is faced not only with the paradox of how to theorize mothering while
recognizing the impossibility of motherhood, but also the paradox of how to
theorize subjectivity while recognizing the impossibility of being a subject. To
put this in Kristeva's terms, however, I conclude that these two impossibilities
are "just the way it is," and I believe that, in accepting this, feminist theory
"gnaws at the symbolic's almightiness" (1986: 185). So clearly, neither I nor
any other feminist theorist is in a position to resolve once and for all the paradoxes of embodiment, gender, and representation and solve the dilemma of
difference in theorizing mothering. Rather, feminist theorists must recognize
that, given the hegemony of individualism and essential motherhood,
accounts of mothering will inevitably be characterized by inconsistencies and
contradictions, and feminist theory will inevitably include multiple accounts
of mothering that will contradict each other and nonetheless contribute
something important to our understanding of mothering. Furthermore,
accounts of mothering characterized by inconsistencies and contradictions
can nonetheless be politically enabling and useful. Feminist theory will have
to focus on which (incomplete and contradictory) account of mothering provides the best alternative to essential motherhood in specifically defined contexts or at specifically defined moments for advancing specific feminist social
and political goals (Fraser and Nicholson 1990). In its current ideological context, U.S. feminism can only offer an inevitably paradoxical politics of mothering. A politics of mothering that recognizes the simultaneous impossibility
and ideological significance of motherhood may actually be the most reason-
able position to take in a political culture that fetishizes motherhood and

childhood and preaches family values while providing little or no material and social support for actual mothers and children.

— a paradoxical politics of mothering —

A politics of mothering that accepts the impossibility of motherhood and the impossibility of individualist subjectivity, and that does not require for its foundation a univocal, coherent, and exhaustive position on mothering, might instead make possible multiple and overlapping positions of resistance to individualism and essential motherhood, and might show how to achieve or constitute the possibility of movement among such positions. Such a politics of mothering might create the conditions for strategic movement among contradictory positions on mothering in response to different articulations of the intersection of individualism and essential motherhood in different contexts and at different times. It would consciously include both an identity-based challenge to sexism and male dominance and a difference-based challenge to individualism (as do most of the accounts of mothering I have considered) in order to sustain a multifaceted resistance to both essential motherhood and individualism. This might allow feminism to take advantage of those moments when the intersection of individualism and essential motherhood is most open to critique, subversion, and rearticulation.

What, then, are some of the paradoxes of mothering that such a politics would have to encompass? In general, a paradoxical politics of mothering would take up a wide variety of issues related to conception, pregnancy, birth, and child rearing, but it would recognize that it cannot offer a completely coherent and consistent position on these issues. Because such a politics would especially look to the complex material, social, and ideological over-determination of mothering and the inconsistent material, social, and ideological effects of the intersection of individualism and essential motherhood, its responses to these inconsistent effects are likely to be inconsistent themselves. But this sort of interplay of inconsistency may do more to subvert and rearticulate dominant ideological formations than the attempt to construct a univocal and coherent response to the contradictions of mothering as it is theorized, organized, and experienced in the context of individualism and essential motherhood. For example, a paradoxical politics of mothering would recognize the great variety of ways in which people can take responsibility and care for children. It would recognize different kinds of families and theorize the specificities, for instance, of single parenting, step-parenting, and gay and lesbian parenting, without delegitimizing these kinds of families and parents. It would also recognize that some kinds of care are required by all children, but also that all children require some kinds of care that are specific to them and/or their circumstances, for instance, as Ruddick's account of maternal practice argues. It would also consider a wide variety of outcomes as acceptable results of child rearing. Such a politics of mothering would strive to destabilize the distinctions of mothers, fathers, and people who are "childless" so as to create even more variety of ways that all persons can participate in caring for children, as Collin's account of African-American traditions of mothering does. But a paradoxical politics of mothering would also recognize that some persons, including some women, will have little or nothing to offer in caring for children, and some persons, including some women, will want little or nothing to do with it, and support this position in relationship to mothering as well.

The issue related to mothering that perhaps most widely engages U.S. political culture at the moment is the difficulty many women, and a small but growing number of men, face in caring for children while also working for pay to provide financially for them. The sort of paradoxical politics of mothering that I imagine would strive to create new ways for mothers to care for children while also engaging in work for pay, and to challenge employers, schools, local communities, and other institutions to respond to the needs of mothers and other child rearers employed for pay. It would insist that paid work, and the supports necessary to engage in it, must be available to all persons engaged in child rearing, for example, as both Gilman and Beauvoir argue. This politics would also recognize and strive to serve the needs of paid child care givers for good working conditions and adequate wages for their work. At the same time, it would demand the possibility of full-time child rearing, and advocate the material and social support of this form of child rearing, as Key advocated. But, more so than Key, it would advocate ways of enabling full-time child rearers to be as independent and as free as possible from the control of other individuals, organizations, and the state. A paradoxical politics of mothering would also take into account the difficulties and risks of combining child rearing with paid work and of full-time child rearing, depending on their social organization. This politics of mothering would support the choice of full-time child rearing while theorizing how, in modern industrialized capitalist social contexts, the option of full-time child rearing is not realistically and practically available to many people and full-time child rearing has meant the risk of economic dependency and thus disempowerment for those who engage in it. But it would also support the choice to combine paid work with child rearing while theorizing how, in modern industrialized capitalist social contexts, this form of child rearing is not a choice but a necessity for many persons, and this choice risks insufficient attention to the needs of children and the overworking of mothers and other child rearers who make this choice. A paradoxical politics of mothering would insist on public support of mothering, including material support, while resisting public control of mothers and child rearers. This politics would theorize both the risks of public support for mothering, which easily slips into public control of mothers, and the risks of public disengagement from mothering, which can leave mothers and child rearers without sufficient material and social support.

An issue related to mothering that has very much engaged feminism in particular is the development of many different ways of consciously intervening in the processes of conception, pregnancy, and birth, or what have come to be called reproductive technologies.[3] This issue makes a number of demands on a paradoxical politics of mothering. It requires the recognition that reproductive technologies can greatly enhance women's options with respect to mothering. But it also demands the acknowledgment that, in modern, industrialized capitalist social contexts, these technologies are not equally accessible to all women and that these technologies can be used both to control and exploit women, particularly by putting some women in the position of being able to exploit other women, for instance in the case of surrogate and adoptive mothers. So a paradoxical politics of mothering would work for the equal access of all women to reproductive technologies while also working to prevent their use in ways that control and exploit women. It would recognize that the greater use of reproductive technologies risks the recuperation of essential motherhood's view that all women are meant to be and want to be mothers. It would also analyze how the greater use of reproductive technologies risks delegitimizing some ways of becoming mothers, such as adoption, and some children, such as disabled children, by valorizing children with some biological and/or genetic connection to their parents and children without characteristics that traditional medical practices see as defects to be corrected or eliminated. A paradoxical politics of mothering would also resist the tendency to settle the problems raised by these reproductive technologies in individualist terms, for instance, by developing and enforcing surrogacy contracts, in order to resist recuperating the individualist concept of subjectivity and the material, social, and ideological circumstances supported by this concept of subjectivity.

Since I have argued that the naturalization of maternal heterosexuality and the denial of the possibility of lesbian mothering is a deeply embedded element of essential motherhood, it might seem that an unambiguous support for and encouragement of lesbian mothering would be one of the best ways for feminism to resist essential motherhood. But even in this case, a paradoxical political position on lesbian mothering might be more effective at undermining essential motherhood. A paradoxical politics of mothering would not only support the rights of lesbians to become mothers and the rights of lesbian mothers, it would recognize and respond to the fact that lesbians can be and become mothers in a variety of ways. It would articulate the specificities of the variety of lesbian experiences of mothering, and critique the constraints and obstacles lesbian mothers may face without valorizing and/or romanticizing lesbian mothers as mothers and/or as feminists. But a paradoxical politics of mothering would also encompass the concern that the small but growing trend toward lesbian mothering and its greater public visibility constitute a "domestication" of lesbianism (Robson 1992). This concern recognizes that lesbian mothering is not inevitably or unambiguously resistant to essential motherhood. Indeed, lesbian mothers might try harder and be more successful at mothering as essential motherhood defines it precisely because their mothering is delegitimated by essential motherhood. This concern also recognizes that lesbian mothering may weaken or detract from the resistance to essential motherhood, as well as to other forms of male dominance, implicit in a lesbian refusal to engage in mothering (Card 1996).

In describing these elements of a paradoxical politics of mothering, it is important to emphasize that the particular stances that feminism might take on issues related to mothering, the specific ways in which feminism might elaborate these concerns and act on them, cannot be anticipated in advance with much clarity or specificity. Like so much else of feminist practice, this paradoxical politics will often find itself in a reactive position, grappling with elements of dominant ideological formations and struggling to subvert and rearticulate them; interacting with dominant institutions and struggling to reconstruct them; confronting dominant social policies and practices and struggling to change or redeploy them. And these efforts will always have contradictory results, some rather easy to foresee, others not. To express this more concretely, a paradoxical politics of mothering might find itself defending a minor girl's right to an abortion without parental consent one day, and defending a mother's right to determine her child's health care the next. And the paradoxical politics of mothering that I describe will have to struggle with many contradictions of this sort. In the ideological context in which feminism in the United States operates at present, resisting and countering the contradictory effects for mothers and women of the intersection of individualism and essential motherhood depends on recognizing the impossibility of motherhood—the impossibility of being a mother as essential motherhood specifies motherhood and the impossibility of being both a mother and a political subject as individualism defines subjectivity—and accepting the paradoxical politics of mothering that follows from this recognition.

NOTES

Chapter One
1 Althusser 1969, 1971; Gramsci 1971; Laclau and Mouffe 1985; Hennessy 1993.
2 Althusser 1969: 89–127; Larrain 1983: 180–97; Laclau and Mouffe 1985: 97–105; Hennessy 1993: 29–30.
3 The question of the extent to which the concept of the discursive is sufficient to conceptualize what exists and is effective has of course been very much debated in recent feminist theory and in other theoretical practices. Without purporting to settle this question in its entirety, my concept of ideology resists the distinction of the discursive and the nondiscursive, especially versions of this distinction that read discursivity as immateriality and materiality as nondiscursivity (Laclau and Mouffe 1985: 107–113). Instead I try to maintain a view of discursivity as enmattered and materializing, and a view of materiality as a process of ongoing discursive constitution and enactment (Butler 1993: 1–12, 27–31). Nonetheless, my conceptualization of ideology, like the feminist accounts of mothering I analyze, is both dependent on and undermined by the dominant discourse of individualism on which I, like all theorists, must rely in an individualist ideology context. Thus, my attempt to articulate what I mean by "ideology" and how I understand it to operate in terms of concepts of discursivity and materiality inevitably imports the implicit distinction of the material and the immaterial. I am sure that the tendency to read these conceptions of discursivity and materiality in these terms is inevitable, but I believe it is also resistible.
4 Eisenstein and Jardine, eds., 1985; Scott 1988; Minow 1990; Rhode, ed., 1990; Bock and James, eds., 1992.
5 The literature of critiques of essentialism in feminist theory is quite extensive. See, for example, Scott 1988, 1991; Spivak 1988a; Riley 1988; Fuss 1989; Fraser and Nicholson 1990; Butler 1990, 1993; Grosz 1994; Nicholson 1994. For an analysis of this critique in relationship to mothering, see DiQuinzio 1993.
6 The literature of feminist critiques of this individualist theory of knowledge is also quite extensive. See, for example, Hartsock 1985, Harding 1983, 1991; Lloyd 1984; Keller 1984; Grimshaw 1986; Bordo 1987; Gatens 1991; Haraway 1991.
7 On 'interpellation', see Althusser 1969; De Lauretis 1987: 12; Spivak 1988a: 204; Hennessy 1993: 75; Weedon 1987: 30–32.
8 Rubin 1975; Unger and Crawford 1992; Bem 1993; Lorber 1994; for analyses of the use of the concept 'gender' in social constructivism, see Scott 1986; Nicholson 1994; Hawkesworth 1997; McKenna and Kessler 1997; Smith, Steven G. 1997; Scott 1997; Connell 1997.
9 On feminist standpoint epistemologies, see Hartsock 1985, 1997b; Harding 1983, 1991, 1997; Haraway 1991; Alcoff and Potter, eds., 1993; Hirschmann 1997;

Hundelby 1997; O'Leary 1997; Welton 1997; Collins 1997; Hekman 1997; Smith, Steven G. 1997; Smith, Dorothy E. 1997. Feminist reinterpretations of psychoanalysis include Mitchell 1975; Chodorow 1978; Gallop 1982, 1985; Kofman 1985; Spregnether 1990.

Chapter Two
1 Key 1912a, 1913.
2 Gilman 1911, 1913a, 1913b, 1913c, 1913d, 1913e, 1913f, 1914a, 1914b, 1914c, 1915a, 1915b.
3 See also Havelock Ellis's introduction to *Love and Marriage* (Key 1911: xv–xvi).
4 Thanks to Barri Gold, Muhlenberg College, for this point.

Chapter Three
1 But see Oliver 1993: 163–68, for the problematics of the categorization "French feminists."
2 Ruddick's first work on maternal thinking appeared in print in the summer of 1980, and so may not have been available to Elshtain at the time of writing *Public Man, Private Woman*. Elshtain's source for Ruddick's work is a graduate seminar paper written by Christine de Stephano at the University of Massachusetts, Amherst, in 1979.

Chapter Four
1 Those who have criticized Beauvoir's theory of embodiment in these terms include McCall 1979; Seigfried 1984; Hartsock 1985; Gatens 1991. A critique of Beauvoir's theory of embodiment that focuses on its effects on her account of mothering is O'Brien 1981. Those who have argued that Beauvoir's theory of embodiment resists or challenges dualism, or contributes something to such resistance and challenge, include Butler 1986; Young 1989; Ward 1995. But see also Butler 1990. See Pilardi 1995, for a good survey of this discussion.
2 On over-determination, see Althusser 1969: 89–127; Larrain 1983: 180–97; Laclau and Mouffe 1985: 97–105; Hennessy 1993: 29–30.

Chapter Five
1 For example, Thorne and Yalom 1982; Nicholson 1986; Okin 1989; Folbre 1994.
2 On feminist standpoint theory, see also Harding 1983, 1986, 1991; Haraway 1991; Alcoff and Potter 1993; Hartsock 1985, 1997; Hirschmann 1997; Hundelby 1997; O'Leary 1997; Welton 1997.
3 My analysis of how the concept of experience operates in Ruddick's argument relies on Scott 1991; see also Mohanty 1992. For a discussion of the use of the concept of experience that specifically considers Ruddick's work, see Grant 1987.
4 As I see it, feminist standpoint theory does better to argue for its political rather than epistemological superiority. See Tronto 1993 for such an argument. This is also true of Ruddick's claim that, with respect to mothering, she "makes it up" (1989: 61–64).

5 Note the slippage that excludes "those mothers who are" *men* from one of the criteria Ruddick articulates here. This has the effect of repudiating the implication of the concept of maternal practice that men can be mothers, and maintaining a connection of femininity and mothering.
6 Adams and Minson 1978; Weedon 1987; Haraway 1991: 190–201.

Chapter Six
1 Kristeva 1984: 22–23, 58–61, 99–106, 138–39, 143–44, 208–13; see also Oliver 1993: 12–14, 182–88.
2 The question of the essentialist implications of the figure of the mother in Kristeva's work has much occupied other feminist theorists. See Leland 1992; Butler 1990; Grosz 1990; Stanton 1989; as well as Rose 1986; Ziarek 1992, Oliver 1993. For an argument that Beauvoir provides a less essentialized account of maternal subjectivity than does Kristeva, see Zerilli 1992.
3 See also Hirsch 1989; Spregnether 1990.
4 See also Kofman 1985; Spregnether 1990.
5 See also Fraser 1992; Leland 1992; Myers 1992, for more broadly focused critiques of the adequacy of psychoanalysis as a basis for feminist theory and politics.
6 See Haraway 1990, for a similar critique of the desires at work in theorizing origins in terms of mothering.

Chapter Seven
1 See also Roof 1991: 90–118, where she argues that both Kristeva and Chodorow tend to assume a far more homogeneously heterosexual female identity than either Freud or Lacan.
2 See also Chodorow 1978: 194, where Chodorow is quick to point out Balint's assumption of women's heterosexuality in her explanation of the processes of identification that occur in heterosexual intercourse.

Chapter Eight
1 See Gallop 1988, for her deployment of Rich's call for "thinking through the body" to launch a very different approach to the complexities of identity and difference in feminist theory.
2 The expectation that the autobiographical thread of *Of Woman Born* will include some account of Rich's experience of lesbian mothering is also raised by reading *Of Woman Born* in light of some of her other work from the same time period, especially " 'It is the Lesbian in Us . . . ' " read at the Modern Language Association meetings in December 1976 (1979 [1976]), and "The Meaning of Our Love for Women Is What We Have Constantly to Expand," a speech from 1977 (1979 [1977]).

Conclusion
1 For an interesting step in this direction, see Laqueur 1990 and Ruddick 1990.
2 See, for example, Haraway 1990; Hennessy 1993: 74–99; Hartsock 1997a, 1997b; Hekman 1997.
3 See Purdy 1996; Ginsburg and Rapp, eds., 1995; Raymond 1993; Rowland 1992; Lasker 1987; Stansworth, ed., 1987; Corea 1985.

REFERENCES

Adams, Parveen, and Jeff Minson. 1990. "The 'Subject' of Feminism," in Parveen and Cowie, eds., *The Woman in Question*. Cambridge: MIT Press.

Alcoff, Linda, and Elizabeth Potter, eds. 1993. *Feminist Epistemologies*. New York: Routledge.

Althusser, Louis. 1969. *For Marx*. London: Penguin.

———. 1971. *Lenin and Philosophy*. New York: Monthly Review Press.

———. 1979. *Reading Capital*. London: Verso.

Badinter, Elizabeth. 1980. *Mother Love: Myth and Reality*. New York: Macmillan.

Beauvoir, Simone de. 1989 [1952]. *The Second Sex*. New York: Vintage.

Bem, Sandra. 1993. *The Lenses of Gender: Transforming the Debate on Sexual Inequality*. New Haven, CT: Yale University Press.

Bernard, Jessica. 1972. *The Future of Motherhood*. New York: Bantam Books.

Bock, Gisela, and Susan James, eds. 1992. *Beyond Equality and Difference: Citizenship, Feminist Politics, and Female Subjectivity*. New York: Routledge.

Bordo, Susan. 1987. *The Flight to Objectivity: Essays on Cartesianism and Culture*. Albany, NY: State University of New York Press.

Braidotti, Rosi. 1989. "The Politics of Ontological Differences," in Brennan, ed., *Between Feminism and Psychoanalysis*. New York: Routledge.

Buhle, Mary Jo. 1981. *Women and American Socialism, 1870–1920*. Urbana: University of Illinois Press.

Butler, Judith. 1986. "Sex and Gender in Simone de Beauvoir's *The Second Sex*." *Yale French Studies* 72: 35–49.

———. 1990. *Gender Trouble: Feminism and the Subversion of Identity*. New York: Routledge.

———. 1993. *Bodies That Matter: On the Discursive Limits of 'Sex.'* New York: Routledge.

Card, Claudia. 1996. "Against Marriage and Motherhood." *Hypatia* 11 (3): 1–23.

Chodorow, Nancy. 1978. *The Reproduction of Mothering: Feminism, Psychoanalysis and the Sociology of Gender*. Berkeley: University of California Press.

Cixous, Helene. 1976. "The Laugh of the Medusa," in Marks and de Courtivron, eds., *New French Feminisms*. New York: Schocken.

———. 1985. *The Newly Born Woman*. Minneapolis: University of Minnesota Press.

Collins, Patricia Hill. 1991. *Black Feminist Thought: Knowledge, Consciousness, and the Politics of Empowerment*. New York: Routledge.

———. 1997. "Comment on Hekman's 'Truth and Method: Feminist Standpoint Theory Revisited': Where's the Power?" *Signs* 22 (2): 375–81.

Connell, R. W. 1997. "Comment on Hawkesworth's 'Confounding Gender' Restructuring Gender,." *Signs* 22 (3): 702–7.

Corea, Gena. 1985. *The Mother Machine: Reproducing Technologies from Artificial Insemination to Artificial Wombs*. New York: Harper and Row.

Cott, Nancy. 1987. *The Grounding of Modern Feminism*. New Haven: Yale University Press.

Daly, Mary. 1978. *Gyn/Ecology: The Metaethics of Radical Feminism*. Boston: Beacon Press.

De Lauretis, Teresa. 1987. *Technologies of Gender: Essays on Theory, Film, and Fiction*. Bloomington: Indiana University Press.

Derrida, Jacques. 1974. *Of Grammatology*. Baltimore: Johns Hopkins University Press.

———. 1978. *Writing and Difference*. Chicago: University of Chicago Press.

———. 1981. *Dissemination*. Chicago: University of Chicago Press.

———. 1982. *Margins of Philosophy*. Chicago: University of Chicago Press.

Dietz, Mary G. 1985. "Citizenship with a Feminist Face: The Problem with Maternal Thinking." *Political Theory* 13 (Spring): 19–37.

———. 1987. "Context Is All: Feminism and Theories of Citizenship." *Daedalus* 116 (Fall): 1–24.

Dinnerstein, Dorothy. 1976. *The Mermaid and the Minotaur: Sexual Arrangements and Human Malaise.* New York: Harper Colophon.

DiQuinzio, Patrice. 1993. "Exclusion and Essentialism in Feminist Theory: The Problem of Mothering." *Hypatia* 8 (3): 1–20.

———. 1995. "Feminist Theory and the Question of Citizenship: A Reply to Dietz' Critique of Maternalism." *Women and Politics* 15 (summer): 23–42.

Donovan, Josephine. 1985. *Feminist Theory: The Intellectual Traditions of American Feminism.* New York: Continuum.

Echols, Alice. 1989. *Daring to Be Bad: Radical Feminism in America, 1967–1975.* Minneapolis: University of Minnesota Press.

Edelstein, Marilyn. 1992. "Metaphor, Meta-narrative, and Mater-narrative in Kristeva's 'Stabat Mater,'" in Crownfield, ed., *in Julia Kristeva.* Albany, NY: State University of New York Press.

Egan, Maureen L. 1989. "Evolutionary Thought in the Social Philosophy of Charlotte Perkins Gilman." *Hypatia* 4 (1): 102–19.

Eisenstein, Hester. 1983. *Contemporary Feminist Thought.* Boston: G. K. Hall and Co.

Eisenstein, Hester, and Alice Jardine, eds. 1985. *The Future of Difference.* New Brunswick, NJ: Rutgers University Press.

Elshtain, Jean Bethke. 1981. *Public Man, Private Woman.* Princeton, NJ: Princeton University Press.

———. 1982a. "Antigone's Daughters." *Democracy* 2 (April): 46–59.

———. 1982b. "Feminism, Family and Community." *Dissent* 29 (fall): 442–49.

———. 1990. *Power Trips and Other Journeys: Essays in Feminism as Civic Discourse.* Madison: University of Wisconsin Press.

———. 1991. "Against Gay Marriage II: Accepting Limits." *Commonweal,* November 22: 685–86.

———. 1994. "Single Motherhood: Response to Iris Marion Young." *Dissent* (winter): 267–69.

Evans, Sara. 1979. *Personal Politics: The Roots of Women's Liberation in the Civil Rights Movement and the New Left.* New York: Vintage.

Ferguson, Ann. 1989. *Blood at the Root: Motherhood, Sexuality, and Male Dominance.* London: Pandora.

Firestone, Shulamith. 1970. *The Dialectic of Sex.* New York: Bantam.

Folbre, Nancy. 1994. *Who Pays for the Kids? Gender and the Structures of Constraint.* New York: Routledge.

Foucault, Michel. 1980. *The History of Sexuality,* Volume 1. New York: Vintage.

———. 1987. *Language, Counter-Memory, Practice: Selected Essays and Interviews.* Ithaca, NY: Cornell University Press.

Fraser, Nancy. 1992. "The Uses and Abuses of French Discourse Theories for Feminist Politics," in Fraser and Bartky, eds., *Revaluing French Feminism: Critical Essays on Difference, Agency, and Culture.* Bloomington: Indiana University Press.

Fraser, Nancy, and Linda Nicholson. 1990. "Social Criticism Without Philosophy: An Encounter between Feminism and Postmodernism," in Linda Nicholson, ed., *Feminism/ Postmodernism.* New York: Routledge.

Freud, Sigmund. 1923 [1961]. "The Infantile Genital Organization of the Libido," in *The Standard Edition of the Complete Works of Sigmund Freud,* Volume 19. London: Hogarth.

———. 1924 [1961]. "The Dissolution of the Oedipus Complex," in *The Standard Edition of the Complete Works of Sigmund Freud,* Volume 19. London: Hogarth.

———. 1925 [1961]. "Some Psychical Consequences of the Anatomical Distinction Between the Sexes," in *The Standard Edition of the Complete Works of Sigmund Freud,* Volume 19. London: Hogarth.

———. 1931 [1961]. "Female Sexuality," in *The Standard Edition of the Complete Works of*

Sigmund Freud, Volume 21. London: Hogarth.

Friedan, Betty. 1963. *The Feminine Mystique*. New York: Norton.

Fuss, Diana. 1989. *Essentially Speaking: Feminism, Nature, and Difference*. New York: Routledge.

Gallop, Jane. 1982. *The Daughter's Seduction: Feminism and Psychoanalysis*. Ithaca, NY: Cornell University Press.

————. 1985. *Reading Lacan*. Ithaca, NY: Cornell University Press.

————. 1988. *Thinking Through the Body*. New York: Columbia University Press.

Gatens, Moira. 1991. *Feminism and Philosophy: Perspectives on Difference and Equality*. Bloomington: Indiana University Press.

Gilligan, Carol. 1977. "In a Different Voice: Women's Conceptions of Self and Morality." *Harvard Educational Review* 47, 4 (November): 481–517.

Gilligan, Carol. 1982. *In a Different Voice*. Cambridge: Harvard University Press.

Gilman, Charlotte Perkins. 1898 [1966]. *Women and Ecomomics*. Boston: Small, Maynard and Company [New York: Harper and Row].

————. 1910a. "Genius, Domestic and Maternal." *Forerunner* 1 (June): 10–12 and (July): 5–7.

————. 1910b. "Comment and Review." *Forerunner* 1 (December): 25–26. [Review of Key, *The Century of the Child*.]

————. 1911. "Comment and Review." *Forerunner* 2 (October): 280–82. [Review of Key, *Love and Marriage*.]

————. 1913a. "On Ellen Key and the Woman Movement." *Forerunner* 4 (February): 35–38.

————. 1913b. "Education for Motherhood." *Forerunner* 4 (October): 259–62.

————. 1913c. "Ellen Key's Attack on 'Amaternal Feminism.'" *Current Opinion* 54 (February): 138–39.

————. 1913d. "Charlotte Perkins Gilman's Reply to Ellen Key." *Current Opinion* 54 (March): 220–21.

————. 1913e. "The New Mothers of a New World." *Forerunner* 4 (June): 145–49.

————. 1913f. "Illegitimate Children." *Forerunner* 4, (November): 295–97.

————. 1914a. "As to 'Feminism.'" *Forerunner* 5 (February): 45.

————. 1914b. "The Conflict Between Human and Female Feminism." *Current Opinion* 55 (April): 291.

————. 1914c. "Feminism or Polygamy." *Forerunner* 5 (October): 260–61.

————. 1915a. "Birth Control." *Forerunner* 6 (July): 177–80.

————. 1915b. "Pensions for 'Mothers' and 'Widows.'" *Forerunner* 5 (January): 7–8.

Ginsburg, Faye D., and Rayna Rapp, eds. 1995. *Conceiving the New World Order: The Global Politics of Reproduction*. Berkeley: University of California Press.

Gramsci, Antonio. 1971. *Selections from the Prison Notebooks*. New York: International Publishers.

Grant, Judith. 1987. "I Feel Therefore I Am: A Critique of Female Experience as a Basis for Feminist Epistemology." *Women and Politics* 7 (3): 99–114.

Grimshaw, Jean. 1986. *Philosophy and Feminist Thinking*. Minneapolis: University of Minnesota Press.

Grosz, Elizabeth. 1990. "The Body of Subjection," in Fletcher and Benjamin, eds., *Abjection, Melancholia, and Love: The Work of Julia Kristeva*. New York: Routledge.

————. 1994. *Volatile Bodies: Toward a Corporeal Feminism*. Bloomington: Indiana University Press.

Haraway, Donna. 1990. "A Manifesto for Cyborgs: Science, Technology and Socialist Feminism in the 1980s," in Nicholson, ed., *Feminism/Postmodernism*. New York: Routledge.

————. 1991. *Simians, Cyborgs, and Women: The Reinvention of Nature*. New York: Routledge.

Harding, Sandra. 1983. "Why Has the Sex/Gender System Become Evident Only Now?" in Harding and Hintikka, eds., *Discovering Reality: Feminist Perspectives on Epistemology, Metaphysics, Methodology, and Philosophy of Science*. Boston: Kluwer.

————. 1986. *The Science Question in Feminism*. Ithaca, NY: Cornell University Press.

———— 1991. *Whose Science? Whose Knowledge? Thinking from Women's Lives*. Ithaca, NY: Cornell University Press.

————. 1997. "Comment on Hekman's 'Truth and Method: Feminist Standpoint Theories Revisited.'" *Signs* 22 (2): 382–91.

Hartsock, Nancy C. M. 1985. *Money, Sex, and Power: Toward a Feminist Historical Materialism*. Boston: Northeastern University Press.

————. 1997a. "Standpoint Theories for the Next Century." *Women and Politics* 18 (3): 93–101.

————. 1997b. "Comment on Hekman's 'Truth and Method: Feminist Standpoint Theories Revisited': Truth or Justice?" *Signs* 22 (2): 367–74.

Hawkesworth, Mary. 1997. "Confounding Gender," and "Reply to McKenna and Kessler, Smith, Scott, and Connell: Interrogating Gender." *Signs* 22 (3): 649–85 and 707–13.

Hekman, Susan. 1997. "Truth and Method: Feminist Standpoint Theories Revisited" and "Reply to Hartsock, Harding, and Smith." *Signs* 22 (2): 341–65 and 399–402.

Held, Virginia. 1993. *Feminist Morality: Transforming Culture, Society, and Politics*. Chicago: University of Chicago Press.

Hennessy, Rosemary. 1993. *Materialist Feminism and the Politics of Discourse*. New York: Routledge.

Hirsch, Marianne. 1989. *The Mother/Daughter Plot*. Bloomington: Indiana University Press.

Hirschmann, Nancy J. 1997. "Feminist Standpoint as Postmodern Strategy." *Women and Politics* 18 (3): 73–92.

Hochschild, Arlie. 1989. *The Second Shift: Working Parents and the Revolution at Home*. New York: Viking Penguin.

Hundelby, Catherine. 1997. "Where Standpoint Stands Now." *Women and Politics* 18 (3): 25–43.

Irigaray, Luce. 1985a. *Speculum of the Other Woman*. Ithaca, NY: Cornell University Press.

————. 1985b. *The Sex Which Is not One*. Ithaca, NY: Cornell University Press.

————. 1991. *The Ethics of Sexual Difference*. Ithaca, NY: Cornell University Press.

Jaggar, Alison M. 1983. *Feminist Politics and Human Nature*. Totowa, NJ: Roman and Allanheld.

Jardine, Alice. 1985. *Gynesis: Configurations of Woman and Modernity*. Ithaca, NY: Cornell University Press.

Keller, Evelyn Fox. 1984. *Reflections on Gender and Science*. New Haven, CT: Yale University Press.

Key, Ellen. 1909. *The Century of the Child*. New York: G. P. Putnam's Sons.

————. 1911. *Love and Marriage*. New York: G. P. Putnam's Sons.

————. 1912a. *The Woman Movement*. New York: G. P. Putnam's Sons.

————. 1912b. "Motherliness." *Atlantic Monthly* 110 (October): 562–70.

————. 1913. "Education for Motherhood." *Atlantic Monthly* 112 (July): 48–61 and (August): 191–97.

————. 1914. *The Renaissance of Motherhood*. New York: G. P. Putnam's Sons.

Kofman, Sarah. 1985. *The Enigma of Woman: Woman in Freud's Writings*. Ithaca, NY: Cornell University Press.

Kristeva, Julia. 1980 [1977]. "Motherhood According to Giovanni Bellini," in Leon S. Rondiez, ed., *Desire in Language: A Semiotic Approach to Art and Literature*. New York: Columbia University Press.

————. 1982 [1982]. *Powers of Horror: An Essay on Abjection*. New York: Columbia University Press.

————. 1984 [1974]. *Revolution in Poetic Language*. New York: Columbia University Press.

————. 1986 [1977,1983]. "Stabat Mater," in Toril Moi, ed., *The Kristeva Reader*. New York: Columbia University Press.

————. 1987. "Talking About Polylogue," in Toril Moi, ed., *French Feminist Thought*. Oxford: Basil Blackwell.

Lacan, Jacques. 1977. *Ecrits: A Selection*. New York: Norton.

————. 1985. *Feminine Sexuality: Jacques Lacan and the Ecole Freudienne*. Mitchell and Rose, eds. New York: Norton.

Laclau, Ernesto, and Chantal Mouffe. 1985. *Hegemony and Socialist Strategy: Towards a Radical Democratic Politics*. London: Verso.

Laqueur, Thomas. 1990. "The Facts of Fatherhood," in Hirsch and Fox Keller, eds., *Conflicts in Feminism*. New York: Routledge.

Larrain, Jorge. 1983. *Marxism and Ideology*. Atlantic Highlands, NJ: Humanities Press.

Lasker, Judith. 1987. *In Search of Parenthood: Coping with Infertility and High-Tech Conception*. Boston: Beacon.

Lazarre, Jane. 1985. *The Mother Knot*. Boston: Beacon.

Leland, Dorothy. 1992. "Lacanian Psychoanalysis and French Feminism: Toward an Adequate Political Psychology," in Fraser and Bartky, eds., *Revaluing French Feminism: Critical Essays on Difference, Agency, and Culture*. Bloomington: Indiana University Press.

Lloyd, Genevieve. 1984. *The Man of Reason: 'Male' and 'Female' in Western Philosophy*. Minneapolis: University of Minnesota Press.

Lorber, Judith. 1994. *Paradoxes of Gender*. New Haven, CT: Yale University Press.

Lorde, Audre. 1984. *Sister Outsider*. Trumansburg, NY: Crossings Press.

Marks, Elaine, and Isabelle de Courtivron, eds. 1980. *New French Feminism*. New York: Schocken.

McCall, Dorothy Kaufman. 1979. "Simone de Beauvoir, *The Second Sex*, and Jean-Paul Sartre." *Signs* 5 (winter): 203–9.

McKenna, Wendy, and Suzanne Kessler. 1997. "Comment on Hawkesworth's 'Confounding Gender': Who Needs Gender Theory?" *Signs* 22 (3): 650–91.

Meyers, Diana T. 1992. "The Subversion of Women's Agency in Psychoanalytic Feminism: Chodorow, Flax, and Kristeva," in Fraser and Bartky, eds., *Revaluing French Feminism: Critical Essays on Difference, Agency, and Culture*. Bloomington: Indiana University Press.

Minow, Martha. 1990. *Making All the Difference: Inclusion, Exclusion, and American Law*. Ithaca, NY: Cornell University Press.

Mitchell, Juliet. 1975. *Psychoanalysis and Feminism*. New York: Random House.

Mohanty, Chandra Talape. 1992. "Feminist Encounters: Locating the Politics of Experience," in Michelle Barrett and Anne Phillips, eds., *Destabilizing Theory: Contemporary Feminist Debates*. Stanford, CA: Stanford University Press.

Nicholson, Linda. 1986. *Gender and History: The Limits of Social Theory in the Age of the Family*. New York: Columbia University Press.

————. 1994. "Interpreting Gender." *Signs* 20 (1): 79–105.

Nystrom-Hamilton, Louise. 1913. *Ellen Key: Her Life and Work*. New York: G.P. Putnam's Sons.

O'Brien, Mary. 1981. *The Politics of Reproduction*. Boston: Routledge and Kegan Paul.

Okin, Susan Moller. 1989. *Justice, Gender, and the Family*. New York: Basic Books.

O'Leary, Catherine M. 1997. "Counteridentification or Counterhegemony?" *Women and Politics* 18 (3): 45–72.

Oliver, Kelly. 1993. *Reading Kristeva: Unraveling the Double Bind*. Bloomington: Indiana University Press.

Pateman, Carole. 1988. *The Sexual Contract*. Stanford, CA: Stanford University Press.

————. 1992. "Equality, Difference, Subordination: The Politics of Motherhood and Women's Citizenship," in Bock and James, eds., *Beyond Equality and Difference: Citizenship, Feminist Politics, and Female Subjectivity*. New York: Routledge.

Patterson, Yolanda Astarita. 1986. "Simone de Beauvoir and the Demystification of Motherhood." *Yale French Studies*, 72; 87–105.

Pilardi, Joanne. 1995. "Feminists Read *The Second Sex*," in Simons, ed., *Feminist Interpretations of*

Simone de Beauvoir. University Park, PA: Pennsylvania State University Press.

Poovey, Mary. 1988. *Uneven Developments: The Ideological Work of Gender in Mid-Victorian England*. Chicago: University of Chicago Press.

Purdy, Laura M. 1996. *Reproducing Persons: Issues in Feminist Bioethics*. Ithaca, NY: Cornell University Press.

Raymond, Janice G. 1993. *Women as Wombs: Reproductive Technologies and the Battle over Women's Freedom*. San Francisco: Harper San Francisco.

Register, Cheryl. 1982. "Motherhood at the Center: Ellen Key's Social Vision." *Women's Studies International Forum* 5 (6): PAGES.

Rhode, Deborah L., ed. 1990. *Theoretical Perspectives on Sexual Difference*. New Haven CT: Yale University Press.

Rich, Adrienne. 1976. *Of Woman Born: Motherhood as Experience and Institution*. New York: Norton.

———. 1979a [1976]. "'It Is the Lesbian in Us. . . . '" in Rich, *On Lies, Secrets, and Silence: Selected Prose, 1966–1978*. New York: Norton.

———. 1979b [1977]. "The Meaning of Our Love for Women Is What We Have Constantly to Expand," in Rich, *On Lies, Secrets, and Silence: Selected Prose, 1966–1978*. New York: Norton.

Riley, Denise. 1988. *"Am I That Name?" Feminism and the Category 'Woman' in History*. Minneapolis: University of Minnesota Press.

Robson, Ruthann. 1992. "Mother: The Legal Domestication of Lesbian Existence." *Hypatia* 7 (4): 172–85.

Roof, Judith. 1991. *A Lure of Knowledge: Lesbian Sexuality and Theory*. New York: Columbia University Press.

Rosaldo, Michelle Zimbalist. 1974. "Women, Culture and Society: A Theoretical Overview," in Michelle Z. Rosaldo and Louise Lamphere, eds., *Woman, Culture and Society*. Stanford, CA: Stanford University Press.

Rose, Jacqueline. 1986. "Julia Kristeva: Take Two," in Rose, *Sexuality in the Field of Vision*. London: Verso.

Rowland, Robyn. 1992. *Living Laboratories: Women and Reproductive Technologies*. Bloomington: Indiana University Press.

Rubin, Gayle. 1975. "The Traffic in Women: Notes on the 'Political Economy' of Sex," in Rayna R. Reiter, ed., *Toward an Anthropology of Women*. New York: Monthly Review Press.

Ruddick, Sara. 1980. "Maternal Thinking." *Feminist Studies* 6 (summer): 342–67.

———. 1983. "Pacifying the Forces: Drafting Women in the Interests of Peace." *Signs* 8 (spring): 471–48.

———. 1984. "Preservative Love and Military Destruction: Reflections on Mothering and Peace," in Trebilcott, ed. *Mothering: Essays in Feminist Theory*, Totowa, NJ: Roman and Allanheld.

———. 1987. "Remarks on the Sexual Politics of Reason," in Kittay and Myers, eds., *Women and Moral Theory* Totowa, NJ: Rowman and Littlefield.

———. 1989. *Maternal Thinking*. New York: Ballantine.

———. 1990. "Thinking About Fathers," in Hirsch and Fox Keller, eds., *Conflicts in Feminism*, New York: Routledge.

———. 1994. Thinking Mothers/Conceiving Birth," in Bassin, Honey, and Mahrer Kaplan, eds., *Representations of Motherhood*. Cambridge: Harvard University Press.

Rupp, Leila J., and Verta Taylor. 1987. *Survival in the Doldrums: The American Women's Rights Movement, 1945 to the 1960s*. Oxford: Oxford University Press.

Scott, Joan Wallach. 1986. "Gender: A Useful Category for Historical Analysis." *American Historical Review* 91: 1053–75.

———.1988. "Deconstructing Equality-versus-Difference: Or, the Uses of Poststructuralist Theory for Feminism." *Feminist Studies* 14, 1 (spring): 33–50.

———. 1991. "The Evidence of Experience." *Critical Inquiry* 17 (summer): 773–97.

———. 1996. *Only Paradoxes to Offer: French Feminists and the Rights of Man*. Cambridge: Harvard University Press.

———. 1997. "Comment on Hawkesworth's 'Confounding Gender.'" *Signs* 22 (3): 697–702.

Seigfried, Charlene Haddock. 1984. "Gender Specific Values." *Philosophical Forum* 15 (summer): 425–42.

Smith, Dorothy E. 1997. "Comment on Hekman's 'Truth or Method: Feminist Standpoint Theories Revisited.'" *Signs* 22 (2): 392–98.

Smith, Steven G. 1997. "Comment on Hawkesworth's 'Confounding Gender.'" *Signs* 22 (3): 691–97.

Spelman, Elizabeth. 1988. *Inessential Woman: Problems of Exclusion in Feminist Thought*. Boston: Beacon.

Spivak, Gayatri. 1988a. *In Other Worlds: Essays in Cultural Politics*. New York: Routledge.

———. 1988b. "Can The Subaltern Speak?" in Nelson and Grossberg, eds., *Marxism and the Interpretation of Culture*. Urbana and Chicago: University of Illinois Press.

———. 1993. *Outside in the Teaching Machine*. New York: Routledge.

Spregnether, Madeleine. 1990. *The Spectral Mother*. Ithaca, NY: Cornell University Press.

Stacey, Judith. 1983. "The New Conservative Feminism." *Feminist Studies* 9 (fall): 557–86.

Stansworth, Michelle, ed. 1987. *Reproductive Technologies: Gender, Motherhood, and Medicine*. Minneapolis: University of Minnesota Press.

Stanton, Domna. 1989. "Difference on Trial: A Critique of the Maternal Metaphor in Cixous, Irigaray, and Kristeva," in Allen and Young, eds., *The Thinking Muse: Feminism and Modern French Philosophy*. Bloomington: Indiana University Press.

Thorne, Barrie, and Marilyn Yalom, eds. 1982. *Rethinking the Family: Some Feminist Questions*. New York: Longman.

Tong, Rosemarie. 1989. *Feminist Thought: A Comprehensive Introduction*. Boulder, CO: Westview.

Tronto, Joan. 1993. *Moral Boundaries: A Political Argument for an Ethic of Care*. New York: Routledge.

Unger, Rhonda K., and Michelle Crawford. 1992. *Women and Gender: A Feminist Psychology*. Philadelphia: Temple University Press.

Ward, Julie K. 1995. "Beauvoir's Two Senses of 'Body' in *The Second Sex*," in Simons, ed., *Feminist Interpretations of Simone de Beauvoir*. University Park, PA: The Pennsylvania State University Press.

Weedon, Chris. 1987. *Feminist Practice and Poststructuralist Theory*. Oxford: Basil Blackwell.

Weems, Renita. 1984. "'Hush. Mama's Gotta Go Bye Bye': A Personal Narrative." *Sage: A Scholarly Journal on Black Woman* 1 (2): 25–28.

Welton, Katherine. 1997. "Nancy Hartsock's Standpoint Theory: From Content to 'Concrete Multiplicity.'" *Women and Politics* 18 (3): 7–24.

Wittig, Monique. 1969 [1971]. *Les guerilleres*. New York: Viking.

———. 1980. "The Straight Mind." *Feminist Issues* 1 (1): 103–11.

———. 1981. "One Is Not Born a Woman." *Feminist Issues* 1 (2): 47–54.

———. 1985. "The Mark of Gender." *Feminist Issues* 5 (2): 1–14.

Young, Iris Marion. 1984. "Pregnant Embodiment, Subjectivity, and Alienation." *Journal of Medicine and Philosophy* (9): 45–62.

———. 1989. "Throwing Like a Girl: A Phenomenology of Feminine Bodily Comportment, Motility, and Spatiality," in Allen and Young, eds., *The Thinking Muse: Feminism and Modern French Philosophy*. Bloomington, IN: Indiana University Press.

———. 1994. "Making Single Motherhood Normal." *Dissent* (winter): 83–93.

Zerilli, Linda M. G. 1992. "A Process Without a Subject: Simone de Beauvoir and Julia Kristeva on Motherhood." *Signs* 18 (1): 111–35.

Ziarek, Ewa. 1992. "At the Limits of Discourse: Heterogeneity, Alterity, and the Maternal Body in Kristeva's Thought." *Hypatia* 7 (1): 91–108.

INDEX

body, the, 7–8, 10–11, 17, 42, 47, 65–6,
79, 83, 96–9, 110–11, 117–18, 125–8,
146–7, 150, 156–8, 161, 166, 177, 201,
218–19; as a source of knowledge, 98,
126; as situation, 89–114; child's, 156;
in *The Second Sex*, 92–7; male, 17–19,
108, 238; maternal, 125, 146, 149–51,
19, 21, 112, 219, 237; woman's, 16–18,
21, 42, 56, 65, 70, 73, 87, 90, 98, 102,
108, 112, 116–17, 127, 129, 210, 218,
224, 238
boys, 49, 109, 181–2, 185, 192
Braidotti, Rosi, 126
Brown, Murphy, ix
Brunswick, Ruth, 198

C
capitalism, xiv, 6–7, 33, 41–4, 52, 58, 65,
74, 87, 121–2, 177, 179, 182–3, 186,
199, 210–11, 238, 245, 249, 250
caregivers, 75, 122, 131–3, 233, 249
caregiving, 132–3
caretakers, 188
Caribbean, 231
caring: ethic of, 232
castration, 169, 178, 185, 195–6
child custody issues, x, xi
child rearing, xi, xii, xvii, 11, 33, 46, 55–7,
75–7, 80–3, 89, 91, 182–3, 186, 192,
210, 248–9; collective, 190; in the
African-American community, 208–9;
men's equal responsibility for, 12; reorganization of, 109, 187, 190; sex-based
division of labor in, 123; women's
responsibility for, 14, 109–110, 186
child(ren), x, xi, 11, 15, 35–8, 49, 52,
56–8, 63–4, 66–7, 75–7, 80, 82–3, 89,
95, 101–102, 106–7, 108–9, 114,
119–21, 124, 143, 146, 152, 160–1,
164–5, 168, 170–1, 176, 180, 184–6,
189, 194, 200, 203, 205, 207–8,
210–11, 214–17, 223–4, 238, 248–50; -
mother relations, 99, 105–7, 113,
122–3, 143, 145–6, 152, 155; black,

208–9; care, x, 12, 34–7, 55–6, 82, 107,
125, 208, 231; constitution of gender
and sexuality in, 190; development of,
77, 120, 168; father's support of, 52;
identification with same-sex parent,
196; images of, 159–60; installation
into the symbolic, 162–3; sexual orientation of, 192–3
childbirth, 11–12, 15, 65, 73, 89, 91–2, 99,
104, 110, 113, 124–5, 245, 247
childhood, 15, 161–2, 166, 168, 196, 206,
248
Chodorow, Nancy, x, 70, 75, 80–1, 180–3,
188, 197, 199–200, 202–3, 254n 1;
account of mothering, 175, 180, 199,
201–3, 205; account of women's development, 191–2, 199; object relations
theory of, 175, 193; *The Reproduction of
Mothering*, xix–xxi, 144, 173, 174, 187
choice, xii, 12, 67, 97–9
Christ, 149, 155; virgin mother of, 148,
155
Christianity, 43, 148–9, 153
citizenship, 39, 77–8
Cixous, Helene, 70
Collins, Patricia Hill, xx–xxi, 208–10, 239;
accounts of mothering, 211, 213–14,
237–8, 240–1; analysis of relationship
of subjectivity, experience, consciousness, standpoint, and knowledge, 213,
227–37, 246; *Black Feminist Thought*,
207, 212; standpoint theory, 213–14
communitarian theory of politics, 73–4,
122
consciousness, xiii, 6–8, 20–2, 42, 92,
94–5, 112–13, 120, 123, 144, 147,
218–19, 227–37;
experience, 227–37; disembodied, 8, 19,
22, 150, 218; maternal, 22, 113; oppositional, 104, 22, 152; self-, 93, 95;
women's. *See* women, consciousness of
contraception, 12, 107
Cott, Nancy, 30, 59
culture, 14, 124, 146, 149, 151, 168, 185,

13–14, 44, 65, 67, 95, 98, 122, 211; - development, 47–8, 177–8; gendered, 23, 188; in relation, 188
self/other: boundary, 10, 15; opposition of, 95, 211; relation, xix, 91, 122, 151–2, 158, 181–2. *See also* Hegel, relation of self/other
semiotic, the, 144, 147, 149, 154, 169
separation, 180, 192, 211
sex, xii, 6, 17, 22, 45–6, 56, 96, 111–12, 124, 127–8, 135, 152, 184, 201, 219; and relationship to the body. *See* body; in exchange for material support, 51–2; roles, 186
sex/gender: distinctions, 17, 19–20, 34, 46, 50, 112, 127, 237; systems, 185–7, 189–90, 200
sexism, xiii, 48, 87, 133, 187, 209, 211, 222, 237; and male dominance, xvi, xix, 4, 10–11, 15–16, 21, 25–6, 31–2, 37, 47, 49–50, 68–9, 88, 90, 97, 110, 117, 120, 124, 215, 244, 248
sexual: choices, 188–9; desire, 184–6, 200–1; difference, 13–14, 26, 50, 54, 56, 110, 126–8, 145–6, 178, 185, 225; dimorphism, 18–19; freedom, xiii, 49; identity, 178, 188, 191; morality, 45–7, 49; objects, 195, 199; orientation, xi, 189, 194, 234; partners, 152, 185; relationships, 48, 52, 108, 188, 193–4, 197
sexuality, 32, 45–6, 48, 168, 178–9, 181, 186, 187–91, 198, 200–1, 212; effects of shared parenting on, 189; female, 50, 52, 184, 198; reconstructing, 178–9; women's. *See* women's sexuality
sign system, 146, 159, 163, 184
signified and signifiers, 2, 6, 144–7, 150, 154, 158, 178
Silvermarie, Sue, 223–5, 239
sisterhood, 221, 224
slippage of signifiers, 6, 51, 73, 79, 126, 127, 132–4, 136, 152, 153, 168, 187, 213, 215, 220, 223, 234–6, 246, 250

Smith, Susan, ix
social: construction, 17–18, 20, 111; contexts, xv, 2–5, 8–9, 12–15, 17, 21, 24, 39, 44, 64–5, 67, 69, 80–1, 96, 100, 105–6, 111–13, 118–19, 121–3, 131–2, 144, 158, 172, 187, 196–7, 200, 208, 211, 213, 215, 229–30, 233–4, 250; development, 46, 75; difference, 208; evolution, 41, 43, 47, 56; inequality, 121–2; order, 49, 59; organizations, x, xvii, 5, 67, 99, 249; policies, xi, 77, 242, 251; processes, 17–18, 20, 137; relations, xv, xviii, 2–5, 9–10, 13–15, 19, 21–3, 35, 39–41, 43, 45, 65, 67, 73–4, 91–2, 95–6, 103, 108, 112–14, 120–3, 131, 140, 158, 166, 177, 181–2, 201, 211, 245; structures, institutions and practices, xii, 2–3, 6, 8, 10, 13–15, 23, 33, 37, 43–4, 64–8, 87, 124, 131, 179, 183, 186–7, 190, 193, 197–8, 202, 210–11, 229, 232–3; theory, 116, 143, 239–40
social constructivism, 17–21, 124, 200–1
socialism, 40–3, 52, 122
society, 40, 42, 45, 55, 124, 183, 230; American, ix; black, 231; human, 183, 218; industrial capitalist, 83; modern, 183, 185, 197; sexist and male dominated, 99, 106, 193–4; Western, 180; white-dominated, 232
socioeconomic class, xi, 122
sons, 176, 224. *See also* mother–son relations
Spenser, Herbert, 34
standpoint theory, 6, 115–41, 166–7, 170, 213, 227–9, 233–7
subject(s), 138–40, 147, 151, 156, 166–8, 170–1, 203, 206–7, 213, 215–17, 226, 236, 240–1, 245, 247; construction, 23, 171; positioning, 115–19, 129, 135–6, 138–41, 142, 146, 151, 155, 157, 162, 166, 169–70, 184, 220, 224–6, 229–31, 233, 235–7, 239–40, 244–5
subjectivity, xv, xix, xx–xxi, 3, 7, 9–13,

128, 134–5, 137, 141, 143, 149, 153,
167, 169, 172, 176, 181–3, 193, 196–8,
200, 202, 206–7, 211, 214–18, 222,
225, 233, 238–40, 242–4, 249, 251;
African-American, 207–10, 229–36;
analysis of in relation to the family,
72–3, 75–7, 87–8; black, 207–10;
childless, 222, 225; community of,
157, 161–2; containment of, 55, 87;
exchange of, 183, 185–6, 196–7; liberation of, 34, 64, 67, 71, 85, 107–110,
186, 202; oppression of, xi, 4, 13–15,
22–4, 67, 69, 75, 90–1, 94, 96, 98, 185,
187, 198, 202–3, 211, 214–15; pregnant, xi, 102–4, 112; representation of,
25, 215
women's: agency and entitlement, 6, 12,
20, 25–6, 31, 37, 59, 116, 214, 244;
bodies. See body, women's; consciousness, xviii, 22; desire, 51–2, 55, 170,
200;development, 23, 33, 69, 175–6,
195; difference, xvii–xviii, 12–13, 15,
19, 21, 23–5, 27, 31, 33, 40, 44–5, 47,
53, 55–6, 67–8, 78–9, 87–8, 89–91, 96,
108, 110, 116–17, 120, 138, 143,
152–3, 213, 219, 226, 228, 239–40,
246; economic dependence on men,
33–5, 42, 44–6, 50–2, 56, 64, 107, 121,
182, 190; economic independence,
109, 194; equality, xvii, 6, 12, 20, 32,
39–40, 59, 107, 109–110, 122, 202,
244; experiences and situations,
xx–xxi, 6, 12–13, 15–16, 21, 23–4, 27,

29, 58, 62, 65, 68–9, 76, 91, 93, 97,
107, 116–17, 176, 205–41, 243–4, 246;
freedom, xii, 12, 31–2, 39, 44–9, 51–2,
67, 95, 98, 107–8, 110, 122; heterosexuality. See heterosexuality, women's;
identities, xi, 75, 79, 134, 243;
inequality, 4, 13, 23, 121, 198, 202;
movement, ix, 60–1, 63, 242; paid
work, 35, 64–5. See also labor, paid;
politics, xi, 133–4; power, 153, 182;
relations with men, 53, 107–8; relations with other women, 54–5, 161,
170, 194, 200, 202, 224, 233, 239–40;
relationship to others, 23, 193; reproductive capacities, 93–4, 125; rights,
12, 31–2, 38, 40–1, 45, 55, 59, 62, 107;
self-determination, 12, 50; self-development and fulfillment, 34, 37, 39, 41,
53–4, 60; sexual freedom, 44–7, 49–53;
sexuality, xv, 33, 44–50, 52, 55, 59–60,
105, 108; social position, 13, 16, 23,
93–4, 134; subjectivity. See subjectivity, women's; traditional activities and
identities, 72–3, 76–8, 90, 134; transcendence, 93, 97–8, 107, 110
Woodward, Louise, ix
Woolf, Virginia, 221
work. See labor
workers, 41, 65
workplace, 182–3
World War II, 33, 60